The eManager: Value Chain Management in an eCommerce World

Gerhard Plenert

President, Institute of World Class Management

BLACKHALL
Publishing

This book was typeset by
Gough Typesetting Services for
BLACKHALL PUBLISHING
8 Priory Hall,
Stillorgan, Co. Dublin,
Ireland
and
BLACKHALL PUBLISHING
2025 Hyperion Avenue,
Los Angeles,
CA 90027, USA

e-mail: blackhall@eircom.net
www: blackhallpublishing.com

© Gerhard Plenert, 2001

ISBN: 1 842180 08 8

A catalogue record for this book is available from the British Library.

Printed in Ireland by
ColourBooks Ltd

Table of Contents

DEDICATION

To *the gang*

The value network of my life that fills my life with unending changes:

Team Lead in the Value Chain:
Renee Sangray Plenert

Team Members:
Heidi Lynette Plenert
Dawn Janelle Plenert
Gregory Johannes Plenert
Gerick Johannes Plenert
Joshua Johannes Plenert
Natasha Ida Plenert
Zackary Johannes Plenert
Chelsey Jean Plenert

Acknowledgements

To give credit where credit is due, I would have to return to the earliest days of my experience when I worked in a variety of small to medium sized plants in Oregon. Later I worked for NCR Corporation and Clark Equipment Company in plants all over the world — as far away as Indonesia, Malaysia, Singapore, Australia, Chile and Germany and as close as Canada and Mexico. I have worked as Director of Quality for Precision Printers, Inc., a high tech manufacturer in California and as a Senior Principal for American Management Systems where I was part of a team defining the structure and operation of the "enterprise of the future". I am currently President of the Institute of World Class Management. The resulting exposure to a variety of management challenges has given me the professional background for the concepts described in this book. In addition, my academic settings at CSU, Chico and Brigham Young University introduced me to the publication game and I currently have 150 articles and six books under my belt.

I also need to recognize Tony Mason, commissioning editor, and Gerard O'Connor at Blackhall Publishing, who was my mentor and who helped make this book a reality. I further need to recognize my family — my wife, Renee Sangray Plenert, and my children, Heidi Lynette, Dawn Janelle, Gregory Johannes, Gerick Johannes, Joshua Johannes, Natasha Ida, Zackary Johannes and Chelsey Jean — who gave me the time I needed to make this book work.

G. J. P.

Preface

There is nothing permanent except change.

Heraclitus,
Greek Philosopher

Asking "why another management book?" is like asking, "why change?" The only thing in life that is certain is change! And we need to be ready for change by planning for it. An eManager is a world-class manager who *makes change happen* rather than one who is just *effected by change*. The next wave of changes will focus on eCommerce in a supply chain focused world. This is the result of numerous environment-changing events, which include:

- a globalized management style

- a core competency focus of business creating smaller companies

- smaller companies causing more companies in the supply chain

- eCommerce business methodologies

- web based data and information sharing

- advanced planning and scheduling methodologies for supply chain efficiencies

- finite capacity scheduling mathematical tools

- strategic partnerships and alliances

- network based competitive practices

- more indirect selling through web based tools

- more customer customized products

- faster customer service through shorter cycle times

- value chain analysis, which goes beyond materials efficiencies

- motivation focused measurement tools

- an empowered and responsive workforce.

The integration of past values with futuristic technologies creates a value network and the world-class management of the value network defines the role of the eManager. World-class management teaches the world-class eManager how to:

- define goals and strategies
- motivate change in the direction of the goals and strategies
- plan for change
- incorporate systems that will facilitate change
- empower employees to make changes
- reward successful change programs.

A world-class eManager is a manager who realizes that he or she is not broad enough to stay on top of all the changes that are happening within their organization. A world-class eManager realizes that in order to successfully utilize changes to their advantage, they need business partners (employees) that will freely and openly search for changes that can be exploited to the advantage of the organization. They need employees that can quickly react to change. That is why an eManager is one that openly facilitates the changes that are innovated by their employees.

There are many areas of change that need to be continually addressed in today's competitive environment. Key amongst these are issues such as global management strategies, time-to-market/technology development strategies, information/integration strategies, teaming/human resource management strategies, training/education strategies and many more.

An eManager is one who realizes there is not one correct solution for any situation. Rather, there are a series of alternatives and one alternative may be more successful in a specific situation than another. Information and training will help employees to make advantageous choices from amongst the alternatives. The author has implemented many of these principles in his professional life and an example is included as an appendix at the end of Chapter 12.

A world-class eManager is one who realizes that copying will never allow him or her to do any better than to get caught up. Competitiveness requires innovation, not a copycat attitude. For example, the recent fad in the United States for copying Japanese methodologies can never help anyone to do any better than to get equal with the Japanese — and that's just not good enough.

The eManager realizes that eCommerce is defining the future of the procurement process. The web based order process, for both customers and vendors, is a critical element in cycle time compression and waste elimination. Therefore, the eManager utilizes eCommerce to optimize the supply chain. An optimal supply chain manages the linkages from the customer's customer to the vendor's vendor. It plans, schedules and executes product movement performances that are world-class competitive. For example, computer sales will never be the same now that Dell Computer Company has eliminated numerous traditional supply chain linkages by selling computers directly through the web and delivering them directly to customers. The Dell supply chain compresses production and procurement lead-time and reduces cost, thereby giving the customer better service and better prices simultaneously. And that's what value chain management is all about.

This new book teaches us what an eManager is. It discusses the various aspects of world-class management, eCommerce, supply chain management and value chain management, giving explanations and examples of the various concepts. It discusses alternatives for competitive improvement that are available to the eManager. It will also offer the reader sources for the further in-depth study of each of the concepts presented.

You must give up the present to have a future.

Introduction

Nothing is constant but change!
All existence is a perpetual flux
of "being and becoming".

Ernst Heinrich Haeckel

This book focuses on current and future managers who are trying to improve themselves and their job skills. These managers see the future in eCommerce and its rapid change of the business environment. These managers want to become world-class managers of the eCommerce and eBusiness environments that are taking them over. They realize that this requires the management of a network of suppliers, partners and customers in a way that will optimize the value for all members of the network.

This is not a strategy book, although strategy is a very important part of eManagement. It is not a book about goal setting, although, without a clear vision of their mission and goals, eManagers don't have a well-defined target to shoot for. This is a book about *change* — how to prepare for it, how to challenge it, how to take advantage of it and how to use it to gain competitive advantage. This book offers:

1. a discussion of eManagement, world-class management and change models

2. a discussion of eCommerce and eBusiness, supply chain management and value chain management and management styles and techniques

3. a discussion of the key strategy areas that an eManager needs to be involved in, such as global management and information management

4. a detailed discussion of competitive strategies, such as time-to-market strategies

5. a detailed discussion of the characteristics of an eManager

6. a detailed discussion of how the eManager fits into and motivates the enterprise

7. references for further study of the concepts introduced.

This book is a handbook for change that you will want to keep with you as you and your organization grows and changes.

The wise man is satisfied with nothing.

William Godwin,
English minister, reformer and philosopher

PART I

Overview

CHAPTER ONE

eManagement — What Is It?

Once you've chosen the road,
You've chosen the destination.

The farmer heard a loud quacking noise coming from an old, dried-out well. Looking down the well he noticed that one of his geese had fallen in. This was an old but inquisitive goose, always getting into difficult situations. "That darn goose must have jumped over the wall in an effort to see what was on the other side, and it looks like he found out", the farmer exclaimed in frustration.

The farmer thought of putting down a ladder, but the hole was too deep. He then tried to lasso the goose with a rope, deciding that if he ended up choking it, he would at least get a good meal out of the process. But nothing seemed to work. The goose resisted getting caught by the rope and worked against the farmer.

It was getting late so he decided to leave the goose in the well overnight. Perhaps in the morning he would come up with a way to get the goose out. That turned out to be a mistake. All night long he could hear the goose squawking and it kept him awake. In the morning, in frustration, the farmer decided that he would fill up the well with dirt, thereby burying the goose and getting rid of the danger of something or someone else falling in. He started to shovel the dirt into the hole.

At first the goose was stunned by the dirt falling in on him. He didn't like being hit by the dirt and he didn't like the idea of being buried alive. As the dirt fell on him he would fluff his wings shaking off the dirt. Then he would step up on the newly delivered dirt. What the goose initially did out of frustration soon become a repetitive pattern. Each time dirt came down on him he would shake it off and step up, shake it off and step up.

The farmer had long since forgotten the bird and was concentrating on getting the well filled up. Suddenly, much to his surprise, the goose fluttered out of the well. The farmer's attempt to bury the goose had in the end resulted in its freedom. And all it took was shaking off the dirt and stepping up on it.

Today we find ourselves in an environment of continuous change. The speed of this change has become so dramatic that it is difficult for anyone to keep up. Looking back at our first methods of communication — the letter — information transfer could take weeks or even months to deliver, depending on the distance. This was replaced by the first electronic communication revolution — the telegraph. The speed of communications was reduced to minutes. This communication breakthrough has never since been matched. No other technology improvement was able to have as dramatic an impact on communication, based simply on its degree of performance improvements.

As communications methodologies continued to improve, we discovered the telephone, the fax and now the Internet. With each of these revolutions, we encountered dramatic and demanding change. And with each of these changes, we find two types of companies. There are those that would rather sit back stubbornly and hold on to their current position as the dirt of change falls into the well on them. And there are those that have learned to shake the dirt off and step up. The next wave of technology and communications changes will focus on eCommerce in a world focused on a world-class supply chain. This is the result of numerous environment-changing events, which include:

- a globalized management style

- a core competency focus in business thereby creating smaller companies

- smaller companies causing more companies in the supply chain

- eCommerce business methodologies

- web based data and information sharing

- advanced planning and scheduling methodologies for supply chain efficiencies

- finite capacity scheduling mathematical tools

- strategic partnerships and alliances

- network based competitive practices

- more indirect selling through web based tools

- more products customized by the customer

- faster customer service through shorter cycle times

- value chain analysis that goes beyond materials efficiencies

- motivation focused measurement tools

- an empowered and responsive workforce.

The eManager is a leader who has learned not just how to shake and step, but how to take the dirt and use it to build a new future. From this we can come up with a definition:

> The eManager is a shaker and stepper in a leading edge competitive environment of eCommerce and eBusiness.

THE NEW BUSINESS MODEL

Web based businesses have changed the business model of the future. Traditional financial based models, which focused on return on investment (ROI) and profitability, don't fit because they use short-term metrics and are not responsive to the larger investments required of internet businesses. Non-traditional, far-looking models, such as market share domination, have become the basis for investment. Let's take a look at a few examples.

Amazon.com is an online bookstore that started in a small warehouse in Seattle with two employees in 1995, and by 1998 it had revenues of over $600 million. It outflanked the two dinosaurs of the industry, Barnes & Noble and Borders Books & Music, who never knew what hit them until it was too late. Now these dinosaurs are desperately trying to make up for their sleepiness by making their own entrance into Internet sales. While these dinosaurs are struggling to regain their composure, Amazon has moved on to a broader product base, marketing a large variety of consumer products.

Dell is an online, customized computer and peripherals marketer that has rapidly taken the number two place as the supplier of desktop PCs. Dell utilizes an order processing system that allows customers to directly order computers in over 6,000 configurations. It offers seamless linkages between its online systems configuration methodology, its internal process and its inventory planning and replenishment systems.

Dell has eliminated numerous steps in its supply chain by avoiding the retail outlets and the distribution to these outlets. As a result, it has cut 58 days off the system-wide cycle time in a PC industry known to lose one per cent of its product value each week. This reduced lead time also gives Dell a 58 day advantage in new component introductions, allowing it to flush old inventories and introduce new product lines faster. Additionally, Dell boasts just under 26 inventory turns per year, compared to less than eight for Compaq.

Dell's cycle time reductions have allowed it to minimize its inventory holding costs. Additionally, Dell charges for the computer at the time of configuration, not at the time of delivery. The result is that Dell has successfully created a cash float where the consumer is financing the inventory costs during the five days between order placement and delivery. The combination of lower inventory levels and riding on the customer's cash float has placed Dell into an enviable position that allows it to sell PCs at costs that are lower than the average computer retailing outlet.

Dell utilizes Internet based, build-to-order manufacturing processes and a web-linked order entry system to schedule and pass order information directly from customers to suppliers. Dell has established a close supply chain collaboration with suppliers like Intel and Microsoft. For example, Sony ships Dell monitors directly from the Sony factory with a Dell label and the Dell facility never comes into contact with the unit.

Dell's focus on the supply chain, and on making the purchasing process easier by the use of the Internet and corporate intranets, made it one of the few profitable dot.com companies in the 1990s.[1]

THE EMANAGEMENT STYLE OF MANAGEMENT

The best leaders . . . almost without exception and at every level, are master users of stories and symbols.

Tom Peters,
Business Writer

When Tasha (aged fourteen) was asked to define an eManager, she drew what we see in Picture 1. She saw the eManager as a type of superhuman, someone who could do anything and accomplish it at Internet speed. And, to some extent, she is right. The eManager needs to know what is technologically new and relevant, and how to maximize the effectiveness and performance of it all. An eManager also needs to be able to optimize his or her management

---

1. Hughes, Jon, Mark Ralf and Bill Michels, *Transform Your Supply Chain: Releasing Value in Business* (Boston: International Thomson Business Press) 1999.

style and techniques. An eManager can be defined as:

> A leader that optimizes the efficient use of eCommerce and web based technologies in a World-class Management environment.

Using this definition as a basis, it is helpful to review the development of management styles. Initially, management styles focused on the authoritarian, domineering, *Theory-X* style of management which was very hierarchical in structure where power tended to reside on the top. The next phase of management development focused more on an employee involved style of management where relationships between management and the employees were considered to be important. This was referred to as *Theory-Y* management. But the hierarchical structure tended to remain and that power continued to reside at the top. The next phase of management style development was the *Theory-Z* style, which focused on the active participation of the employees. This approach looked at the value of the employees and sought their suggestions. The level of suggestion implementation turned out to be a measure of how "Theory-Z" a company really was.

Each step in the management evolutionary process was driven by technology. The move from Theory-X to Theory-Y was the realization that machines could perform the repetitive brute labor and that the role of employees was becoming more mental than physical. The move from Theory-Y to Theory-Z was the realization that automation was managed on the production floor where day-to-day decisions had to be made rapidly. It was ineffective to wait for ideas and decrees to come from management only.

Beyond these initial stages of management philosophy, and as technology continued to develop, particularly with the advancement of the computers, information began to drive a need for responsiveness. This introduced a new generation of managers who realized that the employees knew more about what was going on than the managers. For example, Ricardo Semler's book *Maverick* is an excellent example of this trend. Employees were no longer idea generators where management still held all the power — they were now the selectors and implementers of the ideas. The hierarchical structure was replaced by a structure that was extremely flat and the traditional departmental silos began to erode. Employees, not managers, were starting to run the companies. Decision power was being distributed down the corporate structure.

Competitive pressures internationally, and a focus on core competencies (doing what you do best), encouraged organizations to look outside of themselves for services. Centralized control was being replaced by distributed supply chain management. This introduced more steps in the vendor to customer linkage, making the management of this process more complex. This trend focused on developing a supply chain where an organization would develop a relationship with shippers, vendors and customers, so that all the linkages in the supply chain could be effectively integrated.

Soon management realized that time responsiveness was not the only important element in customer satisfaction. The supply chain linkages also had a cost element and resource efficiency element associated with them. This realization generated a need for value chain management, which is the management of all the linkages of the supply chain in the most resource efficient way. Time and financial resources became just as important to manage as labor, materials or logistics resources. Sometimes this includes the elimination of elements of the supply chain. For example, web marketing has eliminated the need for retail outlets in some areas.

Value chain efficiency was facilitated by eCommerce. With the introduction of web based marketing, the need for retailing and travelling sales personnel was significantly reduced. Links in the supply chain were starting to disappear, eliminating unnecessary elements of process waste. Value chain efficiencies were able to outperform the traditional supply chain in both cost and time performance. This level of technology opened the door for a new type of manager who understood world-class management principles as well as eCommerce technologies — the eManager.

Returning to our definition, eManagers have some key characteristics. These are:

- empowered employee base — employees have involved ownership of the process and have the authority to take corrective action, employees are the focus of the day-to-day action and with the availability of integrated scheduling information they are capable of making immediate adjustments and improvements

- web based corporate strategies — eManagers understand the utilization of eCommerce technologies including eMalls, web based marketing and strategic information interfaces between all levels of the supply chain; the web becomes the basis of scheduling and value-chain optimization

- integrated value chain planning and scheduling — the planning of work and the scheduling of the flow of work through the entire supply chain needs to be integrated together utilizing finite capacity scheduling methodologies — this planning and scheduling integrates the logistics systems, the manufacturing processes, the wholesaling processes and the materials sourcing processes taking into consideration all elements of capacity to assure the successful on-time deliveries of all customer orders; time to market and cycle time reduction become critical planning pieces and expanding this into the value chain brings in the integration of financial and strategic information that is shared with all links of the supply chain

- open and fully accessible information — a total sharing of all information including strategic tactical and operational, with all other elements of the supply chain, done through a secure web based environment

- full resource management — the analysis of resource demands and the capacity management of all resources including labor, materials, facility, logistics, equipment, financial, engineering, etc. along the entire supply chain

- world class management techniques — the utilization of leadership methodologies including globalization strategies, teaming and goal setting in order to facilitate organizational success.

Global eManagement success requires that managers have a thorough understanding of five pillars:

1. International web-based eCommerce and eMail management.

2. Functionality of optimizing the international supply chain focusing on the efficient utilization of all resource elements to the competitive advantage of the supply network.

3. World-class strategy development based on specific, measurable goals — the eManager needs to be able to define and develop a values statement, core competencies, vision statement, mission statement, strategic initiatives, a strategy and a plan of operation, and to develop a measurement system that motivates co-ordinated responses to these goals.

4. How to create successful innovation and change management frameworks utilizing tools like concept management and breakthrough thinking.

5. Successful time management by compressing the cycle time of the entire supply chain.

These eManager pillars are built on a foundation of world-class management tools such as:

- eCommerce integration and web development

- a supply chain information network that is web based

- a team based empowered workforce that takes ownership in its processes

- globalized goals integrated locally

- a focused measurement system that motivates goal-directed responsiveness

- a technology strategy that balances an organization in all phases of the product life cycle

- an open and sharing participative management style

- a value based organization

- a learning organization that focuses on all elements of training and education including that of the vendors

- a value-adding, waste-eliminating continuous improvement strategy.

IT'S THE *START* THAT *STOPS* MOST PEOPLE

Why Another Management Book?

The purpose of this book is to take management theory and management practices into the year 2000 by discussing world-class value chain management techniques in an eCommerce environment. This book will be a blueprint for international eManagement success.

Global eManagement success focuses on five pillars, which I have already outlined above — understanding eCommerce, optimizing the international supply chain, world-class strategy development, successful innovation and change management and successful time management.

The purpose of this book is to prepare the next generation of managers by showing them how to integrate and coordinate these tools into an effective competitive strategy.

> Well, if there's no time for fun doc, then what are we trying to save the planet for?

> Major West,
> *Lost in Space*

SUMMARY

International competitive changes will force a change in management style into the next millennium. These changes will result in the creation of world-class management tools in a supply chain and value chain environment that utilizes eCommerce efficiencies. This next generation of management will know how to shake off the dirt and step up — it is known as eManagement.

> Thee Lift Me And I'll Lift Thee, And We'll Ascend Together.

> Quaker Proverb

SUGGESTIONS FOR FURTHER READING

You might like to do some further reading on this subject. Some suggestions are:

Plenert, Gerhard and Bill Kirchmier, *Finite Capacity Scheduling* (New York: John Wiley & Sons, Inc.) 2000.

Plenert, Gerhard and Shozo Hibino, *Making Innovation Happen: Concept Management Through Integration* (Boca Raton, FL: St. Lucie Press) 1998.

Plenert, Gerhard, *World Class Manager* (Rocklin, CA: Prima Publishing) 1995.

CHAPTER TWO

eCommerce

Give me a place to stand and I will move the world.

Archimedes,
Greek mathematician

In 1969 the United States Department of Defense established ARPANET (Advanced Research Agency Network) in response to a need to have an open line of communications between all nodes of a communications network. They didn't want the network to be dependent on a single physical line of communication. They wanted the communication system to be free and independent, allowing the network to establish flexible information routes regardless of disruptions of any type. The result was a network of computers and communications lines that allowed universal access across multiple transmission routes. Originally intended as a military communications system, the network quickly developed into a messaging system that included civilian messages. By 1983, ARPANET had become MILNET and the remains of the original network became known as the Internet. By the mid 1990s the original four ARPANET sites had blossomed into 6.6 million Internet computer sites worldwide.

The Internet network of computers still required the users to be able to identify which computer node they wanted to address. This frustrated a British physicist Tim Berners-Lee who was trying to search for specific pieces of information without knowing which computer node to address. He established links called hypertext, which helped users identify the information they were looking for. By 1990 he linked hypertext to an online addressing system called Uniform Resource Locator (URL) and he called the link the World Wide Web (WWW). In 1991 he made the WWW freely available to the public and the Internet age exploded.

By 1996, about 40 million people around the world were connected to the Internet with 627,000 domain servers. By the end of 1997, more than 100 million people were connected and the Internet had grown to 1.5 million domain servers. Worldwide Internet commerce sales revenue had reached $10.6 billion. Internet traffic doubled approximately every 100 days for the last three years of the 1990s. By 2001, Internet revenues are projected to reach $223 billion.[1]

---

1. Helms, Marilyn M, "Electronic Commerce", *Encyclopedia of Management* (Gale Group Publishers) 1999, pp. 237-241.

What had started as a simple, computer linked message switching system was rapidly expanded into a system used to perform business transactions.

We have entered a new competitive era of business development — web focused businesses. Not only are traditional business transactions performed through the use of the Internet, but also new methods of business and new types of business are rapidly developing. New companies have sprouted up in all the traditional avenues of marketing and operations. And the old dinosaur companies have felt the pain of rapidly losing market share to these new up-starts. In order to hold on to markets that they traditionally dominated, these dinosaurs are now painfully moving into web based enterprises as well, even if it sometimes seems excessively expensive. This new era of business has been labeled eCommerce, or, as IBM would refer to it, eBusiness.

> eCommerce represents an unprecedented challenge and opportunity for AMS clients – global leaders in telecommunications, financial serv-ices, insurance, healthcare, and government. eCommerce technology and business models are propelling the reinvention of business rela-tionships and even the restructuring of entire industries.

> Paul Brands,
> Chairman and Chief Executive Officer
> Reginald Foster,
> Vice President and Chief eCommerce Officer, AMS

DOT.COM START-UP COMPANIES TAKE OVER

In 1998, 25 per cent of Dell Computer's revenues came from online sales. By 1999 it had jumped to 30 per cent and in 2000 it is expected to become 50 per cent.

In the first quarter of 1999, Travelocity.com, an Internet travel agency, had gross sales of over $128 million, which was a 156 per cent increase over the previous year. During this time they registered 1.2 million new members.

During the first quarter of 1999, Piper Jaffray, an investment bank, added 1.2 million new accounts and $100 billion in new assets. Its number of trades per day had increased by 49 per cent.[2]

Cisco, the leader in internetworking equipment, produces routers and switching equipment. Responding to the rapid change of the Internet world, Cisco has learned how to overhaul its product line every two years. The rapid-ity of change in the computer industry inspired Cisco's Stanford University founders, Leonard Bosack and Sandra Lerner, to develop an organization based on innovation management.

---

2. *Ibid.*, pp. 237-241.

Cisco believes that continuous innovation demands that its organization be:

- built on change, not stability
- organized around networks, not rigid hierarchies
- based on interdependencies of partners, not self sufficiency
- constructed on technological advantage, not old-fashioned bricks and mortar.

From its starting point of working literally out of a garage in 1984, Cisco sold its first router in 1986. By 1987 its sales were $1.5 million, in 1989 it had hit $28 million and by 1991 it had hit $183 million. As the Internet came of age, Cisco's head start had made it unstoppable. The rest of the 1990s were focused on strategic growth acquisitions, thereby strengthening Cisco's position in its marketplace.[3]

DEFINING ECOMMERCE

When Zack was asked to define an eManager, he came up with Picture 2. For

---

3. Kalakota, Dr Ravi and Marcia Robinson, *eBusiness: Roadmap for Success* (Reading, Massachusetts: Addison-Wesley) 1999, pp. 73-76.

him, even at the age of eleven, an eManager is someone who lives with one finger on the Internet and uses the other hand to wave to his or her employees. An eManager knows eCommerce and eBusiness and optimizes the performance of his or her business through the use of these tools. So, what is eCommerce anyway? eCommerce can be defined as:

> The performance of business transactions (eBusiness) through electronic, primarily web based, means. It is the exchange of electronic transactions (i.e., commerce) between autonomous organizations, consumers, and/or vendors.

Traditionally commerce involved material sourcing, distribution systems, manufacturers, wholesalers, retailers and the eventual customer. As shown in Figure 2.1, each of these steps in the supply chain network required the transfer of information, usually in the form of printed documents. Transactions were kept at a distance. The transfer involved numerous documents such as requisitions, orders, bills of lading, picking documents, receiving documents, invoices and checks. Each document transfer process required extensive lead-time for document preparation and document transfer, usually measured in days. It also involved the costs associated with the transfer, such as postage, paper, labor, equipment and so on.

Figure 2.1: Traditional Value Management

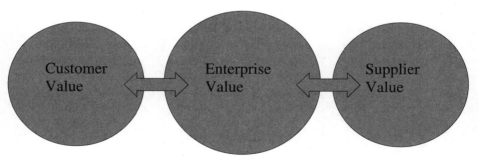

The movement to eCommerce attempted to speed up the vendor-to-customer cycle time while simultaneously reducing the costs of these activities and of the financial transactions. As shown in Figure 2.2, eTechnologies brought the transfer of information closer together. Initially this involved electronic data transfer systems like electronic data interface (EDI) or electronic funds transfer (EFT), or through the use of fax machines in order to send order-placement documentation. More recently this has involved web based environments. As the data linkage tightened (see Figure 2.3), suppliers were able to access customer information so that the supply chain linkage from the customer's customer through to the vendor's vendor could be more responsive.

Figure 2.2: eTechnologies Applies to Traditional Value Management

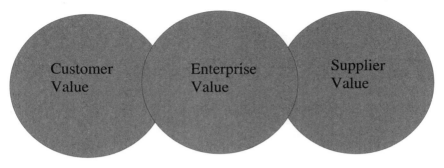

Figure 2.3: eTechnologies Introduced to eManager Value Management

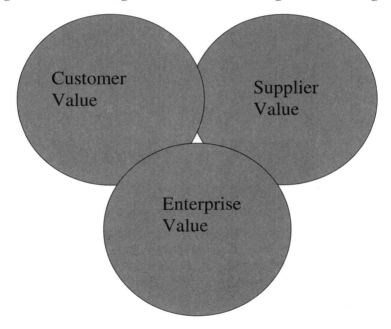

Eventually we see the linkages shown in Figure 2.4 where total information integration exists. For example, traditionally purchasing a computer would require the involvement of component vendors from all over the world, shippers, assemblers producing a standardized generic product package, wholesalers, distributors and retailers where the customer ultimately goes to select and purchase the computer. Dell Computers has changed this process, dropping a multitude of warehousing and logistics steps and by eliminating the retailer. Dell offers online computer configuration and purchasing. Now a

Figure 2.4: Supply Chain Integrated eManagement Value Management

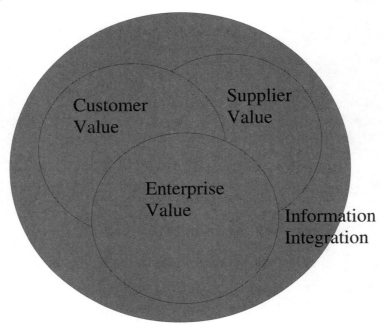

customer can purchase a customized product directly from the assembler and have it shipped directly to their location. The advantages of this eCommerce transaction is that there is significantly less paperwork and fewer steps in the process, thereby reducing cost. Additionally, the customer gets a customized product that he or she won't have to transport. Even the payment process is handled online through a secured web process.

eCommerce has come to be more than just the business transaction. It also incorporates all the activities that surround the transaction. A broader definition could be:

> Electronic commerce is a multidisciplinary field that includes technical areas such as networking and telecommunications, security, and storage and retrieval of multimedia; business areas such as marketing, procurement and purchasing, billing and payment, and supply chain management; and legal aspects such as information privacy, intellectual property, taxation, contractual and legal settlements.

> Adam, Dogramaci, Gangopadhyay and Yesha,
> *Electronic Commerce: Technical, Business, and Legal Issues*
> (Prentice Hall) 1999, page xi

eCommerce has affected all areas of business, including online stock purchasing, online banking, even, for example, online web based video renting and delivery. Food, household goods and even cleaning services can be acquired through paperless means. For example, the traditional bookstore has been replaced by organizations like Amazon.com, which can be accessed through the web. Here you can search through a book list for specific topics, titles, authors, etc. You can order and purchase the selected book and have it delivered directly to your location. If you have a specific book in mind, this web based book ordering process can be a tremendous timesaver over finding the time to go to a bookstore and then searching the bookstore for your book. Web purchasing avoids having to stand in line to pay for the book, or finding that the book you want isn't in the store and you have to order it anyway. This entire process can be handled online in minutes through a web based eBusiness transaction.

Additional elements of the eCommerce environment include eMail where messages can be sent immediately to anywhere around the world at relatively no cost when compared to traditional postal systems. There is also the eMall, where you can do your shopping online and make purchases and payments directly over the Internet. Another form of eCommerce is the enterprise resource planning (ERP) environments that integrate entire organizations through an intranet environment. These could be government organizations, businesses, financial systems, commercial systems or even countries. This intranet can access Internet environments like eCatalogs where purchase contracts have already been negotiated. Subscribers can have supplies or services drop-shipped directly at their location, saving time, transport costs, warehousing costs and paperwork.

> If senior executives don't have reasonably detailed answers to the "future" questions, and if the answers they have are not significantly different from the "today" answers, there is little chance that their companies will remain market leaders.
>
> Hamel and Prahalad[4]

There are numerous objectives behind the eCommerce push. eCommerce has created an entirely new way to do business, which offers a new form of convenience, speed and market efficiency in the delivery of goods and services. eCommerce has empowered people to explore new directions of competitiveness through supply chain efficiencies, new employment opportunities and a new international economics. For example, governments are looking for ways to streamline their processes, like the electronic filing of taxes or web

---

4. Hamel, Gary and C K Prahalad, "Competing for the Future", *Harvard Business Review*, (July-August 1994) pp. 122-128.

based renewal of vehicle registrations and licenses. And companies are transferring order information and engineering information using eMail and the Internet. eCommerce will:

- streamline the order placement process
- reduce product development cycle times
- reduce product delivery cycle times
- facilitate order customization
- empower small business to reach large markets
- create new services and businesses
- facilitate supply chain optimization
- facilitate improved planning and scheduling
- allow for the accessibility and sharing of information to a level never before deemed possible and at speeds previously considered unrealistic.

The Internet will catastrophically collapse in 1996.

Robert Metcalfe,
inventor of the Internet

FedEx is an impressive example of Internet implementation success. As far back as 1994, FedEx put its package tracking service online making the information accessible to its customers through the FedEx web site. Customers could track order information in detail at their own convenience without the need to work with telephone operators and service centers. FedEx supplied software for its customers that allowed them to access the Internet tracking system directly. What had previously been enterprise "private" information was now publicly accessible. The result was a greater degree of flexibility for the customers, increased customer confidence in FedEx and $2 million per year savings for FedEx.

The entry of FedEx into the Internet was the same as most other companies, through the order placement and tracking process. Soon they moved beyond order tracking into an intranet development that included personnel information tracking, tax forms, employee evaluations, project management information, the publication of technology reports and help-desk support.

KEY ELEMENTS OF AN ECOMMERCE ENVIRONMENT

In spite of the numerous eCommerce success stories, there are still far too many failures. The majority of the failures occur because many companies don't see eCommerce as a serious strategy tool. Rather, they see web sites as an opportunity to convey information about the company and its products, much like an online brochure. Companies like Barnes & Noble and Borders Books realized far too late that web sites could also be used for order placement and general customer servicing. It wasn't until companies like Amazon.com had started to significantly eat into their market share that they realized that a web customer servicing presence is critical for competitive success. The competitive standouts in eCommerce have realized that some of the key elements of an eCommerce environment should include systems that focus on:

- paper management — the elimination of paper whenever possible, not necessarily by creating electronic substitutes, but by totally eliminating paper when redundancy or duplication exists

- funds management — electronic financial transactions like the EFT environments

- time management — the elimination of waste steps in the processing of the transactions and the movement of goods; cycle time reduction for processing goods and the elimination of steps can be critical and, additionally, the transfer of information, like engineering drawings, can be performed utilizing email at speeds and efficiencies which were previously impossible

- responsiveness — giving the customer what they want, when they want it, and customizing it for their use — this is the primary competitive advantage for eCommerce business over traditional commercial environments

- cost efficiency — taking advantage of the cost reductions that are available through the use of electronic tools, like paperless or retail-less environments

- supply chain/value chain management — the management of all the steps in the supply chain, starting with the vendor's vendor through to the customer's customer and also focuses on the realization that all these steps are governed by an entire series of resources, each of which has demands and capacity limitations placed on them to resist their efficient performance; value chain management is the optimization of all the resources, including the financial resource, along the supply chain

- waste elimination and value-added transactions — this challenges all steps in the system and questions their value to the overall transaction — anything that does not add direct value to the overall process should be considered for elimination as a waste item

- customer support systems — true eCommerce focuses on customer satisfaction or customer relationship management (CRM) systems and customer satisfaction should be the primary reason for eCommerce existence; with that in mind, a customer support system allowing for feedback, complaints, questions and any other type of interaction must become a critical piece of the eCommerce environment.

American Management Systems (AMS), an IT consulting organization, developed a list of recommendations for successful CRM implementation. These include:

- focus on relationships and relationship pricing. AMS engages a relationship manager as well as a project manager for each of their consulting projects

- create innovate bundles of products and services

- provide superior customer service

- develop a compelling experience for customers

- customize and personalize

- convince customers that they need to return — make the web site a resource for information and/or entertainment, as well as a tool for business

- make routine tasks simple through re-engineering

- strive to match constant increases in customer expectations.[5]

> The philosophers have only interpreted the world, in various ways; the point, however, is to change it.
>
> Karl Marx

ECOMMERCE INTEGRATION

Amazon.com is commonly recognized as being one of the Internet success stories in that it boasts one of the highest sales volumes of all web based businesses. Its initial offering of books has expanded into music, toys, electronics products and software. However, Amazon.com's biggest play in the Internet world is its customized customer database. It collects information about each customer's buying patterns and is able to customize the presentation to the customer on its web site to fit the needs of every customer, even to the point of addressing them by name and offering them a list of recommended purchases.

Companies like Amazon.com have raised the level of customer expectation. Customers expect an integrated response from organizations that offer web services.

---

5. Helms, Marilyn M, op. cit., pp. 237-241.

Areas of eCommerce integration include:

- institution management (government, education, commerce, financial, etc.) — eCommerce can be used to integrate any of these institutional structures into an internal intranet which contains linkages out into the Internet environment

- network management (corporate, supply chain, inter-government agency, etc.) — eCommerce can be used to manage large networks of information or resource flows

- process management (ordering, contracting, production, sales/marketing, invoicing/payment, credit investigation, etc.) — eCommerce is an excellent tool for the management and integration of systems like the functional business systems of any institution.

Dell Computer Company also uses customer relationship management tools like personalization and customization. For its corporate customers it has a special customized premier page, which lists the products and services that are under contract with that particular customer. The page includes any special pricing, discounting or delivery arrangements. Ford Motor Company has reported a saving of $2 million in only one year by using Dell services.[6]

I think that there is a world market for maybe five computers.

Thomas Watson,
Chairman, IBM (1943)

FUTURE ECOMMERCE ENHANCEMENTS

640,000 bytes of memory ought to be enough for anybody.

Bill Gates (1981)

eCommerce development has already gone through several evolutionary iterations, but there is a lot more still to come.

Electronic signatures are just starting to become commonplace but the key problems are in the security of the signature and legal acceptance of the transaction. In security, preventing unauthorized use of the signature is still a problem. The other block to electronic signatures is a legal acceptance of the signature as if it were handwritten. In the future, electronic signatures will significantly reduce the processing of numerous financial and legal transactions.

---

6. *Ibid.*, pp. 237-241.

With digital cash, the ability to pay cash over the Internet is being explored. There are still legal and governmental concerns, but the bankcard has reduced some of these concerns. True electronic cash is still under consideration.

Encryption systems are another enhancement, as Internet security is still a major concern. Many of the Internet prophets predict that the next wave of Internet enhancements will be triggered by Internet fraud. Insufficient security systems, poorly managed firewalls, etc. exist throughout the Internet. An entirely foolproof way to prevent someone from intercepting Internet transactions has not been found. Currently, complex encryptions are very sophisticated, expensive, slow and need continual updating and modification. Tools like smart cards are being explored, but there is still a lot that needs to be accomplished. Likewise, robust infrastructure, an eCommerce infrastructure, which includes a system of standards, needs development.

The government policy makers have still not figured out how to get a handle on the Internet. As soon as they do, we can expect a system of taxation and a series of transaction regulations. These regulations will cover the movement of funds, the legal issues of interstate and inter-country commerce, the marketing tools and techniques and the morality issues that have already come under intensive discussion.

We have only begun to explore the potential of eCommerce. There are numerous ideas that have not even been thought of which may entirely change the way we utilize the Internet. For example, the medical, legal and government professions have not even seriously considered its potential and huge growth will most likely occur in each of these areas. Internationally, the Internet has not yet experienced the type of growth that it has seen in the United States and a similar growth is expected. Additionally, crime on the Internet has not yet been fully explored and we will most likely be in for a few surprises in this area. It is far too early to predict the future of the Internet.

We have reached the limits of what is possible with computers.

John van Neyman (1949)

SUMMARY

As with faith, in the Internet world, seeing is not believing. If you wait till you see, you're too late. Rather, "believing is seeing".

Gerhard Plenert

Recently NASA lost the Mars Climate Orbiter. Two labs were working on it — one using the metric system and the other using the US system of feet and inches. No one tested, checked or even thought to ask about the consistency of the measurement system — the orbiter crashed into Mars. What is the lesson we can all learn from this? Never underestimate the importance of communication. Today we receive e-mail, voice mail, snail mail, FedEx envelopes, beepers, cell-phones, faxes and, of course, the Internet, both at home and at work. We have no lack of information tools. Yet we still have the orbiter crashing into Mars because of a trivial communication error. Sometimes it is not the lack of information that creates the problem, it is the lack of common sense.

The Internet and eCommerce has just started to identify itself as a key world player in defining the competitive position of businesses. However, the successes of companies like Dell Computers, Amazon.com, FedEx, America on Line (AOL) and Cisco has demonstrated how quickly companies can lose their competitive position and their market share if they adopt a "wait and see" strategy to web development. eCommerce is no longer in the future, it has become part of the present, taking with it a transformation of the management structure. Traditional managers must now become eManagers who are expert eCommerce strategists if they are to maintain a competitive foothold.

> In five years, there won't be any Internet companies because they will all be Internet companies. Otherwise, they will die.
>
> Andy Grove,
> Chairman, Intel, (in USA Today)

SUGGESTIONS FOR FURTHER READING

As well as the reading material suggested by the footnotes, you might like to consult the following publications:

Kosiur, David, *Understanding Electronic Commerce* (Redmond, WA: Microsoft Press) 1997.

Plenert, Gerhard, *Making Innovation Happen: Concept Management Through Integration* (Boca Raton, FL: St. Lucie Press) 1998.

Plenert, Gerhard, *World Class Manager* (Rocklin, CA: Prima Publishing) 1995.

Chapter Three

Value Chain Management

As highlighted by the success of revolutionary companies such as Cisco and Dell, success is often measured in terms of supply chain versus supply chain.

Kalakota and Robinson,
eBusiness: Roadmap for Success

When eight year old Chelsey was asked to define an eManager, she drew Picture 3 of Eric who had everything in his life working so well that the sun was shining, rainbows were out and his feet weren't even touching the ground. This eManager is ready for the future. He knows the role of his supply chain and he has it under control to the point where it is an excellently performing value chain.

I asked friends to define a supply chain for me and a Chinese friend told me the proverb of how it takes 10,000 people to make bread. In this example you have the person who sells the bread, but behind that person is:

- the one who delivers the bread
- the one who bakes the bread
- the store that sells the grain
- the one who collects the ingredients
- the miller who mills the grain
- the farmer who grows the grain
- the farmer who milks the cow
- the toolmaker who makes the shovel
- the steel smith who makes the steel
- the carpenter who makes the handle
- the logger who cuts the tree
- the toolmaker who makes the saw
- the stonemason who cuts the grindstone
- the builder who builds the mill
- the seamstress who makes the uniforms
- the carver who makes the buttons
- the weaver who makes the cloth
- the weaver who makes the thread
- and so on!

From this example we see why it takes 10,000 people to make a loaf of bread. This entire network of materials movement is what is referred to as the supply chain. A definition of the supply chain could be:

> Supply Chain Management is the integration of all sub-processes that enable the exchange of information and the movement of goods between the suppliers' suppliers and the customers' end customers, including manufacturers, distributors, retailers, and any other enterprises within the extended supply chain. It is composed of three sub-processes: Demand Planning, Supply Planning, and Demand Fulfillment.

Although the concept of supply chain management is easy to conceptualize, the management of the supply chain becomes increasingly complex depending on the company size, the number of companies in the network, the diversity of the product mix, the number of variations (options) on products and the intensity with which the company pursues a global sourcing and delivery strategy.

Complexity is further compounded when we consider that a company may be associated with multiple supply chains concurrently. A manufacturer of plastics, for example, may simultaneously be a part of the supply chains for mechanical goods, industrial products, aircraft parts and automotive parts.

Despite the interdependent nature of these parts, many managers have viewed the components of the channel as separate entities or "islands of information", rather than as parts of a continuous system. From a standpoint of ownership, the components are separate, but from a business standpoint, the pipeline or channel is composed of naturally linked entities that function as partners. Thus, when one component within the channel experiences a change in business level, all processes in the component upstream or downstream will be affected. The affect can be magnified or reduced depending upon whether or not the item is being pushed or pulled because of operational or financial considerations.

Although every business has a supply chain, not all businesses manage their supply chain for competitive advantage. An example of this can best be illustrated by looking at Scott Paper. Upon acquisition of Scott Paper, Kimberly Clark performed a full review of inventory levels and replenishment policy within the newly acquired operations. Kimberly Clark noted that inventory levels within Scott Paper were inconsistent with the known consumer demand pattern. Subsequent analysis confirmed that Scott Paper's inability to anticipate sales at the end user level, coupled with an inadequate fulfillment policy, greatly minimized top line numbers. This lack of visibility resulted not only in inaccurate forecasts, but also excessive or constrained capacity, reduced customer service and excessive or insufficient inventories. Kimberly Clark was subsequently beholden to orders from resellers to create product forecasts, plan capacity, manage inventory and schedule production until a new supply chain strategy could be implemented.

Various studies have confirmed that inventories in many consumer packaged goods companies may be as high as 100 days of supply and, when considering raw materials, the total chain for some products could contain more than one year's supply of inventory.

Customer order changes, equipment failures, acts of god, employee unrest and competition have historically wreaked havoc on the business cycle. Traditionally, companies have responded by increasing inventory to offset this uncertainty. Today's business environment does not afford companies the luxury of preparing for this uncertainty through such means. High inventories translate to increased carrying costs and exposure to obsolescence that can limit a company's flexibility. Hence the only good reason to maintain inventory is that a condition exists that makes it less costly to have inventory than to not have it. Anytime inventory can be reduced, the company decreases costs and improves profitability. In fact, an efficient consumer response study, published by the Food Marketing Institute, concluded that 42 days could be removed from the typical grocery supply chain, freeing up $30 billion in current costs and reducing inventories by over 40 per cent. Decreasing the amount of time required to move inventory from one level of the chain to the next also shortens the cycle time of the entire chain and thereby increases competitiveness and customer satisfaction.

Companies practicing supply chain management (SCM) include, for example, Kimberly Clark, Dell Computers, Southwest Airlines, Hewlett Packard, Warner Lambert and Siemens. All have reported significant cost and cycle time reductions due to the implementation of SCM. Typical results show increased inventory turns, decreased out of stock occurrences and a replenishment cycle (cycle time) that has moved from weeks to days to, in some instances, hours.

There are numerous reasons contributing to the growing interest in supply chain management including:

- new collaboration technologies
- mass customization of products/services
- increase in short lead-time, customer responsive business
- shortened product life cycles
- increasing supplier delivery complexity
- cost reduction pressures
- globalization
- mergers and acquisitions
- smaller, core-competency focused companies
- functionality dispersion placing more companies into the network.

As we see in Figure 3.1, SCM is an integrated collection of linkages. The efficient management of those linkages is what constitutes SCM performance success. Companies like Wal-Mart Stores Inc. claim that the secret to their competitive success is found in their effective management of their supply chain. When a product is purchased in a retail outlet, the transaction is immediately reported to the warehouse and the replenishment process occurs with the replacements being sent out often that same evening.

> The ultimate difference in a company that manages its supply chain is their focus shifts from what goes on inside each of the links, to include the connections between the links.
>
> Marilyn M Helms, Editor,
> Encyclopedia of Management

SCM takes traditional enterprise management techniques and moves them "outside" the enterprise. Internally, as well as externally, many companies operate in silos. Internally we find separate divisions that treat each other with

Figure 3.1: Supply Chain Management

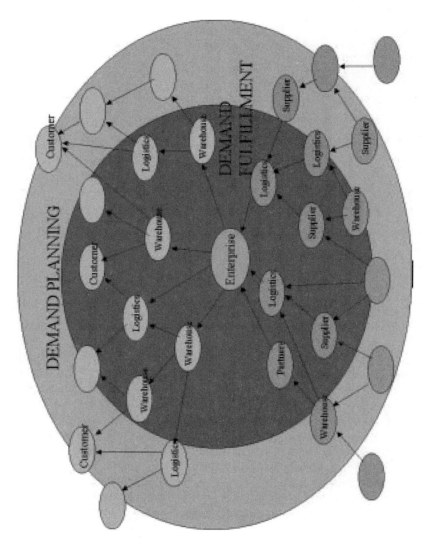

an "over-the-wall" approach to management. Similarly, externally, companies traditionally treat each other with this same avoidance and distance.

With SCM, the focus is no longer on what is happening internally, but rather the focus is on what is happening in the external network of materials movement and information exchange (see Figure 2.4 on page 16). Each of the functions or enterprises in the traditional network of enterprises is no longer an isolated individual entity. Rather, each function is managed as part of an interrelated and integrated network of entities. What happens to one entity directly effects what happens to all the other entities. Poor performance by one entity reflects badly on the entire network. Customers do not accept intra-network fingerprinting. A failure of one part of the network is a failure of the entire network. Therefore, all links in the network must "manage" and be able to collect information about all the other links in the network. Effective supply chain management is the development of the information and materials movement bridges that will allow network management.

SCM performance is highly recognized as the key to eManagement success. It is not enough to have a web presence. If you can't respond to that web presence at Internet speed, your customer base will rapidly erode. This performance is measured by the customers in terms of:

• product development cycle time
• product delivery cycle time
• on-time delivery performance
• market share performance.

Simultaneously, the SCM network of enterprises expects performance in stock evaluation, profitability, inventory and asset investment and utilization and financial ratios and measures.

The need to balance these performance areas is the focus of supply chain optimization. To achieve competitive advantage in today's markets, business needs to ensure that all levels of the supply chain collaborate effectively. By ensuring that all levels of the supply chain are working from the same information and enabling them to work in a manner best suited to their requirements, organizations can reduce time to market and stock inventory levels while minimizing bottom-line costs through resource optimization. Lack of effective collaboration affects an organization's ability to meet time-to-market constraints, affects bottom line costs and minimizes top line profitability. Conversely, well-implemented and controlled collaboration can provide a major business differential against competitors by offering the means to be highly responsive to market conditions. The future will see an emergence of techniques and technologies that will ensure that the customer receives the right product at the right location at the right time and at the right price while simultaneously optimizing the resource utilization of all entities in the supply/value network.

Many of the most impactful eBusiness solutions are aimed at transforming less glamorous but extremely important processes like supply-chain management, customer service and support, and distribution.

Louis V Gerstner,
CEO, IBM (October 1999)

THE VALUE CHAIN

Moving from the supply chain to the value chain requires an expansion of perspectives and direction. SCM focused on materials movement and information movement. Value chain management (VCM) expands that perspective to optimize all the resources with a focus on the "critical resource" for defining optimal performance. For example, in a service supply chain, or in an asset management/maintenance supply chain, materials are rarely the critical resource. In these cases, the critical resource often revolves around the technical abilities of the labor resource.

VCM takes a look at total factor productivity, which is the productivity of all the resources in the SCM and, based on Pareto's 80-20 Rule, selects the resource(s) that is the most critical to successful SCM performance. By focusing on the critical resource, the total productivity of the network can be optimized.

In Figure 3.2, the primary SCM components of materials flow management and information flow management can be seen at the bottom of the chart. We also see the network elements of suppliers, maintainers, service providers, operators, manufacturers, distributors, retailers and customers. VCM adds the total factor productivity optimization to the diagram. eCommerce adds the business-to-business (B2B) and the business-to-customer (B2C) dimension to the information integration. The result is a new paradigm for management — the eManager's network for performance optimization.

VCM has been defined as follows:

Value Chain Management (VCM) is the integration and optimization of all resources starting with the vendor's vendor. It integrates information, materials, labor, facilities, logistics, etc. into a time responsive, capacity managed solution that maximizes financial resources and minimizes waste, i.e. optimizes value for both the Supply Chain Network and the customers' customer.

Using this definition as a basis, it is helpful to review how VCM was developed. Traditional industries focused on vertically integrated operations. For example, if you manufactured a product you wanted to control the material sources, the transportation, the warehousing, the production and possibly even the retailing of your product. The theory was that the more vertical elements

Figure 3.2: SCM/VCM

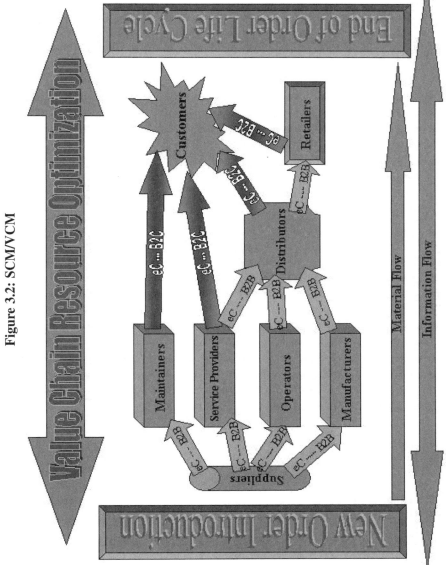

that were under your direct control, the more efficiently you were able to perform.

Competitive pressures internationally caused organizations to realize that they weren't good at everything. Organizations started to focus on what they did best and so they focused on their core competencies. This shift away from vertical integration encouraged organizations to look outside of themselves for services. For example, a manufacturer would have a shipping company do all their packaging and shipping. This introduced more steps in the vendor to customer linkage, making the management of this process more complex.

The trend toward operational diversification focused organizations on developing a supply chain where an organization would establish a relationship with shippers, vendors and customers so that all the linkages in the supply chain could be effectively integrated. These interrelationships became extremely complex to manage. Initially, the management of these relationships and linkages was primarily performance based. Having too many linkages in the supply chain would often cause poor responsiveness to customer demands. Time-to-market became the buzzword of successful competitive position. The organization that managed its supply chain the most effectively tended to have the competitive advantage.

Soon management realized that time responsiveness was not the only important element in customer satisfaction. The supply chain linkages also had a cost element and resource efficiency element associated with them. This realization generated a need for value chain management, which is the management of all the linkages of the supply chain in the most resource efficient way. Sometimes this includes the elimination of elements of the supply chain — for example, web marketing has eliminated the need for retail outlets.

Returning to the definition of value chain management, we can now look at the key aspects that are incorporated in VCM. These include integrated supply chain planning and scheduling, full resource management, cycle time responsiveness, chain-wide resource optimization and information integration. These can be considered in more detail.

Integrated Supply Chain Planning and Scheduling

The planning process for managing the supply chain is easy and has existed for many years. Systems like material requirements planning (MRP), manufacturing resources planning (MRP II), distribution requirements planning (DRP), theory of constraints (TOC), just-in-time (JIT), critical path methodology (CPM) and project evaluation and review technique (PERT) have performed the planning process effectively for the last 30 years. However, under these environments, capacity has been treated as an afterthought and therefore scheduling has been plagued with performance challenges. The introduction of capacity management tools like finite capacity scheduling (FCS) into the existing planning environments has allowed us to develop schedules that were optimizable both in timing and in cost. Most planning systems still do not include these scheduling elements and therefore focus on achieving delivery performance through the utilization of an overriding expedite process. FCS enhancements are a key piece in the development of efficient VCM environments.

Full Resource Management

Traditional environments focused on managing only the materials resource, assuming all the other resources had an infinite capacity. This fallacy in logic came from the limitations of the planning systems that were already discussed. In a centrally controlled environment where authoritarian rule existed, the expediting process could make this management style operational. Unfortunately, in a multi-stage supply chain integration, the scheduler needs to make sure that capacity limitations are considered at all steps in the supply chain. Expediting across the links of the supply chain was extremely difficult if not impossible. For example, the constrained resource at one link in the supply chain may be entirely different than the constrained resource at another step in the supply chain. For one step it could be labor while at another step it could be truck capacity. Therefore, a scheduling system that analyzed all the resource elements at all steps and constrained all these elements became a critical piece in value chain management.

Cycle Time Responsiveness

Total cycle time measures are needed because they have, in many cases, become more important than cost when it comes to competitive advantage. Strategic positioning requires a supply chain to be able to supply a customized product at speeds quicker than anyone else can supply the same product, even if it is not customized. Therefore, a measure of cycle time performance, measuring the time from when the order for a customized product is placed until it is delivered to the customer, becomes as important as price.

Chain-wide Resource Optimization

Value chain management adds the evaluation of not only all the traditional resources such as labor, materials and machinery but it also includes the optimal management of the time and the financial resources. Realizing that the supply chain has more steps than existed in the traditional vertical model, the margins of each step are smaller because each step needs to share a smaller piece of the overall margin pie. In order to accomplish this, value chain management focuses on value-added optimization (also referred to as waste elimination). Some organizations have interpreted this to include the elimination of steps in the supply chain, like the elimination of retailers in the online eMall. The efficient performance of all the remaining links in the supply chain is also carefully evaluated by each link.

Information Integration

Value chain management is meaningless if a total sharing of information does not exist amongst all elements of the supply chain. This includes all levels of information, from the operational information which includes capacities and work loads, to the strategic levels which includes vision and mission statements. This sharing of information has to be fully accessible and interactive, which suggests some sort of web based database. Each link of the supply chain will need to be able to evaluate the efficiencies and performances of all the other links in the supply chain. However, this information network should not be available to elements outside of the immediate supply chain, like competitors. The shared information within the chain will primarily be utilized by each of the elements of the supply chain for their specific planning and scheduling. It will also be utilized by the sales/marketing functions to generate realistic schedules for the customer and end consumer of the supply chain process. An overall finite capacity scheduling process will be necessary which must project realistic and feasible schedules while simultaneously optimizing cost and timing.

In summary, value chain management increases the number of steps in the supply chain by focusing on core competencies. VCM attempts to optimize the integrated efficiency of these steps in the management of resources, including the response time and the cost resource.

> If you focus just on the buyer-seller transaction, or the procurement aspect, or just on the customer-facing part of the organization, a lot of the advantage to be gained from managing value chains is left out of the picture.
>
> Gordon Swartz,
> Oxford Associates Inc.[1]

THE ENTERPRISE OF THE FUTURE

> There's no doubt that technology accounts for only about ten per cent of the entire effort to adopt a value-chain model. . .The other ninety per cent concerns cultural issues.
>
> Andrew White,
> Longility Inc.[2]

---

1. Sheridan, John H, "Managing the Value Chain for Growth", *Industry Week* (6 September 1999) pp. 50-66.
2. *Ibid.*

All companies have a supply chain, but very few manage it effectively. As we look to the future we see enterprises that have the following characteristics:

- globalized management style
- core competency focus of business creating smaller companies
- greater tendency to outsource non-core competency functions
- smaller companies cause more companies in the supply chain
- eCommerce business methodologies
- web based data and information sharing
- advanced planning and scheduling methodologies for supply chain efficiencies
- finite capacity scheduling mathematical tools
- strategic partnerships and alliances
- network based competitive practices
- more indirect selling through web based tools
- more customer customized products
- faster customer service through shorter cycle times
- value chain analysis which goes beyond materials efficiencies
- motivation focused measurement tools
- empowered and responsive workforce
- competitors in one supply chain may be partners in another supply chain.

All of these characteristics point to two eventualities — SCM and VCM are critical to competitive success and the SCM will become more complex, thereby requiring more sophisticated management structures.

Technology is fueling revolutionary changes in our world. At the same time, business is facing global competition, convergence, deregulation and the consumer's growing appetite for personalized services. Savvy organizations are riding this wave of change to unprecedented levels of success. These enterprises of the future *or next generation enterprises* (NGE) are leading the charge — using sophisticated technologies and innovative business models to embrace customers, suppliers, partners and employees in a new model of collaboration.

A next generation enterprise is an enterprise that successfully integrates business and technology to provide unprecedented value to customers on their own terms and with astounding efficiency. Technology is necessary to become a next generation enterprise, but it is not sufficient. An enterprise must go beyond using new technology within an existing framework. It must rethink its fundamental business model.

A next generation enterprise is actually a value network — a network of enterprises — that operate in such an integrated fashion that traditional organizational boundaries are blurred. These value networks share data (for example, capacity, sales, cost, lead time and inventory data) and optimize its use across the entire network to ensure that the network, rather than individual organizations, perform to peak efficiency.

Next generation enterprises, and the value networks that they represent, will lead their industries in the years to come. Value networks, rather than individual organizations, will compete against each other. They will operate in a dynamic global environment with few barriers to competition. They will have the potential to reach a vastly larger customer base. They will succeed in an environment where customers expect instant access, day or night, to customized products and services.

How do you recognize a next generation enterprise? Next generation enterprises are characterized by their:

- integration — they integrate and align with customers, suppliers and partners
- leverage — they leverage organizational resources
- maturity — they embrace the concept of the value network.

> Just as the assembly line symbolized the industrial age, the supply chain
> will become the symbol of the Internet age.
>
> Richard Karpinski

Integration—Align with Customers, Partners and Suppliers

A next generation enterprise collaborates and inter-operates with partners, suppliers and customers to an unprecedented degree. It achieves this high level of integration through customer value management, supplier value management and enterprise management.

Customer value management — a next generation enterprise focuses on its customers (which can be consumers or other businesses) and strives to increase the value that it provides to them and derives from them. It extends the boundaries of its own organization to embrace its customers — to provide them with direct access to information, products and services. It actively listens to its customers and responds to their needs and desires.

Supplier value management — a next generation enterprise knows that it cannot stand alone. It expands its boundaries to encompass its business partners and suppliers. From simple information sharing, it progresses to enhanced customer service, supply chain management and collaborative products.

Enterprise management — feedback and learning within the organization serve to enhance the value of customer and supplier relationships and to respond to market trends with new and improved products and services. A next generation enterprise fully leverages the knowledge that it possesses and nurtures the ongoing process of knowledge creation. It considers knowledge a key competitive advantage. It promotes knowledge acquisition, delivery and storage. It actively uses knowledge (for example through data mining, decision engines and online analytical processing) and strategic intellectual capital.

Leverage—Use Organizational Resources to Advantage

A next generation enterprise leverages:

- people — employees are empowered to increase productivity and effectiveness through collaboration and innovation, and performance is measured in terms of the value that an individual adds to the enterprise

- process — process follows function; every element, every procedure, every structure of a next generation enterprise exists to contribute to the value network and to support the attainment of shared business goals; the management hierarchy is flattened; the primary role of managers is to support, rather than direct, highly productive and empowered employees; the work setting maximizes productivity

- technology — new technologies enable product and service innovation, they support knowledge leverage across the organization and enable the efficient movement of information

- organization — the organization fully leverages its competitive abilities, reaches out to its partners in the value network to complement its strengths and embraces its customer's goals as its own.

Maturity—Embrace the Value Network

The concept of a next generation enterprise continues to evolve as business gradually absorbs successive technological advances. During each of the past three decades, we have witnessed movement toward global, extended enterprises. These can be labeled *ad hoc,* independent enterprises, coordinated enterprises, relationship value network and business redefinition.

Ad hoc — in the 1960s and earlier, prior to the rise of computer-based business automation, organizations were insular and protective. Their processes were manual and highly sequential. The flow of information was limited and decision-making was hierarchical.

Independent enterprises — during the 1970s, enterprises were mainly independent entities (see Figure 3.3). They concentrated on automating internal processes. Even large, global corporations defined their boundaries very narrowly. Interactions with suppliers and partners were localized, rigid and at arms length. Customers were often served through intermediaries. The flow of resources and information was restricted and hierarchical — even within organizational boundaries.

Co-ordinated enterprises — during the 1980s, advances in electronic data

Figure 3.3: Independent Enterprises

interchange led to widening links to suppliers and partners, as shown in Figure 3.4. Large organizations began to realize new efficiencies related to direct interaction with suppliers and partners. For example, large retail organizations provided key suppliers with direct access to inventory status, streamlining the reordering process and enabling them to optimize onsite inventory. For the most part, however, links to suppliers and partners were achieved by automating existing manual processes and the underlying processes and relationships did not change fundamentally.

Relationship value network — in the 1990s, the Internet revolutionized the relationship between organizations and their customers by providing a direct, personal link (see Figure 3.5). This openness spawned a new ability to know the customer, interact directly, customize products and services and get immediate feedback on the relationship. In addition, links to suppliers and partners were widened. Organizations began re-engineering and redefining their relationships — to customers, suppliers and partners — rather than merely automating existing manual links.

Business redefinition — in the coming years, these relationships will be enriched and expanded, forming seamless extended enterprises (see Figure 3.6). New value networks will be defined. Distinctions between suppliers, partners and enterprises themselves will be blurred. The result will be a network of extended enterprises that work together to offer exceptional value and responsiveness to their customers, while achieving remarkable success for their employees, partners and stockholders.

**Figure 3.4: Co-ordinated Enterprises with Links to
Suppliers and Partners**

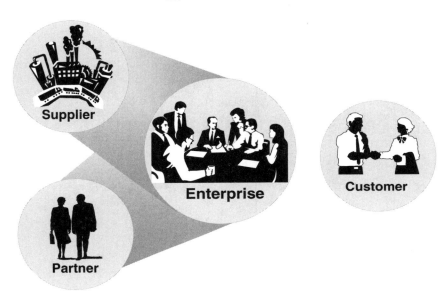

Figure 3.5: Links to Customers Forge Relationship Value Networks

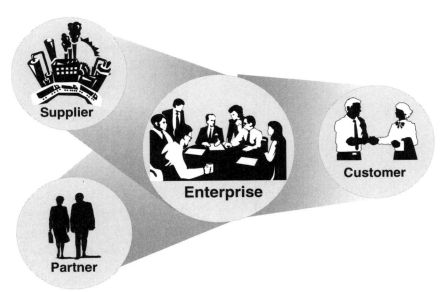

**Figure 3.6: Business Redefinition through Networks of
Extended Enterprises**

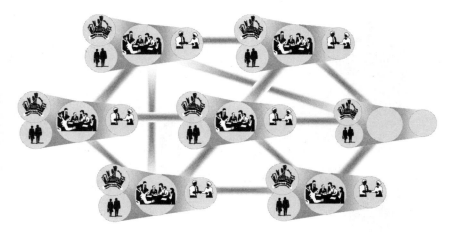

While the trends are clearly visible, all enterprises are not at the same level of maturity with respect to this evolution. In the future, business success will depend on the enterprise's ability to transform itself along this continuum and to mature into a next generation enterprise.

In summary, the enterprise of the future requires three key elements:

• technologies — like eCommerce
• SCM and VCM optimization methodologies
• eManagers that know how to integrate these processes and tools.

Make it so!

Captain Picard,
Star Trek — The Next Generation

PLANNING AND SCHEDULING

It's a supply-chain versus supply-chain world today. Companies don't only compete with each other but with an extended web of suppliers.

Rob Rodin,
CEO, Marshall Industries

The enterprise resources planning (ERP) systems fad, now finally passing, introduced management and information transfer systems within the enterprises. From this base of information, ERP systems were able to develop a number of planning tools like rough cut capacity analysis and aggregate production planning (sometimes referred to as aggregate production scheduling). However, we need to draw a distinction between planning and scheduling tools. A planning system is a forward-looking system that makes projections on demand and resource availability, primarily based on history. Tools like forecasting, the business plan and aggregate production planning are planning tools. A scheduling system is one that focuses on the present. For example, if I receive a customer order today, when is the actual date on which I can have the product shipped to that customer?

A planning system works based on history and averages. A scheduling system works on actual current demand on capacity and the actual remaining available-to-promise capacity. Planning systems focus primarily on the internal enterprise, whereas scheduling systems focus initially at the internal enterprise, but soon find themselves integrating the entire supply chain network into the scheduling process. ERP systems are planning systems.

The next wave of competitive development is in the efficient scheduling of the supply chain/value chain. The tools of the future will be advanced planning and scheduling systems and on finite capacity scheduling. For example, under existing ERP systems an order for a product will be placed and an average, estimated lead-time will be quoted as the delivery date. Additionally, based on the actual decided-upon delivery date, a production schedule is generated that will push the start of the production/supply process based on this estimated date. It can almost be guaranteed that this estimated lead-time will be incorrect. This date may be unrealistic because the capacity needed to produce this product is already allocated and is no longer available. Or, another failure of the system can be that the capacity exists in abundance and the product is completed way too early in the process. The result is that the company will need to inventory the completed item until it is time to ship the product. Either situation is unacceptable. Hence, scheduling systems are now being developed that will facilitate the analysis of the actual demand on resources against the actual availability of resources. These systems need to incorporate the actual schedules and capacities of the suppliers, shippers and warehouses and so on — in other words, the entire supply chain.

The future performance of the supply chain hinges on the efficient performance of the scheduling tools utilized to manage the supply chain. Expanding this efficiency across all resource areas creates the field of value chain management and ultimately, when the customer perceives an increase in their value, they will respond accordingly causing the supplier to customer relationship to improve.

In the vast tract of online business-to-business eCommerce – projected to speed past $1 trillion in annual revenue by 2003 – supply chain management is slowly taking center stage: AMR Research of Boston predicts the online SCM market growing forty-eight per cent annually over the next five years. Revenues in 1999 of $3.9 billion will swell to $19 billion in 2003 . . .

Walid Mougayar,
Business 2.0 Magazine

SUMMARY

A candle loses nothing by lighting another candle.

Father James Keller,
Founder, The Christophers

Supply chain management is the Borg Collective (*Star Trek*) of interactive networking wherein all members of the collective share equally in the information and materials exchange. The collective increases its power through the information assimilation process. Value chain management takes the collective to the next level, wherein each member is rewarded (or penalized) through the synergistic performance of the collective. A special set of tools are introduced so that the collective's performance is evaluated and optimized.

Supply chain management and value chain management are a strategy and methodology that considers the combined impact of components and processes required to meet customer demand. This includes the procurement, purchasing, warehousing, production and distribution of the associated products and services from the "vendor's vendor to the customer's customer". The ultimate goal of supply chain management is thus to ensure that the customer receives the *right product* at the *right location* at the *right time* and at the *right price* while simultaneously optimizing the resource utilization of all entities in the supply/value network.

An eManager is capable of creating a SCM/VCM Borg Collective through the efficient optimization of eCommerce tools. This manager is simultaneously an innovative leader in both technology and management methodology. This book will now discuss management methodologies that are necessary for the eManager of the future.

. . . the alarming reality is that for many companies, their supply chain suffers from its weakest – offline – links, and can't fully support an eBusiness with the speed and flexibility the Net economy demands. But not for long.

Walid Mougayar

SUGGESTIONS FOR FURTHER READING

For further reading on this topic, you might find the following publications useful:

Hughes, Jon, Mark, Ralf and Bill Michaels, *Transform Your Supply Chain* (London: Thomson Business Press) 1999.

Kalakota, Dr Ravi and Marcia Robinson, *e-Business: Roadmap for Success* (Reading, Mass.: Addison Wesley) 1999.

Plenert, Gerhard and Shozo Hibino, *Making Innovation Happen: Concept Management Through Integration* (Boca Raton, FL: St. Lucie Press) 1998.

Plenert, Gerhard, *World Class Manager* (Rocklin, CA: Prima Publishing) 1995.

Plenert, Gerhard and Bill Kirchmier, *Finite Capacity Scheduling* (New York: John Wiley & Sons, Inc.) 2000.

PART II

World-class Management

CHAPTER FOUR

Management

> . . . for a conscious being, to exist is to change, to change is to mature, to mature is to go on creating oneself endlessly.
>
> Henri Bergson,
> French philosopher

As a farmer was walking through one of his fields one day, he came across a frightened baby eagle clumsily stumbling, trying to run to escape. He felt sorry for the bird. It looked as though its parents had abandoned it and it was too young to be able to fly. The farmer picked up the little bird, took it back to the farm and placed it with a flock of baby turkeys that had recently hatched. The eagle grew up eating turkey food, walking like a turkey, talking with turkeys, learning from turkeys and thinking that being a turkey was the best thing to be.

One day the farmer decided the eagle was old enough to return to the wild on its own and so he took it out to the field to show it that it could fly. He picked up the eagle and threw it up in the air. But the eagle, still thinking like a turkey, fell back to the ground. The farmer tried again, throwing the eagle higher. He reasoned that if the eagle saw that it hurt to hit the ground, he might be forced to spread its wings and fly. But again, the eagle hit the ground. The farmer repeated this process over and over for several days until one day the eagle, frustrated and tired of hitting the ground, spread its wings and realized it wasn't a turkey after all. It could fly. It was an eagle.

Many of us have been raised like managerial turkeys, thinking that the way we were taught to do things is the best way and that we shouldn't question anything. It is time to quit falling to the ground and to realize that we are eagles. We may hit the ground a few times before we realize it, but *we are eagles*, and we can fly. This book will help us fly. We need to:

- be leader who motivate and direct change
- be world-class eManagers.

World-class management and flying like an eagle are related. Actually they are quite similar, but you'll have to read this entire chapter to find out all the ways they are similar. First, we must start by establishing a better definition of what a world-class eManager is. To accomplish this we need to:

- figure out where we are at (point A)
- figure out where we want to be (point B)
- develop a strategy (travel plan) to get us from point A to point B
- consider the tools that are available to help us reach our destination.

The process begins! The first step is to look at some of the different types of management styles that exist so we can figure out what type of manager we are.

> Now here, you see, it takes all the running you can do, to keep in the same place. If you want to get somewhere else, you must run at least twice as fast as that.
>
> Lewis Carroll,
> *Through the Looking Glass*

THE TYPES OF MANAGERS

There are several types of managers and there are numerous ways to categorize them. For example, there is the *sunrise manager* who has a view towards the future, as opposed to the *sunset manager* who fights fires in the here-and-now. We often think of the sunrise manager as the dreamer with the wild ideas that never go anywhere, whereas the sunset manager is the workaholic who is great at getting things done in a hurry. Another way of looking at these managers is to consider the sunrise manager as a progressive, leading edge, technology-minded manager. This type of manager is brought into an organization when it is looking for growth or change. A sunset manager is brought in when an organization is trying to stabilize a current situation. For example, trying to revive or sustain existing programs that are starting to falter would be a good reason to hire a sunset manager. Are you a sunrise manager or a sunset manager?

Another way to classify managers is to consider their attitudes toward their subordinates. The two extremes are the *authoritarian manager* and *participative manager.*

Authoritarian managers are typified by being secretive, having their fingers in everything that happens, always having the final word and telling, rather than asking. This type of manager is often referred to as the *Theory-X manager.*

Participative managers value employee opinions. They spend more time listening than talking during a meeting. They look for ideas from the bottom, realizing that employees have the best understanding of day-to-day operations. These managers use these bottom-up ideas for top-down management and implementation of the ideas for change. They are concerned about employee job satisfaction and rewards. This type of manager is often referred to as a *Theory-Y manager*.[1]

There is a second type of participative manager. These managers tend to empower employees to make their own decisions and to implement their own ideas. This form of participative management is referred to as the *Theory-Z manager*.[2] In this management style we switch the top-down decision-making process that is characteristic of the Theory-X or Theory-Y management style, to a bottom-up, decision-making process characteristic of the Japanese management style. In the Theory-Z style we are heavily involved in teaming, like the quality circles of old (a Japanese methodology for empowerment and teaming) and we use the teams to develop, approve and implement ideas. Managers take on the role of facilitator, being responsible to make sure the approved ideas get implemented timely and correctly. These managers are no longer the decision makers and drivers of forward progress. Theory-Z managers keep their teams focused and present them with areas that need consideration and evaluation, but let the team make their own improvement decisions. So, are you a Theory-X, Theory-Y or Theory-Z manager?

A third way to classify managers is to use the *five Cs*. These are cash, crisis, conflict, cool and change managers.

Cash manager — cash managers focus on costs and budgets and have probably come through the accounting or finance ranks. This type of manager tends to be risk-averse and looks toward stability rather than opportunity. Cash managers find it advisable to patch-and-repair old technology, as opposed to replacing it with new technology, primarily because it would be too difficult to cost-absorb it all in one or two fiscal years. This management style is why we still have so many outdated factories in the United States when we know they cannot be competitive in the long run. However, since the old factories are still demonstrating some minor profit levels, they are kept and maintained until they are totally unprofitable. Then the plants are transferred overseas, where labor costs are cheaper. The cash manager feels the need to look for short-term profitability rather than long-term competitiveness.

Crisis (or crash) manager — crisis managers believe you shouldn't fix anything that isn't broken. This style of manager, like the cash manager, strives toward stability, looking at problems as disruptions that need to be conquered, rather than as opportunities for future improvements. These managers attack

1. For more information about Theory-X and Theory-Y managers, including some very interesting examples, read the book: McGregor, Douglas, *The Human Side of the Enterprise* (New York: McGraw-Hill) 1985.
2. Theory-Z management is explained nicely, including examples, in Pascale, Richard Tanner and Anthony G Athos, *The Art of Japanese Management* (New York: Warner Books) 1982; Joiner Jr, Charles W, "Making the 'Z' Concept Work", *Sloan Management Review* (Spring 1985) pp. 57-63.

problems without considering the roots of the problems, thereby fixing only a symptom and not the cause. Often the fix includes the installation of another "system" to monitor the problem and catch it if it happens again.

Conflict manager — conflict managers look at the workplace as a battlefield of competing players. They always feel the need to take and maintain the upper hand through whatever means necessary. Control is the primary tool of power and intimidation is the primary motivating force. This type of manager is the reason unions were formed.

Cool manager — cool managers believe the work force is best motivated by giving it whatever it wants. These managers try to bribe their way into the hearts of their children, which is how they view their employees. They want to be everybody's best friend and want everyone to smile at them as they walk by. The cool manager often has wishy-washy management style that results in more confusion than direction.

Change manager — change managers search for challenges in competitiveness. These managers thrive on positive, goal-focused changes, seeing them as the opportunities that make work exciting. Changes are viewed as opportunities for growth. They see problems as opportunities for change. Rather than trying to fix problems, change managers spend time looking for the roots of the problems and attempt to generate the necessary changes that will make the problems disappear.

Using the five Cs to define a management style requires integration with the other classifications. For example, you could have a manager that is sunrise, cool and Theory-X. This would be a happy, smiley, bossy dreamer. Have you identified yourself yet? Let's add one more classification category before we integrate the management styles.

A last but important method for classifying a manager is to compare the "boss" to the "leader". A boss directs employee traffic, whereas a leader shows the way using appropriate examples and by stepping out into the traffic in front of the employees. Bosses manage, but leaders tend to lead out and search for a difference. Bosses see themselves as "King of the Hill" and want to keep the hill for themselves, whereas leaders show and help everyone get to the top of the hill themselves. Bosses strive with a "do as I say" philosophy, whereas leaders use the "do as I do" technique. With leaders, employees tend to have a clear definition of what is expected of them because the example set by the leader who has shown them their objective. Simply put, bosses provide stability and governance, while leaders open the door for innovation.[3]

The boss is someone who has to be there for the business to run correctly. Without the boss, the employees lose the decision-maker. It's often a situation

---

3. Many good articles discuss the role of leaders in a changing, growing organization. For example, Senge, Peter M, "The Leader's New Work: Building Learning Organizations", *Sloan Management Review* (Fall 1990) pp. 7-23. This article focuses on the need for an

where "while the cat's away, the mice will play". Alternatively, leaders are people who, if they did not show up to work for a few days, they would not be missed. All the employees would know how to keep the business functioning and the leader's absence would hardly be noticed. Good leaders are people who manage themselves into obsolescence.

Insecure managers create complexity. Real leaders don't need clutter.

John F Welch, Jr,
Chairman and CEO, General Electric[4]

WHAT TYPE OF MANAGER ARE YOU?

Now it's time for you to classify yourself. You need to integrate the different types of management style in order to define your own personal style. What type of manager do you think you are? Are you a Theory-X, sunset, cash manager, which would be a bean-counting, bossy, fire-fighter telling everyone what to do, how to do it and when to do it and insisting that no one does anything until directed? Or are you a Theory-Y, sunrise, cool leader who loves everyone, likes to show rather than tell everyone how to do their job and shares your schemes of grandeur with your employees? Figure out what type of manager you are. Remember:

Before you can figure out where you're going, you have to know where you're starting from.

Use Figure 4.3 on page 80 to evaluate yourself. Mark an N, O or Y next to each of the management types in order to get a clear picture of where you are now. Now that you have classified yourself, have your peers evaluate you using Figure 4.3 as a grading sheet. Next, have your employees evaluate you using some form of blind vote. You may be surprised to find out what kind of manager others think you are.

Now you know a little more about yourself. You know what your man-

---

organization to be "continuously learning" through leadership. Kotter, John P, "What Leaders Really Do", *Harvard Business Review* (May-June 1990) pp. 103-111. This article stresses that "good management controls complexity; effective leadership produces useful change." The article observes that "management controls people by pushing them in the right direction; leadership motivates them by satisfying basic human needs" and offers three interesting leadership examples (American Express, Eastman Kodak and Procter & Gamble).

4. Jack Welch's opinions about what makes a good manager (business leader is the term Jack prefers) is discussed in an interesting article — Tichy, Noel and Ram Charan, "Speed, Simplicity, Self-Confidence: An Interview With Jack Welch", *Harvard Business Review* (September-October 1989) pp. 112-120.

agement style is right now. The next step toward being a world-class eManager is to define your management style *goal*. After that, we need to set a travel plan that will take you from where you are and get you to where you're going. We'll spend the rest of the book doing that. But for now, let's take a close look at our target.

The road to world-class leadership is not a journey, it is a race!

THE WORLD-CLASS EMANANGER

Another chart has been created in an attempt to help you to classify yourself in your present state and to help you clearly define your target. With four different methods for classifying management styles, a diagram representing all of the management options would require four dimensions. Unfortunately, a sheet of paper limits us to two dimensions. Even Steven Spielburg has difficulty showing us four dimensions on a two-dimensional surface (the movie screen). Figure 4.1 breaks down the two most complex management style classifications. From Figure 4.1 we see all sorts of mixes and matches of management styles. These mixtures of styles are detailed in Figure 4.4 on page 81.

World-class is being a Theory-Z change manager. Looking at Figure 4.1, it doesn't matter where we find ourselves now, we should strive toward Theory-Z change manager status. Now let's take a look at the last remaining two classification categories. As a world-class eManager, we want to be a sunrise rather than a sunset manager, always looking for alternatives and options for improvement, but realizing that many of these options will fail. Also, as a world-class eManager we want to be leaders rather than bosses, motivating and guiding our employees by our hard work and our farsighted examples.

Finally, we know what a world-class eManager should look like. A world-class eManager should be a:

- sunrise manager — long-term orientation looking for the "better way"
- Theory-Z manager — having employees involved with and guiding the business process through participative and empowered team efforts
- change manager — guiding a dynamic, evolving business organism that capitalizes on change opportunities
- leader — being a character building, motivational example.

The wicked leader is he who the people despise.
The good leader is he who the people revere.
The great leader is he who the people say, "We did it ourselves."

Lao Tsu

Figure 4.1: What Type of Manager Are You?

	Theory-X	Y	Z
Cash	Totally Impersonal Quick to Fire	Calculated but Sharing	Cost-Conscious Employees
Crisis	The "General"	Self-Directed Fire Fighting	Frustrated Employees
Conflict	The "Boss"	Confusion	WAR
Cool	Decision with Confusion	Self-Directed Confusion	No Direction
Change	Enforced Improvements	Overriding Motivation	On the Right Track

Having categorized world-class eManagers and determined how to "slot" them, let's now decide why we want to fit into this slot. It's like saying we should be eagles, when most of us are quite happy being turkeys and thinking that a turkey is a good thing to be. A world-class competitive stance will not allow us to be anything but world-class eManagers. World-class eManagers look to the future: a highly competitive future; a future full of changes. World-class eManagers realize that their employees are the key to motivating successful change and that employees are led, not bossed. Turkeys walk into the future, tripping over change as it happens to them, but eagles fly over the changes and out into a successful hereafter.

WORLD-CLASS MANAGEMENT EXAMPLE

Numerous organizations are attempting to move themselves toward world-class management status. For example, Tridon-Oakdale placed its management team in a hotel to get them away from the everyday bustle of fire fighting. The goal given to these managers was to "work out a new vision for Tridon". The result was a complete turnaround in both management style and output performance.

Some of the changes that occurred included the following:
- an organization chart turned upside down with employee teams on the top
- a new quality standard, which far exceeded that of Tridon's competitors
- "legendary customer service"
- competitive pricing
- reduced inventory and lead times
- a $6 million turnaround.

Some of the keys to success included a new mission statement with a commitment to change, an improved focus on building relationships between all employees, employee participation and the goal of having "everyone speak", total quality control, Kanban "just-in-time" manufacturing, "smart change" management that focused on doing the right things and, finally, a focus on technology improvements.[5] Total quality will be discussed in more detail in Chapters 6 and 13.

Tridon has demonstrated that world-class management works, but it considers itself as just getting ready for the next wave of improvements.[6]

> Now that we are in a constant state of change, nothing will ever remain the same.

> Don Green,
> Chairman, Tridon

THE WORLD-CLASS EMANAGER

A world-class eManager views the future as an opportunity. The here and now is adequate for the past, but just not good enough for the future. This manager views all aspects of the enterprise — systems, production philosophies and even management styles that were in existence 20 to 30 years ago — as wholly deficient for today and especially inadequate for the future.

By their very nature, world-class eManagers are risk takers, since change always involves risk. Additionally, the long-term perspective of world-class eManagers often makes them unpopular in the short run. World-class mangers enjoy the excitement of being leading edge innovators, despite the occasional failures they will suffer on this risky management road.

---

5. Later in this chapter we will discuss the Toyota production system as an example of continuous change and innovation. Toyota developed the Just-in-Time (JIT) production process, which uses a production control tool called the Kanban card. This card tracks and controls the quantity of products through the production process.
6. For an interesting article on Tridon, see Tonkin, Lea, "Workshop Report: Canadian Region — Building on the Past at Tridon-Oakdale", *Target* (Summer 1990) pp. 34-37.

World-class management is soaring with the eagles. It's finding the eagle within you and changing your lifestyle so that you can soar. It's the ability to *change yourself* faster than the *changes that are trying to affect you*. World-class eManagers are in control of change, rather than letting change control them. They are innovators and adventurers. They have the ability to listen, when listening is wiser than talking.

World-class management is motivating positive, goal directed change. It is being in control of change. It is using change to your advantage. But being in control of change is not a simple task. There are many facets to change. To be effective users of change, we need to consider all these facets, plan for them, strategize their usage and utilize them to our advantage.

All change is not positive change. Changing just for the sake of changing is foolish. Thinking through the consequences and effects of changes is as important as implementing the changes. Changes need to make a positive contribution toward goal achievement, without sacrificing the value system (ethics and integrity) of the enterprise. However, not changing for fear of making a mistake is the same as deciding not to be world-class.

To manage change, we need to be innovators and creators. An innovator searches for opportunities to change. An innovator sees opportunity in every problem and looks for ways to take advantage of opportunities. Innovators work with others, as team players, because they understand the synergistic ideas created by teamwork. The creator takes newly found opportunities and turns them into defined projects, activities or programs that will take advantage of the recent discoveries.

The management of change also takes an adventurer and a general. The adventurer is not afraid to take a chance on change and looks for the opportunity to do battle, to take an idea and to drive forcefully forward. An adventurer despises the routine and mundane and looks for opportunities to break away, always searching for new areas to discover. Generals know that they can't win the battle alone. Even Michael Jordan (formerly of the Chicago Bulls), who was probably one of the greatest basketball players of his time, as great a player as he was, could not have won one basketball game without four other players on the court.

Two basic questions still need to be answered:

1. Why should we go through the change process? Change is inevitable and will run you over if you're not ready for it. This book will teach you how to get ready for change.

2. Why is change necessary? There are several reasons for change. The first reason is competition, whether from domestic or foreign competitors. We need to improve to stay on top of our competitors. Another reason for change is to take advantage of technological advancements, such as automation or computerization. Still another reason for change is the changing habits of our customers. Customer awareness programs,

environmental consciousness, resource scarcity, governmental regulations and economic swings affect the way customers think and act and force us to change the way we manage.

To live is to change, and to be perfect is to have changed often.

John Henry Newman,
English Cardinal and Writer

At this point, having a somewhat clearer view of the characteristics of a world-class eManager, we are ready to take a look at why change is such an important part of the lifestyle of this manager.

A DISCUSSION OF CHANGE

One day a man was leading his donkey down the street. After a short distance, the donkey decided he didn't want to travel any farther. He stopped in his tracks, put his rump on the ground and wouldn't budge. The man tugged at the donkey's rope and tried to coax it to get up and walk. The coaxing soon turned to name calling and threats involving glue factories. The donkey didn't move. A neighbor was passing by and stopped to help the frustrated donkey owner.

"The only way you're going to get that donkey to move is by talking nice to it," the neighbor advised.

Indignantly the donkey owner challenged his neighbor to see if he could do any better with the stubborn critter. The neighbor picked up a two-by-four that was lying by the side of the road and proceeded to give the donkey a swift, hard wallop right between the eyes. Then he pulled on the rope softly and asked the donkey to get up. The donkey immediately stood up and followed the neighbor down the street.

"Didn't you say I should talk nice to the donkey?" the donkey owner protested.

"Of course! And I did," said the neighbor, "but first I had to get his attention."

Sometimes managers are like donkeys. Sometimes we need to be hit by a two-by-four on the side of the head before we will start paying attention.[7] Often, change brings out the donkey in all of us. Remember:

Change and innovation are not stifled by the way things are but by the way we perceive things.

---

7. Some of you may catch this pun on the best-selling book *A Whack on the Side of the Head* by von Oech. The book stresses creativity and open-mindedness in our thinking. von Oech, Roger, *A Whack on the Side of the Head* (New York: Warner Books) 1990.

Change is as old as time and as leading edge as the future. Even the rate at which changes are occurring is changing. But as prevalent as change is, we often want to resist it with all the effort we can muster. Perhaps if we understand change better, we will tend to be more like eagles.

Let us contemplate the two sources of changes:

1. the changes that come from us

2. the changes that happen to us.

Treating the second source of change first, we need to be prepared for changes that will happen to us. We need to watch for these changes and use them as opportunities to improve. World-class eManagers watch for and use growth and development opportunities. This brings us to another thought:

> It doesn't matter how far in front of the pack you are, if you're not moving fast enough you'll get run over.

Change is innovation; it is developing leading edge competitive strategies; it is moving forward. Remember:

> It doesn't matter how fast you're moving, if you're not moving in the right direction you'll never achieve your goal!

The first type of change, the change that comes from us, requires us to originate the change. For some managers, this type of change is a little harder to manage because of the effort involved in creating the changes. It suggests that we need to find and generate our own opportunities for change and our own innovations. This is harder to achieve because most organizations tend towards bureaucracy, which suppresses change. Most organizational structures are motivated by measurement systems that stifle and often punish change. We need measurement systems that motivate the discovery of change.[8] The measurement and motivation of change is a major topic of Chapter 12. The

---

8. Other organizations and authors have wrestled with this issue. See, for example, the work of Eli Goldratt and Bob Fox who strongly support a Socratic process for the discovery, creation, and stimulation of change. They believe in the participate development of change (a team process), and they believe that imposed change is ineffective change. Additionally, an incorrectly developed measurement system will block, rather than motivate, the change process. Some additional reading by these authors includes: Fox, R E, "Theory of Constraints", *NAA Conference Proceedings* (September 1987); Goldratt, Eliyahu M, and Jeff Cox, *The Goal* (Croton-on-Hudson, New York: North River Press Inc.) 1986; Goldratt, Eliyahu M, *The Haystack Syndrome* (Croton-on-Hudson, New York: North River Press Inc.) 1990; Goldratt, Eliyahu M, and Robert E Fox, *The Race* (Croton-on-Hudson, New York: North River Press Inc.) 1986; Goldratt, Eliyahu M, *What is this Theory called Theory of Constraints?* (Croton-on-Hudson, New York:

search for change opportunities can mean a structural reorganization as well as a mental reorganization of your enterprise.[9]

This book focuses on both types of change. Your organization needs these changes, not only to stay ahead, but also to survive in a competitive environment. This book will help you become a leader who can help your organization manage change; it will motivate you to find and implement positive changes in a goal-oriented direction and turn you into a leader who motivates and directs change. Finally, this book will help you become a world-class manger.

To get the most out of this book, read it all carefully. What you are doing is hunting for ideas. Mark the ideas that fit you best, and, after reading the book, reread those ideas that impressed you the first time through. Then search for ways to implement these ideas into your management style. The last step in the use of this book is to total quality manage (TQM) the review process by repeating this process every six months to one year. As your goals and job function change, so will the information and tools you need to help you through the change process. Reviewing this book regularly will help you reanalyze your position and put it into perspective, both for you individually and for you within your role in the company as a whole.

> The single greatest power in the world today is the power to change ...
> The most recklessly irresponsible thing we could do in the future would
> be to go on exactly as we have in the past ten or twenty years.
>
> Karl W Deutsch,
> Professor of International Peace, Harvard

North River Press Inc.) 1990. See also Plenert, Gerhard J, "Bottleneck Scheduling for an Unlimited Number of Products", *Journal of Manufacturing Systems*, Vol. 9, No. 4, pp. 324-331; Plenert, Gerhard J, and Terry Lee, "Optimizing Theory of Constraints When New Product Alternatives Exist", *Production and Inventory Management Journal* (Third Quarter 1993) Vol. 4, No. 3, pp. 51-57.

9. Articles discussing change and change management are endless. Here is a listing of a few of the better ones: Schaffer, Robert H and Harvey A Thomson, "Successful Change Programs Begin with Results", *Harvard Business Review* (January-February 1992) pp. 80-89. This article stresses that we focus on results, not activities. Kanter, Rosabeth Moss, "Change: Where to Begin", *Harvard Business Review* (July-August 1991) pp. 8-9. This articles encourages the following steps — begin with use-directed, action oriented information, be willing to build on platforms already in place and encourage incremental experimentation that departs from tradition without totally destroying it. Beer, Michael, Russell A Eisenstat and Bert Spector, "Why Change Programs Don't Produce Change", *Harvard Business Review* (November-December 1990) pp. 158-166. This article focuses on how "effective corporate renewal starts at the bottom, through informal efforts to solve problems".

MODELS FOR CHANGE

There are numerous models for implementing change, from the slow and systematic, such as total quality management (TQM), to the fast and radical, such as process re-engineering (PR). Both concepts are discussed in Chapter 13. There are models that motivate change through their measurement process and there are measurement systems that discourage change (see Chapter 12 for more information on the measurement of change). Correctly implemented, change models give us an entirely new focus on what change can do for us.

When we manage change, rather than letting change manage us, our focus becomes more global, technology-oriented, flexible and customer-responsive. We need to focus on competitive, customer-oriented areas of change (see Chapter 5).

I spent most of my working years dealing with technology transfer to industrial settings all over the world. One of my favorite questions to ask is — how do you deal with change and innovation, such as the implementation of new technology in your environment? Another question I often ask is — how do you motivate innovation? Many answers are similar to this — innovation is great and we like it, as long as it has already been tried somewhere else. The attitudes of most people in response to my question is similar to:

> The innovator makes enemies of all those who prospered under the old order, and only lukewarm support is forthcoming from those who would prosper under the new.
>
> Machiavelli,
The Prince[10]

Innovation is seldom rewarded and only in the case of extreme success is the innovator thanked for risk-taking. The result is a fear of innovation and change, as shown in the following model where we see that time causes change to occur, which builds uncertainty, which causes fear.

Time *leads to* change *leads to* uncertainty *leads to* fear.

We need to conquer the fear by demonstrating that the model can be changed to one where time causes change, which is viewed as an opportunity for innovation.

Time *leads to* change *leads to* opportunity *leads to* innovation.

---

10. If you want to read a real negative approach to business and government decision making, this book is for you: Machiavelli, Niccolo, *The Prince* (New York: Penguin Classics) 1984.

Change is forced upon us through problems and errors, but problems and errors are also the seeds of opportunity and innovation. A world-class eManager focuses on the opportunities rather than the problems. Problems and errors bring the opportunities to our attention, but the world-class eMananger will resist solving the problem and will prefer to focus on the opportunity for change. Alone, these statements sound idealistic. However, what this really means is that problems or errors occur because there is some basic need that is not being taken care of properly. The "problem" can be solved by measuring and identifying the root source of the problem more effectively. The "opportunity" to fix the root cause offers us the chance to build a better mousetrap that avoids the cause of the problem. One example of this is the creation of post-it notes, which started as a problem — attaching notes to a letter, book or report without destroying it the way staplers or tape do. The problem was converted into an opportunity — develop a new adhesive that allows for easy removal — and the opportunity has now been translated into a major product and market segment.

We need to establish an environment of motivated innovation within our organizations by removing the fear of change. We need to *focus* on innovation in our enterprises and this can only be achieved with properly motivated changes.

Small companies and countries, which are often the companies and countries that are innovating, are upsetting large companies and countries, which tend to be slow to move. Let's consider some examples.

1. If you want process innovation, where do you go? For a long time Japan has demonstrated its international competitiveness through its ability to reduce production lead times and production costs. The Japanese were considered small at one time.

2. If you want to introduce a new product into the market quickly, where do you go? Taiwan has become the time-to-market innovation leader.

3. Minimum cost and maximum flexibility steel production has been taken over completely by the small steel companies in the United States, which have, for a long time, been successful in beating out the big guys, both foreign and domestic, in competition and quality.

We have defined world-class management in terms of the style of management and the role of change. Let's next take another look at world-class management, this time addressing the role of innovation and creativity.

INNOVEERING

A world-class organization is an innovative, creative, goal-oriented organization. A world-class eManager motivates the positive innovative and creative thinking process, what I refer to as *innoveering*, which means "creatively innovated changes". Changing, just for the sake of changing, only creates turmoil. Changing, to move positively forward towards a goal without sacrificing the integrity of the organization, is world-class.

Recently the topic of creative thinking has become very popular. Books such as *Breakthrough Thinking* and *A Whack on the Side of the Head* have stressed the importance of imagination in the change process.[11] For example, von Oech stresses the need for creativity to discover new solutions to problems and to generate new ideas when old ones become obsolete.[12] Stephen R Covey, in his book *The Seven Habits of Highly Effective People*, focuses his second habit on creativity.[13] Peters, Waterman and Austin, in their search for eight common characteristics of excellent companies, focus on employee innovation within the corporate value system.[14]

Innoveering is innovative change engineering. It is change that uses technology (see Chapter 7), integration (see Chapters 12 and 14) and innovative strategies (see Chapters 12 through 13) and focuses on a continuous improvement model (Chapter 13). Again, change, in and of itself, is not necessarily good. We need positively directed, goal oriented, innovative, creative change. Then we have innoveering. That's when we become world-class.

One of the best examples of innoveering is the Toyota just-in-time production system. Just-in-time (JIT) is a production planning philosophy developed in Japan that focuses on waste minimization through inventory reductions. But JIT didn't exist before being developed by Toyota. JIT wasn't copied; it was innoveered.

After World War II Japan was trying to rebuild its industry. The Japanese tried copying Western (primarily United States) production methodologies,

---

11. I have already referenced both of these books, but there are numerous other works available on creativity, such as: Stimson, Judith A, "Unleashing Creative Thinking for Change", *APICS 37th International Conference Proceedings* (Falls Church, VA: APICS) 1994, pp. 665-666; Abair, Robert A, "'Dare to Change': Revolution versus Evolution", *APICS 37th International Conference Proceedings*, op. cit., pp. 40-41.
12. I've already listed von Oech's book *A Whack on the Side of the Head*. Another good book by the same author is von Oech, Roger, *A Kick in the Seat of the Pants* (New York: Harper & Row) 1986.
13. Covey, Stephen R, *The Seven Habits of Highly Effective People* (New York: Simon & Schuster) 1989. Another excellent Covey book that discusses important issues related to the lifestyle and habits of a leader is Covey, Stephen R, *Principle-Centered Leadership* (New York: Summit Books) 1991.
14. See Peters, Tom and Robert Waterman, *In Search of Excellence: Lessons from America's Best Run Companies* (New York: Harper & Row) 1985; Peters, Tom and Nancy Austin, *A Passion for Excellence* (New York: Harper & Row) 1985.

which were considered the best in the world, but they soon encountered problems:

- the Japanese lacked the cash flow to finance the large in-process inventory levels required by the US batch-oriented production systems
- the Japanese lacked the land space to build large US style factories
- the Japanese didn't have the natural resource accessibility that the US had
- Japan had a labor excess rather than a labor shortage, which meant that labor efficiency systems weren't very valuable.

The Japanese innoveered these problems into opportunities. They realized that their competitive problem was a process problem, not a product problem. They proceeded to copy product technology and worked diligently to innovate *process technology* oriented around materials efficiency rather than labor efficiency. The result was the flow-through JIT production methodology for which Toyota has now become famous. But Toyota will be the first to admit that it wasn't easy. Toyota officials scoff at United States attempts to copy JIT after two or three years of implementation. They will readily say it took them 30 years to develop JIT. But they got there one innoveering change at a time.

The result was that the Japanese built smaller factories (about one-third the size of their United States counterparts) in which the only materials that were in the factory were those on which work was currently being done. (Note, however, that the Japanese work with single digit batch sizes — one to nine units — whereas US batch sizes can range in the hundreds of units. For each batch, only one item in the batch is worked on at a time; the rest of the batch is inventory. Therefore, a batch of 100 units creates a continuous, on-going inventory of 99 units. Unfortunately, the batch is often not being worked on and is just idle inventory. This batch size difference between the United States and Japan creates a tremendous difference in inventory levels). In this way inventory levels were kept low, investment in in-process inventory was at a minimum and the investment in purchased natural resources was quickly turned around so that additional materials were purchased.[15] The focus was on materials (inventory) efficiency rather than labor efficiency.

But the Toyota innoveering process has not ended. It continues, focusing on changes and improvements, both in the product and in the process areas. Toyota continues its innoveering through a continuous improvement process referred to as *waste elimination*. The company views waste as anything that does not add value to the product. Waste can occur in labor, materials,

---

15. Numerous books detail the Toyota production philosophy JIT — see Shingo, Shigeo, *Study of the Toyota Production System from the Industrial Engineering Viewpoint* (Tokyo: Japanese Management Association) 1981 (Shingo has worked with Toyota and has an insiders viewpoint); Wantuck, Kenneth A, *Just in Time for America*, (Milwaukee: The Forum, Ltd.) 1989.

machinery processes or any other aspect of the company. Toyota's seven key areas of waste elimination are the following:

1. waste of over-production — reduce set-up times, process synchronization and visibility

2. waste of waiting — balance uneven work loads

3. waste of transportation

4. waste of processing — why is the product made?

5. waste of stocks — inventory reduction

6. waste of motion — motion for economy and consistency

7. waste of making defective products.[16]

Toyota is determined to continue to improve. Innovative change is constant. Integration involving all levels of employees is critical (discussed further in Chapters 8 and 14). Toyota is an eagle in the world of innoveering.

However, United States businesses are past the point of trying to copy Japan. We need to innoveer beyond what we can copy from anyone if we are to stay competitive. As long as we are playing catch-up, the best we can ever do is to get caught up and that's just not good enough![17] The only way we can get ahead is by innoveering. The Japanese will only stay ahead as long as we, by focusing on copying rather than innoveering, allow them to.

Imagination is more important than knowledge.

Albert Einstein

HOW DO WE MANAGE CHANGE?

The biggest struggle in learning to manage change is identifying where, when and how to begin. This book will give you the answers to these questions.

Where do we begin? — With you, the reader!
When do we begin? — Immediately
How do we begin? — By carefully laying out a plan for innovation and change.

---

16. More detail is available from Hall, Robert W, *Attaining Manufacturing Excellence* (Homewood, Illinois: Dow-Jones-Irwin) 1987.
17. This concept of innovating yourself rather than copying someone else is the theme of another one of my books — Plenert, Gerhard, *International Management and Production: Survival Techniques for Corporate America* (Blue Ridge Summit, PA: Tab Professional and Reference Books) 1990.

This plan is developed by:

- deciding on a focus or a vision for our change efforts (Chapter 5)
- developing strategies for change that focus on our vision (Chapter 6)
- solidifying each of the strategic areas around the vision — here we discuss how each of the strategies is defined and implemented by looking at quality versus productivity (Chapter 12), global management (Chapter 9), timely mechnology (Chapter 10), integration and measurement (Chapter 12), value added processes (Chapter 11) and training (Chapter 13)
- discussing the characteristics, abilities and traits that a world-class eManager should have to motivate innoveering, including a discussion of the specific change tools available to the manager, such as change models (Chapter 13), management traits, management skills and the role of teaming (Chapter 14) and the integration of the manager in the enterprise, the environment and the changes that affect the manger and the enterprise through time (Chapter 8)
- a wrap up of whether or not you are working towards becoming world-class.

Let's move forward; let's stop being stubborn donkeys that need two-by-fours in order to be motivated to change. Let's learn how to be high-flying eagles, which soar to the greatest heights and view the big picture from their magnificent zenith. We need *world-class management*, which uses goal-oriented, positive-change leadership to motivate and direct the change process. Let's evolve into effective masters of the change process. Let's change, innovate and improve our family environment, our working environment, our enterprise and ourselves.

> The definition of insanity is continuing to do the same things and expecting different results.
>
> Nadler and Hibino,
> *Breakthrough Thinking*

THE PEOPLE

Anthropologists discovered a semi-civilized community living on a remote part of the island of Borneo. Their standard of living, dress and housing was similar to most Western civilizations. However, the anthropologists noticed that what was odd about these individuals was that they didn't wear shoes. The scientists would encounter individuals with severe slashes, bruises and blisters on their feet because of the rough footpaths. But the Borneo residents simply refused to wear shoes.

The anthropologists discovered a shoe factory right in the center of the town. The shoe factory was empty of equipment, but there was a sign out in front of the building that announced a weekly meeting for all those interested in shoes. These meetings had been going on for ten years. The citizens religiously attended these meetings and discussed the benefits of wearing shoes, for example, how they would reduce the pain and make walking more comfortable. But whenever the idea was suggested that they start making shoes in the factory, no one would be interested. So the anthropologists decided to take a pair of shoes and give them to one of the citizens. They got him to try the shoes on and use them for a day. But the next day, they found that this same individual was again walking without the shoes. The anthropologists were baffled and questioned the citizen, "Why aren't you wearing the shoes we gave you?"

He replied, "Oh, I understand that they are good for me, and that they would make me more comfortable. But they're just too much trouble and I'm too busy to put them on." And so he walked off, cutting and bruising his feet as he went.

Do we know anyone who refuses to wear shoes? We probably see them every day, every time we look in the mirror. So where does this stubborn streak come from? *Tradition!* The greatest resistance to change comes from what we already know and from what we already believe. Just look at the small child who is not yet hindered by tradition. The child will learn and believe anything. I'm not asking you to be gullible; I'm asking you to be open minded, like the small child. Learn and understand, before you rush to condemn. Change is especially hard for managers. As we've learned from our quotes, the only thing certain in life is change. But we don't want change to happen to us, we want to utilize and control change to our advantage. A well known anonymous axiom is:

People like things to change but they don't like to be changed.

Stated differently, this means that people like it when changes occur, if the changes are benefiting them. However, people don't like changes imposed upon them.

Federal Express (FedEx), a 1990 Malcolm Baldridge Quality Award winner, is the brainchild of founder and CEO Frederick W Smith who virtually invented the air express industry.[18] The key focus of the FedEx quality program is to achieve 100 per cent customer satisfaction through continuous improvement and change. The continuous improvement process involves the customer in the change process through a survey-feedback-action (SFA)

---

18. The Malcolm Baldridge National Quality Award (MBNQA) is the United States Government national award for quality. [There's an oxymoron for you — "Government Quality".]

program (FedEx, a little of its history, and details of its quality program will be discussed more in later chapters). FedEx has based its quality program on three precepts, the first being:

Customer satisfaction starts with employee satisfaction.

In order to make this precept effective, FedEx has implemented a program called the guaranteed fair treatment program (GFTP). The aim of the GFTP process is to maintain a truly fair working environment, one in which anyone who has a grievance or concern about his or her job, or who feels mistreated, can have these concerns addressed through the management chain, all the way to Fred Smith if necessary.

FedEx considers its employees to be its most important resource and wanted to provide a fair and equitable process for handling grievances. The GFTP philosophy provides an atmosphere for employees to discuss their complaints with management without fear of retaliation. An employee is given seven days to submit a grievance after which time management has ten days to respond. If the employee doesn't agree with the manager's decision, the employee has seven days to appeal the decision up the chain of the review process.

A key element of the GFTP program is that managers get evaluated from both directions, from the top down and from the bottom up. The manager's boss evaluates the manager's ability to implement change through innovation and improvements. The manager's subordinates evaluate the manager's responsiveness to the needs of the employees. A manager must receive favorable ratings from both directions in order to get promotions, raises or bonuses.[19]

From the FedEx quality program we see both an emphasis on change (SFA) and an emphasis on the management-employee relationship aspects of how change is implemented (GFTP). I've had FedEx managers tell me that FedEx is the most challenging, while at the same time the most rewarding company they have worked for because the FedEx program puts the manager into the challenging position of attempting to install change while at the same time not allowing the manager to be excessively forceful in implementing the change. The best managers would be those who implement change by giving the employees ownership in the change.

---

19. FedEx offers a nice document called the *Quality Profile*, which outlines their various quality programs including the GFTP and the SQI. For more information contact:
     Federal Express Corporation
     Public Relations Department
     2005 Corporate Avenue
     Memphis, TN 38132
     (910) 395-3466

I want workers to go home at night and say, "I built that car."

Pahr G Gyllenhammar,
Chairman, Volvo

At this point we have identified that change is inevitable, therefore it is important that change becomes a part of our life and the life of our enterprise. We have also learned that change management needs to be participative, not forced. But why have a section on people in this book? Because, like Steve Young of the San Francisco 49ers football team, you can't complete one touchdown pass without the linesmen to protect you and the receivers to catch the ball and run with it. You need the rest of your team! You can't become world-class alone!

So what do we as managers need in order to be effective motivators of change? What do we need to do to become world-class in people relations? Here's a list of nine key points:

1. the circle

2. goal setting

3. leadership

4. values and ethics

5. add value to society as an enterprise

6. continuous learning

7. innovation and change creation

8. measuring/rewarding

9. stake holders.

Let's take a look at these in more detail.

The Circle

You can make more friends in two months by becoming interested in other people than you can in two years by trying to get other people interested in you.

Dale Carnegie

The circle is a term used to refer to a group working together to achieve a common purpose so there might, for example, be the quality circle, the management circle or the family circle. In order to be a world-class eManager we need to define our circles and make them as effective as possible. And the first quality circle in the life of any manager should be the family circle.

No other success [in life] can compensate for failure in the home.

David O McKay

The family is the first and highest priority circle in anyone's life. The family is your reward structure, it's the reason for working, it's what brings quality into your life. A disastrous home life destroys your work life, whereas, a disastrous work life doesn't seem so bad if you have a successful home life. It is self-destructive to let your work life become your reason for living, because "change" can destroy that life in minutes.

Another important circle of everyone's life is the society they are members of. In the United States, success is measured by individual earning power. In most other parts of the world, success is measured by ones ability to contribute to society. Far too many of us are not contributing (adding value) to society, rather, we are only self-gratifying (trying to fill our own pockets at the expense of others). In reality, how much you work with and help others only increases your own personal value.

The third circles of importance in each of our lives are the circles we work in. These circles are often referred to as teams (see Chapter 14). But are we really forming teams, or are we just grouping? A group is a collection of people thrown together in a room for the purpose of making some kind of decision. A team is a collection of individuals that have worked together over a long period of time and have found a creative harmony and synergy working between them. In teams we find sharing, not domineering, like we do in groups.

In all the circles in our lives, we need to establish quality. I am bothered by terms like "quality time" when referring to our children, as if this phrase is some kind of excuse for spending as little time as possible time with them. There is no "quality time" if an insufficient amount of time is spent, whether it's with the children, the spouse or the employees. The biggest challenge of a world-class eManager is to prioritize his or her time in order to achieve "sufficient quality time" to the extent that it will make a difference in the circles that are important in the manager's life.

Goal Setting

If you don't know where you're going, you'll probably get there.

If you can't see a target, how can you expect to hit it? Unfortunately, far too many people and companies go through life without targets to shoot at. They let changes affect the road they take in life without ever identifying why they're traveling down the road to begin with. If we are only working for money, then money is all we'll ever get out of our work. However, if we work for some greater purpose in life, like a successful family and marriage, or to be the best at whatever it is we do, we'll find that the money comes along as a nice added benefit and we'll have a lot more fun doing it.

We need goals at many levels and at many time frames. Here are just a few areas in which we should have long-range (twenty years +), mid-range (five years +) and short-range goals (one year).

Family goals — sit down with your spouse and children and determine what's important to the family.

Personal goals — what do you want out of life? What will give your life meaning?

Career goals — where do you want your career path to go, realizing that most people change professions on the average of about four times during their life?

Corporate goals — what does your company's business plan state the goals of the company are?

Job function goals — what do you want to accomplish in the job function you are performing? Are you hoping to build better relationships in your circles? Do you want to become world-class? Far too often I have encountered people that, when asked, "How do you decide what areas of your job function you want to perform well in?" I get an answer like, "Whatever it takes to keep my job and get a raise." My reaction is "I'm glad you don't work for me!"

After you have collected these goals together, you then need to do two things.

1. Develop an action plan that will work towards the achievement of the goal.

2. Communicate the goal to all involved. For example, I have encountered numerous organizations where the corporate goals are pretty much kept secret amongst top management. Yet the employees are expected to achieve these goals, which they can not see. You can never over-communicate your goals.

Your personal success needs to be defined. Even playing the lottery requires the selection of numbers and the purchasing of a ticket. Most other goals, like family or work goals, need a more clearly defined game plan. There are several good books available that help in the development of life and work goals. Let me highly recommend the Covey and von Oech books if you haven't already read them.[20]

Recently we have discovered a slight reversal of the goal setting process in organizations. Previously the trend has been for the vision and mission of the organization to be defined by top management. However, we have seen a reversal of this process where the employees are defining the mission of the

---

20. For more lessons on goal setting, see the books by Covey and von Oech, cited earlier.

organization and then a top management vision statement is developed from this employee defined mission statement. For example, Tridon-Oakdale, discussed earlier, brought a team of managers together and had them establish the mission statement of the corporation. This gave the managers an ownership in the goals and an added commitment in achieving the goals of the organization.

Goals define success. Without defined goals, how will you ever know if you were successful in achieving them?

Leadership

> You cannot be friends upon any other terms than upon the terms of equality.
>
> Woodrow Wilson

The most powerful teaching tool has always been the power of example. Every parent has learned this principle the hard way. The children always seem to "do as I do" rather than "do as I say". And the principle is just as correct in the work place as it is in the home. If you are grumpy about changes that are being passed down to you, don't expect your employees to be motivated by changes you pass to them.

Mojonnier highlighted that top management's role in fostering positive organizational change fell into four essential elements:

1. create a detailed vision statement — this is done in Chapters 5 and 6 with a vision and mission statement and a strategic plan

2. assess your current organizations' total culture — this is done as part of the core competency assessment and vision statement process in Chapter 5

3. develop a strategy for achieving your vision (Chapter 6)

4. establish mid-point goals to mitigate your troops — mid-point goals are part of the short-term strategy and the plan of operation (Chapter 6).[21]

The leaders run their organizations using respect, whereas the manager drives his or her people by intimidation. Just ask yourself what environment you would prefer to work under and then give your employees the same level of respect. A leader positively influences and motivates changes. An effective leader helps to position an organization for success.

---

21. This model comes from Mojonnier, Timothy M, "Top Management's Role in fostering and Managing Positive Organizational Change", *APICS 37th International Conference Proceedings*, op. cit., pp. 49-51.

VALUES AND ETHICS

The integrity of men is to be measured by their conduct, not by their professions.

Junius

Values are the glue that keeps us together. We need a value system built on virtue, integrity and ethics if we want to grow old feeling good about what we've done in life, whether it was successful or not. It would be helpful to define some of the terms we are using here:

- values — worth, that which renders anything useful or estimable; excellence

- virtue — worth; moral excellence

- integrity — completeness, wholeness; honesty and sincerity, for example

- ethics — standards of right and wrong; systems of conduct or behavior; moral principles.[22]

The lack of ethics and integrity in the United States has resulted in such a large number of non-trust systems, that often the non-trust systems are more complex than the systems they are trying to protect. A non-trust system is a system established specifically for the purpose of making sure that the original system is not abused. For example, anti-fraud systems like financial auditing systems exist in every organization.

From a psychological perspective, we develop non-trust systems to protect us from having others do to us the types of things we are likely to be guilty of. Otherwise, we probably wouldn't have thought of setting up the non-trust system to begin with. It has been estimated that the non-trust systems that are in existence are costing us more than if we were to just tolerate the occasional fraud that might happen. Our lack of ethics and integrity leaves us morally and financially bankrupt. Chapter 12 discusses these issues in detail.

We can get into a long, drawn out discussion about whether a bribe is less ethical than a tip. However, it really isn't that complicated. If we feel good about ourselves, and if the results leave everyone involved in a win-win situation, chances are the activity was ethical. It's like pornography; we have difficulty defining it, but we know it when we see it.

Internationally, ethics gets very confusing. The United States citizens seem to see everything in life as black or white in the decision-making process, whereas most of the rest of the world sees a lot of gray. For example, Malaysia and Thailand were having a border dispute in a region where a large reserve

---

22. *Webster's New Dictionary* (New York: Russell, Gebbes & Grosset) 1990.

of oil was discovered. The American solution would be to battle it out. But the Malaysia-Thailand solution was to draw a line around this region and to bring in a private developer to develop the oil reserve. Then both countries shared equally in the profits. So what is more ethical, the US way or the South-East Asian way?

We are obsessed with the legalistic. The hand shake is worthless because our legal system has declared it as worthless in court. Technically (on the books), the hand shake has value, but in practice (in the courts) it has no value. This has destroyed our ability to trust each other. If it isn't written down and spelled out in fine print, it legally doesn't have to happen. This brings to mind another interesting ethics example from the South-East Asia region. North America and South-East Asia both have a free trade agreement. For North America it is the North American Free Trade Agreement (NAFTA), which binds three countries, the United States, Canada and Mexico, in a free trade arrangement. For South-East Asia it is the Association of South-East Asian Nations (ASEAN) that have formed a trade agreement involving six countries — Indonesia, Malaysia, Singapore, Philippines, Brunei and Thailand. The NAFTA agreement is 2,200 pages long, whereas the ASEAN agreement, with twice as many countries, is sixteen pages long. It's pretty obvious that our lack of integrity and ethics has made us obsessed with non-trust systems. Show your employees a little more trust and respect and they may surprise you by trusting and respecting you in return.

> It's a shame that the reputation of an honorable profession like that of the legal profession has to be ruined by just five or six hundred thousand bad apples.
>
> Rex Lee,
> Attorney and President, Brigham Young University

Levi Strauss considers the company's most important asset to be its people's "aspirations". This organization has become famous for combining strong commercial success with a commitment to social values and to its workforce. In 1987 it developed the famous "Levi Strauss Aspirations Statement", a major initiative that defines the shared values that will guide both management and the workforce. This Aspirations Statement is reshaping occupational roles and responsibilities, how performance evaluations are conducted, how training is handled and how business decisions are made. The statement, and its focus on the "people" and their values, is credited with making Levi Strauss a flexible and innovative company. More importantly, Levi Strauss has an exemplary record on issues like workforce diversity and worker dislocation benefits.

The Levi Strauss Aspirations Statement focuses on people that are proud and committed; an environment where opportunity exists to contribute, learn and grow; a place where people are respected, treated fairly, listened to and involved. It talks about friendship, balanced personal and professional lives and having fun. The Levi Strauss Aspirations Statement identifies a new type of leadership focused on:

- new behaviors — directness, openness, honesty, commitment to the success of others, willingness to acknowledge problems and errors
- diversity — diversity in age, sex, ethnicity, etc in the workforce
- recognition — financial and non-financial recognition for individuals and teams that contribute to success — "recognition must be given to all who contribute"
- ethical management practices — "leadership that epitomizes the stated standards of ethical behavior"
- communications — employees must know what is expected of them and receive timely and honest feedback
- empowerment — leadership should increase the authority and responsibility of those employees closest to the products and customers.

Levi Strauss has demonstrated the importance of people values and ethics and has taught that these values are critical to world-class management (leadership) status.[23]

> A company's values — what it stands for, what its people believe in — are crucial to its competitive success.
>
> Robert Haas,
> CEO, Levi Strauss & Co.

Add Value to Society as an Enterprise

Being world-class refers to two opposite but equal activities: *eliminating all waste* and *focusing on value-added dimensions.*

Identifying non-value-added activities on a factory floor has always been relatively easy. But this section is focusing on people. This section is focusing on us. How do we identify non-value-added activities in our own lives? Here are a couple of guidelines:

- does the activity help achieve any of the goals that we established just a little earlier in this chapter?
- is the activity we are engaged in of benefit to society or our family (our circle) in any way?

---

23. A detailed discussion of the Aspirations Statement can be found in Howard, Robert, "Values Make the Company: An Interview with Robert Haas", *Harvard Business Review* (September-October 1990) pp. 133-144.

Let me give you a story that will help your understanding of this concept. One time when I was working overseas I got into a discussion of "what is wrong with the United States?" Outsiders always have lots of ideas about what we should be doing differently. However, sometimes, as on this occasion, these insights are thought provoking. The answer was — "the economic decay of the United States is being caused by the fact that you are graduating more and more non-value-added graduates than you ever did before." So I asked for a definition of a non-value-added graduate. The answer was, "anyone working in a profession that does not increase the output of the nation." Individuals who work at professions that simply move the existing resources of the nation around, placing some of them in their own pocket during the process, without adding any value, are non-value added.

On a smaller scale, a lot of the activities we are engaged in only benefit our own pocket books in the short term. We are not creating anything of value to society; and, if we are engaged in activities that add no value, then we are actively engaged in creating waste. In our private or corporate life, we need to refocus our activities, and the activities of our employees, on adding value. We need to eliminate non-value-added processes. We need to add value to society as an enterprise, through the efforts of our employees.

Continuous Learning

It is only the intellectually lost who ever argue.

Oscar Wilde

I believe that you can't learn if you have got your mouth open. You can only learn if you have your ears open and your mouth closed. Chapter 10 goes into detail about training and education. But in this section, what we need to focus on is people learning or sharing between each other.

We have a lot of people that are filled with good ideas and we need to listen to them if we are to benefit from their wisdom. Additionally, being world-class means realizing that improvement only comes about if we open ourselves to changes in the form of new ideas. We need to learn new ideas in order to incorporate them into the things that we do. World-class is giving everyone in the organization opportunities and the appropriate motivation to learn and develop through education and training. We need to build a learning organization.

In this category belongs the need for self renewal, otherwise known as vacation time. Creativity is improved when pressure is removed and drudgery is relieved. Employees need time to get away from it all and they need to be encouraged to do so often.

Innovation and Change Creation

Chaos often breeds life when order breeds habit.

Henry (Brooks) Adams,
American Historian

World-class is breaking out of the ritualistic, mundane things in life. It's real-izing that:

Professionals built the Titanic — amateurs the Ark.

Frank Pepper

Just because an employee is not an expert at something doesn't mean he or she doesn't have worthwhile and valuable ideas. The expression of all ideas, whether by the professional or the amateur, needs to be encouraged. The trick in managing ideas is not to allow egos to get wrapped up in the innovation process. Every idea has to be considered valuable, even if you really think it is a bad one, because you are a prejudiced observer and you don't want to dis-courage the creative process. Additionally, you need to be careful that the "professional" is not offended if the ideas of an amateur contradict his or her professional opinion.

World-class is also the ability to laugh at yourself.

For the Wisdom of the World is foolishness with God.

1 Corinthians 3:19

The books by the author von Oech and Nadler and Hibion (listed earlier) stress this point as being critical in the creative process. Allow your ideas to be destroyed. In fact, do your best to destroy them yourself. How else can you be sure they are fool proof?

Employees need to be involved in and to understand the change process in order to effectively initiate changes. This process is explained in many models similar to the following:

- identifying/recognizing the need or opportunity for change is the first step in making any change
- defining the problem or opportunity that needs to be addressed
- identifying the current company position relative to the problem — you have got to know where you're at before you can determine where to go
- identifying alternative destinations
- identifying the desired destination
- defining a road map to get from where you are to where you want to be
- unfreezing the organization and preparing it for change — this includes training and empowerment

- change implementation
- stabilizing the organization under the new order — this includes the establishment of a new feedback mechanism that will monitor the new status quo.

With an understanding of the change process, organizations and their employees are now ready for innovation and change creation.[24]

This brings us to a critical element of world-class employee innovation and creativity. We need to develop empowered work teams that work together as teams, not groups, and have the authority to implement their ideas (expanded on in Chapter 14). Creativity works best through the synergy of effectively developed and empowered teams. We saw an example of this earlier in this chapter in the Levi Strauss story. Another example can be seen if we look at the Antilock Braking Systems Division (ABS) of General Motors in Dayton, Ohio (formerly Delco Products Company). It did what it was told would be impossible; it developed a world-class empowerment program called employee involvement (EI), starting with a traditional United Auto Workers (UAW) contract. A covenant was established between the union and ABS as it was felt this was the only way it would be in business in two years and that this was necessary if it was to stay even with the continuous improvement programs of its competitors.

ABS supervisors were given new responsibility based on communication and training. A system of trust was established with the workers. This trust is at the core of the EI program. Based on this trust, a set of guiding principles were established which included:

- establishing and maintaining innovative systems that can compete in a world-class climate

- enacting cultural change necessary to insure profitability and job security at the Dayton plants

- running the business as a joint activity seeking contributions from and sharing benefits with all

- providing mechanisms and incentives which promote continual improvement in customer satisfaction

- approaching the covenant as a living agreement, continually reviewing progress and proactively adjusting to maximize competitiveness.

---

24. Another interesting example of the change process is found in the book Bell, Robert R and John M Burnham, *Managing Productivity and Change* (Cincinnati, Ohio: South-Western Publishing Co.) 1991, pp. 10-11.

ABS truly has a world-class empowerment program that is worthy of study and emulation.[25]

Measuring and Rewarding

> Treat people as if they were what they ought to be, and you help them become what they are capable of being.
>
> Goethe

Innovation and creativity need to be stimulated. Recently I was working for a company that had an elaborate total quality management (TQM) program (TQM is discussed in detail in Chapter 11). TQM is a tool for implementing change into an organization. However, the TQM program was failing and they couldn't understand why. I reviewed their measurement system and quickly learned that they were evaluating employee performance based on units per hour efficiency. Bonuses were being paid when employee performance exceeded the standard rates of production. Why would any employee want to spend time implementing changes through TQM if:

- they were being rewarded based on historical rates and historical methodologies?
- there was no reward for implementing the change?
- changes would, in effect, decrease their productive output in the short term and therefore reduce their bonuses?

Let me explain the third point in more detail. When change is implemented, the first thing that happens is a drop off in efficiency. As we see in Figure 4.4, we are working away at a certain level of output and as soon as change is introduced, a loss of productive output occurs. Then, through the process of the learning curve, employees slowly become better and better at the new process, eventually achieving a new, (hopefully) higher level of output. Unfortunately, in the short term, efficiency suffers, and so does the pay check. This company was asking the employees to sacrifice their pay check in order to implement changes. The company didn't want to lose output, but it still wanted the employees to initiate improvements. It was giving the employees mixed signals and the signal that motivated the employees the most was the pay check signal (measurement is discussed more completely in Chapter 12).

To understand this concept completely, let me make a "hang on your wall" statement:

> A measurement system is not for management information — it's for motivating employees.

---

25. For details on the ABS EI program see the article Powell, Jr, Cash, "Empowerment, The Stake in the Ground for ABS", *Target* (January-February 1992) pp. 7-17.

Figure 4.2: What Type of Manager Are You?

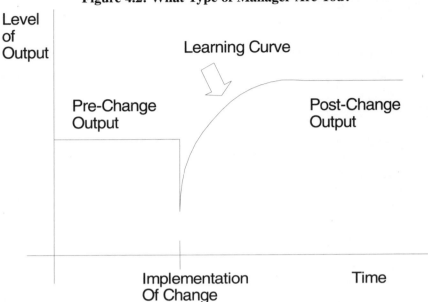

Any measurement system that exists simply for accounting purposes or information gathering purposes is probably counter-effective and is destructive to the company's ability to achieve its goals. A measurement system that is not focused on the goals of the organization is distracting employees away from the goal of the organization. This is because, whether it is true or not, employees believe they are being graded by what they are being measured on. And they will focus their performance in those areas that are being measured. So, select your measurement systems wisely — they may motivate the wrong actions.

Stakeholders

As a world-class eManager you need to identify all the *people* involved in your *circles*. These include family, friends, employees, peers, bosses, customers (both internal and external), vendors and the community.

Taking it from the top, can you satisfy your spouse's needs? Are you making him or her happy? Do they enjoy being with you? How about your children? How about your friends?

Do the people you work with come to you for help or do they avoid you like the plague? Do your customers consider you as someone that can get things done, or as someone that puts things off, or blames things off? Do you identify both your immediate customer (the one you pass product to) and your final customer (the eventual end user) as someone who needs satisfaction? Do you get involved? Do you look to help out your fellow employees and your family and friends, or do you avoid challenging situations? Are you willing and eager to change? Do you avoid wearing shoes because it means you have to change? Simply put:

Are you world-class?

SUMMARY

In Hawaii the native Hawaiians have a sense or feel for each other that supersedes the words of the conversation. They refer to this as the *ha*, which can best be translated as the "breath of life". When Westerners started to visit the islands that *ha* didn't seem to be present. The warmth of the relationship, which is a comfort or a knowing where the other person was coming from, wasn't there. The Hawaiians started to refer to these people as *ha-ole* which is translated "without *ha*." They felt distanced from these foreigners because of this lack of feeling for each other. This lack of feeling created a lack of trust. Today's eManager must learn what Hawaiians already know well. They must learn to have *ha*.

This chapter described the past and future of management styles. It showed a migration of management philosophies showing how competitive markets have forced rapid decision-making processes. This speed has in turn forced decisions to occur at operational levels of the organization rather than strategically. This chapter stressed the importance of strategic goal setting.

In summary, I would like to recommend some reading material for those of you interested in this subject. See the footnote for the references.[26] Without people who are willing and motivated to change, there can be no world-class organization. It is "we the people", which includes you the manager, your bosses, your employees, your customers and your vendors, that makes your enterprise world-class, and just like Steve Young or Michael Jordan, you can't get there without your "circle".

Man is here for the sake of other men.

Albert Einstein

---

26. There are lots of good publications on effective world-class people relations. See Boyst, Jr III, William M, "HRM — Key to the Integrated Management Revolution", *APICS 34th International Conference Proceedings*, op. cit., pp. 354-357; Wallace, Thomas F, *World-class Manufacturing* (Essex Junction, VT: OMNEO) 1994 (see particularly Part III); Plenert, Gerhard, *International Management and Production: Survival Techniques for Corporate America*, op. cit.

Figure 4.3: Find your Management Style

In front of each management style indicate whether you (or the person you are evaluating) fit this description:

N — not really one of these
O — occasionally one of these
Y — definitely one of these

_____ *Sunrise Manager* — has a view towards the future, a dreamer full of wild ideas, progressive, leading edge, technology minded

_____ *Sunset Manager* — spends time fighting day-to-day fires, a workaholic who is great at getting things done

_____ *Theory-X Manager* — secretive, has his or her fingers in everything that happens, always has the final word, tells rather than asks questions

_____ *Theory-Y Manager* — values the opinion of the employees, spends more time listening than talking, looks for ideas from the bottom-up but makes the final decision

_____ *Theory-Z Manager* — tends to empower the employees to make their own decisions and lets them implement their own ideas

_____ *Cash Manager* — cost and budget obsessive, looks toward stability rather than opportunity, prefers to patch and repair rather than replace because it is cheaper

_____ *Crisis (or Crash) Manager* — believes that you shouldn't fix anything that isn't broken, looks at problems as disruptions that need to be conquered, attacks problems

_____ *Conflict Manager* — looks at the workplace as a battlefield of competing players, feels the need to take and maintain the upper hand

_____ *Cool Manager* — feels the workforce is best motivated by giving them whatever they want, wants to bribe their way into the hearts of their employees, wants to be everybody's best friend

_____ *Change Manager* — searches for challenges in competitiveness, strives on changes, innovations, improvements, technology

_____ *Boss* — directs employee traffic, see themselves as "King of the Hill" and wants to keep the hill for themselves, "Do as I Say" philosophy

_____ *Leader* — shows the way using example and by stepping out into the traffic in front of the employees, not afraid to show everyone how to get to the top of the hill, "Do as I Do" philosophy

Figure 4.4: Detailing Figure 4.1

Figure 4.1 breaks down the two most complex management style classifications. From Figure 4.1 we see all sorts of mixes and matches of management styles:

Theory-X Manager-Cash Manager — impersonal and quick to fire – bases all decisions on short-term financial reports

Theory-X Manager-Crisis Manager — the "General" charges his or her troops against the coming enemy, which is often a variety of problems, including the biggest problem of all, change

Theory-X Manager-Conflict Manager — the "Boss" expects the respect of employees and demands immediate response to his or her whims and wishes

Theory-X Manager-Cool Manager — the manager makes the final decisions, but, in an attempt to keep everyone happy, many of the decisions are political and therefore contradictory and result in more confusion than progress

Theory-X Manager-Change Manager — this manager forces change on employees, leaving them rebellious and resistant

Theory-Y Manager-Cash Manager — this manager wants the employees' ideas, but will make the final decision in all cases based on short-term financial viability

Theory-Y Manager-Crisis Manager — this manager expects employees to be self-directed fire-fighters, maintaining the status quo

Theory-Y Manager-Conflict Manager — this manager listens to employees just to satisfy their egos and basically sees employees as a necessary evil requiring toleration

Theory-Y Manager-Cool Manager — this manager solicits the employees' ideas and says "yes" to everyone leaving employees without any real guidance from the top

Theory-Y Manager-Change Manager — this manager wants employees to search for opportunities for change, but reserves the right to override any suggestions, since the manager has the broader insight needed for all decisions made in the enterprise

Theory-Z Manager-Cash Manager — this management style has teams analyzing all changes on a financial basis

Theory-Z Manager-Crisis Manager — here teams work on solving problems with a short-term perspective aimed at getting the problem fixed quickly

Theory-Z Manager-Conflict Manager — here teams continually find themselves having to defend against a management that considers them ignorant

Theory-Z Manager-Cool Manager — this manager is completely employee oriented, but in the effort to keep everyone happy, ends up being an ineffective facilitator, causing frustration and a lack of direction

Theory-Z Manager-Change Manager — this is a manager who facilitates change and motivates employee teams to search for opportunities for change. The teams see themselves as owners of the change and they therefore attempt to implement the change and take pride in the results. Fire fighting is kept to a minimum, and fires are looked at as being caused by some root problem that needs to be identified and changed with a long-term perspective.[27] This is the management style of a world-class eManager.

---

27. Root cause identification is a theme of the book *Breakthrough Thinking*. This book helps Total Quality Management (TQM) teams identify opportunities for improvements — changes! A second, follow-up book expands on this theme. Nadler, Gerald and Shozo Hibino, *Breakthrough Thinking* (Rocklin, CA: Prima Publishing & Communications), 1990. Nadler, Gerald, Shozo Hibino, and John Farrell, *Creative Solution Finding* (Rocklin, CA: Prima Publishing & Communications), 1995.

Chapter Five

Goal and Values Based Strategies

Only those who attempt the absurd can achieve the impossible.

Robin Hood was given a challenge. He was asked to take one bent arrow and with that arrow he was asked to hit three targets at the same time. But, if that wasn't bad enough, he was first blindfolded and spun around a few times. You may say, "How can we expect him to hit a target he cannot see?" or "How can he hit multiple targets with the same arrow at the same time?" But as surprising as it may seem, we are asking our managers and employees to do what even Robin Hood couldn't do, and they are expected to do it every month. Read on and you'll see what I'm talking about.

IDENTIFY THE TARGET

A journey of 1000 miles begins with a single step.

Goals give purpose and direction to what we are doing. We need to focus on a clearly defined target in order to get direction in what we are trying to accomplish. In the development of a goal we have these stages:

- defining the core competencies
- the vision
- the mission
- the strategy
- the plan of operation.

The first step is not really a goal as much as it is an introspective look at what you're good at. Are you good at all these things — sourcing, manufacturing, distribution, retailing and customer service? Probably not. So which one are you really good at, the rest being the necessary evils that you need to tolerate as part of your business. The core competency is the combination of individual technologies and production skills that underlay a company's productive processes.

Some examples of core competencies (sometimes referred to as capabilities) are:

> Sony — miniaturization
> Canon — optics, imaging and microprocessor controls
> Honda — engines and power trains.[1]

After defining the core competency (what you're really good at), we then break the core competency down even more. For example, are you good at distributing everywhere, just in the United States or just in the Pacific Northwest? By going through this process of identification you end up with a clear definition of what your core competencies are. Once you know what you're good at, capitalize on it and build your growth and future around it. This identification step gives you a basis for the development of your goals, which include your vision, mission and strategy.

To become a visionary company you need two things:

1. a guiding philosophy and value system — a vision

2. a challenging short term goal or mission that quantifies the vision.

In each stage of the goal development process we find more detail than at the level before it. For example, the vision is one or two sentences of where the enterprise is going. It is the sense of purpose of an enterprise, its reason for being and its guiding philosophy. A vision builds unity throughout the organization. It doesn't have to be long, but it has to give the organization purpose. The vision should provide employees with a clear image that they can identify with.[2] Some examples are:

> . . . to make a contribution to the world by making tools for the mind that advance humankind.

> Steve Jobs,
> Apple Computer

> To make people happy.

> Walt Disney

Unlike the vague, undefined, timeless vision statement, the mission statement is a series of defined goals for the enterprise that are aimed at the vision. The

---

1. The traditional article in this area is Prahalad, C K and Gary Hamel, "The Core Competence of the Corporation", *Harvard Business Review* (May-June 1990).
2. Some insight on the vision creation process can be gained from the article "The Vision Thing", *The Economist* (9 November 1991) p. 81.

mission has a definite, measurable goal and should be date stamped with a finish line. The mission should be challenging (see the section on the characteristics of good goals later in this chapter). Some examples are:

> . . . achieving the goal, before this decade is out, of landing a man on the moon and returning him safely to earth.

President John F Kennedy (1962)

> Beat Coke!

Pepsi Co.

> We will crush, squash, slaughter Yamaha!

Honda

The next stage of goal development — the strategy — identifies and quantifies goals for each strategic operating area and focuses on bringing that operating area in focus with the mission of the enterprise. Strategy development is the topic of Chapter 6.

The plan of operation is the operating plan for each strategic area detailing how each area will achieve their strategy and mission, and so, in the long run, their vision. The plan of operation requires a detailed tactical plan for executing the strategy in the short term (over the next few months).

This chapter will look at the first big target, the vision, and then the second, more focused target, the mission of the enterprise. The next chapter will discuss the strategic plans. Later in the book we will discuss the operating plans.[3]

The process of establishing goals (*visioning* and *missioning*) takes a class syllabus approach to business. Imagine if in college, when you take a class, the professor comes to you and says "keep doing what you're doing, you're doing great, and at the end of the semester I'll evaluate you". As the semester goes along the professor continues with his vague, direction-less information. Then, when the end of the year rolls around, the professor says, "well, you all did OK so I'll pass some of you and flunk some of you", never indicating why some were passed and some were flunked. If this were true, the students would be screaming and demanding the details of what is expected of them. But this direction-less methodology seems to be an acceptable way to run a business (or the tenure and promotions process in some unnamed colleges and universities). Rather, in college, when you take a class, the professor gives you a class syllabus. This defines what the requirements of the course are, what needs to be accomplished for successful completion of the course and when

---

3. More details about goal setting can be found in Plenert, Gerhard, *The Plant Operations Handbook* (Homewood, Illinois: Business One Irwin) 1993.

the time to do so is up. The class syllabus approach gives everyone in the organization clear objectives and does not leave them blindfolded using crooked arrows. Everyone knows what they're shooting at.

> In an empowered organization, it is a challenge of leadership to make sure each and every employee is involved in creating the vision.

> James J Mapes[4]

In order to discuss goals effectively, we need to discuss the types of goals that exist, and their characteristics. One section of the chapter will focus on the types of goals. Another section will focus on the characteristics of good goals. It is also possible to have secondary goals, but they need to complement, not draw away from the primary goal (see the discussion later in this chapter).

> Where there is no vision, the people perish.

> Proverbs 29:18

TYPES OF GOALS

The goals of an enterprise set the value system of the organization. We, in the United States, have grown accustomed to the idea that there is only one correct goal for a business enterprise — financial. Interestingly, this goal is in the minority when taking an international perspective. From my interaction with businesses around the world I have found four major groupings of goals — *financial, operational, employee based* and *customer based.*

Each of these groupings has specific characteristics. For example, I have listed the goals in order from short-term orientation to long-term orientation. Let's discuss each of these goal types specifically.

Financial Goals

Financial goals include goals such as:
- increase profits
- decrease costs
- increase sales
- increase return on investment
- increase return on net assets
- financial ratios.

---

4. Mapes wrote a fun article that discusses vision and mission statement creation — see Mapes, James J, "Foresight First", *Sky Magazine* (September 1991) pp. 96-105.

Financial goals are very short sighted and tend to be oriented toward quarterly or annual results. The short-sightedness of these goals stems a lot from the lack of trust that we have for each other. For example, stockholders don't trust the board of directors, the board does not trust the CEO, the CEO does not trust the VPs, the VPs don't trust middle management, and so on. The result is that each level monitors the level below it on short-term financial measures. If, for example, the CEO wants to introduce massive technological changes that will take several years to show a return, then he or she will be out of a job after the first or second year of losses. The CEO will have difficulty convincing the board that "the benefits of the change are just around the corner." That's exactly what happened to Florida Power and Light.

Florida Power and Light implemented a total quality improvement — a continuous change and improvement program called the quality improvement program (QIP). The benefits from the improvements were so dramatic that they were the first non-Japanese company to win the Deming Award, which is Japan's most prestigious national quality award. However, the implementation of this improvement program had extensive front-end costs and the result was that after about three years of losses, the board became impatient and untrusting of the CEO. The board threw out the CEO along with his participative management style and all his continuous improvement ideas and installed an authoritarian CEO that keeps everything secret. Suddenly, employees who were formally involved in the organization and its changes now have no idea from one day to the next what's going on within the organization. Short-term financial measures ruled the day at Florida Power and Light, as they do in most United States organizations.

But, in spite of the short-sighted negatives, financial goals can, and often are, used to effect positive growth and change. The key to success seems to be in the realization that long-term visions and missions are not achieved when they are restricted by short-term measures that don't focus on the long-term goals.

Operational Goals

Operational goals have caught on in some parts of Europe. Operational goals tend to be more long term than financial goals. Additionally, achieving operational goals tends to have, as a by-product, the achievement of financial objectives. Operational goals would include (for example):

- improved quality
- improved productivity
- reduced inventory
- increased throughput
- reduced scrap
- improved customer service level.

It is easy to see how achieving each of these goals would improve profits. Additionally, these goals tend to be non-conflicting (see the discussion and example of conflicting financial goals in the section of this chapter that discusses goal characteristics). These goals tend to be long term because success tends to be measured incrementally. For example, a relatively small 10 per cent inventory reduction each year for ten years would lead to an enormous (65 per cent cumulative) inventory reduction after ten years, which, of course, would supply us with a similar increase in profitability.

Employee Based Goals

Employee permanence and stability is an important goal that is used quite often in Japan. The primary reason for the popularity of this goal is that it supports a participative relationship with the employees, rather than the authoritarian one. But there is a lot of misunderstanding about what this goal means and doesn't mean. For example, it doesn't mean that a company should ignore profitability, any more than a successful, profit-oriented company can ignore its employees. It simply means that successful, happy employees create a successful, happy company. Let me explain, through a series of steps, how this goal works.

1. The goal of the company is to give its employees permanence and a steady growth path.

2. To accomplish this you need to be in business longer than any competitor that is building your product.

3. This is achieved by being successful at your product, more successful than any competitor.

4. Product successfulness is measured in terms of market share control.

5. Market share control is captured by whatever means.

6. Once market share control is achieved, you have control of the product pricing, and therefore can recover any losses incurred while attempting to gain market share, hence profitability.

Note that the key goal, the one that started this entire series of events, is employee satisfaction.

> Federal Express, from its inception, has put its people first both because it is right to do so and because it is good business as well. Our corporate philosophy is succinctly stated: People-Service-Profit (P-S-P).
>
> Frederick W Smith,
> Chairman and CEO, Federal Express

Customer Based Goals — Not Quality Based Goals

A customer based goal often gets confused with a quality based goal. Quality is a strategy for achieving any of the goals (see Chapter 12). But quality itself is not a goal because it is defined and interpreted in so many different ways. For example, in the United States most companies who claim themselves to have a "quality product", in fact have only satisfied some internal measure of quality. For most factories, a quality product is defined as one that meets engineering specifications and has absolutely nothing to do with the customer. The international measure for quality, the ISO 9000 certification process, supports this "internal quality" perspective (see Chapter 12 for a more detailed discussion). In Europe, where the ISO 9000 process originated, there is the claim that Germany's quality is higher. But, unfortunately, all this means is that their engineering standards are higher, not that the product is more customer oriented. Therefore, I can be "quality" and still not have satisfied a single customer.

World-class "quality" lies in customer satisfaction, not engineer satisfaction. A world-class quality product would be one about which:

> The customer is so excited that they wouldn't think of going anywhere else to get it!

How do you know if you are customer-goal oriented? You would spend time with your customer at your customer's location and your customer would spend time with you and your employees at your location. You would share, discuss, interact, learn and create ideas (innovate) together. The customer would be an integral part of your planning circle. The reason for all this interaction is because you cannot satisfy a customer if you don't understand what they need or want — how can Robin Hood shoot a target he cannot see?

COMPARING THE TARGETS

I have listed the targets from shortest term to longest term, from easiest to implement to hardest and from most objective to most subjective. Let's take a look at the differences between these goals.

Financial and operational goals are easy to measure. It's all in the data and can be displayed neatly on a graph. Working with employees and customers is vague and not quite as quantifiable. Maybe that's why we shy away from them. However, companies like FedEx and Toyota have found a very definite way to quantify their performance, as we shall see later in the book. It just takes a little more effort. But is it worth it? All the Baldridge and Deming award winners seem to think so. They all fall into one of these last two categories.

What we have achieved, at this point, is the need to establish a goal. This goal takes the form of a vision and mission statement. As discussed briefly in the last chapter, there are two ways to come up with both of these statements — *bottom-up* and *top-down*.

The top-down approach would be to have the CEO, in conjunction with the VPs, develop the vision statement. Then, the mission statement is developed out of the vision generated by the top. The bottom-up approach would be to have middle or lower management define what they see the mission of the organization as being and then define a vision out of this synergistic mission. This helps adapt the organization to its own capabilities, since what works well in one business rarely works perfectly in another. The bottom-up approach has demonstrated ownership and commitment by the employees towards the goals and has therefore become very popular with companies that are employee or customer based in their goal structure.

No matter how the vision and mission statements are developed, the purpose of both documents is to develop a series of back-to-back targets that Robin Hood can shoot with only one arrow. These statements need to fit the employees, they need to be realistic, and they need to be communicated (see the section of this chapter discussing the characteristics of a good target). Often, we find that the employees, when given a say in the visioning process, are tougher on themselves than upper management would have been.

If you fail to plan, you plan to fail.

CHARACTERISTICS OF A GOOD TARGET

If Robin Hood were to pick the ideal target, what would it look like? It would be easy to see, focused (precise enough so that he knows exactly what he's shooting for), well defined and custom designed to challenge his abilities. So why am I making such a big deal out of setting a goal? Because the typical business plan of a company reads like a wish list of all good things and is totally worthless. Having lots of business goals is as useful as not having any if they are not focused on a common vision. The goals soon get in each other's way. Goal setting should not be a process of setting high goals to drive employees to unrealistic ends. Nor should goal attainment result in a compromise of easy to attain steps. A good target should be realistic and attainable. Specifically, there are several characteristics that all goals should have (most goals do not have all of these characteristics, but you should try to include as many as possible):

- participatively created by and matched to the employees
- shared
- non-conflicting

- allows for and encourages change
- simple but not simplistic
- precise
- measurable
- uncompromised
- focused
- achievable yet challenging.

Let's consider these characteristics in more detail.

Participatively created by and matched to the employees — employees that participate in the goal development process maintain an ownership in the goals and feel personally challenged to achieve those goals. The goals are no longer "company" goals, rather they are "my" goals. This is what was meant when we discussed the employees developing the mission statement and then consolidating this into a vision. This is broader than the old concept of management by objectives (MBO) where the employees sit down with their supervisor and set goals for themselves. Participative goal setting is where the employees establish corporate goals, and not just individual goals. Remember the Tridon-Oakdale and Antilock Braking Systems Division (ABS) of General Motors stories? In both cases the employees were actively involved in establishing corporate goals.

Shared — one of the biggest "sins" of goal making is to not communicate the goal to the individuals that are responsible for achieving the goals. I have lost count of the number of companies who have said to me "we don't show our employees our business plan because it is confidential", meaning that only strategic management employees are allowed to look at them (this is where Robin Hood gets blindfolded). My question is, "how can you expect the employees to hit a target they can not see?" Even Robin Hood can't do that. Employees need to know what the goal is, how it is going to be measured, whether or not you are making progress towards the goal and they should receive part of (share in) the reward of achieving the goal.

> A hidden goal is as useful as no goal, for no one will know if you succeeded.

Non-conflicting — financial goals are often conflicting, but non-financial goals can be as well. Let's consider a recent financial example that I encountered. The financial goals of this organization were to increase profits, increase sales, decrease costs and increase the return on net assets. On the surface, this seems like a reasonable set of goals. However, under closer examination we see that these goals are conflicting and therefore impossible to achieve simultaneously. The result is something similar to what we see in Figure 5.1. For about the first 90 per cent of the month we have steady output, working towards minimizing cost and maximizing profit. This is because we are working efficiently. Then, during the last 10 per cent of the month we put on a rush trying to push as much product out the door as possible. We have thrown efficiency, profit and cost reduction to the wind. We send people scurrying around in an attempt to get employees to work in smaller batch sizes so that we can get a few extra product units (orders) out the door. We are now working toward the goal of increased sales. Then we spend the first part of the next month trying to recover from the inefficiency mess created near the end of the previous month. Obviously, from this example, we see that these goals are in conflict. At one time of the month we are working towards one goal while at another time of the month we are working towards another goal. We can't achieve both goals simultaneously. As an additional explanation of this conflict, refer to your elementary economics class where you learned about the production function. This function taught us that the volume at which we produce to achieve maximum sales is not the same volume at which we produce to achieve maximum profits. So which is your goal — sales, profits, cost reductions, market share or return on investment? Several are in conflict with each other. You can't have them all as your goal (unless you're happy with not really achieving any of them). Robin Hood cannot hit multiple, unaligned targets with a single arrow.

Allows for and encourages change — a well-developed world-class goals system realizes that employees need to be able to interact with and initiate change (empowerment). They can't wait for change decisions to come from the top. They need to participate in the change process (participative management). Employees need to be prepared for change (training and education) and motivated toward change (measurement systems). All these points are discussed in detail in later chapters.

> . . . because time and information don't exist or move fast enough for top management to make decisions from the top.
>
> Alvin Toffler[5]

Simple but not simplistic — goals should be simple, the shorter the better. Complex goals are harder to understand and are therefore ignored. Ideally, the vision portion of the goal should be short enough to be wall plaque material and easily remembered and stated by the employees. The vision should stress the core competency of the organization. The mission statement should also be simple, a collection of ten or so sentences, stating how the vision can be operationalized. Similar rules apply to the strategies of the organization.

---

5. Alvin Toffler has written several interesting books about the future and change. The one that started it all off and is well worth your time reading is Toffler, Alvin, *Future Shock*, (New York: Random House Publishers) 1970.

The vision, mission and strategy should not be simplistic, like "We want to get better", or "We want to get richer". These are too vague and employees have difficulty hanging their hat on them.

Precise — goals need to be precise, especially as you get down into the strategies. Goal achievement needs to be measurable. An imprecise goal leads to confusion. The goal needs to be quantifiable and precisely related to each employee telling them what is expected of them.

Measurable — the enterprise needs competitive performance measures to make sure they are staying on top of the competition. Measures like productivity, quality, time-to-market and efficiency are excellent internal operational measures that demonstrate performance on a team basis. Measures on employee satisfaction and customer satisfaction are excellent departmental measures of performance. You have an entire chapter on measurement systems coming up. One important lesson about measurement systems that needs to be learned if we are to achieve world-class status is that a measurement system does not exist for management information or for costing, it exists for motivation.

What you measure is what you motivate!

Don't measure/motivate labor efficiency if what you really want is materials efficiency. And don't measure/motivate labor efficiency if what you really want is quality. You'll receive results in what you measure, not in what you vocalize. And don't try to tell yourself that you can measure labor efficiency, materials efficiency, and quality all at the same time unless you want to:

• confuse employees as to what you're really after, and

• receive average performance in each area as opposed to achieving excellent performance in the area that you really need performance in, which should be your critical resource.

A goal needs to be measured to assure performance and goal achievement, and needs to measure the right things in order to generate the proper motivation.

Uncompromised — a goal needs to be uncompromised. Once established, it needs to be committed to. This is one reason why goal ownership by the employees is so important. Wishy-washy management commitment to goal achievement results in non-achievement. This also refers to goal downsizing. If the employees were involved in goal development, then if they don't achieve the goal we shouldn't go back and say, "Well, you did OK and we'll give you your bonus anyway." That will whitewash the goals and will result in poor goal setting in the future. Goals need to taken seriously and they need to be committed to!

Focused — the company of Figure 5.1 shows a lack of focus. It is basically running the plant two different ways. Since the goals are in conflict, which

Figure 5.1: Conflicting Goals

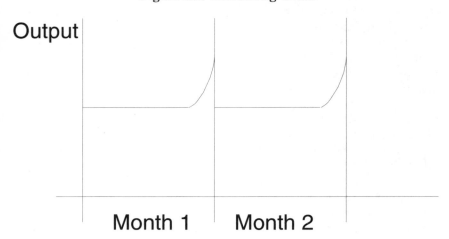

measurement system is appropriate? The one used during the first 90 per cent of the month would be efficiency, productivity and cost of production, the measurement system used during the last 10 per cent of the month would be a sales growth measure. Stressing both will result in the type of chaos shown in Figure 5.1. We need to have focus in our goals, which means we need a target that is well defined and challenging. Set your goal, build a measurement system around it and stick to it.

Achievable yet challenging — the last characteristic of goal setting is that the goal should make us stretch ourselves, but not kill ourselves. We don't want last year's performance to be next year's goal. We want the new goal to be significantly but realistically better than last year's accomplishments, thereby making us better.

Now that we have discussed the characteristics of good goals, let's discuss the role of secondary goals and then take a look at the implementation of a good set of goals.

THE SECOND AND THIRD TARGET

Earlier in this chapter we discussed multiple conflicting goals. We also mentioned that we need a single, focused target to shoot at. Does this mean that secondary goals are bad? Definitely not! As long as they don't conflict with or interfere with the primary goal. Robin Hood can hit multiple targets, if they are nicely laid on top of each other, but not if they are off in different directions.

There is nothing wrong with having secondary goals as long as they strengthen, rather than conflict with, the primary goal. Let me give you an example. If your primary goal is employee permanence and stability, then it would be appropriate to ask what secondary goal would support this primary goal. If we want the employees to have jobs, then we want the plant to be around as long as possible. To do this we need to make sure we manufacture the product as long as possible. We need to control the market and the production of the product. An appropriate secondary goal would be to control market share. Then the next question is, how do we control market share? This may take a little price-cutting or gouging until you control the market. Then you can make the price whatever you want. But a more important way to control market share is by using the definition of quality discussed earlier, which is "to make a product the customer enjoys, likes, and appreciates so much that they wouldn't think of buying from anyone else". A recap of this chain of goals would be:

- primary — employee permanence and stability
- second goal — control market share
- third goal — quality product.

Another type of secondary goal is to break a goal down by departments or management levels. It would be helpful if each department was able to define a sub-goal that would demonstrate that department's efforts towards the primary goal. This sub-goal would be measurable within the organization and would be more useful to the specific organization than the primary goal.

TARGET IMPLEMENTATION

Figure 5.2 briefly outlines what the goal statements of an organization may look like. Note the focus on the core competencies and the strengthening of these core competencies by the development of goals around these. Also note the focus on goals and the development of supportive sub goals that will assist in the achievement of the primary goal.

As we implement the goals, we need to remember:

- goal participation and ownership
- employee preparation and training
- the corporate value system.

Goal participation and ownership — again I need to stress that the most effective goal structure is a participative one, where the employees are involved in the setting of the goals and in the implementation of the goals. Only with employee participation do you achieve employee ownership. And only with employee ownership do we achieve a corporate-wide success commitment.

Figure 5.2: Goal Development

Vision statement

One or two sentences stating what the long-term vision of the enterprise is, focusing on the core competencies of the organization.

Mission statement

A series of goal statements indicating how the organization plans to achieve the vision. This statement specifies what areas the organization plans to change (become better), where it sees its strengths and how does it plan to develop these strengths. The mission should be measurable with a target completion date. The mission statement, like the vision, should focus on the core competencies of the enterprise.

Strategy

A focus on the various "strategic areas" of the organization and a quantifiable set of goals stating how each area plans to support and achieve the mission statement. (Strategy development is discussed in more detail in the next chapter.)

Employee preparation and training — it's one thing to set goals, it is entirely another thing to make sure that the employees have the tools necessary to achieve the goals. Sometimes this means technology, but often this means training. For example, if quality improvement is a goal, then the employees need to be trained in quality improvement tools; what they are, how to use them, and how they can make a difference. I know a company (name withheld to protect the innocent) that has been using statistical process tracking tools for many years to monitor quality. Recently, I was brought in and asked, "Why are we developing these control charts? What are we supposed to do with them?" Previous management had gotten on a quality control kick and had made employees fill out control charts. Most employees didn't know how to or why. They just did it because they were told to. Is it any surprise that quality didn't improve, in spite of the quality control system?

The corporate value system — the corporate value system needs to be at the heart of all goals and their implementation. Goal achievement should incorporate values, not take a back seat to them. For example, honesty and integrity are often thrown to the wind in order to make the numbers look good. A company that loses its values to numbers will have a long road trying to get its lost integrity back. And, since the numbers weren't realistic anyway, it will also have trouble achieving its realistic goals.

With the necessary commitment and tools, employees will be eager and interested in driving the enterprise towards world-class status.

WHEN GOALS DON'T WORK

If you don't follow the basics of goal development, goals are nothing more than plaques on the wall. For example, a 1991 survey of over 300 electronics companies found that 63 per cent had failed to improve quality defects by as much as 10 per cent. The reason stated was that the programs were not "results driven", they did not have goals that were measured and motivated within a specific time frame. Another example of failure are the many companies who have identified so many activities in so many places in the change process that it required a complex chart just to describe them all (I always leave the name of the company out when the news is bad). In another case, successful change was measured by having 100 per cent of the employees attending a quality-training program. I wonder if anyone cares if they learned anything. In other cases failure occurred because credit wasn't given where credit was due; management sucked up all the credit for what the employees accomplished.[6]

I was asked to visit the plant of a company that had been officially notified of closure. Since the plant was going to close anyway, the management wanted to know what went wrong. It didn't take long to discover a quality improvement system that had all the appropriate control charts and process control tools. The employee training was in place. The plaques about quality were on the wall. So what went wrong? What we quickly learned was that employee performance was measured based on units of output. No one was measured on quality improvements. And so no quality improvements occurred, primarily because quality changes would interfere with productive units produced, which meant that quality improvements would actually reduce, rather than increase the bonus. The employees weren't dumb, they knew how to kiss up to the management fad of implementing quality control systems, while at the same time maintaining the quality of their pay checks. Another instance where goal achievement fails is when the principles and values of the enterprise and its employees are compromised in order to achieve the goals. This makes goal achievement a negative event, rather than an exciting and celebrated event.

Goal achievement can only occur based on the principles and characteristics outlined in this chapter. Otherwise, don't expect world-class results!

---

6. Schaffer, Robert H and Harvey A Thomson, "Successful Change Programs Begin with Results", *Harvard Business Review* (January-February 1992) pp. 80-89.

THE CHANGE PROCESS

Marriage should war incessantly with that monster that is the ruin of everything. This is the monster of habit.

Honore De Balzac,
French writer

Now we are ready to review the change process (mentioned in Chapter 4) in order to see how it ties into the goals and strategies we establish. Our vision and mission should have focused on change (improvement). We will implement this change through a series of strategic steps (next chapter). We will then use any (or several) of a variety of change models in order to implement these changes (see Chapter 13).

In Chapter 4 we discussed two sources of change:

1.   the changes you invoke yourself

2.   the changes that are happening to you.

This chapter has focused on the changes that you invoke yourself. However, there are still those changes that happen to you that require contingency plans. You can't expect everything to roll along perfectly. Life is filled with surprises. The better you are prepared to roll with the punches and the better you are prepared with contingency plans, the more likely you will be able to achieve your eventual enterprise goals.

SUMMARY

To create the new we need to eliminate the old.

Robin Hood needs to have the blinders removed. He not only needs to know where the target is, he needs to participate in the selection and planning of the target. And he needs a target that challenges him, yet is achievable. He needs to be excited about the target. He needs to feel that if he hits the target he will have improved himself.

But goals aren't just for the enterprise. Goals should also be a part of your life and your family's life. What do you want to be when you grow up? What do you want to have accomplished in ten years? Twenty years? How about the goals of your family? World-class means world-class in the home as well as on the job.

Managers, like Robin Hood, need targets in order to measure world-class performance. In this chapter we have discussed core competencies, vision statements and mission statements. Next we will go on to identify what strategic areas we need to have quantifiable goals in, that in turn will focus on the vision and mission of the enterprise.

Chapter Six

Strategies for Change

Men fear thought as they fear nothing else on earth — more than death. Thought is subversive, and revolutionary, destructive and terrible; thought is merciless to privilege, established institutions, and comfortable habits; thought is anarchic and lawless, indifferent to authority, careless to the well-tried wisdom of the ages. Thought looks into the pit of hell and is not afraid . . . Thought is great and swift and free, the light of the world, and the chief glory of man.

But if thought is to become the possession of the many, and not the privilege of the few, we must have done with fear. It is fear that holds men back — fear that their cherished beliefs should prove delusions, fear lest the institutions by which they live should prove harmful, fear lest they themselves prove less worthy to the respect then they have supposed themselves to be.

Bertrand Russell,
Philosopher

Consider the diagram in Figure 6.1. What I want you to do is to determine the length of line BD in the rectangle ABCD, given that line AE (the radius) is ten inches long. It's not intended to be a difficult problem. You can do it with the basic geometry that you learned in junior high school. It should take you about two minutes if you understand the strategy and follow through on the strategy.

The point I am making is that without developing and understanding the strategy, even the simplest goal is impossible to achieve. By the way, the solution to the problem is in the appendix at the end of the chapter.

The problem with strategy is there are about a million different strategy models. I will offer a few and discuss some of the features that are common to all of them. I will also offer you lots of good reading material if you are interested in finding out more about strategy development. However, my focus here is on world-class management, not on strategy development, and so I will focus primarily on those strategic areas that are the most critical to helping you become a world-class eManager.

World-class strategies focus on world-class competitiveness. Some of the competitive trends for the next decade include:

- rapid change in technology and markets
- more global competitors

Figure 6.1: Find the Length of the Line BD

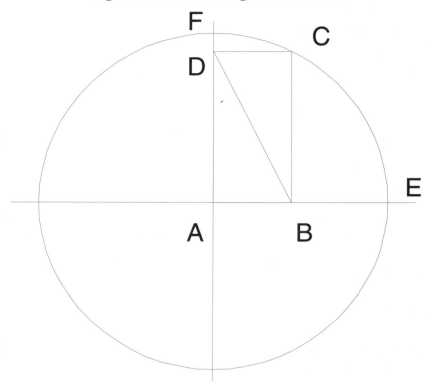

- an increased emphasis on globalization
- an environmental consciousness
- decentralization
- shrinking company sizes (strategic alliances)
- closer links to customers and suppliers
- a competitive emphasis on cost reduction and a customer oriented quality improvement, and a stronger priority on flexibility and time-to-market responsiveness
- borderless companies
- removal of departmentalization.

Some of the key principles of world-class competitiveness include:
- focus on the people (primary employees)

- focus on the customer
- a quality and productivity stance
- a global perspective
- time-based competition
- a technological orientation
- information management
- an integrative stance
- focused measurement
- a value-added decision approach
- continuous training and education.

These trends and principles are the focus of Parts I and II of this book. Both need to be integrated into a strategic plan for the organization. So what is a strategy? Figure 6.2 diagrams the traditional format of a corporate strategy. It shows business units, each of which develop their own strategies in each of the strategic areas. This strategy focuses first on the corporate strategy, which in turn should focus on the mission statement. Both the corporate and the business unit strategies should identify quantifiable, time-based goals at their level. Although somewhat traditional, this process of strategy development is still heavily utilized today. However, the trend toward dropping internal corporate barriers would suggest that soon the corporate strategy and the business strategy would become one and the same.

Figure 6.2: Strategy

The strategy, like the mission and vision statement, should focus on the core competencies of the business unit or corporation. It should contain all the characteristics of goals set in the last chapter. The strategy specifies the scope and boundaries of the business unit. It identifies the basis for achieving and maintaining competitive advantage. It describes how the resources of the business unit will be utilized to achieve the focused corporate mission. It determines the competitive priorities of the business unit, which include:

- cost competitiveness — for example, K-Mart versus Sears, unit costs and delivery costs
- time competitiveness — FedEx versus the US postal system, responsiveness and time-to-market
- quality competitiveness — K-Mart versus Sears, generics versus brand name products, performance and conformance
- dependability — fax versus telegram, the reliability of delivery commitments and service level and responsiveness
- flexibility — Taiwanese businesses versus the US government, adaptability to change and customized products or services
- technology — ability to innovate, new product introduction, tinkering rather than changing and speed and timing of change implementation.

Although these competitive priorities are recognized and accepted as crucial elements in the development of an effective strategy, rarely do they become a part of the measurement/motivation system for the management of an enterprise (see Chapter 12). This is another example of verbalizing a goal without putting any power behind it. The strategy is only as valuable as the power and commitment that is placed behind it.

> Lord, I confess that I am not what I ought to be, but I thank you, Lord, that I'm not what I used to be.
>
> Maxie Dunnan

Now that we have determined what the characteristics of a competitive business strategy entail and what its competitive priorities should focus on, we are now ready to look at some of the strategy models that exist. These models contain areas of consideration that an ideal world-class business strategy should consider.

MANAGEMENT COMPETITIVENESS AND CHANGE

. . . long-range thinking is as rare in the boardroom as in the White House . . .

. . . business is as confused as are the politicians . . .

. . . we are moving from a brute force to a brain force economy . . .

. . . knowledge is the new capital replacing stock or land holdings.

Alvin Toffler

I recently heard the saying that behind every good man is a surprised mother-in-law. Similarly, behind every effective corporate strategy is a surprised manager.

There are numerous models of management competitiveness. Each of these models gives us a slightly different insight into what our competitive strategies should be. However, all of these models focus on corporate excellence through world-class management strategies. These models are all valuable in helping us develop a strategic plan which details out our vision and mission into an area-by-area strategic process. For example, the Hall and Nakane model breaks competitiveness into four quadrants.[1] They are:

1. *technical factors* — the external and worldwide environment factors, such as government policies (fiscal and monetary policy, the taxation system, trade policies, industrial development policies and social and ecological regulatory policies)

2. *technical factors* — internal (within country) factors, such as technical capability, access to capital, technical advance for product design, process design and computer information systems

3. *cultures, philosophy and customs* — external and worldwide environment factors relating to the socioeconomic environment (race, languages and cultures, religions and values, the work ethic, educational systems and values, the health of people, economic and legal systems, support for technical advance and the concept of companies and management)

4. *cultures, philosophy and customs* — internal (within country) factors relating to management philosophies, such as concept and culture of the company, organization structure, human resources management, attitude towards change, competitive strategy, targeting of markets and the method of manufacturing improvement.

---

1. Hall, Robert W and Jinichiro Nakane, "Developing Flexibility for Excellence in Manufacturing: Summary Results of a Japanese-American Study", *Target* (Summer 1998) Vol. 4, No. 2, p. 18.

This model highlights the importance of the global strategy orientation. It also introduces the idea of a company culture, which contains the philosophy, values, aspirations and beliefs that the company has about itself and its people. This is what differentiates it from other firms in the industry.

Another model for world-class management strategies, demonstrated by Burnham, breaks strategic planning into two areas:[2]

1. *external factors* — competition, economic conditions, technology level, change in technology, government regulation, substitutions and the product life cycle

2. *internal factors* — market share, profitability, resources, logistics management and manufacturing.

A third model can be pulled from the publications of Adler, McDonald and McDonald.[3] It would suggest focusing on the following strategic areas:

*   strategic policies — personnel (recruitment, development, evaluation and rewards), technical projects (selection, termination and project management), quality assurance, intellectual properties, funding, facilities and equipment, structure (functional organization and authority), interfunctional linkages, external linkages and regulatory compliance

*   adjustment processes — strength and weaknesses and opportunities and threats.

A fourth model for corporate strategy could be:

*   customer and markets
*   technology and its characteristics
*   performance review systems
*   compensation systems
*   organizational structure
*   competition
*   personnel policies
*   financial position
*   macro and micro economic variables
*   information systems.[4]

---

2. Burnham, John B, "Systematic Improvements in Physical Distribution or 'Why Can't We Just Do It Like We Used To?'" *APICS 34th Conference Proceedings* (Falls Church, Virginia: APICS) 1991, pp. 305-310.
3. You can find out more about this model from Adler, Paul S, McDonald D William and McDonald Fred, "Strategic Management of Technical Functions", *Sloan Management Review* (Winter 1992) pp. 19-37.
4. See Mojonnier, Timothy M, "Top Management's Role in Fostering and Managing Posi-

A fifth model for the development of a corporate strategy focuses on capitalizing on the competitive advantage (core competency) of an enterprise. Michael Porter's model discusses the strategy of diversification and how each business unit needs to define their roles (strategies) and to fit them into the corporate strategy.[5]

> Corporate strategy is what makes the corporate whole add up to more than the sum of its business unit parts.
>
> Michael E Porter

If I were to suggest a model for a world-class corporate or business unit's strategic plan I would suggest the following focus areas, all of which should have goals pointing at the mission statement (or higher level strategic plan) as its target. This plan is probably more than any business unit needs by itself, but the idea is that you would pick and choose those areas that are important for your enterprise to have a defined strategy in. My plan would include the strategic areas of:

- people — employees (education and training, empowerment, teamwork, organizational structure and staff functions), customers (involvement) and vendors (integration)
- integration — information and the elimination of barriers
- globalization
- measurement — internal performance (quality, productivity and efficiency), external performance (added value to society, customer perceived quality, market share), internal factors (capacity, equipment and operational performance), external factors (competition, economic conditions and government regulations), focus and motivation
- continuous change process focused on adding value — elimination of waste, identifying strengths and weaknesses and opportunities and threats
- time-based competition — time to market strategy
- technology — funding and facilities and equipment.

Let's look at these strategic areas in more detail.

People — you need a strategy that identifies, incorporates and empowers people, especially the employees of the business unit. Chapter 4 discusses

---

tive Organizational Change", *APICS 37th Conference Proceedings* (Falls Church, Virginia: APICS) 1994, pp. 49-51.
5. For more information on competitive strategy, see the following publications from Michael Porter: *Competitive Strategy* (Free Press) 1980; *Competitive Advantage* (Free Press) 1985; "From Competitive Advantage to Corporate Strategy", *Harvard Business Review* (May-June 1987) pp. 43-59.

this topic in depth. Next, you need a strategy that relates to customers. Customer satisfaction is the second most important principle to success. Next come the suppliers. Their involvement and integration will help them make better products for you, and will give you valuable insights into how to make your product better.

Integration — you need to drop the internal and external barriers. These include job titles, departments and information barriers. Integration needs to exist physically (mix the different staff functions together in the same room), informationally (don't have separate databases for different departments as the information also needs to flow easily from top to bottom and from bottom to top) and in the processes (your output, information or product, whatever it is you produce, needs to be passed from area to area, not thrown "over the wall" to each other organizationally; keep the employee designations and titles vague and treat everyone as an equal). Chapter 12 focuses heavily on the integration issues.

Globalization — we are part of a big world that is affected by international transactions. We need to be aware of how they affect us. Chapter 9 spends time on this process.

Measurement — defining a measurement/motivational system is at the root of developing a strategic plan. We need to be able to demonstrate, over a defined period of time, that we are able to do our part in achieving the mission of the organization.

Continuous change process focused on adding value — we need to add value to ourselves, our organization and society as a whole. Our strategic plan should motivate us toward adding value, which also includes the identification and elimination of waste.

Time-based competition — time, like change, can be our enemy or our friend. Presently, for most United States firms, time is an enemy because our time-to-market performance is so poor. We are enormously effective at developing technology, but we are lousy at implementing it. For example, who developed the air bag? The United States. Who was first in installing it into their cars? Japan and Europe.

Technology — technology is often the most effective tool for positive change. We need to develop a strategy that defines us as an organization and focuses on long-term technological improvements, as opposed to short-term "patch-it-up and keep-it-running" technologies.

Whatever strategy model you desire to follow, the following rules apply:

1. No one should be left without a goal (strategy). Everyone, from janitor to CEO, should have a goal. For example, Walt Disney Company orients everyone into the big corporate picture and teaches them how they fit in, even if they are only a temporary, six-week employee.

2. Strategies should have short-term (less than one year), mid-term (one to

five years) and long-term (more than ten years) targets. Each of the strategic areas needs a one year and a twenty year target to focus on.

3. The best strategy model to fit your enterprise does not yet exist. You'll have to develop it yourself. You can use the ideas from these example models, but you need to develop your own model.

4. Contingencies need to be established. A strategy is only as good as external influences (changes) allow it to function. Contingent strategies are strategies that help us plan for external changes without giving up the focus on our goals. A contingency is an alternative route to get to our destination. The more thought that is put into our contingency strategies (the more we plan for potential problems), the more likely goal achievement will occur.

> A philosopher was asked, "What do you do when you reach a fork in the road."
>
> He answered very simply, "Take it."

At this point you should have a good feel for the types of areas and goals that your strategy should include. In the next section of this chapter I will discuss one of the most difficult strategies of all, primarily because of its complexity. This is the manufacturing strategy. I will be using this as an example of a functional business units strategy.

WHAT THE STRATEGY LOOKS LIKE

> [The great society] is a place where men are more concerned with the quality of their goals than with the quantity of their goods.
>
> Lyndon B Johnson

Now it's time to combine what we've learned about the strategy. It should:

• be developed at multiple levels — corporate strategy and business unit strategy

• focus on the mission statement or higher-level business strategy

• identify areas of competitiveness within each of the functional strategic areas of your selected strategic model

• focus on the competitive trends and priorities that we listed at the start of this chapter

• integrate the key competitive principles for strategy development listed early in this chapter

- contain quantifiable, time-stamped goals that contain the characteristics of goals discussed in Chapter 5.

Perhaps one of the easiest ways to explain strategies is by using an example. Using Figure 6.2 on page 101, I will discuss what elements should be present in the manufacturing strategy for business unit B. A manufacturing strategy is designed to support the business unit strategy. It needs to compliment the other functional strategies. Using my model, I will again outline the major types (areas) of a manufacturing strategy (goals):

- people — employees (selection and training, involvement and empowerment, compensation, job security, team development, organizational structure and staff functions), customers (involvement, internal to the organization, the final end user, vendors (integration, extent, number and relationships)

- integration — vertical integration (direction), elimination of barriers and information

- globalization

- measurement — of internal performance (quality, definitions, roles and responsibilities, productivity and efficiency, capital budgeting process), external performance (added value to society, customer perceived quality and market share), internal factors, including capacity (amount, timing and type) and equipment and process technologies (scale and level of automation, flexibility versus specialized, size and location of facilities), specialization (operational performance and production control, such as flow and inventory levels and scheduling) and external factors (competition, economic conditions, government regulations, focus and motivation)

- continuous change process focused on adding value — elimination of waste, identifying strengths and weaknesses and opportunities and threats

- time-based competition — time to market strategy

- technology — funding, facilities and equipment and new product development (interface with engineering, marketing and the customer).

> The measure of success is not whether you have a tough problem to deal with, but whether it's the same problem you had last year.
>
> John Foster Dulles

A manufacturing strategy would have short, medium, and long-range goals in each of the categories, focusing on the business unit strategy and the corporate strategy and identifying each of the issues in the above list.

Hayes and Wheelwright developed a model of what they call the four stages of manufacturing's strategic effectiveness role.[6] Manufacturing's role should be to move from Stage 1 to Stage 4 where they are making a significant, value added difference. The stages are described as follows:

Stage 1 — *internally neutral.* The role of a manufacturing strategy is to minimize the negative impact that manufacturing has on the overall organization. Manufacturing is a necessary evil.

Stage 2 — *externally neutral.* Here the strategic role of manufacturing is to achieve parity with its competitors. United States manufacturing is primarily in this category. Manufacturing is strategically competitive as long as the competition plays the same game.

Stage 3 — *internally supportive.* In this stage manufacturing needs to provide a credible supportive role to the overall business strategy. This should focus on continuous positive change and overall goal contribution.

Stage 4 — *externally supportive.* In this role manufacturing has become a significant contributor to the overall corporate competitive advantage. Manufacturing is a major innovator.

Stage 4 is where in-house process development capabilities exist that enable manufacturing to do things that competitors can't do. Internal innovation for modifications and adaptations are motivated. Continuous improvement programs are operational and effective. Integration of the functions at low levels leads to short product introduction cycles. External benchmarking is done to make sure manufacturing performance is ahead of the competition. You find out who is the best, learn from them and then use the innovativeness of your internal work force to accelerate ahead of the competition.

Stage 4 fully utilizes all its manufacturing resources. It knows what its critical resource is and motivates plant operations to effectively utilize the critical resource.[7] Manufacturing is integrated with the other functions of the company to where they see each other as peers; no one function is king. Manufacturing has moved from being a fire fighter to being a strategic planner.

The largest gap exists between Stage 3 and Stage 4. Achieving Stage 4 means that you need to continuously focus on creative change processes. Companies, like Apple Computers, have been known to achieve Stage 4 status and then, through a lack of innovative manufacturing, fall back to a Stage 2 position.

---

6. Wheelwright, Steven C and Robert D Hayes, "Competing Through Manufacturing", *Harvard Business Review* (January-February 1985) pp. 99-109.
7. For additional information on the critical resource, see Plenert, Gerhard, *The Plant Operations Handbook* (Homewood, Illinois: Business One Irwin) 1993.

Within the stages of strategic effectiveness, Wheelwright and Hayes list the major types of manufacturing choices. These are the areas in which world-class strategies should be developed. They are:

- capacity — amount, timing and type
- facilities — size, location and specialization
- equipment and process technologies — scale, flexibility and inter-connectedness
- vertical integration — direction, extent and balance
- vendors — number, structure and relationship
- new products — hand-off, start-up and modification
- human resources — selection and training, compensation and security
- quality — definition, role and responsibility
- systems — organization, schedules and control.

There are numerous excellent articles and books that have valuable information on manufacturing strategy development. For example, the Walters article discusses the integration of engineering, computer integrated manufacturing (CIM) and automated manufacturing technology into the strategy, the focus being on change. Burton stresses globalization, global competition and the development of strategic alliances as the first strategic priority. Landvater, Souza and Wallace focus on the importance of a strategic measurement tool. Gregoire and Delaney stress that the development of good strategy is the key to competitive and world-class success. They stress the need for future vision in the strategy. And last of all, one of the classics in manufacturing strategy is the Skinner article focussing on developing a competitive advantage by task and thereby focusing the factory. He stresses points like:

- there are many ways to compete besides producing at low cost
- a factory cannot perform well on every yardstick
- simplicity and repetition breed competence.[8]

---

8. Walters, Michael F, "Manufacturing Excellence in the1990s", *APICS 34th Conference Proceedings*, op. cit., pp. 425-428; Burton, Terence T, "Manufacturing in the 21st Century", *APICS 34th Conference Proceedings, ibid.*, pp. 454-457; Landvater, Darryl, Steve Souza and Thomas Wallace, "The ABCD Checklist for Manufacturing Excellence: An Integrated Strategic/Operational Measurement Tool", *APICS 34th Conference Proceedings, ibid.*, pp. 458-459; Gregoire, Renee M and Patrick J Delaney, "Manufacturing Strategy: The Key to Competitive Advantage", *APICS 33rd Conference Proceedings* (APICS) October 1990, PP. 9-13; Skinner, Wickham, "The Focused Factory", *Harvard Business Review* (May-June 1974) pp. 113-121. Additional information on manufacturing strategy development can be found in Sheth, Jagdish and Golpira Eshghi, *Global Operations Perspectives* (Cincinnati: South Western Publishing Company) 1989, which contains a number of useful articles.

Additional valuable information that would assist in the development of a manufacturing strategy can be obtained from the national and international quality awards programs that exist. For example, the Baldridge (US national quality award), the Shingo Prize (US award for manufacturing excellence), the NASA (US award for government contractor manufacturing excellence) and the Deming award (Japan's national quality award) offer valuable information. I'm not suggesting that you need to apply for these awards to be world-class. However, you need to be a contender. By looking at these award criteria, we can improve our strategies for change. These award criteria highlight the areas of world-class manufacturing excellence.[9]

The manufacturing strategy example should help you with ideas for the development of your own corporate or business unit strategy. No model is perfect, but the manufacturing example makes a good case study. Every business area has criteria for excellence that are available to them, including awards programs that will assist in defining world-class status.

Another complex area that has enormous opportunities for world-class changes is the logistics area.[10] Customer service and support tends to be a third area that needs overhaul. I'm sure that whatever area you are in, innovation and competitive change are needed. So move forward and see if you can turn your business unit into a Stage 4 world-class enterprise.

---

9. The NASA quality award does not seem to be operating at present. For information on the Shingo Prize, contact:

   Shingo Prize for Excellence in Manufacturing
   College of Business
   Utah State University
   Logan UT 84322-3520
   (801) 797-2279

   For more information on the Deming Prize, see Kilian, Cecelia S, *The World of W Edward Deming* (Knoxville, Tenessee: SPC Press, Inc.) 1992.

   The Baldridge Award criteria are available from:

   Malcolm Baldridge National Quality Award
   National Institute of Standards and Technology
   Route 270 and Quince Orchard Road
   Administration Building, Room A537
   Gaithersburg, MD 20899
   (301) 975-2036

10. An article which may be helpful is Nicoll, Andrew D, "Integrating Logistics Strategies", *APICS 37th Conference Proceedings,* op. cit., pp. 590-594.

STRATEGIC EFFECTIVENESS

. . . seek ye earnestly the best gifts . . .

Doctrine and Covenants 46:8

When I think of strategy development, I think of one of my favorite sayings

If you're not green and growing, you're ripe and rotting.

I know many organizations that seem to be rotting rather than growing. You get comments like, "they've always done it this way", or "they don't see any need for change". They're ripe and rotting. When looking for improvements, you always have to be "green and growing", never thinking you have it all figured out, always looking for a better way or a new idea.

The Saturn automobile manufacturing facility in Spring Hill, Tennessee is one of the premier models of effectively developed and implemented strategies at the corporate level and at the business unit level. Its goal is to build a world-class car, which includes all aspects of the product — sales, service, the entertainment value of the car, the shipping and delivery of the vehicle to the customer, problem correction and employee empowerment. Consider the key elements of their strategy.

1. The importance of people — employees are salaried and involved. Five per cent of an employee's time is spent in training.

2. Commitment to customer satisfaction — they'll travel around the world to fix a problem. They offer no discounting because their customers told them they want the best price the first time, not after extensive negotiations. Additionally, customers don't want to be hassled when they walk into a car dealership, so they have "no hassle" dealerships.

3. A redefinition of the "product" to include the people, the vehicle and the way people are treated.

4. They have an emphasis on building brand equity. They have the highest residual value in their vehicles, even higher than the Lexus and the Mercedes.

5. They have a reliance on partnerships — people working together. This is within and without the organization. In meetings, they pride themselves on not knowing who's who as far as job titles and levels goes.

Saturn focuses on problem acceptance, which is identifying the problem and accepting responsibility for it rather than trying to blame it off and fixing the problem right the first time.

Esso Japan has taken the jump ahead in its strategy development. It has developed a strategy that focuses on a shift beyond commitment to excellence (CTE) feeling that they needed a program that took the next step. It developed a strategy that focuses on:

- creativity and response to changes
- vision and participation
- entrepreneurship and dynamics.

The new strategy program that Esso developed was labelled power to succeed (PTS). It used a diagram similar to the one in Figure 6.3 to utilize the power circles and develop, grow and explode beyond these into PTS. The new challenges that they have developed into their strategies include:

- swift technological changes
- "smart" machines
- low cost factory operations
- value added performance
- developing easier new market entries
- generating stiffer competition.

Esso feels that the keys to this are the innovative and entrepreneurship abilities of its employees. It focuses on empowerment based on a shared vision

Figure 6.3: Esso Japan PTS Program

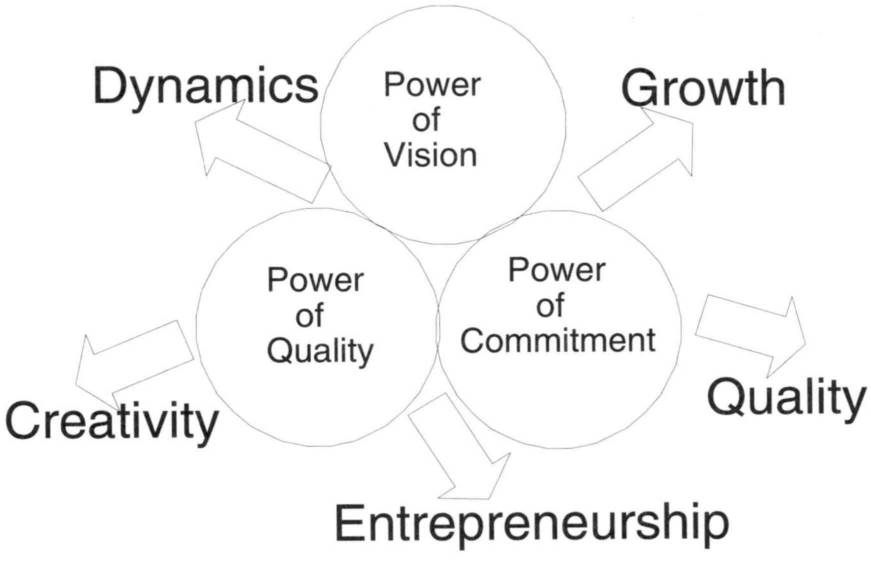

with a minimum amount of bureaucracy and believes that people need to grow in order for the organization to grow. It focuses its strategy on teams, utilizing a total quality management (TQM – see Chapter 7) process to move employees from a status of "work" to a status of "create". It wants employees to be able to "think again".

The Saturn and Esso examples are two examples of world-class enterprise strategy development. By benchmarking (comparing and analyzing) how far these organizations have already come, we can see how far we still have to go in order to become world-class competitive ourselves.

STRATEGY IMPLEMENTATION

. . . press toward the mark for the prize . . .

Philippians 3:14

Strategy implementation focuses on the same considerations that goal implementation did (see the last chapter). These were:

- goal participation and ownership

- employee preparation and training

- the corporate value system.

Some additional implementation concerns in strategy are:

- integration

- measurement and motivation

- innovation.

The strategy should not lose sight of the need for integration. The separate business strategies should not create barriers, but should rather focus on barrier removal.

The fifth important point about strategy implementation is people. The strategy gets closer to the people than the vision and mission statement do. Therefore, the measurement and motivation process also becomes more important.

Strategy is the level at which innovation and change occurs the most. Innovation and change need to be motivated with the appropriate tools and motivations. Refer to the books by Nadler and Hibino mentioned in earlier chapters to open your mind to innovative thinking.

Additionally, there are some key situational variables that need to be considered in strategy implementation. They are:

- the amount and type of resistance
- the trust and power levels of the initiators and resistors of the plan
- the availability of the resources necessary for implementation (data, energy, and so on)
- the stakes involved.[11]

While planning for implementation of the strategy, all players need to be involved in its design and committed to its success, just as they were in the development of the strategy. Otherwise, if they are only involved, then they are passive as to the results. Without commitment, we may be establishing a power struggle and soon territorialism becomes involved and strategy implementation turns into a contest of wills. Involvement needs to build into commitment and commitment builds success. This reminds me of the bacon and eggs breakfast. In the bacon and eggs breakfast, the chicken was involved in the breakfast, but the pig was committed to it. We need commitment in the goal setting process and in its implementation, not just commitment, and definitely not resistance.

STRATEGY SUMMARY

... it is expedient that he should be diligent, that thereby he might win the prize.

Mosiah 4:27,
Book of Mormon

Strategy development is the critical fourth step in the development of goals in an enterprise, the first three being:

1. defining the core competencies

2. the vision

3. the mission.

The strategy gets closer to the employees and is more detailed, identifying specific targets for each business unit. That makes the strategy the key measurement and motivation tool for each of the business units.[12] With strategies,

---

11. See Kotter, John P, Schlesinger L A and Sathe V, *Organization* (Homewood, Illinois: Business One Irwin) 1986, p. 360.
12. See Lowenthal, Jeffrey N, *Reengineering the Organization* (Milwaukee, Wisconsin: ASQC Quality Press) 1994; Wallace, Thomas F, *World Class Manufacturing* (Essex Junction, Vermont: Oliver Wight Publications) 1994.

we now have a tool to handle internally generated changes. With contingencies built into the strategy, we have the capability to defeat imposed (externally generated) changes.

At this point, the world-class eManager should have defined competitive targets for growth, both personally and as part of a corporate entity. In Chapter 4 we discussed where you are now. In Chapters 4 and 5 we have established the target of what we want to become. Now we need to detail the road map of how to make the journey. Part II of the book focuses on the key competitive strategic areas that a world-class eManager should focus on (not forgetting the most important: Chapter 4). Then Part III will focus on the world-class management tools that need to be used within the enterprise setting. Let's move forward detailing the areas that make a manager world-class.

That's one small step for man, one great leap for mankind.

Neil Armstrong

APPENDIX 6.1: BD SOLUTION

The solution to Figure 6.1 is easier than you think. The trick is in realizing that the line BD is the same length as the line AC because these are both diagonals in a rectangle (See Figure 6.4). Next, we see that line AC is the same length as line AE since they are both a radius to the circle. Therefore:

BD = AC = AE = 10 inches

Now that you know the strategy (the trick), you should have no difficulty in solving for line BD in Figure 6.5 if line AE is 20 inches. (BD is 20 inches of course.)

Figure 6.4: Find the Length of the Line BD

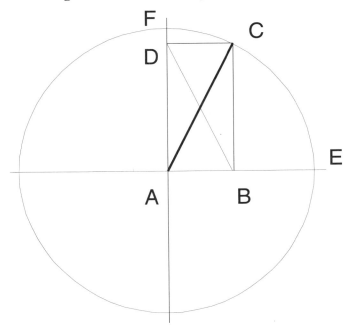

Figure 6.5: Find the New Length of the Line BD

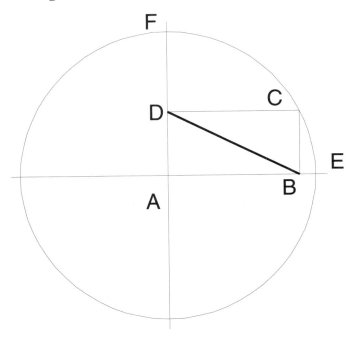

Chapter Seven

Successful Change Management

> The first signs of fundamental change rarely appear among one's customers. Usually they show up first among one's non-customers.
>
> Peter Drucker

The business functions of an organization have, for a long time, focused on stability rather than on change. For example, accounting, finance, personnel, the legal department, most upper management and marketing would love nothing more than to have a steady stable growth. Operations, traditionally, would love a perfectly balanced operation with just the right amount of inventory, just the right workforce and no problems. However, one of the competitive lessons we have learned is that stability breeds failure. If we try to stay where we are, we'll get run over. Just ask the American passenger railroads.

Operations has learned the new competitive lesson, which the remaining functional areas are just waking up to:

> The only way to competitive success is through change management!

The function of the operational organization has changed from one of seeking stability to one of managing change; change in products and their components, change in demand, changes in resources and their availability, changes in operational technology, changes in competitive product makeup, changes in competition, and so on. This is a lesson that needs to be shared with the remainder of the organization.

Continuous improvement (change) is critical in a global economy.[1] Changes should include, for example:

- product innovation
- process innovation (what the Japanese are good at)
- technology innovation
- time-to-market innovation (Taiwan)
- marketing innovation.

But uncontrolled and undirected change can be as disastrous as no change.

---

1. Kobu, Bulent and Frank Greenwood, "Continuous Improvement in a Competitive Global Economy", *Production and Inventory Management* (Fourth Quarter 1991) pp. 58-63.

What we need is to be able to stay ahead of the change process. We need to change ourselves faster than external forces have a chance to change us. We need the change to be focused on a target. And we need to maintain our corporate integrity as we institute change.

To manage change we need to incorporate change models into our business which facilitate the change process. Some of these change models, like total quality management and process re-engineering, will be discussed in this chapter. The problem with the change models is that they are often thought of as another fish story.

> Company (and change models) are like fish — after three days they stink.

Most change models contain some label of quality in them. Quality has become the flag behind which the battle for continuous change is most often fought. But "quality" doesn't fully define everything that is demanded by the change process. Nevertheless, terms like total quality management (TQM) and quality functional deployment (QFD) are change processes that look like they focus on quality. In reality, like all change models, they focus on positive, goal direct changes in all the measurement areas including quality, productivity, efficiency and financial improvements. In this chapter we will discuss and compare several of the "trendy" change models (some aren't really change models even though they get credit for being them). These include:

- quality functional deployment
- total quality management
- process re-engineering
- process re-engineering variations
- benchmarking
- ISO 9000
- award processes.

Before we discuss some of the change models specifically, let's first discuss some of the psychology behind change.

PSYCHOLOGY BEHIND CHANGE

> A man was looking on the ground, brushing the grass aside. A curious bystander asked him, "What are you looking for?"
> The man responded, "My keys."
> The bystander offered, "Where did you drop them? I'll help you find them!"

The man said, "Over there," pointing to a place about ten feet away. "Then why are you looking here?" queried the bystander. "Because it's dark over there and I can't see. The light is much better over here!"

Are we looking for keys (changes) in areas where it's convenient, or are we looking in the areas where we'll get the most benefit for our efforts? Often we take the easy way out when it comes to confronting change. But why do we avoid change? The psychology of change can be summarized in one word:

Resistance

Resistance to change should not be thought of as irrational. Resistance to change is rational behavior. Especially if the change directly effects our job function. Don't fear resistance — work with it. Remember from Chapter 4, all change is not good change. Sometimes the way change is instigated makes the change bad. Sometimes the change fails, no matter how hard we try. But remember also, that without change we are sure to fail because we'll get run over. We need to manage our way around the resistance to change.

In Japan, they use rocks in a river to signify resistance to change. Water flows smoothly down the river until it encounters the rocks, which resist this smoothness. The water must work its way around the rocks in order to successfully move on down the river. When change gets implemented in companies, we also encounter rocks. Consultants have come up with a way to explain the source of the greatest resistance. They say (and quite rightly):

The hardest rocks wear ties (or heels).

The toughest resistance to change comes from managers who are committed to their way of doing things. They learned to do it that way in school, or they've always done it that way and they don't understand why they need to change now. The line workers are used to being jerked around. New changes from management are not something new to them. However, I have seen organizations where over half of management has quit because of a shift from an authoritarian to a participative management style.

So why does this resistance to change occur? Again one word:

Fear

Fear of what? — *The unknown!*

Why is it unknown? — *Lack of education and training!*

Resistance to change should be anticipated and worked with by helping those that fight the change to understand the change and to "buy into" the change. If they feel ownership in the change, the resistance will greatly decrease.

So why don't we get trained and educated in the change process? — *Lack of commitment and appropriate motivation!*

What is the source of the necessary commitment and motivation —*The top!*

OK! If we have the appropriate commitment and motivation from the top, does that imply successful changes? — *No! Because we may not know what we are doing!*

We need tools to help us implement change, like the change models discussed in this chapter. But commitment from the top is a critical beginning. That commitment sets a desire for change throughout the organization. Next we need goals (Chapters 5 and 6) to give the change process direction. Then we need training so that we know what to change, how to change it and when to change it (Chapter 13). Understanding change begins with understanding the change process. Let's take a look at some models of change.

SOME MODELS FOR CHANGE

Remember the change function shown in Figure 4.2 on page 78 and expanded on in Figure 7.1. In Stage A we are operating at a steady state and stable level of operation. Stage B occurs when change is implemented. The level of efficiency drops and a new learning curve kicks in which is signified by Stage C and D. Stage C is the most critical stage because this is the time when many changes are dropped. If Stage C takes too long (point X to point Y) the change may be dropped. This is what has occurred with Florida Power and Light and in many JIT, TQM, or Process Re-engineering implementations. Unfortunately, when a change process is dropped during Stage C, what we see in Figure 7.2 occurs. Most United States companies don't want Stage C to take more than a few months and with larger changes this short time span is impossible. Stage D is where we start to see a return on the change process. The final phase of the learning curve is kicking in. Finally, Stage E is where we have once again achieved stability, hopefully at a higher level of output.

Another model for change shows us as having to work our way through the phases of growth in a change process. The phases are explained below.

Phase I — Recognize the need for change. Invest in new technology or processes. Motivate innovation and experimentation. Encourage learning about new technologies just for the sake of learning.

Phase II — Learn how to adapt technology beyond the initial sought-after results. Keep the ideas flowing.

Phase III — The organization goes through structural changes as process changes occur.

Figure 7.1: Change

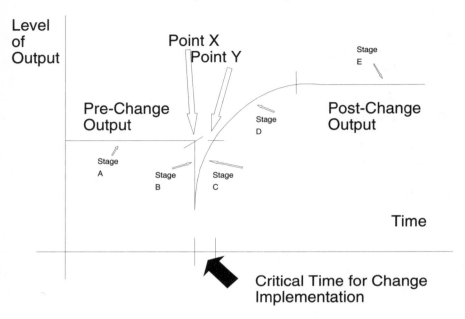

Figure 7.2: Backing out of the Change

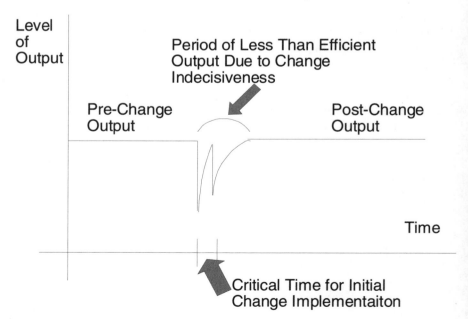

Phase IV — The broad-based implementation of change occurs effecting all aspects of the organization.[2]

The Japanese model for the continuous change process is called Kaizen. It suggests that every process can and should be continually evaluated and continually improved. The primary focus of the improvements is on waste elimination, for example process time reductions, reducing the amount of resources used and improving product quality. Kaizen problem solving involves observing the situation, defining the changes that need to take place and making the changes happen.

One example of the implementation of the Kaizen continuous improvement process is at the Repair Division of the Marine Corps Logistics Base in Barstow, California. Utilizing the Kaizen focus on continuous improvement, it ran a pilot project and received results like:

- 63 per cent reduction in final assembly lead-time
- 50 per cent reduction in work-in-process inventory
- 83 per cent reduction in the distance material traveled
- 70 per cent reduction in shop floor space requirements.[3]

> The process and the system which controls it represent the real problem facing business today, not the people who work within the boundaries set for them by management. . . The improvement efforts and their supporting systems must be directed at the process and not the individual.
>
> H James Harrington[4]

The focus of any change model should be on continuous improvement in the broad sense which includes both the Japanese incremental step perspective and the United States breakthrough business process improvement perspective. The need for change is rarely argued. What is different between the various change models is the speed of the change and the depth at which the change occurs. This is where the Japanese and the United States change methods bump heads.

In comparison, the United States tends to favor:

- fast change

---

2. Gibson, Cyrus F and R L Nolan, "Managing the Four Stages of EDP Growth", *Harvard Business Review* (January-February 1974) p. 76.
3. Szendel, Timothy N and Walter Tighe, "Kaizen American-Style, Continuous Improvement in Action", *APICS 37th International Conference Proceedings* (APICS) October 1994, pp. 496-497.
4. H James Harrington of Ernst & Young, made a presentation titled "Continuous Improvement or Breakthrough Dilema" in Quatemala in November 1994 where these comments were made.

- fast return on investment
- radical and dramatic change
- deep and extensive changes feeling the need to redefine the whole process
- the hunt for the one big change that will fix all the problems
- process re-engineering which is characterized by rapid/radical changes and focuses on change implementation and high-tech solutions.

As well as this, it is slower to get around to making any change because the change process is viewed as being so extensive, dramatic, and upsetting. The result is that there is more resistance to any change process. Change ownership belongs to some change "hero" who quite often is the CEO.

The Japanese, however, tend to favor:

- slow change
- long-term return on investments
- carefully planned out changes
- thinking the change through carefully
- planning before implementing
- small step changes
- total quality management which focuses on analysis and planning in the change process and technology-that-fits-the-situation solutions.

The change process is much less painful, because change involves small, undramatic steps. Therefore, there is much less resistance and, step-wise, small changes are continuously occurring. Change ownership is shared.

> Einstein was asked, if he had sixty minutes left in which to save the world, what would he do? His answer was that he would spend fifty-five minutes planning and five minutes implementing.

Some methodologies have attempted, unsuccessfully, to combine the Japanese and United States approaches by suggesting the implementation of "radical changes without being radical." What they are hoping to do is implement big changes without upsetting the entire organization and developing enormous resistance to the change process. But no one has come up with a good way to accomplish this, probably because no one really understands it. So the conflict between the two change approaches remains. Total quality management (TQM) continues to be viewed as "too slow" by the United States, and process re-engineering (PR) continues to be viewed as "too destructive" by the Japanese.

Let us now consider the most important models for change and discuss the procedures used in implementing these models. The ones we will consider are:

- quality functional deployment
- total quality management
- process re-engineering
- process re-engineering variations
- benchmarking
- ISO 9000
- award processes
- breakthrough thinking
- concept management.

Some of these models only supply us with focus areas of improvement. Others have specific procedures for the change process. The models should not be thought of as exclusive in that if you pick one you can't use any of the others. Rather, they should all be considered as stepping-stones toward your development of your own successful change program.

Quality Functional Deployment (QFD)

QFD is the implementation of continuous improvement process focusing on the customer. It was developed at Mitsubishi's Kobe Shipyards and focuses on directing the efforts of all functional areas on a common goal. In Mitsubishi's case the goal was "satisfying the needs of the customer". Several changes were instituted in order to accomplish this, such as increased horizontal communication within the company. One of the most immediate results was a reduced time-to-market lead-time for products.

QFD systematizes the product's attributes in a matrix diagram called a house of quality and highlights which of these attributes is the most important to a customer. This helps the teams throughout the organization focus on their goal (customer satisfaction) whenever they are making change decisions, such as product development and improvement decisions.

QFD focuses on:

1. the customer

2. systemizing the customer satisfaction process by developing a matrix for:
   (a) defining customer quality
   (b) defining product characteristics
   (c) defining process characteristics
   (d) defining process control characteristics

3. empowered teaming

4. extensive front-end analysis which involves fourteen steps in defining the "house of quality":

(a) create and communicate a project objective
(b) establish the scope of the project
(c) obtain customer requirements
(d) categorize customer requirements
(e) prioritize customer requirements
(f) assess competitive position
(g) develop design requirements
(h) determine relationship between design requirements and customer requirements
(i) assess competitive position in terms of design requirements
(j) calculate importance of design requirements
(k) establish target values for design
(l) determine correlations between design requirements
(m) finalize target values for design
(n) develop the other matrices.

Implementing and using QFD is not an easy process. A great deal of commitment throughout the company is required for the process to be successful. The results of effective implementation are well worth the effort. Reduced product development time, increased flexibility, increased customer satisfaction, and lower start-up costs are just a few of the benefits that can be expected through the use of QFD.

Gregg D Stocker[5]

QFD has been widely recognized as an effective tool for focusing the product and the process on customer satisfaction. A lot has been written on the subject.[6] However, as discussed earlier, QFD is a Japanese approach to focused change and therefore focuses on extensive analysis, utilizing the philosophy that we need to:

Make sure we are doing the right things before we worry about doing things right!

Detailed analysis through the matrices is time consuming, conceptual planning time is much extended by QFD. However, the overall design-

---

5. Stocker, Gregg D, "Quality Functional Deployment: Listening to the Voice of the Customer", *APICS 34th International Conference Proceedings* (APICS) October 1991, pp. 258-262.
6. Another excellent article, like the Stocker article, that focuses on the QFD procedures is written by Dave Henrickson, manager of the Western Region, Motorola Education and Training Center. Additionally, in the Wallace book listed earlier, there are two sections worth looking at: I-3 "Linking Customer to strategies via Quality Functional Deployment (QFD)" by Thomas F. Wallace and II-6 "Quality Functional Deployment: Breakthrough tool for Product Development" by William Barnard. See also Henrickson, Dave, "Product Design as a Team Sport", *Target* (Spring 1990) pp. 4-12.

to-market time should be cut because the design effort focuses on the most important areas.

Dave Henrickson

Total Quality Management (TQM)

Simply put, TQM is a management approach to long-term customer satisfaction. TQM is based on the participation of all members of an organization in improving the processes, products, services and the culture they work in.

Karen Bemkowski[7]

As mentioned earlier, total quality management (TQM) focuses on careful, thoughtful analysis. However, the analysis should be creative, innovative and innoveering oriented. We must be careful when the time comes to implement. We want to make sure that we are implementing positive, goal-focused changes before we move a muscle.

TQM is much broader than QFD. TQM is a change model that is enterprise wide. Some people define TQM in general terms as simply making the "entire organization responsible for product or service quality". This is the way TQM is defined in many organizations and it encompasses everything and anything. However, there is also a specific, proceduralistic version of the definition of TQM. Perhaps the best way to understand TQM is to look at this TQM process. Afterwards we can consider the significance of TQM and its process.

The TQM process

TQM is not just a tool. It has an entire philosophy about how businesses should be run. The philosophy of TQM is filled with ideas and attitudes, such as:

- attitude of desiring and searching out change
- think culture — move from copying to innovating
- do the right things before you do things right
- focus on the goal
- measurement and motivation planning
- top to bottom corporate strategy
- company-wide involvement

---

7. Bemkowski, Karen, "The Quality Glossary", *Quality Progress* (February 1992) pp. 19-29.

- clear definition and implementation of quality
- education, training, and cross training
- integration and coordination
- small, step-by-step improvements.

In TQM, the philosophy behind change is that we become excited about changes. We look for opportunity to change, especially because change should mean that we are becoming better. To be a TQM organization is to become an organization that wants to be the best and realizes that there is always room for improvement.

The success stories for TQM can be found in settings all over the world. TQM successes are measured in terms of the successful implementation of change. This change can take the form of the implementation of new technology, or the correction and improvement of old technology. Often, a successful TQM project results in the ability of employees to work more effectively together. The result is that the measurement of TQM success tends to be an internal success story, and not always externally comparable.

Success in TQM can be found in large organizations like PETRONAS, the national petroleum corporation of Malaysia where, because of its successes, TQM implementation is moving forward on a company-wide basis. TQM, through its systematic implementation of changes, won the Deming Award, a Japanese quality award, for Florida Power and Light, a United States producer of electricity. TQM is receiving nationwide attention in Mexico through a sponsoring organization, Fundameca, the Mexican national productivity and quality improvement organization. Many other Latin American countries are also focusing national attention on TQM implementation, like Guatemala's "II Congreso Nacional Y I Cetroamericano De Calidad Total" meeting. Numerous success stories exist about specific individual companies, like the Solectron story.[8]

In operationalizing TQM there are several points of importance. They are:

- the TQM co-ordinating team (quality council)
- the *three "P" teams* — cross-functional teams
- the TQM project implementation steps
- training programs
- measurement and feedback
- showcasing

---

8. Ramalingam, P Rama, "Making TQM Pay Off: The Solectron Experience", *APICS 37th International Conference Proceedings*, op. cit., pp. 472-476; Bao, Quang and E B Baatz, "How Solectron Finally Got In Touch With Its Workers", *Electronic Business* (7 October 1991); Grant, Linda, "Six Companies That Are Winning The Race", *Los Angeles Times* (17 January 1993); "Solectron Corp.", *Business America* (21 October 1991).

- team building
- systematic problem solving (SPS).

TQM implementations start with a *co-ordinating team*, often referred to as a quality council. This is a team composed of high-level corporate leaders from all the functional areas. This team is appointed by the CEO and operates under his/her direction. The CEO takes an active part in directing the activities of the team. This quality council is then responsible for organizing and measuring the performance of the other TQM teams within the organization. It oversees the installation, training, performance and measurement of the other teams. This team focuses specifically on the corporate goal/vision and definition of quality.

The quality council will organize three different types of teams referred to as the cross-functional three "P" teams. These are *process, product* and *project* teams.

The process teams are ongoing, continuous improvement teams set up at different levels of the organization. They look for improvements in the organization's functioning processes. These teams should be composed of both "insiders" and "outsiders". The insiders know and understand existing functions and operations. The outsiders challenge the status quo.

The second of the three "P" teams are the product teams. These teams are cross-functional but focus on a specific product, product line or service. They are customer and vendor interface teams that are specifically oriented towards the development of new products and the improvement of existing products. Their life span is the same as the life span of the product they represent.

The third of the three "P" teams are the project teams. These teams are limited life teams set up to specifically focus on a specific project, like the construction of a new plant or a computer installation. These teams may be the result of a specific process or product that is being targeted, or they may be set up to research something that the general management team is interested in developing or improving.

The TQM project implementation steps are as follows:

- identify problems (opportunities)
- prioritize these problems
- select the biggest bang-for-the-buck project
- develop an implementation plan
- use operations research and MIS tools where appropriate
- develop guide posts and an appropriate measurement system
- training
- implementation
- feedback — monitoring — control — change
- after successful project implementation and ongoing status, repeat the cycle.

The first function of the team is to identify their function and charter. If you are on one of the three "P" teams, your team's charter is laid out for you by the quality council. If you are the quality council, this charter is laid out for you by the CEO and is aimed at the focused goals of the organization. After understanding their charter, the team will then search for and identify problems that exist and that prevent the organization from achieving this charter. The word "problems" has a negative connotation. A better wording would be to say that we search of "opportunities for improvements". We are not just trying to correct negative effects, we are looking for techniques or tools that will allow us to become better and possibly even best.

Next we take these problems (opportunities) and prioritize them based on their effect on the charter of the team (which should be focused on the goals of the organization). We do a type of ABC analysis (eighty-twenty rule or Parieto Principle) to determine which change would have the greatest effect. Then we select the biggest bang-for-the-buck project and develop an implementation plan for this project. This implementation plan needs to contain guide posts that are based on an appropriate measurement system that points the team towards achieving its charter. The book *Breakthrough Thinking* does an excellent job of discussing opportunity identification techniques.[9]

Training of the implementers and users is critical or else the planned project is doomed to failure. This training makes future users comfortable with the changes. It also offers a bit of ownership since the planned users will now feel comfortable with the changes.

The next step is implementation. The implementation should be a trivial process, if all the planning and training steps are preformed carefully. Part of the implementation is the installation of feedback, monitoring and control mechanisms, as laid out in the implementation plan. Careful monitoring allows for corrective changes to occur whenever necessary.

After successful project implementation, and seeing that the ongoing status of the project is functioning correctly, the team repeats the implementation cycle, looking for more new opportunities for change. If this process is performed correctly, the list of change opportunities should become longer with each iterative cycle. This means that your team is now open for newer and broader opportunities for change.

Training programs need to exist before and after project selection. In the before case, the TQM team needs to understand what tools are available to them. This training would involve an understanding of tools and techniques. Initial training could include programs in areas like operations research/management science tools and techniques, motivational/philosophical training, semi-technical and technical education, the operation of the systems approach,

---

9. Nadler, Gerald and Shozo Hibino, *Breakthrough Thinking* (Rocklin, CA: Prima Publishing and Communications) 1990; Nadler, Gerald, Shozo Hibino and John Farrell, *Creative Solution Finding* (Rocklin, CA: Prima Publishing and Communications) 1995.

and so on. Training programs after TQM team implementation should be user training focused on the changes being implemented. These programs need to be defined (and often conducted) by the TQM team which has the best understanding of the change.

The issue of *measurement and feedback* has already been discussed several times. It is critical to realize the motivational role of the measurement system and that the proper implementation of an effective feedback (reporting) mechanism will assure the ongoing success of the changes implemented.

Showcasing is one of the best techniques for expanding implementation time. What we do here is use the quality council to develop and implement a "sure thing" TQM implementation project. What we are doing is attempting to demonstrate the successes of an organization wide TQM implementation. In the United States, where short-term, quick benefits need to be demonstrated, showcasing becomes a critical part of the selling job of TQM.

There are several types of *teams* required in a TQM environment, like the quality council and the three "P" teams. Understanding which teams need to be organized is just a small part of the problem of team construction. A much bigger problem is making the team effective. For example, team training and team relationship building are necessary for effective interaction and for the synergy of the team (see the Chapter 14 discussion about team building).

One of the biggest downfalls of a TQM system, as far as the United States is concerned, is the implementation lead time of changes (how long it takes to implement the change). Often a decision is made to change and then we start worrying about how to implement the change. *Systematic problem solving* (SPS) is a procedurization of the change process. There is no one perfect model for how this change procedurization should be set up. However, there are a few good examples. Let's take a look at three of them. The first is the one used by Florida Power and Light when they won the Deming Award, the second is the AT&T systematic problem solving (SPS) process and the third is a generalized SPS model called the T-Model.

Systematic Problem Solving (SPS) at Florida Power and Light

In the Florida Power and Light (FP&L) case, the SPS process it used when it won the Deming Award was referred to as its "quality improvement story". This is a series of steps that is standardized and is used to organize and document the change process. The steps are set out below.

1. Team information — here it develops a team project planning worksheet which lists the team members, the meeting schedules and an outline of activities in Gantt chart format. The Gantt chart lists each of the following "quality improvement story" steps and time-lines them.

2. Reasons for improvement — this is a graphic and flow-charted look at why an improvement is desirable. FP&L will analyze which issues are

being addressed, and which are not, in light of some goal that it is trying to achieve. It follows the repeated "why?" questioning process in order to determine the root problems.

3. Current situation — here FP&L will apply Parieto principles to focus on the area that will maximize benefits with the least amount of efforts. It graphs performance history in order to get a better handle on the problem and defines targets and goals for the corrective action that is being planned.

4. Analysis — here the primary tools are fish-bone (cause and effect) diagrams that analyze the possible reasons for the problems being considered. FP&L will develop a *Root Cause Verification Matrix* in order to verify that it is truly working on the root causes of the problems.

5. Countermeasures — here FP&L will develop a countermeasures matrix and an action plan. This is when the change takes place.

6. Results — FP&L will use Parieto diagrams and before and after graphs to validate that the changes are occurring. It will use these to monitor the performance of the implemented changes.

7. Standardization — this section establishes a documented procedure for the ongoing operation of the change using graphical and systems flow-charting tools.

8. Future plans — this is a review of what was learned by this change process. It follows a philosophy of plan-do-check-act. *Plan* is what do you plan to do with regards to this change in the future. For example, are you going to look for even more improvements. *Do* is what will be done next. *Check* is a look at what the feedback mechanism will entail. What do you want to watch for? *Act* is what is the next action to be taken by the team. For example, are we now going to look at the next highest Parieto contributor toward improvements?

Systematic problem solving (SPS) at AT&T

AT&T uses a methodology that includes tasks which are to be performed in four distinct stages. These are:

- ownership — team responsibility for the activities
- assessment — clear definition of the process
- opportunity selection — analyze how process problems effect customer satisfaction and rank them in order of opportunity for improvement
- improvement — implementing and sustaining the change.

The ownership, assessment and opportunity selection stages are considered management processes. Then, based on the overall four stages, grouped under management and improvement, AT&T developed a series of steps called the management and improvement steps which focus on the SPS process. They are:

(a) establish process management responsibilities

(b) define process and identify customer requirements

(c) define and establish measures

(d) assess conformance to customer requirements

(e) investigate process to identify improvement opportunities

(f) rank improvement opportunities and set objectives

(g) improve process quality.

Note that the AT&T process follows the Japanese model closely. More detailed information is available about this process through publications put out by AT&T.[10]

Quality excellence is the foundation for the management of our business and the keystone of our goal of customer satisfaction. It is therefore our policy to:

> Consistently provide products and services that meet the quality expectations of our customers.
>
> Actively pursue ever-improving quality through programs that enable each employee to do his or her job right the first time.

Robert E Allen,
Chairman and CEO, AT&T

The T-Model

The third systematic problem-solving example that we are going to discuss is called the T-Model. This model is a systemized model for change which has a philosophical as well as a procedural aspect and which follows systems analysis principles. Philosophically, this model looks for rapid, continuous

---

10. AT&T Bell Laboratories, *AT&T's Total Quality Approach* (Publication Center of AT&T Bell Laboratories) 1992; AT&T Bell Laboratories, *AT&T Process Quality Management & Improvement Guidelines* (Publication Center of AT&T Bell Laboratories) 1989. These publications and additional information are available from:
      AT&T's Customer Information Center
      Order Entry Department
      P. O. Box 19901
      Indianapolis, Indiana 46219
      1-800-432-6600

improvement, change implementation. Procedurally, the T-Model follows a series of basic rules or steps. The basic rules of the T-Model are:

(a) define the area of change

(b) define the purpose of the change — don't ask why the change should be made and don't do an analysis of the change and its requirements — the purpose of the change needs to be defined first

(c) evaluate the purpose — does it eliminate waste and improve the value added component of the product?

(d) define the constraints — such as environmental, customer, cultural

(e) evaluate the techniques available for solving the problem

(f) implement the change

(g) monitoring, feedback and data collection

(h) corrective action — here we are reacting to the feedback. If the feedback is not what we want, then we return to step (b) above and rethink our corrective action.

The T-Model is more general than the Florida Power and Light example because it is not applied to a specific situation. There are no specific tools assigned to each of the steps. However, as the T-Model is applied to a specific example, such as in the Florida Power and Light situation, it would become more focused, detailing specific tools and procedures that should be used.[11]

The Good News About TQM

TQM was the first stage of realizing that we need to take "quality" (or the search for positive change) out of the quality department and make it a company-wide program. TQM is a strategy towards continuous, corporate-wide change, it is a philosophy, an operationalized process and a fad. It becomes a fad if we expect quick results and become disenchanted because we are not "like the Japanese" in the first two months. TQM is a strategy towards becoming leading edge and world-class.

TQM differs from the other quality tools like TQC, SPC, or ILQC (see Chapter 12) in that it is not as directly focused as these other systems on a specific procedure. Rather, TQM is a continuous search for problems (opportunities) that eliminate waste and add value in all aspects of the organization, and makes these improvements one small step (5 to 10 per cent improvements) at a time.

---

11. Plenert, Gerhard and Shozo Hibino, "The T-Model: A Systematic Model for Change", *National Productivity Review* (Autumn 1994) Vol. 13, No. 4, pp. 543-549.

In spite of its slowness, TQM has been extremely successful internationally and is getting ever increasing attention. References to TQM and its leadership abound.[12] TQM is a very specific process improvement step in a drive towards world-class status.

Process Re-engineering

Wisely, and slowly. They stumble that run fast.

William Shakespeare,
Romeo and Juliet

Process re-engineering (PR) is rapid, radical change. It is not downsizing, which many companies are using it for, rather it is work elimination. It is positive, growth-focused change, looking for opportunities to eliminate waste and improve value added productivity, often through the implementation of technology such as image processing (see Chapter 12).

In 1994, $32 billion was invested in re-engineering of which two-thirds of the re-engineering projects will fail. Why? Because the change process builds up a lot of resistance thereby forcing its failure. Secondarily, because PR is used as an excuse for downsizing, often the downsizing results in the elimination of critical employees that will be difficult to replace. The downsizing process is not carefully thought through, it has been rushed through and the results are disastrous.[13]

However, just like any tool, there are some extremely positive aspects to process re-engineering that make it worthy of our attention. The first is that PR focuses on change implementation at the top of the corporate hierarchy. It generates more of a top-down change culture. And it focuses on process oriented changes.

PR's focus on the process emphasizes that the process, not the products, holds the secrets for the most dramatic improvements within an organization. PR focuses on an "all-or-nothing proposition that produces impressive results".

---

12. The organizations that I have referenced in previous appendices are filled with publications and conference information that will help you implement a TQM environment. Some additional readings include: Costin, Harry, *Readings in Total Quality Management* (Fort Worth, Texas: The Dryden Press) 1994; Ross, Joel E, *Total Quality Management: Text, Cases and Readings* (Delray Beach, Florida: St. Lucie Press) 1993; Omachonu, Vincent K, *Principles of Total Quality* (Delray Beach, Florida: St. Lucie Press) 1994. Articles of interest on TQM include a couple from the Wallace book listed earlier: IV-1 "Total Quality Management (TQM)" by Joseph Colletti and IV-2 "Tools for Total Quality Management (TQM)" by Bill Montgomery.

13. Plenert, Gerhard, "Process Re-Engineering: The Latest Fad Toward Failure", *APICS — The Performance Advantage* (June 1994), pp. 22-24.

PR is defined as:

> The fundamental rethinking and radical redesign of business processes to achieve dramatic improvements in critical, contemporary measures of performance, such as cost, quality, service, and speed.
>
> Hammer and Champy[14]

The principles of re-engineering include:
* organize around outcomes, not tasks
* have those who use the output of the process perform the process
* subsume information processing work into the real work that produces information
* treat geographically dispersed resources as though they were centralized
* link parallel activities instead of integrating their results
* put the decision point where the work is performed and build control into the process
* capture information once and at the source.

There are three R's of re-engineering:

Rethink — is what you're doing focused on the customer?

Redesign — what are you doing? Should you be doing it at all? Redesign how it can be done.

Re-tool — re-evaluate the use of advanced technologies.

Some characteristics of process re-engineering include:
* several jobs are combined into one
* workers make the decisions — empowerment
* "natural order" sequencing of job steps
* processes with multiple versions depending on the need
* work is performed where it makes the most sense
* checks and controls are reduced
* reconciliation is minimized
* "empowered" customer service representation
* hybrid centralized/decentralized organizations.

---

14. Hammer, M, and J Champy, *Re-engineering the Corporation* (New York: Harper Business) 1993.

Like TQM, the focus of the re-engineering effort is the team. Departments are replaced by empowered process teams. Executives change their role from scorekeeper to leaders. Organizational structures become flatter. Managers change from supervisors to coaches.

PR has the following steps or phases in the change management process:

1. mobilization — develop a vision, communicate the vision, identify champions and process owners, assemble the teams

2. diagnosis — train and educate, current process analysis, select and scope the process, understand the current customer, model the process, identify problems, set targets for new designs

3. redesign — create breakthrough design concepts, redesign the entire system, build prototype, information technology

4. transition — finalize transition design, implementation phase, measure benefits, the role of communication to avoid resistance, you cannot overcommunicate.

PR has many of the procedural characteristics of TQM but is more philosophical. PR focuses on being competitive via the rapid and the radical and it stresses the process as the key to successful change. There are numerous books available that discuss the philosophy of PR. The best is still the original, by the gurus of process re-engineering, Hammer and Champy. SME/CASA has put out an excellent booklet focusing on manufacturing processes that can be re-engineered. *OR/MS Today* also has an excellent article that discusses first and second generation re-engineering programs.[15]

---

15. Hammer, M, and J Champy, "The Promise of Re-engineering", *Fortune* (May 3 1993) pp. 94-97; Hammer, M, "Re-engineering Work: Don't Automate, Obliterate," *Harvard Business Review* (July-August 1990) pp. 104-112; Jason, R, "How Re-engineering Transforms Organizations to Satisfy Customers", *National Productivity Review* (Winter 1992) pp. 45-53; Marks, Peter, *Process Re-engineering and the New Manufacturing Enterprise Wheel: 15 Processes for Competitive Advantage*, CASA/SME Technical Forum (Dearborn, Michigan: Society of Manufacturing Engineers) 1994; Harbour, Jerry L, *The Process Reengineering Workbook: Practical Steps to Working Faster and Smarter Through Process Improvement* (White Plains, New York: Quality Resources) 1994; Cypress, Harold L, "Re-engineering", *OR/MS Today* (February 1994) pp. 18-29; Ravikumar, Ravi, "Business Process Reengineering — Making the Transition", *APICS 37th Annual International Conference Proceedings*, op. cit., pp. 17-21; Miller, George, "Re-engineering: 40 Useful Hints", *APICS 37th Annual International Conference Proceedings*, op. cit., pp. 22-26; Melnyk, Steven A and William R Wassweiler, "Business Process Re-engineering: Understanding the Process, Responding to the Right Needs", *APICS 37th Annual International Conference Proceedings*, op. cit., pp.115-120; Boyer, John E, "Re-engineering Office Processes", *APICS 37th Annual International Conference Proceedings*, op. cit., pp. 522-526; Stevens, Mark, "Re-engineering the Manufacturing Company: 'New Fad or For Real'", *APICS 37th Annual International Conference Proceedings*, op. cit., pp. 527-530.

Process Re-engineering Variations

Numerous variations have sprung up in an attempt to correct some of the problems of re-engineering. I will list several of these and offer some brief information about each of them. I will include references for additional information. The benefits of each of these variations has still to be proven.

John Lipscomb has developed a program that focuses on re-engineering improvements utilizing quality systems deployment (QSD). QSD is a variation of QFD focusing on customer directed systems development. The contradiction is that re-engineering is "rapid and radical" and QSD is systematic and carefully defined. However, this blending attempts to end up with a change process that falls somewhere in between the two and attempts to utilize the benefits of each.[16]

Lowenthal stresses that the re-engineering of the organization should focus on the core competencies and that it is the organization itself, and not just the processes within the organization, that need re-engineering. The enterprise needs to take advantage of its core competencies when it focuses its organization-wide business process improvements. Organizational re-engineering is defined as:

> The rudimentary rethinking and redesign of operating processes and organizational structure, focused on the organization's core competencies, to achieve dramatic improvements such as reduced cost, increased product and service quality, and increased market share and profitability.
>
> Jeffrey N Lowenthal[17]

Aetna is re-engineering vital business functions across all its business units. The focus of these efforts is on the customer. It is replacing the traditional systems with new, re-focused processes. Chairperson and CEO Ronald E Compton of Aetna stresses that there are several commandments inherent to any re-engineering effort, as outlined below.

1. You have to give people a mission, a clear understanding of how to achieve that mission, and a road map for choosing the appropriate steps for action.

2. Either service the customer superbly, or don't even try.

3. Change is not something that happens. It's a way of life. It's not a process, it's a value. It's not something you do, it engulfs you.

---

16. John R Lipscomb, President of Lipscome and Associates of White Lake, Michigan has made presentations with the title "Re-engineering Continuous Improvement Through Quality Systems Deployment."
17. Lowenthal, Jeffrey N, *Reengineering the Organization: A Step-by-Step Approach to Corporate Revitalization* (Milwaukee, Wisconsin: ASQC Quality Press) 1994.

4. Technology is never really a problem. The problem is how to use it effectively.

5. The wrong answer rarely kills you. What it does is waste time. Further, time is a limited resource — the only absolutely limited one.

6. The weak link in re-engineering is will. Re-engineering is a huge job and it is agonizingly, heartbreakingly tough.

7. Once people catch on to re-engineering, you can't hold them down. It's a lifetime venture.

Compton states that Aetna is expecting to save over $120 million annually from streamlining its processes.[18]

ISO 9000

ISO 9000 is a model that is often advertised as a model for change and improvements. However, the ISO 9000 process tends to focus on stability. The ISO standard was developed by Europe in an attempt to standardize the quality of goods coming into Europe. For many companies it seemed like a trade barrier. The reason why is because ISO 9000 focuses on quality in the internal process of the organization, assuring that what was designed is what is actually built. It does not focus on the customer. Nevertheless, the ISO standard has become an international standard for quality and systems performance that many companies are utilizing.

ISO has come to define quality, not change. It is a set of standards for quality based on two main foundations:

- management responsibility and commitment to quality which should be expressed in a formal policy statement and implemented through appropriate measures
- a set of requirements that deal with each aspect of the company activity and organization that affects quality.[19]

ISO can be used as a standard for improvement and the ISO quality system requirements can become the focus of change systems. In this way, ISO criteria can be integrated into a change process. However, in and of itself, ISO is not a change model as is frequently believed.

---

18. Rijkin, Glenn, "Reengineering Aetna", *Forbes ASAP*. A Technology Supplement to *Forbes Magazine*, Sidebar (7 June 1993): 81.
19. The Wallace book mentioned earlier has an article by Robert L Jones and Joseph R Tunner titled "ISO 9000: The International Standard for Quality." ISO information can be obtained from any of the quality and productivity organizations mentioned in earlier chapters. The ISO organization, International Organization for Standardization, is located in Geneva, Switzerland.

Award Processes

The award programs, like the Baldridge, Deming and Shingo Prizes (contact information listed earlier) all have an excellent base of standards from which to build change models. Like the ISO criteria, these award program criteria are an excellent basis for developing a focus for your change program. For example, the Shingo Prize organization focuses on continuous improvement processes through total quality systems and the Deming award focuses on demonstrated improvements resulting from a continuous improvement process. The Baldridge has the following list of improvement criteria for award evaluation:

- leadership — senior management's success in creating and sustaining a quality culture
- information and analysis — the effectiveness of the company's collection and analysis of information for quality improvement and planning
- strategic quality planning — the effectiveness of the integration of quality requirements into the company's business plans
- human resource utilization — the success of the company's efforts to utilize the full potential of the work force for quality
- quality assurance of products and services — the effectiveness of the company's systems for assuring quality control of all operations
- quality results — the company's results in quality achievement and quality improvement, demonstrated through quantitative measures
- customer satisfaction — the effectiveness of the company's systems to determine customer requirements and demonstrated success in meeting them.

Within these seven categories there are 33 examination items and 133 sub items. As with the ISO process, the award process is not a change process, but it greatly assists an organization in establishing the criteria that should be incorporated into an effective change model. Going through the award process motivates the development of effective change procedures.[20]

Breakthrough Thinking

To solve difficult problems and find creative solutions, our present thinking paradigm and process must change. Gerald Nadler and Shozo Hibino published *Breakthrough Thinking* in 1990 and *Creative Solution Finding* in 1993. In these two books, they defined a Japanese developed paradigm shift in thinking. They called this new thinking paradigm "breakthrough thinking" (BT). From a historical viewpoint, our thinking paradigms have been continuously

---

20. The Wallace book also has an article titled "The Malcolm Baldridge National Quality Award Program" by Stephen George.

shifting over time. Our conventional thinking paradigm (Descartes thinking), is out of date with a rapidly changing world and needs to shift again to a new thinking paradigm. In the 21st century, we have to be multi-thinkers who are able to use three thinking paradigms — *God thinking, conventional (Descartes) thinking* and *breakthrough thinking* (BT).

God thinking focuses on making decisions based on God's will. For some decisions, there is no need for analysis. Behavior is firmly dictated by God's will, our values systems and our life philosophies. For example, morality or ethical issues are decided and are not open for discussion. Conventional thinking starts with an analysis process that focuses on fact or truth finding. When we make a decision, our behavior is based on the facts or on scientific truth. We need the facts in order to make our decisions. Breakthrough thinking starts with the ideal or ultimate objective. When we make a decision, we base our behavior on this objective.

The three thinking paradigms are completely different and each has a different approach. We have to select and utilize each of these paradigms on a case by case basis. Someone who uses and interchanges these thinking paradigms is referred to as a "multi-thinker".

Since there is no future which continues along the same lines as our past and present (because of the drastic changes going on in the world), we cannot find futuristic solutions based on past and present facts. Our thinking base should be changed away from facts and refocus on the substance, essence or ideal.

To identify the substance of things is not easy. We have to transform ourselves from having a conventional machine view to a systems oriented view. The traditional perspective of conventional thinking is to view things as a reductionistic machine, breaking everything down into elemental parts and neglecting the "whole" organic view.

The epistemology of breakthrough thinking is that "everything is a system" which focuses BT on a "holonic view". If we define everything as a system, then everything is a "Chinese box", which means that a bigger box (system) includes a series of smaller boxes (systems). A small box (system) contains still smaller boxes (systems) and so on. Each box (system) has its purpose(s). If you repeatedly ask, "What is the purpose?" and then "What is the purpose of that purpose?" and then "What is the purpose of that purpose of that purpose?" and so on, you can reach the biggest box which is "wholeness". You can view everything from the perspective of this wholeness. BT calls this search the "purpose expansion".

Breakthrough thinking consists of a thinking paradigm and thinking process. The thinking paradigm of breakthrough thinking is the opposite of the paradigm of the conventional thinking. Its main points are expressed as seven principles:

1. *Uniqueness Principle* — always assume that the problem, opportunity or issue is different. Don't copy a solution or use a technique from elsewhere

just because the situation may appear to be similar. In using this principle, we have to think about the locus or solution space of the problem. This locus is defined using three points:

(a) Who are the major stakeholders? Whose viewpoint is most important?
(b) What is the location?
(c) When (what is the timing)?

2. *Purposes Principle* — explore and expand purposes in order to understand what really needs to be accomplished and identify the substance of things. You can tackle any problem, opportunity or issue by expanding purposes, if you change your epistemology to a systems view. Understanding the context of purposes provides the following strategic advantages:

(a) Pursue the substance of things — we can identify the most essential focus purpose or the greater purpose, often referred to as the substance (core element) of things by expanding purposes.
(b) Work on the right problem or purpose — focusing on right purposes helps strip away nonessential aspects to avoid working on just the visible problem or symptom.
(c) Improve the ability to re-define — re-defining is usually very difficult. Once you've re-defined, you can have different viewpoints, each of which enables you to solve problems from different directions
(d) Eliminate purpose/function(s) — from systems theory we learn that a bigger purpose may eliminate a smaller purpose. By focusing on the bigger purpose, you can eliminate unnecessary work/systems/parts, which means that you can get more effective solutions.
(e) More options, more creative — if you have a purpose hierarchy, you have a lot of alternative solutions.
(f) Holonic view — take a "big picture" perspective.

3. *Solution-After-Next (SAN) Principle* — think and design futuristic solutions for the focus purpose and then work backwards. Consider the solution you would recommend if in three years you had to start all over. Make changes today based on what might be the solution of the future. Learn from the futuristic ideal solution for the focus purpose and don't try learning from the past and present situation.

4. *Systems Principle* — everything we seek to create and restructure is a system. Think of solutions and ideas as a system. When you see everything as a system, you have to consider the eight elements of a system in order to identify the solution.

(a) purpose — mission, aim, need
(b) input — people, things, information

(c) output — people, things, information
(d) operating steps — process and conversion tasks
(e) environment — physical and organizational
(f) human enablers — people, responsibilities, skills, to help in the operating steps
(g) physical enablers — equipment, facilities, materials to use in the operating steps
(h) information enablers — knowledge, instructions.

5. *Information Collection Principle* — collect only the information that is necessary to continue the solution finding process. Know your purposes for collecting data and/or information. Study the solutions, not the problems.

6. *People Design Principle* — give everyone who will be affected by the solution or idea the opportunity to participate throughout the process of its development. A solution will work only if people know about it and help to develop and improve it.

7. *Betterment Timeline Principle* — install changes with built-in seeds of future change. Know when to fix it before it breaks. Know when to change it.

The breakthrough thinking process is an approach of reasoning toward a situation specific solution and a design approach. It is an iterative, simultaneous process of mental responses based on the purpose-target-results approach (PTR approach). PTR's three phases are:

1. purpose — identifying the right solution by finding focus purposes, values, measures

2. target — targeting the solution of tomorrow; ideal SAN vision and target solution

3. result — getting and maintaining results towards implementation and systematization.

Concept Management

Concept management (CM) is a Japanese movement which integrates breakthrough thinking (BT), world-class management (WCM) and total quality management (TQM). BT is the technique utilized to develop ideas. It moves away from the slowness and costliness of traditional root cause analysis commonly used in the United States and Europe. WCM offers the formal structure around which the ideas are turned into goals and a measurement/motivation system. TQM is the process for team based idea/change implementation.

CM is an idea generation and implementation process used by companies like Toyota and Sony that breaks away from the traditional, analytical thinking common to companies such as the Ford Motor Company (which uses the TOPS program) or the Russian TRIZ program. Instead, it focuses on forming a purpose hierarchy through a series of steps.

Concept management uses the term *concept* to mean innovative purpose-driven change creation and management to mean leadership. Therefore, concept management is "innovative, change-oriented, purpose-driven (goal focused), creative leadership". This leadership occurs through the integration of ideas, primarily the ideas expressed in two leading edge philosophies — breakthrough thinking (just discussed) and world-class management.

The three thinking paradigms are completely different and each has a different approach. We cannot neglect any of these three thinking paradigms because each has an influence in the decision-making process. We have to select and utilize each of these paradigms on a case by case basis. Someone who uses and interchanges these thinking paradigms is referred to as a "multi-thinker".

World-class management is broad in its application and numerous publications discuss the subject in detail (see my book *World Class Manager* or *Making Innovation Happen; Concept Management Through Integration*). However, in order to get a clear understanding of how world-class eManagers manage change, the focus would be on:

1. people — employees and stakeholders are the source of change opportunities and they need to be motivated properly through an appropriate measurement system in order to drive change

2. customers — customers are the reason for change and in order to be competitive we need to give our customers a clear reason why they should not buy from anyone else but us

3. performance — performance requires focus on a goal, whether it is financial or quality or some other focus and we need to measure, monitor and offer feedback information about our performance

4. competitors — competition creates fear, but it also creates opportunity; competitors need to be analyzed and understood in order to be defeated

5. future — the future is coming whether we're ready for it or not, and if we're not ready for it, it will pass us by, along with our customers and competitors

6. integration — through integration everyone and everything work together — managers are not merely bosses, they are leaders and facilitators by example and work side by side with the employee.

World-class management is not a system or a procedure, it is a culture. It is a continually molding process of change and improvement. It is a competitive strategy for success.

In the United States, TQM has fallen into disfavor because of its analytical approach to change. The analysis process is deemed too slow to be competitive. But that is primarily because TQM utilized root cause analysis. With breakthrough thinking we can revisit our use of TQM.

There are two major aspects to TQM: philosophical and operational. From the philosophical we get guidelines and from the operational we get techniques. Traditionally, the philosophy of TQM could be stated as "make sure you're doing the right things before your worry about doing things right". Total quality management (TQM) focuses on careful, thoughtful analysis. However, the analysis should be creative, innovative and innoveering oriented. It wants to make sure that we are implementing positive, goal-focused changes before we move a muscle.

TQM is an enterprise-wide change model. Some people define TQM as making the "entire organization responsible for product or service quality". To some TQM is a behavior-based philosophy of motivation and measurement. TQM does, in fact, require a cultural shift for all members of an organization in that it uses an entire philosophy about how businesses should be run. TQM is filled with ideas and attitudes:

- attitude of desiring and searching out change
- think culture — move from copying to innovating
- focus on the goal
- measurement and motivation planning
- top to bottom corporate strategy
- company wide involvement
- clear definition and implementation of quality
- education, training and cross-training
- integration and co-ordination
- small, step-by-step improvements.

TQM implementation starts with a coordinating team, often referred to as a quality council. This is a team composed of high-level corporate leaders from all the functional areas, usually at the vice-president level. This team is appointed by the CEO and operates under his/her direction. The CEO actively directs the endeavors of the team and is often an active team member. This quality council is then responsible for organizing, chartering and measuring the performance of the other TQM teams within the organization. It oversees the installation, training, performance and measurement of the other teams. This team aims to keep all teams focused on the corporate goal and vision.

Concept management works in a series of stages.

Concept creation — the development and creation of new ideas through the use of breakthrough thinking's innovative methods of creativity.

Concept focus — the development of a target which includes keeping your organization focused on core values and a core competency. Then, utilizing the creativity generated by concept creation a set of targets are established using world-class management and a road map is developed helping us to achieve the targets.

Concept engineering — this is the engineering of the ideas, converting the fuzzy concepts into usable, consumer oriented ideas. TQM through the use of a focused, chartered team and through a managed SPS process helps us to manage the concept from idea to product.

Concept in — this is the process of creating a market for the new concept. We transform the concept into a product, service or system, using world-class management techniques. We may utilize breakthrough thinking to help us develop a meaningful and effective market strategy.

Concept management — both the management of the new concepts as well as a change in the management approach (management style) is effected by the new concept. Concept management is the integration of the first four stages of the concept management process (*creation, focus, engineering* and *in*).

WHICH MODEL IS BEST?

I'm always doing what I can't do yet in order to learn how to do it!

Vincent Van Gogh

There is no "best" change model. The best for you is the one you build yourself, fitting your organization and utilizing your goals and focus. However, some of the model alternatives are better than others. A world-class change model should focus on effective, customer and employee oriented change management that offers competitive innoveering strategies. World-class change management is total quality management or a modification of the process re-engineering model which includes an additional focus on the analysis process. TQM offers the most structure and tends to be the least resisted.

Concept management integrates the best of TQM and breakthrough thinking into a structure change process that has demonstrated impressive successes. Therefore, I would tend to prefer it over the other alternatives. However, I need to stress again, that the best change model for you is the one you customize for yourself. Some literature that has tried to solve this "best change model" problem has been included.[21]

---

21. Allen, Dan J, "Work Re-engineering and Total Quality Management: Synergy or Conflict", *APICS 37th International Conference Proceedings*, op. cit., pp. 506-507; Abair, Robert A, "'Dare to Change': Revolution vs. Evolution", *APICS 37th International Conference Proceedings*, op. cit., pp. 40-41.

Once we understand that "what worked in American Industry for two hundred years won't work any more," we can begin to "Think Weird" and to challenge paradigms.

Robert A Abair

CHANGE MODEL IMPLEMENTATION

Things do not change; we change.

Henry David Thoreau

A short but hard working blacksmith had been watching the new lady school teacher in town very closely. Neither he nor the lady were married and he felt that if he didn't get married soon he would be past his prime. One day this school teacher came by his shop and asked him to do some repairs. He eagerly did the work and when he was asked how much it cost he told her he would do it for free if she would go out on a date with him. She eagerly agreed since she also found herself mildly attracted to him.

Near the end of their date they were strolling through a grove of trees and the blacksmith asked her if he could give her a kiss on the cheek. She eagerly agreed but told him "just one!"

The blacksmith had been hoping for just such an opportunity and so he had brought an anvil with. He set the anvil down on the ground next to her, stepped up on it, and gave her a kiss. Then he said, "Since the kissing is over (after all — she said just one) I guess I won't be needing this anvil any more."

Implementing change cannot end with one kiss, even if the boss said, "just one." Change is a continuous, ongoing, never-ending challenge that we need to eagerly take control of. This chapter has given us an anvil, and, although it may be heavy, we can't discard it. However, we should always look for ways to make it lighter (altering the change process can also be positive).

The keys to change model implementation, as we have stressed throughout the book, are:

- focus on a goal and develop a vision, mission, strategy and operating plan for change built around this goal and the enterprise's core competencies
- get the commitment for change from the top — this commitment includes a commitment to training and education and also involves a commitment to empowerment, thereby placing the employees in charge of their own changes
- select a change model and customize the model for your organization
- develop change building blocks, implementing change without discarding old ideas, rather, building on them
- open your mind to breakthrough thinking (review the Nadler and Hibino books listed earlier)

- utilize measurement to motivate change
- develop a feedback mechanism to track and improve upon change performance
- develop internal and external change contingencies (not all changes work out as planned) — internal change contingencies are contingencies against internally planned changes and external contingencies involve external (outside of your influence) changes.

None of these steps can be left out. Change implementation is important, but it has to be done right! Why? Because it directly effects your future!

The first step to change is found in changing ourselves.

SUMMARY

All that is essential for the triumph of evil is for good men to do nothing.

Edmund Burke

World-class change is managed, focused change. A world-class eManager is one who takes advantage of change rather than letting change take advantage of him or her. To do nothing is to fail. However, to change is not necessarily to succeed. Change needs the characteristics discussed in this book. But remember:

With no change you get nowhere!

My picture of a world-class change oriented eManager is one who utilizes concept management and quality functional deployment processes to define what changes are needed, to carefully plan out the change implementation, to work around and with resistance, to develop commitment and to make a difference. A world-class change eManager is a manager who makes world-class changes.

Chapter Eight

The Integrated Enterprise

If a guest at the Boston Ritz-Carlton requests six hypoallergenic pillows, the hotel's knowledge-based system will make sure she will have them waiting for her at any Ritz in the world.

Davis and Botkin[1]

This chapter is about the functions of the enterprise. No, I'm not talking about the Starship Enterprise, but I do plan to "beam you up" so that you can get the big picture of these functions and how they integrate together. What we need, as world-class eManagers, is a "beam me up" attitude about all aspects of the company. We want to look at the big picture so we can see how all the pieces fit together.

This chapter does not discuss each of the aspects of the enterprise in detail. Rather, this chapter shows the interaction and integration of these aspects so the reader understands the importance of the enterprise functions.

ENTERPRISE FOCUS

To live is to change, and to be perfect is to change often.

John Henry Newman

When Dr Robert Oppenheimer, supervisor of the creation of the first atomic bomb, was asked by a congressional committee if there was any defense against the weapon, he quickly responded "Certainly".

"And that is . . .?" inquired the committee.

Dr Oppenheimer looked over the hushed, expectant audience and subtly whispered, "Peace."

How often do we prepare ourselves for corporate warfare and how seldom do we look for peace? Is the purpose of the enterprise to fight a war, or is it to win the prize? Winning, for a competitive, world-class eManager, takes co-operation and teamwork, not bloodshed.

---

1. Davis, Stan and Jim Botkin, "The Coming of Knowledge-Based Business", *Harvard Business Review* (September-October 1994) pp. 165-170.

The enterprise should focus on the key competitive strategy areas:

- the customer — external (spouse and family), internal (fellow employees), immediate (the manufacturer you ship to) and final (the end user of your product)
- change
- value-adding and waste elimination
- trust — eliminate the intimidating non-trust systems.

Enterprise focus needs a target to shoot at. The focus of the world-class enterprise should include:

- a definition of the core competencies
- a vision
- a mission
- a corporate and divisional strategy
- an operating plan
- a definition of the critical success factors
- a measurement/motivation system
- an empowered, team-based work force
- productivity and quality improvements
- a global perspective
- a technology policy
- a training program.

Deciding the enterprise focus needs to be a joint effort. This focus should incorporate all the characteristics discussed in this book. In an article on enterprise failures, the following five factors were given as playing a major role in the decline defined as a slowdown in competitive momentum:

1. *entrapment and self-deception* — a resistance to change, a comfortableness with the status quo, a self-justification that everything is going along as it should even when outsiders disagree

2. *hierarchical orientation* — the business bureaucracy dominates over the basic competitive business drive

3. *cultural rigidity* — tight administrative control which inhibits rapid, timely change

4. *a desire for acceptance through conformity* — a "don't rock the boat" attitude throughout the organization

5. *too much consensus and compromise* — no one is willing to take the bull

by the horns, no one wants to take a risk at making a decision because the mistake will then come back to haunt them.[2]

The world-class eManager is one with a focus on focusing the enterprise. And the world-class eManager's integrity and trustworthiness is seen as a critical element in his or her effectiveness as a manager. Without a focused manager, it's impossible to build a successfully focused enterprise.[3] But now that we have focus, let's look at the functions of the enterprise.

> The preservation of the means of knowledge among the lowest ranks is of more importance to the public than all the property of all the rich men in the country.
>
> John Adams

THE FUNCTIONS OF THE ENTERPRISE

It is impossible, in one short chapter, to discuss all the functions of an enterprise. However, I will highlight a few of the basic ones here so that I can demonstrate the need for functional enterprise integration. The functions of the enterprise include the business processes, the identification of appropriate business interactions, the understanding of all the perspectives of the different enterprise organizations and the recognition of the integration mechanisms and how the integration should work.

A world-class eManager understands the abilities of individuals across all functional areas. He or she may not be able to do the job, but the manager will be familiar with how each of the functions fit into the big picture (the "beam me up" attitude we discussed earlier). Enterprise functional understanding encompasses many areas, discussed below.[4]

The business processes — these include:

- customer interaction (sales and marketing functions and customer support services)

- technology development (product design and development and process and industrial design and development)

---

2. Lorange, Peter and Robert T Nelson, "How to Recognize — and Avoid — Organizational Decline", *Sloan Management Review* (Spring 1987) pp. 41-48.
3. Weiner, Edith, "Business in the 21st Century", *The Futurist* (March-April 1992) pp. 13-17.
4. The American Production and Inventory Control Society (APICS) has developed an integrated enterprise manager certification program (Certification in Resource Management) which includes similar components — see Appendix 12.2).

- production processes (facilities planning and production)

- logistics (purchasing and the receiving function, shipping and product distribution and internal product movement and inventory)

- support/information functions (quality management, human resources management, finance and accounting and maintenance).

The identification of appropriate business interactions — who interact with whom, and how (see Figure 8.1).

The understanding of all the perspectives of the different enterprise organizations — this involves continuous training and education.

The recognition of the integration mechanisms and how the integration should work.

A detailed understanding of any of these topics can be quite extensive, especially if we consider all the potential areas for change. For example, in human resources management (HRM), certain procedures need to be understood such as:

- career development

- environmental changes — for example, regulations and OSHA

- recruitment and termination

- training and education

- performance measures

- technologies.

Additionally, certain concepts need to be understood — management by objective (MBO), individually and by team; empowerment; matrix management; and teaming.

> The CEO as a strategic guru is a thing of the past. CEOs must now focus on finding and motivating talent.
>
> Bartlett and Ghoshal[5]

In a recent presentation, Boyst outlined the key HRM strategies for enterprise success. They are:

- continuous improvement

- the new workplace environment

- rethink performance evaluations

- team building

---

5. Bartlett, Christopher A and Sumantra Ghoshal, "Matrix Management: Not a Structure, A Frame of Mind", *Harvard Business Review* (July-August 1990) pp. 138-145.

- planned job changes
- life long learning
- cross-training
- compensation planning.

> The future consists of a perpetually changing environment and workplace. A company must maintain its competitive skills and so must the employee . . . it is people that make things happen . . . HRM will be one of the keys to the 1990's integrated management revolution.
>
> William M Boyst Jr, III[6]

Later in this chapter, we will consider manufacturing as a more detailed example of enterprise functions, improvements and integration.

> The human resources of an organization represent its most important, sustainable, competitive advantage. It is vital then, that our systems for managing our people help us maintain their commitment, their trust, enhance their development, and direct their effort toward outcomes of strategic importance to the organization.
>
> Thomas C Tuttle,
> Maryland Center for Quality and Productivity[7]

ENTERPRISE INTEGRATION

Figure 8.1 shows an idealistic example of the business interactions. In it we see the customer as the center of all interactions, feeding the development of technology (product technology) and the sales and marketing functions. In response, the customer receives the product delivered from the logistics system. Technology develops products and processes required to produce the products and deliver this information to production. Sales delivers projected customer demand to the production organization. Production utilizes the purchasing function to supply its raw materials, which is delivered by the logistics department.

The support functions integrate with all these operating departments. For example, HRM interacts with all the departments because there are employees in each department. Information systems (IS) collects and feeds back all

---

6. Boyst Jr III, William M, "HRM — Key to the Integrated Management Revolution", *APICS 34th International Conference Proceedings* (APICS) 1991, pp. 354-357.
7. This is taken from a presentation by Tom Tuttle titled "Reengineering Human Resources". The MCQP is located at the University of Maryland in College Park, Maryland.

the appropriate information needs of the departments. Finance and accounting manage the costs and assets of the organization and the quality function validates the products and the processes throughout the organization.

Ideally, these functional circles will not exist in a world-class enterprise. Rather, an integration will exist where teams of employees will be established that integrate all these functional processes. For example, a TQM product team would include technology, customer, sales/marketing, quality, production, logistics and purchasing representatives along with some "external" representation (see Chapters 7 and 14).

Other models for world-class enterprise integration exist. For example, enterprise resource planning attempts to integrate the planning functions, from the business plan down through the production processes, with the financial and accounting functions.[8] Another model builds the integrated information flow model of enterprise integration and looks at the integration process from an information perspective.[9] Additionally, some expansions of the integrated enterprise model as defined by APICS (discussed earlier) are expanded on to show how teaming, leadership and motivation play important roles in the integration process.[10]

Another way to look at integration is through the measurement/motivation process.

Companies that measure together, motivate together.

There are numerous areas of measurement that can be integrated into an enterprise wide perspective. For example:

• measures of quality — such as reduced complaints

• measures of operation costs — such as reduced inventory levels

8. Blevins, Preston, "Enterprise Resource Planning (ERP) — an Executive Perspective", *APICS 37th International Conference Proceedings* (APICS) October 1994, pp. 138-142.
9. See a number of my articles — "An Overview of JIT", *International Journal of Advanced Manufacturing Technology* (1993) Vol. 8, pp. 91-95; "Integration — Manufacturing's Hidden Buzzword of the 1990s", *International Productivity Journal* (Fall 1991) pp. 11-16; "Decision Support Systems in Manufacturing", *Malaysian Journal of Operations Research* (December 1992) Vol. 1, No. 2, pp. 37-43; "Manufacturing Management — a World Model", *Production Planning and Control* (1992) Vol. 3, No. 1, pp. 93-98; "The Integration of Information Flow into an Expert System Using a Decision Support Systems Base", *Fourth International Conference on Systems Research Informatics and Cybernetics Proceedings* (August 1988); "Decision Support Systems", *Seventh International Congress of Cybernetics and Systems Proceedings* (September 1987) pp. 149-435.
10. Gregoire, Renee M and David M Lehman, "Integrated Enterprise Management (IEM)", *APICS 37th International Conference Proceedings*, op. cit., pp. 155-159; Proescher, Jay, "Leadership in the Integrated Enterprise", *APICS 37th International Conference Proceedings, ibid.*, pp. 181-184.

- measures of flexibility — such as reduced product cycle time
- measures of reliability — such as equipment effectiveness
- measures of innovation — such as time-to-market reductions
- measures of productivity — such as improved output to input performance
- measures of teaming and empowerment — such as increased suggestions per employee.[11]

Perhaps one of the most important measures of integrated enterprise performance is the measure that validates if the enterprise has achieved the *we* status. It's one thing for management to think they are integrated and it's entirely another thing for the employees to feel that they are integrated. A *we* status measurement is taken by simply listening to the employees when they talk to each other, or outsiders like customers. Do they talk about *us* and *them* (referring to different management levels or functional areas in the company) or do they talk about *we*, when referring to their place of employment. When the *we* status is achieved, the company is well on its way to becoming world-class.

One last comment on integration touches at the constant upheaval of the structure of companies. It is best expressed by comparing it to the Japanese concept of integration and unity.

> Companies that stay together, grow together.
>
> Dave Savona[12]

Companies that constantly redefine their structure build insecurity into the workforce. This is especially visible during mergers and acquisitions. The employees become more worried about keeping their jobs than about growth.

> Write the vision, and make it plain upon tables, that he may run that readeth it.
>
> Habakkuk 2:2

---

11. For further information on performance measures I would recommend Buker, David W, *Top Management's Guide to World Class Manufacturing* (Kansas City, Missouri: The Lowell Press, Inc.) 1993; Plenert, Gerhard, *The Plant Operations Handbook* (Homewood, Illinois: Business One Irwin) 1993.
12. Savona, Dave, "America's Keiretsu", *International Business* (November 1994) pp. 46-63.

MANUFACTURING AS THE EXAMPLE

As an example of the complexity of functional understanding I will review the functional aspects of manufacturing (see the production circle in Figure 8.1). World-class eManagers would not be experts at each of these, but would at least have some background on how they function and how they integrate into the "beam me up" perspective. Let's consider some of the issues that manufacturing functionality incorporates.

Facilities management —

- objectives and strategic issues — cost effectiveness, employee safety, regulation compliance, management of internal and external interfaces, quality and productivity, and change and value-added management

- responsibilities — equipment maintenance procedures, preventive maintenance procedures, facilities maintenance procedures, subcontractor services and technological change implementation

- measures — downtime, budgets and safety records.

Figure 8.1: Business Interactions

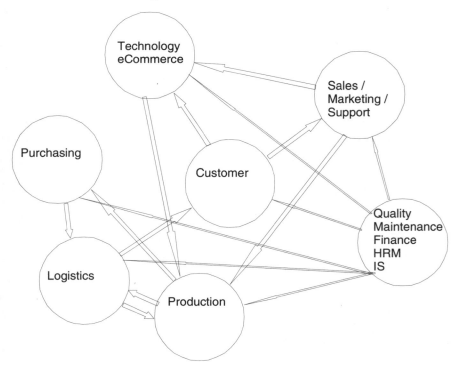

Process management —

- objectives and strategic issues — develop and update product processes, match processes to available equipment, new technology introduction, cost effectiveness, quality and productivity, and change and value-added management

- responsibilities — process design, costing, tooling and equipment, plant layout, material handling, testing, methods and standards, budget/cost management, total quality management and the introduction of technology such as just-in-time (JIT), computer integrated manufacturing (CIM) and computer aided design/computer aided manufacturing (CAD/CAM)

- measures — yield, scrap, cost, time to market, productivity, quality and change efficiency.

Production management —

- objectives and strategic issues — continuous improvement, meeting product specifications and schedules, efficient use of all resources, focus on the critical resource, new technology introduction, cost effectiveness, quality and productivity, and change and value-added management

- responsibilities — resource selection, teaming, training, communication, continuous improvement, budget/cost management, technology introduction, TQM

- measures — time, cost, productivity, quality, change efficiency, flexibility and inventory levels.

Integration management —

- objectives and strategic issues — between facilities management and process (design of equipment, facilities acquisition and process considerations), between process design and manufacturing (workforce, equipment, timing and production and process methods), between facilities management and manufacturing (maintenance and environmental), continuous improvement, safety planning, new technology introduction, cost effectiveness, quality and productivity, and change and value-added management

- measures — throughput, cost, time, productivity, quality, change efficiency and flexibility.

"World-class manufacturing" is a term that has come to be identified with leading edge manufacturing philosophies, such as those outlined below.

Strategic philosophies —
- information sharing/integration

- international focus (global management)
- long-term strategy
- manager versus leader/facilitator
- time to market strategies
- MRP II or JIT philosophies
- simplification and focus.

Employee involvement philosophies —
- teaming
- empowerment
- shorter organization charts
- gainsharing
- job security
- cross training and job rotation.

Improvement philosophies —
- planning for change
- continuous improvement
- total quality management (TQM)
- benchmarking
- risk and uncertainty assessments.

Quality philosophies —
- Deming Principles (or Juran or Crosby)
- TQM
- total quality control
- quality circles
- in-line quality control
- statistical process control.

Production planning philosophies —
- just-in-time production philosophies
- theory of constraints
- bottleneck allocation methodologies
- bill of energy.

Computerization/automation philosophies —

- computer integrated manufacturing (CIM)
- decision support systems (DSS)
- expert systems (ES)
- artificial intelligence (AI)
- computer aided design /computer aided manufacturing (CAD/CAM).[13]

> Where there is no vision, the people perish.
>
> Proverbs 29:18

An additional focus of world-class manufacturing places the emphasis on integration. The largest improvements in the manufacturing process are made by the white-collar employees (engineers, marketing/sales, purchasing and scheduling). Senior management is often surprised that it is them, and not the manufacturing floor, that is slowing down the output of the factory. It is important to make these individuals a part of the manufacturing team so that the team members can directly influence each other.[14]

The manufacturing example that we have discussed in this section of the chapter is not intended to scare you. It is intended to challenge you. To be world-class we need to understand the enterprise and its functions. Let me give you a few additional resources that will help you outline and understand manufacturing's functions in a footnote.[15] The Hayes and Wheelwright articles are somewhat dated but have become classics in manufacturing strategy. Similar resources are available for any of the functional areas of an enterprise.

---

13. Details of these concepts can be found in *The Plant Operations Handbook*, cited earlier.
14. Nicol, Ronald and Harold Sirkin, "Manufacturing Beyond the Factory Floor: The White Collar Factory", *Target* (Winter 1991) pp. 28-35.
15. As mentioned earlier in this chapter, details about the functional processes in manufacturing can be gained from the CIRM study aids from APICS, and you can also refer to the books by Buker, Wallace and Bell and Burnham, listed earlier. A few more references that might be of interest are Dertouzos, Michael l, Richard K Lester and Robert M Solow, *Made in America: Regaining the Competitive Edge* (Cambridge, Massachusetts: The MIT Press) 1991; Miller, William B and Vicki L Schenk, *All I Need To Know About Manufacturing I Learned In Joe's Garage* (Walnut Creek, CA: Bayrock Press) 1993; Kelleher, James P, "Total Quality Management in Production Planning and Control", *APICS 34th International Conference Proceedings,* op. cit., pp. 180-181; Grant, Robert M, R Kirshnan, Abraham B Shani and Ron Baer, "Appropriate Manufacturing Technology: A Strategic Approach", *Sloan Management Review* (Fall 1991) pp. 43-54; Wheelwright, Steven C and Robert H Hayes, "Competing Through Manufacturing", *Harvard Business Review* (January-February 1995) pp. 99-109; Hayes, Robert H and Steven C Wheelwright, "Link Manufacturing Process and Product Life Cycles", *Harvard Business Review* (January-February 1979) pp. 133-140; Ross, David F, "Aligning the Organization for World-Class Manufacturing", *Production and Inventory Management Journal* (1991) pp. 22-26.

At the Advanced Manufacturing Center of Schlumberger Technologies a five-year plan for achieving world class manufacturing status was developed. The program required:

- total commitment and high level involvement

- all employees participate in a total team effort

- complete employee involvement and dedication

- a mission statement that is committed to customer satisfaction

- continuous improvement through employee buy-ins to changes

- a focus on supplier excellence.[16]

NCR-Ithaca converted its plant from "an embarrassment" to the "pride of the company" through world-class manufacturing strategies that focused on process improvements and teamwork. It now dominates 24 per cent of the worldwide printer market. It instituted a change in management philosophy that stressed that quality was now the responsibility of everyone in the organization, focused on self-directed teaming and reduced the management overhead from 1 supervisor for 24 employees down to 1 supervisor for 100 employees. It also instituted JIT and TQC production methodologies. Job flexibility was improved through cross training and operator flexibility was increased from 2 job skills per operator to 8 job skills each. The results of these changes are impressive. Inventory on hand went from 111 days down to 21 days (from 2000 printers in process down to 400). Manufacturing cycle time went from 60 days down to 8 days. Manufacturing floor space went from 45,000 square feet down to 19,000 square feet. And the successes go on and on. But most important, NCR-Ithaca sees its biggest challenges for competitiveness and change in its future.[17]

> Education is a danger . . . At best an education which produces useful coolies for us is admissible. Every educated person is a future enemy.
>
> Martin Bormann,
> German Nazi leader

16. Beddingfield, Thomas and Thomas Waechter, "Attaining World Class Manufacturing Status", *APICS 34th International Conference Proceedings,* op. cit., pp. 472-476.
17. Labach, Elaine J, "No Screws, No Glue, No Adjustments", *Target* (Winter 1989) pp. 23-30.

MOVING FROM THE ENTERPRISE TO THE ENVIRONMENT

. . . of more value than harsh discipline.

Saint Augustine

The business enterprise is a very intricate, integrated entity, much like the Starship Enterprise. There are lots of systems pieces, all of which need to be understood in order for everything to work together effectively. However, don't let any system become your god, whether it's the computer system, the production control system, the accounting system or your data collection system. The system is yours to use, not yours to be controlled by. And, believe it or not, if used correctly, it can be an enjoyable experience. A world-class eManager understands the functions of the enterprise. He or she utilizes them in innovative ways in order to achieve the goals of the enterprise. This manager searches for the "beam me up" approach, looking for the big picture in all situations and then utilizes his or her knowledge and experience base to make changes happen.

A dog was carrying a bone in his mouth when he happened to pass by the edge of a river. He stopped to look down into the slow moving waters and saw his reflection. The dog was convinced that this second dog, his reflection, was carrying a bigger bone than he was so he dropped his bone to try to steal the larger bone. But as his bone drifted away down the river, he realized that the other dog had dropped his bone as well and now they were both left without any bone.

Do we ever chase mirages or reflections? One such mirage is that the larger the computer you have, the better. Another is that the enterprise exists in an isolated shell, unaffected by the world around it. A world-class enterprise does not exist in a shell, it exists in a community, a society, a country and a world.

Nowhere is this more evident then in a global setting. The "shell" perspective on life often exists in the United States, but, in most of the rest of the world, the enterprise is a critical element of the community. The enterprise is expected to "add value" to the society where they are established, to the people in the community and not just to themselves. They need to plan and think globally, but act locally. They need to set up a global target, but allow the local organization to utilize local processes for achieving those targets. And, in the end, they need to improve the environment in which the organization exists.

The shoe that fits one person pinches another; there is no recipe for living that suits all cases.

Carl Jung

STAKEHOLDERS

I have long thought that the aging process could be slowed down if it had to work its way through congress.

Speech writer for George Bush

Upon being dismissed from his government job in the custom house, Nathaniel Hawthorne arrived home in deep despair. With his head hung he told his tale with all hopelessness to his wife who didn't waste a minute before she set pen and ink on the table, lit the fireplace and sat him down. Putting her arms around his shoulders she said "Now you will be able to write your novel." Which, of course he did. This story is often used to demonstrate that out of adversity comes new opportunity — an important and valuable lesson. However, I also see a lesson of how an inspired leader (his wife) took a negative opportunity and turned it into a positively great one. There is no question that his wife had a lot to do with the results, even though she put very little ink to paper. This wife was a stakeholder who took her commitment to her husband seriously.

In life, as in business, we have numerous stakeholders. These include:

• in life — your spouse, children, relatives, friends, neighbors and community

• in business — your fellow employees, suppliers, customers, community, your country, the communities and countries you interact with and your owners.

It is your function *as an individual* to add value to all the stakeholders in your life. It is your function *as an enterprise* to add value to all the stakeholders in your business community.

Globally, adding value may include schools, government involvement, medical facilities, sports and family involvement, like subsidized recreational activities, housing or stores. Adding value means improving the future of the children of your employees. Adding value includes improving the living standard of the employees and their families.

Tellabs feels that for managers who are "striving for world-class status, people involvement programs are the bull's-eye" of the target. Starting with a pilot project of twelve employees, it soon expanded the involvement project to three plants. It focused on building flexible people involvement and people systems and on integrating performance management and compensation systems. Internally, it took seven job levels with 52 job titles and flattened them down to one level with one job title. The results? At its Lisle, IL location, turnover has gone from 46 per cent down to 8 per cent.[18]

---

18. Neusch, Donna R, "How Tellabs Took Aim at People Involvement", *Target* (Spring 1991) pp. 4-13.

ENVIRONMENTAL CONSIDERATIONS

A person who buries his head in the sand offers an engaging target.

Mabel A Keenan

American factories are often moved from one part of the United States to another because the regulations aren't as tight. Now, with the NAFTA agreement, this movement often includes Mexico or Canada. However, in the past we have moved plants to India or Latin America to get around safety and pollution restrictions. This type of behavior is not world-class — it is cowardly. World-class behavior is ethical. World-class eManagers make a difference in the lives of the stakeholders and not just a difference in the pocketbook.

The new buzzword for social consciousness in the environment is "green manufacturing". This is where the company designs and plans their plant to be environmentally appropriate to the community. Green manufacturing is where pollution concerns are part of the planning process, not an after-thought implemented because the government forces them to.

When considering technology improvements, we need to make sure that the cost of the technology is not higher than the benefit. This is part of Schumacher's message in his book *Small is Beautiful* (listed earlier). An example of technology cost is that the energy generated through the entire existence of the Chernobal Nuclear Power Facility was not worth the cost that the whole world has to pay for that plant's melt down. Now, I'm not opposed to nuclear energy, but, as a thoughtful example we should consider whether the cost of "cheaper" nuclear energy is really worth it in the long run. For example, if the price that we had to pay for nuclear generated energy also included a cost element that paid for the breakdown and disposal of the waste products, would nuclear energy really be cheaper than other forms of energy? A world-class environmentally conscious enterprise should include disposal costs of plutonium, plastics, glass or any of the packaging and products sold. I realize that this would destroy competitiveness, since your product would now have to have a higher price. Or would it? Is lack of environmental consciousness a reason for a lack of competitiveness or is it just an excuse? An innovative technologist would be able to turn this "disadvantage" into a competitive advantage and still be considered "green". Some problems are easier to avoid, then to solve. When the avoidance has detrimental effects on society, that's not world-class. This reminds me of the old saying:

It's easier to be forgiven than to get permission!

It may be easier, but is it ethical? Is it world-class?

I'm not going to spend a lot of time talking about all the different kinds of pollution, such as air, water, noise, pollution, pornography, violence and so on. I will simply say:

> If it ain't uplifting, if it ain't adding value (in the long run — all things considered) it ain't worth it!

Entertainment and television can be very value-added or it can be very degrading. Walt Disney is the master of value-added entertainment. You always come out of his movies feeling better than when you went in. Focus on adding value in your life. Similarly, focus on adding value in your business.

> What bothers me about TV is that it tends to take our minds off our minds.

As frustrating as it may seem at times, there are good things happening that improve our environment. Top executives from companies like Dow, DuPont, AIG, Amoco and Monsanto have gone on the road to discuss environmental stewardship. These companies are spending advertising dollars to support the environmental agenda and developing waste management programs, recycling programs, pollution prevention programs and environmentally conscious product development programs.

Cynics claim this is an attempt to win sympathy and would suggest that we should not support their hypocritical attempts at environmental consciousness, but I frankly don't care. Anything that will improve my standard of living, and the standard of living for my children, deserves my support. I'd rather support someone who is branded a hypocrite, but who is moving in the right direction, than to support nothing. This industrial support is just the beginning. It's not even enough to be called the tip of the iceberg. We have a long way to go. But at least we are starting to move in the right direction.[19]

HOW TIME MOVES THE ENTERPRISE

> Corporation: an ingenious device for obtaining profit without individual responsibility.
>
> Ambrose Bierce

The environment includes all the things around us, whether it's the air, the water or the people (like customers and employees). A world-class enterprise

---

19. Siwolop, Sana and Amy Barrett, "Business and the Environment", *Financial World* (23 January 1990) pp. 40-42.

needs to add value to, not detract from, all elements of the environment. There are numerous value added components in all stages of industry. For example:

- technology development
- technology implementation through engineering
- product production
- product accessibility and timeliness through logistics
- retail accessibility and convenience
- service institution appropriate services.

The key to world-class environmental success in each of these value-added states is the individual integrity of the individual world-class eManager to do what is right, not what is profit advantageous.

In 1870 the Methodists were having an annual conference in a college in Indiana. The presiding bishop was asking the group for an interpretation of current events, when the president of the college volunteered, "I think we are in a very exciting age."

When asked to continue the president said, "I believe we are coming into a time when we will see, for example, wonderful inventions. I believe men will fly through the air like birds."

Bishop Wright was visibly disturbed by this statement. He said, "This is heresy, this is blasphemy; I read in my Bible that flight is reserved for angels. We will not have such talk here in my area."

After the conference, Bishop Wright returned home to his two young sons, Orville and Wilbur.

This book is about world-class change eManagement. And change is a direct result of time. Like the bumper sticker says:

Change Happens

Without time, everything would stay the same forever. With time, we have change, and with change we have opportunity.

> Where you're at in life isn't near as important as in what direction you are going.

> The journey of a thousand miles begins with one step.

> Lao-Tse

MANAGEMENT THEORY AND TIME

Some theories of business are so powerful that they last for a long time.
But eventually every one of them becomes obsolete.

Peter Drucker

Things change! Change changes! Even the best way to manage change,
changes! This is evident by the series of management philosophies that have
inundated our management styles. Each philosophical stage was the key to
competitiveness during a particular era. These have included:

Guilds — still very effective in Europe and many developing parts of the
world

Industrial revolution — Henry Ford and assembly lines

Scientific management — Frederick Taylor, the father of time studies

Humanistic (human relations) management — Hawthorne studies on human
behavior

Japanese management — Edward Deming and inventory efficiency

Productive technology — automation replacing workers

Information technology — computers

Change management — change and time efficiency.[20]

One of the most interesting ways to show this change in management processes is through the migration that has occurred in production systems. In
Figure 8.2 we see how production control philosophies have migrated through
a series of stages to where now we have an innumerable number of "right"
ways to run a factory. Of course there is no one right way that will work for all
factories — the correct way for any one factory needs to be matched to the
needs of the factory.

In Figure 8.2 we see the *2-Bin* inventory control system is the earliest
control system. Even today it is still the most common system among small to
mid-sized manufacturers. Next we have economic order quantity (EOQ) and
linear programming (LP) used for production control. After World War II we
had an explosion of production system technologies. Computers made material requirements planning (MRP) feasible and integer programming (IP) possible. Japan developed just-in-time (JIT) out of the EOQ model. And Israel
created optimized production technology (OPT). Then, about ten years ago,

---

20. For further reading, see Roth, William, *The Evolution of Management Theory* (Orefield,
Pennsylvania: Roth and Associates) 1993.

Figure 8.2: The Migration of Production Control Systems

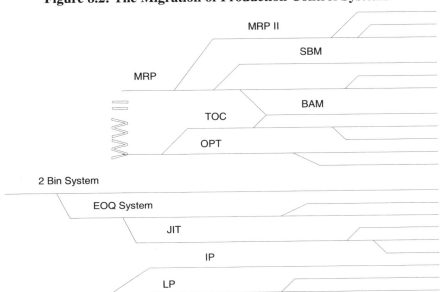

theory of constraints (TOC) came out of OPT and manufacturing resources planning (MRP II) came out of the integration of MRP and the accounting functions. More recently, schedule based manufacturing (SBM) and bottleneck allocation methodology (BAM) have been developed which are improvements and refinements on some of the problems that existed in some of the other production planning systems.

As a result, we now have a multitude of management philosophies and a multitude of production planning processes, all of which are still being used. Each is competitive when placed in an appropriate environment. Time has blessed us with an enormous bag of competitive tricks and there will be more, rather than less, in the future. The only disadvantage of all these alternatives is that we have to understand them in order to use them properly.

One man's sunset is another man's dawn.

An American Tail — Fievel Goes West

THE TIME LINE OF THE ENTERPRISE

There is a well-known and often discussed corporate life cycle. This life cycle is similar for nations and for products. In Figure 8.3 we see this life cycle diagrammed out. The length of the cycle averages at about 600 years for a nation. For the United States, we are somewhere in the maturity stage, and, some would argue, starting down the decline.

For companies this cycle averages around twenty years. However, it is getting shorter and shorter all the time. For some companies the cycle is only as long as the life of a specific product they were established to produce. For the company, birth often revolves around some piece of technology, or some entrepreneur's idea of a profitable business. After birth the cycle shifts to start-up where it is still run primarily by the entrepreneurs. However, at some point the company becomes too large to be run by a sole entrepreneur and professional managers are brought in. For most businesses this is somewhere around 30 to 50 employees. With a professional management staff, the entrepreneur often phases out of the picture and the company jumps into its growth phase. Unfortunately, with growth and a professional management staff comes the search for stability which results in bureaucracy. We have now entered the maturing phase of the organization. With maturity often comes complacency and a resistance to change. Without change the company starts to lose it's vigor and drive resulting in decline.

For products, the life cycle can be as short as just a few months, especially in the high-tech industries. Alternatively, it can be as long as hundreds of years. A company's life, or even a nation's life, can be tied to the life of a product. In the case of a nation, many have grown and died around a natural

Figure 8.3: The Time-Life Cycle

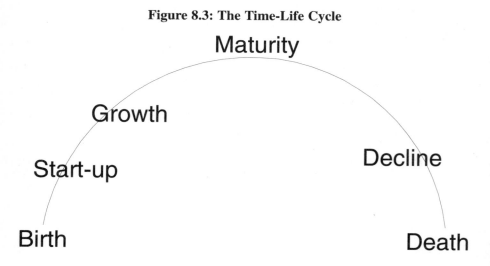

resource. When the resource is depleted, prosperity ends and the nation is overthrown. In the case of a company, it is set up to produce a new piece of technology and it's entire existence revolves solely around the production of the product.

Fortunately, the time-life cycle does not have to signal the end of the enterprise. In Figure 8.4 we see how repeated product life cycles can be utilized to maintain the growth that has been established. Recently, because of the recession and because of competitive pressures, many companies like IBM have found themselves in decline and have decided to downsize and regroup, searching for new products with new product life cycles on which they can hang their growth maintenance. If they don't successfully find new products, death is inevitable.

From Figure 8.3 we see that time and change will eventually kill you unless, as in Figure 8.4, you innovate and re-innovate, change and change again, keeping yourself on the top of the time-life cycle near maturity. In Figure 8.4 we see how, when curve A is in decline, curve B is in maturity, curve C is in growth and curve D is in start-up. To be a growth maintenance company we need to have products in each of the stages of the time-life cycle all the time. We cannot focus our efforts on just one product. This is done with the following teams:

- the new product innovation team needs to focus on identifying new product ideas
- the new product development team needs to focus on making the product producible in a timely and profitable fashion
- the marketing team needs to focus on market expansion during the growth phase of the product; production needs to focus on adequately planning productive capacity
- during maturity, marketing needs to focus on market maintenance and the innovation team needs to look at product modification searching for new product life cycles in the old products
- during decline phase-out occurs — the product is generally profitable but losing its customer appeal and new innovation needs to take its place.

Figure 8.4: Growth Maintenance

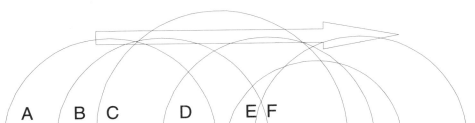

The time-life cycle teaches us that enterprise growth maintenance is dependent upon repeated change and repeated innovation. Stability leads to stagnation, which is a sure sign of enterprise death.

FUTURE COMPETITIVE POWER

People who say it cannot be done should not interrupt those who are doing it.

Anonymous

The competitive power in the future depends on whom you're talking to. For manufacturing, as we have considered in previous chapters, the competitive power of the future is in:

• rapid product changes

• time-to-market efficiency

• product cycle time reductions

• a commitment to customer satisfaction

• employee empowerment and teaming

• stakeholder integration

• quality and productivity initiatives.

Manufacturing is a critical value-added element, third only in importance to agriculture and pure technology development. Manufacturing controls the product development engineering function, the production function and is a key to customer satisfaction. Maintaining this value-added status is a critical competitive edge in the future (see Chapter 11).

Boldrin claims that the competitive future of manufacturing lies in the efficiency of material flow, cycle time reductions and employee empowerment. He cites examples of how Hargrove, a manufacturer of gas fireplace logs, reduced floor space by 80 per cent and cut cycle time by 50 per cent by re-engineering and simplifying the production floor.[21]

Burton sees the future of manufacturing requiring:

• the full emergence of the global corporation

• virtually instantaneous operations (customer responsiveness combined with very short cycle times)

• total supply chain integration

21.Boldrin, Bruce J, "Breaking the Time Barrier to Achieve World Class Manufacturing", *APICS 37th International Conference Proceedings,* op. cit., pp. 662-664.

- engineering and manufacturing integration
- new age of quality
- more rapid continuous improvement
- a growth in strategic alliances
- flat, unstructured organizations.[22]

In retailing we find that it has long been believed that the new competitive power base is the retailer. Customers trust the store more and more and the manufacturer less and less. We are getting a confidence shift. It is the retail establishment that guarantees the quality of the product. However, the competitive edge in retailing in the 1990s and beyond is not in marketing, rather, it is in logistics. Accessibility and timing are the competitive strategies of the future. Future value-added growth comes in the form of getting the customer what they need when they need it and in the form (product type) they want to get it in.

The integration of the logistics function into the other functions of the retailer, often referred to as speed sourcing, has been identified by stores such as Target and WalMart as a critical success factor. Technological investment into this ability is a key to the speed sourcing strategy for companies like J C Penny.

In retailing and other forms of service organizations such as banking, customer service was forgotten for a long time, being considered too costly. Marketing was considered to be more important. However, customer service is becoming fashionable again, being considered a strategic competitive edge. Stores like Target and Nordstrom are re-focusing on customer service. They are building service into product returnability and even into the way the store is structured and laid out. Similarly banks are improving their hours and accessibility.

Daniel J Sweeney, vice-chairperson of the Retail Service Industry Group, Price Waterhouse, a retailing industry consultant and a member of the National Advisory Council of Brigham Young University, identified four future vectors for retailing and the service industries:

1. Globalization will effect 90 per cent of all retailers — retailing will be changed by the new emerging middle classes in developing countries which tend to have a strong family focus (the model for effective retail globalization is IKEA of Sweden).

2. Optimization, such as taking advantage of scale economies, is growing (WalMart is the grand master in this area).

---

22. Burton, Terence T, "Manufacturing in the 21st Century", *APICS 34th International Conference Proceedings,* op. cit., pp. 454-457.

3.   Electronification, such as greatly improved home shopping and CD-ROM catalogs, is on the increase.

4.   Personalization, such as anticipation marketing, is making its mark.

The future is coming. The world-class eManager will be ready for it!

> Don't worry about people stealing your ideas. If your ideas are any good, you'll have to ram them down people's throats.
>
> Howard Aiken

HOW THE WORLD-CLASS EMANAGER CHANGES OVER TIME

I was trying to explain a management concept to a plant manager and we were interrupted numerous times, which disrupted our train of thought. After what seemed like the fiftieth interruption, the manager looked at me in disgust and said, "At work I spend all my time listening to customers, managers, employees and vendors. At home I spend all my time listening to my spouse, my children, the TV, radio, and movies. I just don't seem to have any time to listen to *reason!*"

What scared me most about what the plant manager said is that I could sympathize with him. I occasionally have the same problem myself. We just don't have time to listen to reason. And the key action word here is "time". I temporarily left the working world and joined academia (I was sure that they didn't do anything) just to get a little "time". I had spent so much of my time fighting fires that I never had the chance to look for the source of the fire. In academia I got a chance to be "beamed up", to take a look at the big picture and to get paid for it. The ironic part about it all is I always believed that:

> If you know how to do a job, you do it; and if you don't know how to do it, you teach it!

I found out that you learn more about a job by teaching it than you do by doing it, especially when some feisty student questions some of your "we've always done it that way" philosophies. Now, when I go out and "do it" I have a much clearer perspective on what I'm doing. Teaching gave me a chance to "listen to reason". Everyone should try it some time. Whether you're teaching your fellow employees, at the local junior college or at a university, the challenge of getting challenged is invaluable.

You can't become a world-class eManager unless you take time to listen to reason. Therefore, the keys to becoming a world-class eManager are:

1.   taking *time*

2.   to *listen* (training)

3. to reason (ideas)

4. so we can become better (change).

So, after saying this, the question I get first is, "Where do I begin? What do I change first?"

My answer is always "The point of least resistance". There are lots of things to change. Review the world-class management test in the next chapter to see all the areas of change. Identify the areas where you need improvement. Sequence the needed changes to see where you would:

*   have the most fun to least fun

*   need the most help

*   have the biggest benefit on your future performance.

You need positive feelings about your efforts, so do those things that will make you feel the most successful first. Then go on to the next. You can't do it all at once but you can get started, one small step at a time.

In his book *The Evolution of Management Theory* (listed earlier), Roth takes a look at the future of management theory. He proposes the organizational structure which includes six dimensions. This is the "multilevel, multidimensional, modular-organization" of Gharajedaghi and includes:

*   output units — manufacturing and logistics

*   input units — supplier or even competitor sourcing

*   environmental units — government and stakeholder relationships

*   planning/decision-making unit — the integrative unit where all other units are represented

*   control unit — monitor, feedback, data collection

*   management unit — facilitating decisions.[23]

Roth suggests that the key future issues of the organization are:

*   organization size and design

*   marketplace pressures

*   socioeconomic doctrine

*   the changing role of stakeholders

*   private sector involvement.

---

23. Gharajedaghi, Jamshid, "Organizational Implications of Systems Thinking: Multidimensional Modular Design", *European Journal of Operations Research*, August 1984.

An expert is someone called in at the last minute to share the blame.

Sam Ewing

CONTROLLING TIME

Figures 8.3 and 8.4 showed us the need for constant innovation and change development. Figure 8.5 shows us how change occurs. What we need to do is integrate change over time by building transition bridges between the change phases. Figure 8.6 shows how these transition bridges occur in a company's growth path. It shows that growth is not as smooth as Figure 8.3 would like us to believe. Rather, there are stages of growth where we switch roles between change implementation (Stages B and C in Figure 8.5 or Stage F in Figure 8.6) to change stabilization (Stages D and E in Figure 8.5 or Stage G in Figure 8.6). Figure 8.6 shows that the change implementation process is not always a smooth transition — there are often rough spots.

From these charts we learn that change over time is not as easy as stability. In fact, we will often feel like the change wasn't worth it (Stage C of Figure 8.5 or the Florida Power and Light story), but without it we will die as an enterprise.

Figure 8.5: Change Function

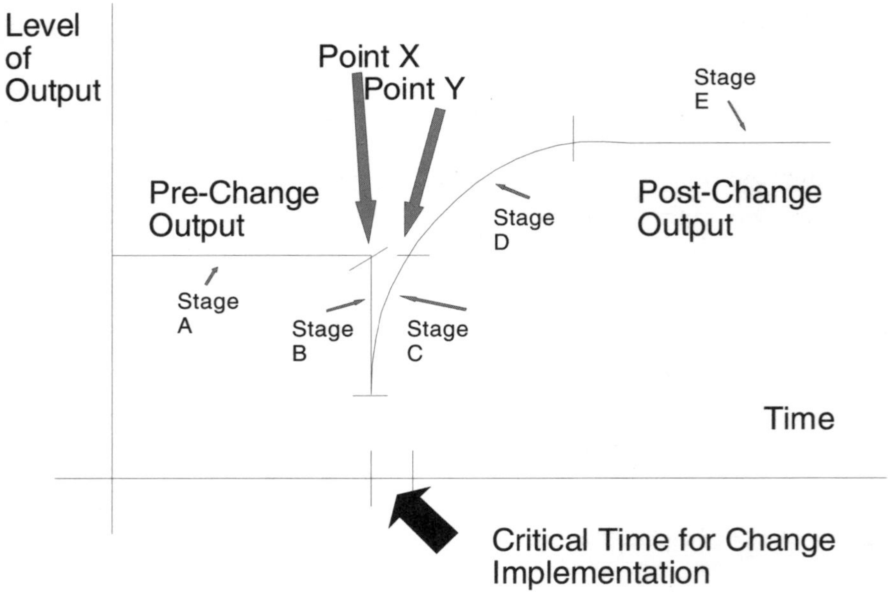

Figure 8.6: Growth Transitions

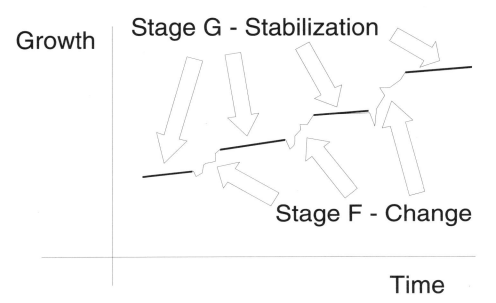

The tools for change are immeasurable, as we have seen throughout this book. Probably the best tool for world-class change implementation is the TQM process outlined in Chapter 10. But we cannot forget that we need to change the individual before we can change the enterprise.

Why do parents spend the first year of a child's life trying to get the newborn to walk and talk, and then spend the next nineteen years telling the child to "shut up and sit down?" Similarly, why do we get excited about new ideas during the start-up phase of a company but get offended by them during the growth and maturity stages of a company? The attitude that motivates change should be constant and continuous. We shouldn't be like the grandfather who said:

> The older I get, the better I was!

If we work toward positive, goal-directed change as we go along, then we won't have to pretend we did after we are forced into it.

> Few people blame themselves until they have exhausted all other possibilities.
>
> Francis Duffy

SUMMARY

A world-class eManager is a manager who is continually changing over time. A world-class eManager utilizes time to his or her advantage, understanding that time can both make an enterprise great or kill it. Stability cannot exist. Change will happen. The question is — as time goes on, will you control it or will it control you?

> The best way to convince a fool that he is wrong is to let him have his own way.
>
> Josh Billings

Chapter Nine

A Global Management Strategy Integrated Locally

I was made to work; if you are equally industrious, you will be equally successful.

Johann Sebastian Bach

A man had been working at a lumber mill for years. Every Friday night he would go home from the factory with a wheelbarrow full of sawdust. The security guard at the plant gate became real suspicious about this man and his sawdust and started to question him. The guard had a hard time believing that anyone could find any use for that much sawdust. The guard would search through the sawdust expecting to find something hidden in the sawdust, but always came up empty. After this man had been retired for several years, the security guard came to him and asked, "I know you were stealing something from the plant all those years, what was it you were stealing?"

"Wheelbarrows!"

Do you ever spend time digging around in the sawdust and not seeing the wheelbarrows? One of the great wheelbarrows of industry today, one that is keeping it from being world-class, is globalization. We dig around trying to find competitive opportunities in the sawdust and miss the really big opportunity. Let me give you a little test in your ability to spot a wheelbarrow. Connect all the nine dots in Figure 9.1 using only four straight lines. You can't lift up your pencil between lines — the lines have to be connected. The solution is found in Appendix 9.1.

If you don't want to win, no one will stop you.

GLOBALIZATION — WHAT IS IT?

Globalization is looking beyond the nine dots. It's realizing that there's a big world out there, that reaches far beyond our small little community and that this world is getting closer to us all the time. Globalization is the realization that, whether we like it or not, this big world is becoming an ever increasing factor in our daily lives. And, being world-class in this global environment means that we are looking beyond the sawdust to see the wheelbarrows; it means looking beyond our small, isolated environment to identify competitive

Figure 9.1: Nine Dots

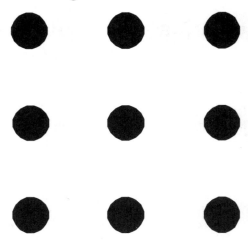

opportunities on a much larger scale than we ever previously imagined.

This chapter will offer a brief outline of globalization and its dynamics. Like many of the topics of this book, I can only offer a brief "big picture" perspective of this topic. Numerous books exist that offer detailed explanations of the topic.[1] Globalization requires careful strategic planning because it can become very complex depending on where and what you are working with. However, the benefits are enormous, as you shall see. You must consider globalization as a critical strategic requirement in your drive to become world-class.

The wise learn many things from their foes.

Aristophanes,
Athenian poet

THE GLOBAL ENTERPRISE

A global enterprise is one that is involved in international transactions. These

---

1. Three books that I have drawn from for parts of this chapter, and which included excellent expansions of much of the material that is found in this chapter are Daniels, John D and Lee H Radebaugh, *International Business – Environments and Operations* (Reading, Massachusetts: Addison-Wesley Publishing Company) 1994; Sheth, Jagdish, and Golpira Eshghi, *Global Operations Perspectives* (Cincinnati, Ohio: South-Western Publishing Co.) 1989; Plenert, Gerhard, *International Management and Production: Survival Techniques for Corporate America* (Blue Ridge Summit, PA: TAB Professional and Reference Books) 1990.

transactions can take many forms and might include, for example, vendors, subcontractors, customers, subsidiaries, plants and financing (banks and private investors).

Almost every company, no matter how small, is either directly or indirectly globally influenced in some way. Even if you don't have direct international transactions, it is highly likely that components of what you purchase, or the end user of your output, will be internationally influenced. Often one of your primary competitors will be international.

Ignoring the global perspective is not seeing the wheelbarrow or not connecting the nine dots. Being a global manager is understanding and effectively manipulating foreign markets, whether they are consumer markets, labor markets or vendor markets. For example, Ohmae goes so far as to say that seeing and thinking globally is the world-class eManager's first task.[2] Information has allowed global managers around the world to speak a common language of business.

Globalization does not remove the need for localization. The products and services we provide still need to be culturally distinct. For example, when Mexico decided to market shoes called "Jesus boots" (a direct translation from the Spanish) in the United States, sales went stale. However, by renaming the sandals, sales quickly took off. When United States auto manufacturers were faced with the Kimono regulations of Japan, where bumpers had to be wrapped back into the body of the car so that the long Kimonos would not get caught in them, they cried "trade barrier" and fought it all the way. A global enterprise and a world-class global manager understands the need for product and service localization within a global environment.

The global enterprise is an "insider", not an "outsider". It understands how localized markets work from the inside, whether it is in, for example, North America, Europe, Japan or Latin America. It realizes that there are differences within each region (compare the United States, Canada and Mexico) and within the regions of each country (compare the west of the United States with the north-east, the south or Alaska, for example). A global enterprise focuses on the localization within each of these sub regions.

The result is that a global enterprise develops a global strategy, which builds on localized independence. It develops global visions and missions, but realizes that home office solutions very seldom are workable locally and that the local organizations need to be empowered to make its own decisions. A global enterprise is one that recognizes that all customers, including those that are rarely or never heard of in the home office, are equally important.

> When things go really well — or very badly [in your business] — misplaced home-country reflexes start to intervene. . . Too many entrenched

---

2. Ohmae, Kenichi, "Managing in a Borderless World", *Harvard Business Review* (May-June 1989) pp. 152-161.

systems work against collaborative efforts . . . Customer needs have globalized, and we must globalize to meet them.

Kenichi Ohmae

Global management has been the focus of numerous studies. For example, 31 major trends were listed as shaping the future of American business. Industrial globalization directly affects the majority of these, including issues such as:

- time control — time responsiveness
- dramatic growth in home shopping
- the environment
- labor relations changes
- defense spending shifts
- government regulations to increase
- permanent damage to the nuclear industry
- the budget deficit won't go away
- reversal of tax cuts for wealthy.[3]

Another study suggests that the first characteristic of 21st century industry is the emergence of the global corporation. Some of the features of the global corporation are:

- virtually instantaneous operations
- integrating the supply chain
- flat, unstructured, modular organizations
- growth of strategic alliances
- a renewed focus on quality.[4]

Another study which focuses on global marketing stresses four critical success dimensions, each focusing on the global effects:

1. business strategy

2. product strategy

3. market mix strategy

4. country strategy.[5]

---

3. The Roper Organization, Inc., *The Public Pulse* (1991) Vol. 2, No. 1, pp. 1-8.
4. Burton, Terence T, "Manufacturing in the 21st Century", *APICS 34th International Conference Proceedings* (APICS) October 1991, pp. 454-457.
5. Quelch, John A, and Edward J Hoff, "Customizing Global Marketing", *Harvard Business Review* (May-June 1986) pp. 59-68.

> The big issue today is not whether to go global but how to tailor the
> global marketing concept to fit each business.
>
> Quelch and Hoff

Still another study stresses that the effective global competitor must understand the nature of the global customer, which includes:

- the cultural differences (discussed later in this chapter)

- the political ideology — such as government stability and degree of government control, tariffs

- the business climate — such as business practices and protocol, banking,
  technological sophistication

- the demographic infrastructure — such as population makeup, education,
  health, urbanization.[6]

The world-class global manager realizes that he or she does not have all the
answers. They realize that they do not have a localized perspective for every
region in which their enterprise is involved. For example, Whirlpool International's management committee is made up of six people from six different
nations and this is typical of most world-class global enterprises. Asea Brown
Boveri (ABB), the European electrical engineering giant based in Zurich,
Switzerland has grouped its entire product line of thousands of products into
50 business categories or business areas (BA). The leadership team for each
BA is given global responsibility for developing the business unit strategy for
its area. This includes the incorporation of global responsibility, selecting product development priorities and allocating production among countries. None
of the BA teams are located in Zurich, rather, they are distributed throughout
the world.[7]

Hewlett-Packard moved the headquarters of its personal computer business
to Grenoble, France. Siemens A G, Germany's electronics giant, moved its
medical electronics division to Chicago, Illinois. Ford's world-class engine
factory, where Mexican engineers and technicians produce 1,000 engines per
day at world-class quality levels, is located in Chihuahua, Mexico. Texas
Instruments' most complex wafer production facility is in Sendai, Japan. Intel
is establishing one of its prime strategic research centers in Penang, Malaysia.
Most consumer electronics products marketed in the United States by American
companies such as General Electric, RCA and Zenith are manufactured abroad.
Chrysler has reduced its domestic capacity to 40 per cent and now buys the

6. Albin, John T, "Competing in a Global Market", *APICS - The Performance Advantage*
   (January 1992) pp. 29-32.
7. For more detail on global relationships see Reich, Robert B, "Who is Them?", *Harvard
   Business Review* (March-April 1991) pp. 77-88.

majority of the automobiles it markets under its brand name from Mitsubishi in Japan. Sears, K-Mart and J C Penney procure a large percentage of their merchandise from foreign manufacturers. Non-US companies such as Shell, British Petroleum, Hoechst, Toyota, Nissan, Honda, Sony and Mitsushita have, through acquisitions and new facilities, introduced production facilities in North America. Other successful global competitors include IBM, GE, McDonalds, Philips, Toys-R-Us, KFC, NCR, AT&T, Unilever and Proctor & Gamble. The list goes on and on. These companies have all discovered the globalization advantage. They are focusing on strategic global relocations. They are becoming global citizens. World-class management requires that you become a global citizen also.

> . . . change is the nursery of musicke, joy, life, and eternity.
>
> John Donne,
> English poet

REASONS FOR GLOBALIZATION

So far in this chapter we have discussed why it makes good sense to be globally oriented. I will now review some specific strategic reasons why you may want to make globalization a part of your corporate or business unit strategy. My own personal list of specific strategic reasons for globalization would include:

- cost competitiveness
- time-to-market competitiveness
- manufacturing processes
- information processes
- government policy
- competitive markets
- technology transfer
- competitive lessons we can learn.

Cost Competitiveness

Cost competitiveness is usually one of the first and, often, the wrong reason for globalization. As we have already discussed in previous chapters, cost cutting is a short-term financially oriented decision motivator. Almost always, the relocation decision is based on labor cost and labor cost is typically 10 per cent or less of the value-added cost of the production process. Relocation decisions based on cutting labor costs can only detrimentally affect the total cost reduction. In the past, labor cost competitiveness has caused plants to be shifted to Latin America, East Asia and more recently South-East Asia. Fortunately the mistake of labor cost competitiveness has been recognized and labor-cost-only shifts do not occur as often.

> The truth is that many accounting systems are not designed to provide information to answer the questions managers face in today's market. Worse, the information is still used and catastrophic decisions are made because the accounting information indicates it is the smart thing to do.

> Howell and Soucy[8]

However, if total cost or value-added cost competitiveness is the basis for globalization, then the global strategy, although still short-term oriented, at least has potential merit. Often, in these cases, materials sourcing costs are the dominating factor. For example, if locating a plant in Asia, in spite of the increased shipping and inventory carrying costs and in spite of the potentially lower productivity and quality levels, still results in a net production cost reduction, then the move is a good one. Products like electrical components, compressors, electric motors, metals, agricultural materials, some chemicals, petroleum and its products, are cheaper overseas than when purchased in the United States.

Another cost competitive issue that has motivated globalization is transportation, shipping, tariffs and exchange rates. For example, Coca Cola and Pepsi bottle their product as close to the consumer as possible. Then, the only thing that is imported is the high value-added item of the syrup. The bulky items like the bottles and the soda water are locally sourced. Similarly, Japanese companies have decided to manufacture in the Untied States or Canada because of the Japanese yen and US dollar relationship (see the discussion on exchange rates).

Recently, with the introduction of NAFTA, there have been many surprises. For example, the movement of Toys-R-Us and WalMart into Canada has resulted in the closure of some major Canadian toy retailers. Additionally, labor-intensive production processes like agriculture, which should favor the low labor costs of Mexico, have in fact resulted in agricultural products being shipped from the United States to Mexico and, surprisingly, Mexican farmers, rather than United States farmers, have been displaced. In both the Canadian and Mexican cases, cost competitiveness was the issue. The lowest total cost producer won the lions share of the market.

---

8. Howell, Robert A and Stephen R Soucy, "Determining the Real Costs of Doing Business in a Global Market", *National Productivity Review* (Spring 1991) pp. 157-165.

Time-to-Market Competitiveness

One of the strategic disadvantages of the United States is its inability to react quickly to market changes. However, some Asian countries like Taiwan and Hong Kong have developed a strategic niche by being able to react quickly. For example, if you are trying to produce fad clothing items, or if you are trying to react to a sudden trend shift in the toy market, these Asian producers would be able to quickly adjust their production output to meet your needs. A similar shift in the productive output of a United States, European or Japanese plant could take months to make.

Manufacturing Processes

Improvements in the manufacturing processes have created mini-factories that are more efficient and less costly than their previous counterparts. These mini-factories are easily relocated overseas opening the doors for new market opportunities.

World-class global quality is Level "A" societally-oriented quality. And world-class productivity is value-added, waste-eliminated productivity. Productivity and quality strategies need to be integrated into a global strategy.

Information Processes

Tools like telecommunications, faxes, teleconferencing and computer networking have reduced or eliminated the distance barriers. These tools have become increasingly important to the financial and retailing industries.

Government Policy

Countries like Mexico and many of the previous communist countries have initiated enormous privatization programs. These programs offer opportunities for new markets and have become part of the globalization strategy of many companies.

Many countries like Malaysia, Singapore, Mexico and Ireland offer enormous incentive packages for companies interested in developing operations in their country. These packages often include reduced tax incentives and duty-free trade zones for the manufactured products.

Competitive Markets

Markets for your products exist all over the world. Globalization is often driven by the desire to enter these markets. Often, opening new markets also requires the globalization of the manufacturing process. For example, in Europe you need to have a production facility within the borders of the European Union (EU) in order to avoid certain tariffs and trade restrictions. Therefore, for companies who want to access the European markets, the European production facility becomes part of their marketing globalization strategy.

> ... the [international] service sector will become a major target of productivity improvements in the 1990s.
>
> Blumberg[9]

Technology Transfer

The exchange of technology between countries is often the primary basis for globalization. Japanese firms have, for a long time, transferred technology to Japan by establishing a facility in the United States and then staffing that facility with the best of America's workforce. The Japanese would then learn the technology and transfer it back home.

Ideally, however, the exchange of technology is not as one-sided as the Japanese example. World-class technology transfer is where the exchange is two-way, where the United States shares with Europe or Asia and they in turn share their insights. This strategy forces us into a discussion of perspectives. There are many different perspectives on when and what technology should be transferred. A few are outlined below.

US, Japan or Europe out to a developing country

The US perspective on why we should transfer to a developing country is because we are kind and generous. We want to help their economy grow, giving them jobs and a market for the products that are produced and in return, we are getting cheaper products.

Developing countries in from the US, Japan, or Europe

The developing country sees the US (or Japan or Europe) as an opportunist who is looking for cheap labor that can be utilized to operate outdated technologies. For example, Malaysia has a negative unemployment rate, they already have more jobs than people and they import people from other countries to cover the increasing demand.[10] Another example, Thailand, like many of these countries, has a positive trade balance. They wonder, if manufacturing is so good for the economy, why doesn't the United States keep its manufacturing and build up its own economy? These developing countries feel that the US and Japan are systematically trying to keep them twenty years behind

---

9. Blumberg, Donald F, "Improving Productivity in Service Operations on an International Basis", *National Productivity Review* (Spring 1991) pp. 167-179.
10.Plenert, Gerhard, "Technology Transfer – A Developing Country Perspective", *IAMOT Newsletter* (September 1994) pp. 5-6.

technologically. For example, when the US wants to transfer a plant to a developing country, it transfers old, inefficient technology in the hopes that the cheaper labor rates will turn the inefficient machinery into a positive financial gain. This twenty-year old technology is how the United States systematically holds the developing country level of technology down.

Japan is a little more open about keeping the developing country behind. When the Japanese transfer technology to a developing country, they bring in their own technocrats and never give the developing country any leading edge technology. For example, the Proton Saga is a Malaysian built car being produced in a plant that is the combined effort of Mitsubishi and the Malaysian government. However, rather than bringing in leading edge manufacturing technology, like that used in Japan, the Japanese set the plant up using outdated technological production methods, similar to that used in older United States plants. The Japanese didn't want the Proton Saga to become an international competitor.

A technology exchange is where both sides of the exchange benefit. We would assist the developing country in technological growth and they in turn would help the US develop new technologies. These types of exchanges are why so many companies are setting up technology development centers in many parts of the world. An interesting, although controversial, book discussing the developing country point of view is *Small is Beautiful*.[11]

Technology transfer is an important element of a globalization strategy and needs to be considered carefully in ways that every newspaper reporter is familiar with (see below).

Who to transfer to — some countries offer financial incentives and others offer a highly educated work force (Malaysia and Hong Kong).

What to transfer — some companies select to only transfer their support functions and not their core competencies. Others transfer in areas where they hope to learn from the country transferred to (Europe or Japan).

When (the timing or turn-around of the transfer) — some countries are quicker at technology implementation (for example Taiwan). On other occasions, the technology transfer may be timed to specific events, like market entries (Mexico and NAFTA).

Where — location of the transfer. Some countries offer strategic opportunities in their location (Singapore and shipping or Hong Kong and banking for example).

How — the transfer process. Does transferring require the movement of large amounts of equipment or personnel? Does the new location require large amounts of resources (heavy equipment or energy)?

---

11. Schumacher, E F, *Small is Beautiful: Economics as if People Mattered* (New York: Harper Perennial) 1989.

Why — does technology transfer make strategic sense? Is the transfer justified financially or logistically, for example.

A study was done looking at the transfer of bicycle technology within three classes of countries, the developed countries (DC — United States, Japan), newly industrialized economies (NIE — South Korea, Singapore) and less developed countries (LDC — Mexico, Indonesia). A comparison was made based on several criteria, including cost. The results are that NIEs are the most cost competitive countries for bicycle manufacturing. The introduction to state-of-the-art technology results in detrimental consequences for LDCs and the complex, machine technology introduced should be more mass production, rather than hi-tech oriented. The large production gains occurred in each category of country after the introduction of advanced technology processes like the quality control process or the introduction of flexible production methodologies. None of these findings are surprising, but this study quantifies these results with supportive data.[12]

Competitive Lessons We Can Learn

After World War II, Japan and Germany both went through all three stages of development, from LDC to NIE to DC. If we learn no other lesson, we should at least learn about the competitive characteristics of enthusiasm, drive and commitment shown by these countries.

> One of the greatest pains to human nature is the pain of a new idea.
>
> Walter Bagehot,
> English economist

One of the primary tools used for analyzing the growth of nations and, additionally, of the development of industries within these nations, is benchmarking. Benchmarking is an analysis of national, industrial or corporate numbers to see how the different industries compare. The primary basis for comparison is financial and operational numbers, although these don't always tell a complete story. For example, the innovative potential of your employees is hard to quantify. The American Productivity and Quality Center (APQC) and the International Productivity Service (IPS) both have data collection services that can be utilized to help you compare yourself to the rest of the world (addresses for both are listed in Appendix 12.2). Additional in-country services are available, like the Canadian interfirm comparisons or the United States Standard Industrial Classification (SIC) classified financial statistics.[13]

---

12. Suri, Rajan, Sanders Jerry L, Rao P Chandrasekhar and Ashoka Mody, "Impact of Manufacturing Practices on the Global Bicycle Industry", *Manufacturing Review* (March 1993) pp. 14-24.
13. The Canadian statistics can be received from the Industry, Science and Technology

A focused program in Canada called the Interfirm Comparison Program is sponsored by the Industry, Science and Technology Canada Organization (see Appendix 9.2). This program focuses on benchmarking for Canadian firms. Similar programs exist in many other countries.

Harley-Davidson was in serious trouble in the early 1980s. In fact, it wasn't expected to survive. This last surviving United States motorcycle manufac-turer was being devastated by the Japanese with a market share loss of from 75 per cent in 1973 to less than 25 per cent. But Harley has recovered and has come back to control 50 per cent of the market share. Here is an example where a banker (Citicorp) badly misjudged a company's potential by looking only at the numbers. What happened? It's simple. Harley learned from the competition and it learned its lessons well.

In the early 1980s Harley quality was awful and manufacturing was a mess. It thought it could rely on a dedicated and committed customer forever, but it was wrong. Managers bought the company and made a dramatic turna-round. They told their own story in the book *Well-Made in America*.[14]

> We were being wiped out by the Japanese because they were better managers. It wasn't robotics, or culture, or morning calisthenics and company songs — it was professional managers who understood their business and paid attention to detail,
>
> Vaughn Beals,
> Harley-Davidson

Harley-Davidson used world class management tools like empowerment and globalization to make a difference in sales, profits and return on equity. But the numbers that eventually made Citicorp happy only came after Harley understood and beat the competition.

One of the lessons that we learn from globalization is that most countries have moved away from the concept that there is one, perfect right answer to all problems. The "one right answer" way of thinking seems to be characteristic of Christian cultures. In the Middle East and Asia, there is the realization that "one right answer" does not exist, rather, alternatives exist. Two plants running side-by-side producing the same product may have different "right" answers to the same problem. This may occur because one has an authoritarian management style and the other has a participative management style.

Canada (see appendix 9.2). The United States classifies all their industries by a Standard Industrial Classification (SIC) code. This coding scheme exists internationally, unfortunately, there are major discrepancies internationally as to what categories of products are allowed into each classification. Tables for the United States are available which show the average financial data for small, medium, and large firms within each SIC classification. One such table is *Industrial Norms and Key Business Ratios* put out by Dun and Bradstreet Information Services.

14. Reid, Peter C, *Well-Made in America* (McGraw-Hill) 1990.

In the United States and Europe, the search for the "one right answer" causes us to have an all-or-nothing attitude to changes. For example, in our attempt to copy Japan, we went through a series of all-or-nothing right answers. About ten years ago quality circles were the fad. Everyone thought that by implementing quality control (QC) circles they would have the perfect answer to competing with the Japanese. When this didn't provide the desired results within two years, it was thrown out and statistical process control (SPC) was deemed the perfect solution. Again, after two years, this was thrown out and the next fad was introduced. We went through in-line quality control (ILQC), just-in-time production (JIT), total quality management (TQM) and many more such fads, trying, implementing, short-term testing and then rejecting the technique. But in our search for this perfect answer, the search for the trick of the Japanese, we never asked the Japanese what their secret was. The Japanese would have eagerly told us that their secret is none of the above. Rather, it is all of the above. It is the integration of all of these processes over a long period of time (20-30 years) that brings about the desired results. But we in the United States still go on looking for the one perfect, two-year answer to our differences.

Many developing countries have learned the building-block approach to improvements. They have given up on the idea of a quick fix and are looking at alternatives for improvements, implementing the change, saving and incorporating the elements that work, integrating them into the process and then finally moving on to another idea for change. Tools like SPC or QC or JIT are not tested and rejected — the good elements of each are accepted and integrated into the process. They have the approach that all of these tools are building in a long-term, planned-out solution, not a quick-fix solution.

Developing countries have also learned another lesson from change implementation which is that changes don't work unless we follow them through to completion. A change is not fully implemented until it achieves Stage E of the implementation process (see Figure 9.2). Stage E may be two months, two years, or 20 years, but you don't reject the change process the way Florida Power and Light did just because your two years are up and you're still in Stage C, or sometimes even D.

This is a lesson all world-class eManagers need to integrate into their way of thinking — change processes need to be followed through to completion and each change needs to be thought of as a building block toward some larger goal, not as the total solution in and of itself.

Globalization has taught us another lesson:

As long as you're playing catch-up, the best you can ever do is get caught up. And that's just not good enough.[15]

---

15. That is the major message of my book *International Management and Production: Survival Techniques for Corporate America,* cited earlier.

Figure 9.2: Change Function

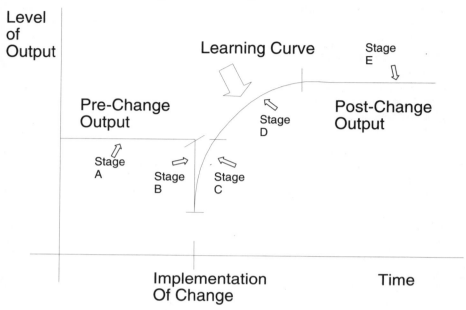

As long as we're playing copycat, we won't get ahead. Copycatting only has value if you're way behind or just beginning. But if you're head-to-head with your competition, you need to innovate ahead of the competition. This innovation can take many forms, for example:

- product innovation
- process innovation (what the Japanese are good at)
- technology innovation
- time-to-market innovation (Taiwan)
- marketing innovation.

It is innovation that makes you competitive, not copying. And part of the lesson that the global competitors have learned is that it is often the unique, surprise innovation that will capture the customer's eye.

The reason for continual change is so we are always adding value to the output we generate. Time erodes value-added through competition. However, change, such as innovation, increases value-added. We can not stay in business and sell our product at cost. It is the value-added portion of what we produce that allows us to cover our mistakes, breakdowns and surprises. The more value-added content we have, the more profit we have. Similarly, I could relay almost the same message to you if I said that the reason for continual change is to eliminate waste in the process. Waste elimination adds value.

We have an unlimited number of lessons that we can learn from globalization. I have highlighted a few that I have found to be important. I hope you incorporate these in your drive to become a world-class eManager.

> When asked what he thought of Western civilization, Mahatma Gandhi replied, "I think it would be a good idea".

THE GLOBAL-CULTURAL DIFFERENCE

We often use "culture" as the excuse for our lack of a competitive stance. We say that "culture" is the reason that the Japanese are better at teaming, or that "culture" is the reason the Chinese are the business entrepreneurs of Asia. We say that "culture" explains a difference in the work ethic of one country when compared to another. Unfortunately, most of these "cultural" excuses are nothing more than that — excuses. The key to cultural differences and taking advantage of these differences is in understanding them. I will discuss some of them now, so that you will have a better understanding of why business transactions and ethical systems work differently.

The biggest key to cultural differentiation is religion. In my statements about these religions I am not saying that this is the correct interpretation of a religious philosophy. Rather, I am saying that a business attitude and culture can be seen as developing around a particular aspect of the religion.

The religious basis of the United States, Canada, most of Europe, Australia, South Africa and a few more countries including many of the eastern block (former Soviet Union countries like Russia) tends to be right wing Christianity. Right wing Christianity is characterized by Jesus Christ and claims of the one true religion, the one right answer and the one God. But this God is a God that we use as a tool to help us get what we want. In this environment, it is the individual and individual rights that are most important.

The religious basis for most Latin American countries, Spain, Portugal and Italy, is left wing Christianity. This is characterized by Jehovah of the Old Testament and the one God who is more of a condemning God that will squash you if you don't stay on track. In this culture it is the family unit that tends to be the most influential.

The Middle East, North Africa, Indonesia, Malaysia and a few other countries are predominately Muslim. The Muslim God is a God of fear. Strict rules must be complied with. Allah wants us to fight for what is right, often to the obliteration of all else that is considered to be wrong. In this culture it is the religion that is the most important and an attack on religious doctrine is suicide.

The Jewish God Jehovah is also a God of fear. He is quick to destroy the evil doers. However, in the end, He will forgive all. What you find is a strategy of "don't do onto others what you don't want them to do onto you." This is also characterized as, "it is easier to get forgiven than to get permission." This makes them aggressive and adventurous risk takers.

In the Far East, like Thailand and surrounding areas, we find Buddhism. Here we tend to find a compromising, second chance attitude to life where if you mess up the first time and don't achieve Nirvana, you'll come back to earth and get a second chance. The little stresses of day-to-day life don't matter much in the big picture of the eternities. What matters most is the larger (family or societal) unit.

In China we find Communism tainted with Buddhism and Taoism. What's important is the success of the societal unit and an individual who is not contributing to society is a disgrace.

In India and surrounding regions the dominant religion is Hinduism. Hinduism is a world of many gods and finds acceptance and good in all gods. This culture is characterized by tolerance and compromise. The most important unit is the clan or cast (extended family).

Looking at these religious differences we see a few things immediately. One is that the individual dominates in importance only in right wing Christianity. This tells us that an individual-rights oriented ethical system is not universal. There are even extreme cases where the religion requires that if an individual is an embarrassment to the larger unit by not being an active participant and adding value to the unit, the individual should be removed (cast out).

Considering the religious influence, we also notice that some cultures focus on compromise as opposed to a fight-for-what-is-right attitude. For example, there is a piece of land on the border between Malaysia and Thailand that was the subject of a dispute for the two countries. Then oil was found in this region. The American way would be to punch it out over this piece of land. The Asia way was to draw a line around the region and set up a separate entity to manage the region and the oil. Both countries then shared in the profit.

Often, in societal oriented cultures, it is the relationship that is the focus of business transactions. The trust between individuals is more important than the transaction. The *word* is more important than the *paper* (contract). In the United States we have developed such elaborate non-trust systems (accounting, finance, auditing, personal, information, legal, etc.) that the cost of these non-trust systems is often higher than if we were to get rid of them all and suffer the occasional fraud. The US way to handle business transactions is to not let anyone get away with anything. We protect ourselves by developing elaborate documents.

As stated, in societal cultures, the word is more powerful than the paper. This is true even in court. It is not the contract, but rather, it is the "understanding" that influences court decisions. Additionally, no matter how complete you think your contract is, if you are not willing to demonstrate your trustworthiness by spending time with whomever it is you are trying to do business with, then you're simply not going to get the business.

I don't intend this discussion of cultural differences to be anything close to complete. I only expect it to be enlightening and to open your eyes to the diversity that exists. Cultures vary dramatically between countries and between regions within a country (for example compare the United States South-East bible belt with the left-over hippies of the Pacific North-West). A more complete study of the localized culture of the specific country is important in order for you to be an effective world-class player.

DEFINING A GLOBALIZATION STRATEGY

A globalization strategy is an element of the corporate or business strategy that focuses on internationalization. As discussed at the beginning of this chapter, internationalization can take many forms. In one study of internationalization practices it was found that nearly all the globalized companies required major organizational changes, primarily in decentralizing. Ninety-four per cent of the globalized companies strongly agreed that competition is heating up globally and the pace of innovation has quickened. Some additional points of the study included:[16]

- half of the companies felt that exports are the best globalization strategy and the other half felt that investment was the best strategy

- about three-quarters of the companies felt that globalization is best accomplished using joint ventures

- the relationships with customers and suppliers had to change dramatically to where they were working much more closely with each

- 85 per cent of the surveyed companies felt that empowerment is not a buzzword and should be used for decision making.

A second study stresses that the competitive advantage of a company determines the value-added in the global market place. The existence of both determines a successful globalization strategy.[17]

In yet a third study, successful global (referred to as transnational) companies require the integration of efficiency, customer responsiveness and the

16. Chilton, Kenneth, "Changing Structures and Strategies: Survey of American Manufacturing Executives", *Center for the Study of American Business, Washington University, St. Louis, Missouri* (September 1993) Working Paper 151.
17. Kogut, Bruce, "Designing Global Strategies: Comparative and Competitive Value-Added Chains", *Sloan Management Review* (Summer 1995) pp. 15-28.

ability to exploit learning (employee training and innovation) in order to be successful.[18]

Having considered these elements of a globalization strategy, we also need to recognize some risks. The biggest risk is of pushing too much toward one of the extreme ends of the integration-diversification spectrum. Too much diversification will cause segmentation. These types of organizations tend to have unique foreign and domestic branches, each with their own objectives and value system. The other extreme is equally as bad. This is where the global and domestic arms of the company are so integrated that effective localization is lost. These types of organizations treat, and expect, everyone to act the same. A happy balance between these extremes is needed, where globalization is part of the vision, mission and strategy of the corporation, while, at the same time, the localization aspects where we work closely with the country and the culture are not lost.

ELEMENTS OF A GLOBALIZATION STRATEGY

This is not an attempt to dictate what is required in a globalization strategy. Rather, this is a list of suggestions of elements that should be included, such as:

- ethical considerations
- international trade theory
- international financial transactions
- political and legal environments
- types of international relationships
- modification of goals
- relocation decisions.

Ethical Considerations

Ethics are discussed in Chapter 14. However, in a globalization strategy it is important to recognize that cultural differences translate into ethical differences. For example, we often encounter the age-old debate of why a tip is considered ethical and a bribe unethical in American culture, whereas this conflict does not exist in other cultures.

In a globalization strategy, other issues also come into play, such as, is it ethical to relocate a plant to India so that we don't have to be concerned about health risks to the employees? Or is it ethical to move a plant to Latin America

---

18. Bartlett, Christopher A and Sumantra Ghoshal, "Managing Across Borders: New Strategic Requirements", *Sloan Management Review* (Summer 1987) pp. 7-17.

so that we don't have stringent pollution regulations? Are employee safety and pollution cost reductions considered legitimate cost savings for plant relocations?

Another ethical dilemma is that of nationalism. At home, off-shore plant relocations cost American jobs but save the American consumer money. Overseas, nationalism may mean that the relocated plants build schools, roads or other infrastructure items in order to support the community and thereby become an integral and accepted part of the society.

> When in Rome, do as the Romans do.
>
> St Ambrose

Determining what is ethical is a judgmental evaluation based on background and experience. However, we must adhere to some ethical legal basis for our activities. What I'm stressing is not that we should disregard our ethics, but we should recognize that we don't have the one right ethical system any more than we have the one right way to run a factory.[19]

International Trade Theory

International trade theory stresses the law of comparative advantage. This law basically states that if I'm better at growing apples (if I can grow them cheaper) than you and you're better at building boxes than I am, then we should each do what we are comparatively better at and trade. In the end we will each end up with the desired number of boxes and apples, but the total cost of boxes and apples for each of us will be cheaper than if we each grew our own apples and built our own boxes. The principle of comparative advantage supports the benefits of job specialization and economic efficiency.

International Financial Transactions

There are numerous forms of international financial transactions that need consideration for the globalizing enterprise. For example, what form of investment is best? The forms of foreign investment that are preferred differ dramatically from one country to the next. Within each country there is a United States embassy and within each embassy there is a foreign commercial officer. The purpose of this officer is to help United States investors determine the best form of foreign investment for them. Investment may include the direct investment of capital in resources like plants or equipment, it may mean

---

19. A detailed discussion of international ethical dilemmas can be found in the Daniels and Radebaugh book referenced in this chapter. The book also contains a detailed discussion of trade theory and world financial transactions.

the development of partnerships or it could include the establishment of strategic alliances. The foreign commercial officer can also help you come into contact with existing businesses that have already suffered the foreign investment experience. For example, in Malaysia the foreign commercial officer arranges monthly breakfasts where foreign visitors can meet with many of the leaders of American businesses in Malaysia and discuss their experience with them. You can't get any better information than to get it directly from those who have gone through the experience already.

Another critical element of the foreign financial transaction is the foreign exchanges process. This is a lot like playing the stock market. Foreign currencies are a lot more sporadic in their activities than the US dollar. Exchanging dollars for Mexican pesos, or Malaysian ringgits, or any other currency, can create a boom or a bust. Timing the investment correctly, like timing in the stock market, is the key to success or disaster. Because of this, many companies require all transactions to be made in US dollars, thereby assuring themselves some level of protection.

Currency exchanges become especially risky in countries where the inflation rate is enormous, like many Latin American countries, or where the government is unstable. For example, in one day the Turkish lira took a 28 per cent plunge in value.[20] However, investment in the currencies of aggressively growing countries, like South East Asia, can generate substantial profits beyond what the United States investment would have returned. Currency exchange transactions need to be managed carefully unlike in one recent, unnamed, developing country that nearly lost their entire treasury because of a poor currency investment decision.

Political and Legal Environments

The political and legal environments play a large role in strategic globalization. The stability of the government may discourage commitment. For example, China's lack of consistent policy has made some companies gun shy. Other countries have been known to nationalize (take over) the companies. However, countries like Mexico and many of the eastern block countries are privatizing (eliminating the government control of) many of their industries, which opens opportunities for foreign investment.

As discussed earlier, the legal environments in many countries focus on trust, not on contracts. Having it "in writing" may be important for the United States, but the "understanding" is more important in many other countries.

The government also gets involved in control issues like regulations, taxes and tariffs. In some countries, Brazil for example, it is extremely difficult to bring product in and profits out. Other countries are extremely open having tariff and tax free zones for export production, such as Singapore.

---

20. Landau, Nilly, "Managing Exotil Risks", *International Business* (May 1994) pp. 62-66.

Some countries require partnerships. For example, Mexican coastal properties can only be owned by Mexicans. Therefore, a partnership needs to be arranged with a Mexican national if you want to build a coastal resort. Trading partnerships are springing up all over. The initial trading partnership was the European Economic Community (now the European union, or EU) where the European nations banded together to eliminate barriers to the flow of goods across national borders within Europe. The North America Free Trade Agreement (NAFTA) is a trading partnership between the United States, Canada and Mexico. NAFTA has so far proved to be a real boom for American industries. Industries, like agriculture, that the United States was expecting to lose turned out to be gainers. Other trading partnerships are also springing up in South-East Asia, Africa and Latin America. The advantage of the partnership is that, for example, if you want to trade within Europe, you only need to establish a relationship with one country, in order to be able to trade with them all. The disadvantage of the partnerships is that they each have their own political agenda, such as ISO 9000 certification in Europe, and this has to be worked with.

Unfortunately, whenever a trading partnership is formed and two countries agree to trade more with each other, they are also, by default, saying they are going to trade less with other countries. Some alliances even set up barriers to trading with countries outside the partnership. For example, the EU established the ISO 9000 quality certification program, requiring that anyone who wants to trade within the EU must be certified. This blocks many countries from trading in Europe. Economically, however, any time a trading barrier is dropped through a partnership, it is ultimately the consumer that benefits from cheaper products.

The world's major trade liberalization program is the General Agreement on Tariffs and Trade (GATT), which has 117 member nations. GATT has generated a basic set of rules for trade negotiations and offers a mechanism for ensuring that the rules are implemented. The most recent round of negotiations, the Uruguay Round, which lasted eight years (ending in 1993), agreed on provisions that took effect in mid-1995. The GATT process has equalized trade between nations and has significantly reduced the average tariffs of industrialized countries (from about 40 per cent in 1947 to around 5 per cent currently). The results of these negotiations have been to significantly reduce the costs of consumer goods, and to offer open and freer trading for developing countries, which is vital for their economic growth.

Types of International Relationships

There are many different forms of international partnerships that have developed, such as company buy outs or joint ventures. The one partnership arrangement that is being given the most attention recently is the formation of strategic alliances. A strategic alliance is where an enterprise focuses on their core competencies and then orients their business strategy around that core competency. There are many examples of recently established strategic alliances. For example, FedEx is utilizing its logistics capability to act as the inventory and distribution agent for other enterprises whose core competency is manufacturing. It has established a Business Logistics Services division, which forms a unique alliance with companies like Laura Ashley to restructure and manage its distributions systems. FedEx is the master of logistics, and Laura Ashley was the master at producing products with English charm. Neither could do the other function well. The strategic alliance formed between the two gave each the best of both worlds. As a result, Laura Ashley can resupply its 540 shops anywhere within the world within 24 to 48 hours.

FedEx provides similar services for National Semiconductor Corporation, who wanted to stay within its core competency of building semiconductors. FedEx also provides its logistics services for the House of Windsor. FedEx provides the logistics services that offer time-definite delivery within two working days and additionally they provide inventory tracking and control, which includes pulling, packing, shipping and monitoring the inventory movement process.

Another example of a strategic alliance is Solectron, a Malcolm Baldridge Award winner, which is one of the world's premier electronics companies. It has shunned advertising, minimized product research and development, and focused entirely on manufacturing and customer service. And because Solectron is so good at it, it is getting more business than it can handle and being choosy about who it will accept.[21]

Strategic alliances mean sharing control of some aspects of the company. This is difficult for some managers to accept. However, backing off of the things you're not good at and doing even better at the things you are good at is the focus of the strategic alliance gamble. And most companies that have attempted these alliances have found them to be successful. For example, the FedEx strategic alliances are a critical element of customer service and satisfaction for the companies FedEx supports.

Company buy outs or joint ventures involve the enterprise in new areas that are often not part of their core competency. This may be a good strategy for control, but it is often not as effective toward profitability as the strategic alliances where the enterprise focuses on its core competency. Unfortunately, these alliances don't work on the basis of ownership or control, they work only on the basis of partnership, effort and commitment.

> To compete in the global arena, you have to incur — and defray — immense fixed costs. You need partners. . . With enough time, money,

---

21. Savona, Dave, "The Invisible Partner", *International Business* (November 1994) pp. 64-68.

and luck, you can do everything yourself. But who has enough? . . . Having control does not necessarily mean better management.

Kenichi Ohmae[22]

Collaboration is the best form of education. By working in strategic alliances you benefit financially, learn strategically, and you save a lot of time and money doing it.

It's not devious to absorb skills from your partner — that's the whole idea.

Hamel, Doz and Prahalad[23]

Modification of Goals and Value System

When globalizing, we need to rethink our goals. The vision, mission and strategy of the enterprise needs to reflect the focus on globalization. Our core competencies and core processes need to be evaluated in light of the new globalized agenda.

Centralization with Diversification

The vision, mission and corporate strategy need to be centralized but the business strategy needs to be diversified (localized). The localization process needs to be done carefully, considering local attitudes and cultures, or the investment will be a failure. For example, in the case of plant relocations, the approach for justifying the plant relocation can make the difference between success and failure. Most relocations are still done on a labor-cost approach, forgetting issues such as increased inventory carrying costs or relocation overhead costs. Much better approaches exist, like the total-cost approach, the value-added approach or the critical resource approach. In the total-cost approach, all costs of relocation are considered, including overhead or burden costs. In the value-added approach, the products selected for relocation are those that contribute the least to overall corporate profitability. The high value-added products are kept at home so that the home company and country can maximize the profitability of the products. In the critical resource approach, the resource that is the most critical in adding value to the product is evaluated

---

22. Ohmae, Kenichi, "The Global Logic of Strategic Alliances", *Harvard Business Review* (March-April 1989) pp. 143-154.
23. Hamel, Gary, Doz, Yves L and Prahalad, C K, "Collaborate with Your Competitors — and Win", *Harvard Business Review* (January-February 1989) pp. 133-139.

to see if the relocation will reduce the costs of this critical element. If so, then relocation is considered desirable.[24]

The balance between centralization of goals and diversification of control is critical. All business units need to be focused on the same targets, but not all will achieve that target using the same types of bows and arrows.

Developing the Strategy

Several excellent sources exist that specifically assist in the development of a globalization strategy. These should be used if you feel the need for more detailed information than I have presented you with. Yip's article is specifically written to "globalize an individual firm's corporate strategy".[25] The Daniels and Radebaugh book listed in this chapter offers a detailed explanation of global strategy development.

> Ninety per cent of the politicians give the other ten per cent a bad reputation.
>
> Henry Kissinger

CHARACTERISTICS OF A WORLD-CLASS GLOBAL MANAGER

The world-class global manager incorporates all the strengths discussed in this chapter. They include:

1. the *big picture* perspective

2. globalizing the vision, mission and corporate strategy

3. utilizing international transactions to add value and minimize waste

4. understanding global markets and competitors

5. centralizing with a localized perspective

6. global corporations

7. understanding cultural, political, demographic and business climate differences and their effects on the business transaction

8. understanding when globalization is good, and when it isn't

---

24. Plenert, Gerhard, "Plant Relocation: How Decisions Are Made Today", *Industry Forum* (March 1994) pp. 1-3; Plenert, Gerhard, "Technology Transfer — A Developing Country Perspective", *IAMOT Newsletter* (September 1994) pp. 5-6.
25. Yip, George S, "Global Strategy . . . In a World of Nations?", *Sloan Management Review* (Fall 1989) pp. 29-41.

9. understanding the differences in perspective

10. understanding technology transfer

11. utilizing comparative tools such as benchmarking

12. moving from a copycat to an innovation mentality

13. learning from the enemy (competitors)

14. utilizing strategic alliances

15. utilizing step-by-step building blocks towards improvements

16. supporting free trade and avoiding protectionism.

The *Harvard Business Review* has conducted a number of surveys on the characteristics of a world-class global manager. The one common characteristic that they have learned is that "change is indeed everywhere — regardless of country, culture, or corporation". They also learned that culture, more than geography, is the major determinant of a manager's views. These studies are ongoing and strengthen many of the points made in this chapter.[26]

> Were it not for imagination, Sir, a man would be as happy in the arms of a chambermaid, as of a duchess.
>
> Samuel Johnson,
> English lexicographer, essayist and poet

SOURCES FOR ADDITIONAL INFORMATION

For a general information publication on what's going on in the world, I would recommend the *Christian Science Monitor*. For a business look at the world I would recommend the magazine *International Business* which includes articles focused on the events within specific countries or regions, as well as summary information like the Dave Savona article about trade and trade changes (for example, in August 1994 there was information about US trade and the import increase rankings of countries featuring China, the September issue featured the Caribbean and in November, India's growth was discussed and country imports were ranked).[27] There is also a useful *Worldwide Business Practices Report* put out by International Cultural Enterprises in Deerfield, IL.

---

26. Kanter, Rosabeth Moss, "Transcending Business Boundaries: 12,000 World Managers View Change", *Harvard Business Review* (May-June 1991) pp. 151-164; "The Boundaries of Business: Commentaries from the Experts", *Harvard Business Review* (July-August 1991) pp. 127-140.
27. Savona, Dave, "World Commerce", *International Business* (August 1994) p. 42; (September 1994) p. 38; (November 1994) p. 18.

The productivity and quality organizations listed in Appendix 12.3 can open the door to courses, consultants and certification programs if desired. I have included a few more North American regional organizations in Appendix 9.2. Organizations like these also offer excellent conferences and conference proceedings. There are hundreds of helpful conference articles available, for example, the Albin article presented at an APICS conference comments on *Fortune Magazine's* global competitors and discusses ten successful global strategies. Or the Peters article describes the business strategy for the rapidly developing Asia-Pacific nations.[28] The Academy of International Business (AIB) is also an excellent source for international business conferences and proceedings.

There are also a few books worth mentioning which include *International Business — Environments and Operations, International Management and Production: Survival Techniques for Corporate America* and *Global Operations Perspectives.*[29]

What luck for rulers that men do not think.

Adolf Hitler

SUMMARY

A bus driver and a minister died at the same time and they both met Peter at the pearly gates of heaven. Peter interviewed each of them, then he sent the bus driver to the highest place in the heavens and the minister to the lowest. The minister protested and asked "I dedicated my whole life to spreading the word of God. Why does a bus driver get the high place and I get such a low place?"

Peter answered "When you preached, everyone slept. But when the bus driver drove his bus, everyone prayed."

I'm a little worried that I might be like the preacher when it comes to globalization. Rather, I would prefer this chapter (and the entire book) to effect you like the bus driver. I want you to feel like you are on a whirlwind tour bus ride that motivates you to pray for a rebirth. I want you to be reborn into a world-class management realization that without a globalization strategy, your enterprise will have difficulty achieving and maintaining a competitive stance.

---

28. Peters, Andru M, "The Pacific Rim Nations' Business Strategy for the Next Ten Years", *APICS 37th International Conference Proceedings*, op. cit., pp. 226-231; Albin, John T, "Competing in a Global Market", *APICS 37th International Conference Proceedings*, op. cit., pp. 244-248.

29. *International Management and Production* and *International Business - Environments and Operations* have already been listed. The third book is Sheth, Jagdish, and Golpira Eshghi, *Global Operations Perspectives* (Cincinnati, Ohio: South-Western Publishing Co.) 1989.

SUGGESTIONS FOR FURTHER READING

The references throughout this chapter will have given you a wealth of information on this subject. As well as the publications listed below, you might like to see three articles of mine:

"Production Considerations for Developing Countries", *International Journal of Management* (December 1988) pp. 358-364.

"Productivity in a Developing Country Factory", *APICS 37th International Conference Proceedings* (November 1994) pp. 712-715.

"The Development of a Production System in Mexico", *Interfaces* (May-June 1990) Vol. 20, No. 3., pp. 14-23.

You might also be interested in an article by Jan Stoddard and Ramona Memmott "Going Global by Working Together", *APICS 37th International Conference Proceedings*, pp. 709-711.

APPENDIX 9.1: NINE DOTS SOLUTION

The solution to Figure 9.1 is easy once you see the strategy. We tend to limit the scope of our vision, and that seems to be the common problem with the solution to Figure 9.1. Looking at Figure 9.3 we see how, by looking beyond our own little, isolated world of the nine dots, and extending the lines beyond this region, we can easily connect the dots in four continuous lines by drawing them in the sequence A-B-C-A-D.

Figure 9.3: Nine Dots Solution

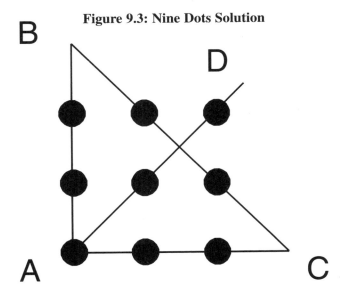

APPENDIX 9.2: NORTH AMERICA REGIONAL QUALITY AND PRODUCTIVITY ORGANIZATIONS

For Canada contact:

Interfirm Comparison Program
Industry, Science and Technology Canada (ISTC)
Ottawa, Ontario K1A 0H5
Canada
(613) 954-4971

or:

Productivity Improvement Service
Services to Business Branch
Industry, Science and Technology Canada (ISTC)
235 Queen Street
Ottawa, Ontario K1A 0H5
Canada
(613) 954-4969

For Mexico contact:

Fundacion Mexicana Para La Calidad Total, A. C.
FUNDAMECA
Loma Bonita #24 Col. Lomas Altas
Mexico, DFCP 11950
525/570-3989 & 525/570-7483

For Central America contact:

Instituto Centroamericano de Investigacion y Tecnologia Industrial
(ICAITI)
Programa de Gestion de Calidad y Productividad (PGCP)
Ave. La Reforma 4-47, Zona 10
Gautemala 01010
Central America
502/2 31 06 31

Chapter Ten

A Technology Management Strategy

The guts to attack yourself mercilessly is what counts.

Tom Peters

The computer is an utter and complete failure! Or is it? If the development of a piece of technology does not achieve its initial goal, is it a failure? Often, the initial development of a piece of technology does not turn out to be its primary area of usefulness. For example, NASA technology centers developed hundreds of medical advances like the incubators, fire retardant materials like fire suits, and optical materials like night vision, which have little to do with the initial reason for the development of the technology. The initial reason for the development of the computer was to predict the weather. And we all know how accurate weather prediction has become since the introduction of the computer. So is the computer a failure? You be the judge.

Technology development has always been a strong point in the United States. The US government, through its technology development centers, develops more technology than any other organization in the world. Unfortunately, the development of all this technology has little gain if it can't be turned into consumer products. For example, the US was the developer of the air bag, but the Japanese and the Germans had it installed in their cars first.

Technology developed by the US is, by law, available to everyone and anyone who wants to make copies of it. There is an enormous library of this technology in Washington, D.C. where anyone can go to learn about developed technology. There are employees of the US federal government that work for this library and whose function it is to assist anyone interested in finding the desired technology. Unfortunately, the biggest users of this library are foreign businesses and foreign governments, not US business or US state and local governments. The US government develops the technology, but US business never gets around to applying its share of the technology. We can't seem to get it out to the market in time to be competitive.

In today's new business order, the spoils of corporate warfare belong not to the biggest companies, but to the quickest — those firms that consistently speed quality products or services to the marketplace and respond instantly to their customers' needs.

Philip R Thomas

Technology is improvement and leading-edge technology requires change. When considering the operation of a world-class enterprise, technology improvement, and its rapid implementation, is continuously required in all areas. World-class management is continuous change through innovative technological improvement.

There are several areas of technological competitiveness. Few countries are competitive in all these areas. They are pure research technology, time-to-market technology, product technology, process technology, technology transfer, facilities and equipment technology, systems and procedures technology, information technology and services, and customer support technology.

Pure Research Technology

This is the primary area of United States technological leadership. The US technology data banks develop so much technology that it would take more resources than we have available to develop it all. However, US industries tend to avoid this technology because they cannot maintain proprietary rights. Anyone can copy it, especially international competitors who don't honor our patent laws. However, in the high-speed competitive world that we live in today, self-development of technology takes too long. We should let the experts at technology development create the technology for us, as they are so willing to do (similar to strategic alliances). This would generate faster technology implementation, which is one of the keys to world-class competitiveness.

There is a network organization that links to all the federal technology centers. This network organization, the Federal Laboratory Consortium for Technology Transfer (FLC), exists solely to assist business in finding already developed technology that can be applied to satisfy their needs. They publish a free newsletter called *News Link* that updates technology users on available resources. They receive funding from each of the technology labs and matching grants from the White House. Some of the technology available includes:

- fiber optic connector advances
- vaccine improvements
- electromagnetic analysis tools
- airborne mapping systems for agriculture
- integrated circuit technology
- improved lasers for manufacturing
- solid oxide fuel cells to power electric cars
- computer security systems.

NASA is one example of the many technology labs. NASA has a library of 3,000 patents available for licensing by businesses and individuals. These include aerodynamics, chemicals, electronics, optics, medical research, test and measurement equipment, sensors, computer software, materials, mechanics, mathematics, life sciences, fabrication technology, machinery, manufacturing and physical sciences. They publish a free monthly summary of a small part of the technology that is developed and available for private industry called *NASA Tech Briefs*. This magazine contains a list of NASA technology transfer services (including contact names, addresses and phone numbers). They have technology transfer centers all over the country. Some recent examples of the hundreds of thousands of NASA technological developments include:

- *COSMIC* — a NASA library of thousands of computer software applications like CARES which is used by Mitsubishi Motors to predict the probability of failure for a rotating ceramic turbine rotor
- medical advances such as a cool suit for MS patients that improves vision and reduces fatigue
- robotics so dexterous that they can play the piano
- icing buildup sensors for aircraft.

Appendix 10.1 contains contact information for the FLC, NASA and other technology organizations.

Time-to-Market Technology

As already mentioned, time-to-market technology is the primary area of weakness for the United States and it is the primary strength of many Asian countries. In today's competitive world-class environment — *timing is everything.*

The development of technology is only one small step for mankind. The second step is to find commercial applications for the technology. The third step is to engineer the technology into a consumer product and the fourth step is to manufacturing engineer the product so that it is rapidly, flexibly and low cost producible. Then we have to produce the product and get it out to the customer. Delays in any of these steps will destroy your competitiveness. All areas need innoveering (innovative engineering — see Chapter 4). Volumes have been written about the importance of an innoveered time-to-market effort for US industry and I can't attempt to reproduce it all here. However, when it takes the US manufacturers three to four months to build a bicycle, the same bicycle that can be produced in a couple hours in a Asian plant, we can envision the magnitude of the problem. Other examples of the time differences include the automotive fender-forming machine that is used in the US, Sweden and Japan. The setup time for this machine in the US is six hours, for Sweden it's five hours, for Japan it's twelve minutes. Or how about the new product introduction time of four to five years in the US and less than a year in most Asian countries (a couple months for Taiwan). The United States has a long way to go. But we can do it, and there are many examples to prove it. For example, Motorola reduced its invoice processing from 3.6 days to 30 minutes.

World-class enterprises realize that long-term strategies and short-term technology implementations and operations are the competitive advantage for the next decade. The opposite, short-term strategies and long-term technology, is currently an ingrained part of the United States' method of operation. The most difficult part of this shift is a change in attitudes and culture.[1] For example, IBM, with its development of the IBM Proprinter, was being hammered by its Japanese competitors and recognized that it had to find another way of doing things. It redesigned, with a "fast to market" philosophy. This included changes like a *design for automated assembly* (DFAA) philosophy, which included a new set of rules (like their "no-fasteners" rule), needed in order to satisfy robotics limitations. It incorporated concurrent development, knocking eighteen months off the product development time, and adjusted the testing process so that it starts sooner and ends sooner. The bid and quote purchasing practices of tooling were suspended because they delayed tooling availability. And the changes went on and on effecting all areas of technology deployment. In the end, the Proprinter cut 40 per cent off normal development time.[2] We can do it! Remember:

> Be bold and courageous. When you look back on your life or the life of your company, you'll regret the things you didn't do more than the ones you did.

Product Technology

Product technology ideas originate from several sources. For example, the customer may have defined a need that we will try to develop. Or the vendor may have determined an improvement to the products we produce. Employees are also an excellent source for product innovations, if we would just ask them for their ideas. And sometimes product ideas come from pure research technology ideas that are just begging for consumer application. Whatever the source of the technology may be, it needs to be transformed into a consumer product through the efforts of the product-engineering people.

1. Bodinson, Glenn, "Time-based Competition is the Competitive Advantage of the 1990s", *APICS - The Performance Advantage* (December 1991) pp. 27-31.
2. March, Artemis, "Meeting Time and Cost Targets: The IBM Proprinter", *Target* (1991) pp. 18-24.

A world-class product technology strategy requires several important aspects:

- time — time-to-market efficiency
- quality — the product needs to be exciting to the customer and needs to satisfy customer requirements
- productivity — the product needs to be efficiently producible in our production environment
- teaming — it's not just engineers that develop a world-class product, it's also customers, vendors and employees, and this implies a new culture.

There are numerous strategies that will affect and improve the product design process. One good example is the Henrickson article that lists "forty things to do for more competitive product designs".[3]

> A fundamental change must occur in your company culture and in the way you conduct business.
>
> Dave Henrickson

Another example of product technology development is the Adler, Riggs and Wheelright article which focuses on improving competitive position. This focuses on management's frustrations with product development projects and suggests improvement strategies.[4] Product technology development needs to be faster (time-to-market) and more customer satisfaction (quality and productivity) focused. And it needs to be a team effort to be world-class.

Process Technology

Whereas product technology development has always been a strength in the United States, process technology development has always been the strength of the Japanese. The Japanese have often been known to copy US products exactly, but they improve the methodology and speed of production to the point that they obliterate their American competitors in cost and quality. This is true in the automotive, electronics and many other industries. Process has simply never been a focus of concern in US manufacturing. We always left it to the process engineers to come up with the best way to build products and we never did what the Japanese do so very well — we never asked the employees who do the production process if they could think up any improvements. The difference is demonstrated in the six hour compared to twelve minute set up times for the fender-forming machines mentioned earlier. To

---

3. Henrickson, Dave, "Product Design as a Team Sport", *Target* (Spring 1990) pp. 4-12.
4. Adler, Paul S, Riggs, Henry E and Wheelwright, Steven C, "Product Development Know-How: Trading Tactics for Strategy", *Sloan Management Review* (Fall 1989) pp. 7-17.

look at another example, Sony has zero changeover time. New products begin on the assembly line while preceding models are still coming off the end of the line. Tool and die changes are made in minutes as the assembly line is running.

> The objective, I think, is not to reduce the time it takes to run a part; the objective is to reduce the time it takes to set up the machine to run the part. We've never told (the engineers) that before.
>
> Richard Crowser,
> Rank Xerox

> We (in the United States) have setups that last anywhere from fifteen minutes to eight hours, and by matching the Japanese capability of making quick changeovers . . . we saw — three, six, ten minutes or less.
>
> Bob Bamber,
> Caterpillar[5]

Let me give you another example where process technology (also affecting product technology) was significantly transformed when the employees got involved. This is a case where the engineers were made to work alongside the employees for a period of time, making their own products. The engineers learned a lot from their temporary co-workers. They also learned from the frustrations they personally felt while building their own products. Figure 10.1 shows a small example of one of the effects of this project. Product A of Figure 10.1 shows an initial work table which was part of a much larger product. The work table was composed of sixteen structural pieces (four legs, eight angle braces and four sides, no top). It was spot welded at each of the overlapping connection points. Product B of Figure 10.1 shows the redesign of this table using one sheet of folded sheet metal (folded down the legs at the

Figure 10.1: The Table

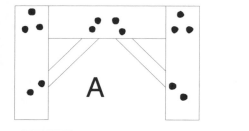 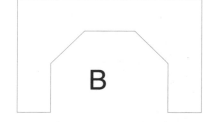

---

5. Taken from Bell, Robert R, and John M Burnham, *Managing Productivity and Change* (Cincinnati, Ohio: South-Western Publishing Company) 1991, p. 49.

corners) and having only one line of spot welds where the ends joined together. Product B is cheaper to produce, and much stronger.

Obsolete processes need updating and innovating; they need to be changed.

You won't become world-class utilizing obsolescence!

Nearly all of the information that is available about process improvements comes from two sources — the theories of the Americans and the tools of the Japanese.

American theorists who are experts in process improvements go back to Henry Ford and his assembly line, or Frederick Taylor and his book *The Principles of Scientific Management*.[6] Although these individuals have fallen into some disfavor, a reading of their original teachings will show that their philosophies, especially with regard to employee relations, aren't that different from what we are trying to copy from the Japanese today. It's the abuse of their philosophies over time that has caused them to seem outdated. More recently, American authors like Deming, Juran and Crosby, and Japanese authors like Shingo, Ishikawa and Taguchi, have taught us a lot about process improvements (see Appendix 12.1).

Some more recent publications focus on process changes. For example, Belt discusses the tools available for process technology change implementation. Belt has a book out that discusses the benchmarking of the process (comparing it with other organizations). Mody, Suri and Sanders focus on the organizational changes that are required for effective process change implementation in order to maintain a steady pace of change.[7]

One dilemma which seems to be a contradiction and which exists in process technology is the speed of technological change. The Japanese look for the small, incremental changes developed and implemented by their employees through the process of empowerment. The United States tends to think of change as a big surge of innovation, replacing production lines and even factories. Is the rapid change better then the incremental step toward improvement? See Chapter 13 for a discussion of the alternative change methods. One thing is for sure, change is critically necessary. But the US approach of looking for the big innovative step unfortunately often results in

---

6. Taylor, Frederick Winslow, *The Principles of Scientific Management* (New York: W W Norton and Company) 1967; Ford, Henry, *Today and Tomorrow* (Cambridge, Massachusetts: Productivity Press) 1988.
7. Belt, Bill, Brooks, Roger and Burris, Rick, "Management Technologies for World-Class Manufacturing", *APICS 37th International Conference Proceedings* (APICS) October 1994, pp. 143-147; Camp, Robert C, *Business Process Benchmarking* (Irwin) 1994; Mody, Ashoka, Rajan Suri and Jerry Sanders, "Keeping Pace With Change: Organizational and Technological Imperatives", *World Development* (1992) Vol. 20, No. 12, pp. 1797-1816.

no change being made at all because of the long-term pay-back of large changes.

> Behold the turtle. He only makes progress when he sticks his neck out.
>
> James B Conant

Is American industry a turtle looking for the big innovation that never happens?

Technology Transfer

Technology transfer, or technology exchange, has become a critical world-class strategy. As discussed in the last chapter, technology partnerships with other companies or countries, like the use of strategic alliances, allows a company to focus on its core competencies, letting it do what it's best at. See the discussion of these types of technology transfer in the last chapter.

Surprisingly, some of the poorest technology transfers occur within our own companies or countries. The intercompany communications need "rapid, radical change". There is still too much "over the wall", departmentalized mentality within companies. We waste a lot of time, money and effort when two facilities develop similar software packages or work out technology implementation procedures independently.

Technology substitution is an excellent form of technology transfer. For example, a process developed in Russia, known in the US as group technology, focuses on identifying similar parts that could be interchangeably used as substitutes for each other. Group technology avoids the unnecessary design, development and production of similar, interchangeable products by different parts of the organization. I have encountered situations where engineers working right next to each other have designed very similar (interchangeable) products and triggered the making of tools, dies and the cataloging of procedures to make these similar products. They each had their own setups and schedules. This has no value-added and is a blatant waste of resources.

Facilities and Equipment Technology

When considering areas for technological advances, we often consider only product technologies. I have now discussed the importance of time-to-market and process technologies. However, facilities and equipment technology is also a forgotten piece of technology that can make a big difference in world-class performance. Items such as the building, materials movement equipment and preventive maintenance program, all improve the productivity of the organization. For example, the Japanese focus on factories that are one-third to one-half the size of American plants. They use equipment that is small and specifically task functional (and much cheaper) and avoid the mega-machine that does everything. They produce the same output and have the same size labor force. However, they have less materials movement and materials storage space.

The organization of the facilities and equipment is also a factor. The US tends to departmentalize similar equipment all within the same area. The Japanese tend to sequence the equipment in the sequence in which it will be utilized by the manufactured product. A world-class technology strategy would consider alternatives in facilities and equipment technology.

Systems and Procedures Technology

A focus on systems improvement is not new. Systems include production planning, logistics planning, inventory planning, accounting and billing systems. Systems technology means having the systems tools available for product and process improvements. Most of the Deming Award winners focus on systems improvements, like the documentation of all processes including the reporting and feedback mechanisms. They continually study *what*, *why* and *how* a process is carried out. They look for value-added, trying to eliminate waste steps in any procedure. They use tools like flow charting and wall pasting to review all the steps and the length of time a particular process takes. This often includes the implementation of quality process control tools.

The Japanese stress that "big systems mean big trouble" and that the movement into robotics or other sophisticated, automated technologies should only occur after the operating bugs are worked out. Often, in the US, the implementation of a system is sold based on the philosophy that the system will solve the bug. In reality, the only things most systems do is speed up the error creation process. Things can now go wrong faster. I have been involved in numerous implementations where a computer and a software tool was introduced with the promise to improve the discipline of the employees and reduce the number of errors. However, the employees didn't understand that they needed to do things differently and in the end the system failed. The system was blamed for the failure, not the poor installation process. The Japanese would suggest that until the employees understand and do the process correctly, speeding up the process will only speed up the errors. The focus should be on understanding, training and keeping it simple.

Information Technology

With many organizations, information technology is beyond being a solution; it has become an obsession. We run to automate everything and anything, losing any focus on why we should automate. Goals and caution are thrown to the wind and software technologies are brought in and out of companies as if they were toys. An information technology strategy needs to be a part of the over all company strategy, keeping it focused on the mission and vision of the company.

Having expressed my word of caution, let me stress that there are numerous areas of information technology that can be extremely helpful and time saving. These are just a few examples:

- electronic data interchange (EDI) — the ability to transfer order and billing information between customers and vendors without extensive written documents
- networking — the interconnection and data sharing between all organizations and people within a company
- the personal computer (PC) — computer power at every desk for analysis and planning
- image processing — the ability for anyone to review source documents on the computer screen from anywhere in the computer network
- digital technology — improved accuracy in the data collection and storage process, for example voice messaging.

Tools like multimedia marketing allow flexible technology tools. However, the high prices of this technology may make it prohibitive.[8] Other information technology tools provide for international data sharing and information integration. In a recent research study, 82 per cent of the companies studied plan to increase their information technology, which is higher than for any other type of technology.[9]

Information technology is a very positive growth influence, but it needs to be kept focused on value-added and waste-elimination opportunities. I recently visited a company where I was asked to review their statistical process control (SPC) methodology. Apparently they had been collecting data for about a year. Some consultant had told them that SPC was a good thing, so they implemented it. Each department had set up their own data collection criteria, but only a few departments had any idea why they were going through the process at all. Data collection for the sake of data collection is a

---

8. Seideman, Tony, "Multimedia Marketing", *International Business* (August 1994) pp. 26-28.

9. *International Business* had a special section in the September 1994 issue called "Information Technology Special Report". The technology study reported the following anticipated investments in technology:

	Decreases	Stay the Same	Increases
Information	1%	17%	82%
Manufacturing			
Equipment	7%	31%	62%
Research	3%	34%	63%
Distribution	4%	39%	57%
Facilities	18%	40%	42%

waste, it adds no value. Similarly, I have worked in factories where, every once in a while, we would not deliver the month-end reports, or deliver them late on purpose, just to see who would scream. Those who screamed used the reports. For the others (about 80 per cent) we were generating waste. Perhaps it's time to review the value-added influence of your information system.

> Common sense is not common.
>
> Will Rogers

Services and Customer Support Technology

Ultimately, technology advances should be focused on the customer. However, we often forget the interfaces that are needed to integrate technology with the customer. Improved customer communication, whether it's an 800 number for complaints or problems, or people from our organization working out at the customer site to understand the customer's needs better, is a form of technology that can be just as critical as the other forms of technology discussed. Often, this is the only thing the customer sees and it is a vital element for customer satisfaction and repeat business. We need to make a good impression on the customer via an effective customer interface.

A TECHNOLOGY STRATEGY

> I never did anything worth doing by accident, nor did any of my inventions come by accident. They came by work.
>
> Thomas A Edison

The key to a technology strategy is the customer. Occasionally, technology development for the sake of technology (like the post-it notes) generates benefits. But most often, it is technology development focused on customer satisfaction that brings the biggest rewards. This translates into a technology strategy that focuses on quality, timeliness, productivity, service and competitiveness.

A customer oriented technology strategy requires:

- customer, employee and vendor tie-ins
- a keep-it-simple strategy
- a focus on how much technology, when to introduce the technology and where, or in what areas, to do the introduction
- a corporate culture shift toward motivating innovation and invention.

One of the toughest areas for technology strategy development is in the area of new product development. However, there have been numerous recent studies to assist with planning such a strategy. For example, the Roberts and Berry article stresses a framework for a new product entry strategy that focuses on enterprise future growth and profitability. The Wheelwright article focuses on why development projects go wrong and suggests that they are reactionary (respond to problems) rather than planning a strategy for technological implementation.[10]

> ... the organization fails to plan sufficiently for the requisite skills and resources, to define the project and its purposes appropriately, and to integrate the development project with other basic strategies.

> Steven C Wheelwright

Another study by Lewis and Linden stresses that sometimes we are wasting time and money unnecessarily by focusing on technological development when it is not part of our core competency. We need to focus our development efforts.

> Much of the money and effort spent today on research and development at the corporate level is wasted . . . (it is) necessary only if a company is following a technology leadership strategy . . .

> Lewis and Linden

There is also the concern in the Erickson, Magee, Roussel and Saad study that stresses the focus on short-term profitability derails vital research and development programs. This study states that incremental, innovative technological improvements in existing product lines and innovating to adapt old products to new markets tends to be the most profitable.[11]

> A program to develop a radically new technology must be approached with great caution; it can be a strategic trap . . .

> Erickson, Magee, Roussel and Saad

As a last point, *The Economist* has done an interesting survey of manufacturing and process technologies in order to identify cutting edge technology strategies. This study stresses that information technologies will tend to be the

---

10. Roberts, Edward B, and Charles A Berry, "Entering New Businesses: Selecting Strategies for Success", *Sloan Management Review* (Spring 1985) pp. 3-17; Wheelwright, Steven C, "A Rubber Mallet and a Two-by-Four: The Concept of Development Strategy", *Target* (Fall 1991) pp. 4-16.
11. Lewis, William W, and Lawrence H Linden, "A New Mission for Corporate Technology", *Sloan Management Review* (Summer 1990) pp. 57-67; Erickson, Tamara J, John F Magee, Philip A Roussel, and Kamal N Saad, "Managing Technology as a Business Strategy", *Sloan Management Review* (Spring 1990) pp. 73-78.

technology that is the most fruitful. It also focuses on the effective utilization of time-to-market and process technologies, such as robotics, as a strategic advantage.[12]

Integrated engineering change management, which eliminates over the wall technology or engineering departments, promotes interaction and time focused change. Time focused change is the world-class competitive strategy of the future.

Positive, goal-focused technology development is change — and change is competitive advantage. Without an aggressive technology development strategy, whether it focuses on all the technological areas listed or just on one core competency area, we cannot stay competitive.

> It is a bad plan that admits of no modification.
>
> Publilius Syrus

A TIME-TO-MARKET STRATEGY

A time-to-market strategy should really be a part of a technology strategy. However, it is so competitively critical that I want to stress it by bringing it into a point all by itself. Our corporate and business unit strategy must incorporate a plan for being time competitive. This includes the time elements for all the technological aspects discussed at the start of this chapter. This includes:

- time to develop pure research technology
- time to develop product technology
- time to incorporate the necessary process technology
- time savings through technology transfer
- time savings and waste elimination through facilities and equipment technology
- time savings with systems and procedures technology
- time improved information technology avoiding waste-generating data and reports
- time response oriented services and customer support technology.

Some supportive literature would include recent conference articles like the ones by Arenberg and Vesey, which stress engineering focus and efficiency in the time-to-market process. There are also excellent books available, like the Thomas book which focuses on time-to-market reduction in the production

---

12. "Survey — Manufacturing Technology: On the Cutting Edge", *The Economist* (5 March 1994) pp. 3-19.

and process technologies areas. See also the Peters article which stresses ten "must dos" for a world-class eManager in a time-competitive environment. These are:

1. pioneer the application of information technology inside and outside the firm

2. a revolution in organization structure — a flatter organization with no borders or barriers

3. total process revision (TPR) — eliminating unnecessary administration

4. measurement — make time the principle basis for measurement

5. wholesale empowerment

6. decentralization

7. adversary to partner — networking like strategic alliances based on trust (see Chapter 9)

8. no job descriptions (see Chapter 14)

9. wholes, not parts — networking and the big picture

10. way of life — time-obsessed competition needs to be entrenched into the enterprise.[13]

> To compete in time, the average front-line employee must be encouraged to go anywhere, talk to anybody, to get any information.
>
> Tom Peters

ADDITIONAL READING

There are a couple more books which will tell you more about competitive strategies in technology. One is by Betz which discusses core competencies, goal setting and technology planning. It then goes through all potential areas that a technology strategy may cover. The other book is by Wallace which offers a chapter on infrastructure and technology.[14]

---

13. Arenberg, Thomas E, "Engineering Productivity — JIT in the Product Delivery Function", *APICS 34th International Conference Proceedings* (APICS) October 1991, pp. 271-273; Vesey, Joseph T, "The New Competitors: They Think in Terms of 'Speed-to-Market' ", *APICS 34th International Conference Proceedings*, op. cit., pp. 274-277; Peters, Tom, "Time-Obsessed Competition", *Management Review* (September 1990) pp. 16-20; Thomas, Philip R, *Competitiveness Through Cycle Time: An Overview of CEOs* (New York: McGraw-Hill Publishing Company) 1990.
14. Betz, Frederick, *Strategic Technology Management* (New York: McGraw-Hill Engineering and Technology Management Series) 1993; Wallace, Thomas F, *World Class Manufacturing* (Essex Junction, Vermont: Oliver Wight Publications, Inc.) 1994.

SUMMARY

Did the microwave oven replace the traditional oven, as was initially planned? No! But most kitchens won't be caught without it. It has become too important for defrosting meat and making popcorn. So, in the end, do we care if the microwave replaced the oven? Yes! Because we now need to focus the microwave on what the customer expects out of it. We need to focus technological advances that will satisfy the customer and possibly open the door to new, expanded, yet undiscovered, technological opportunities. After all, before the microwave existed, no one knew they wanted it. The key question, however, at this point, is not whether the microwave is valuable, but whether the United States can innovate and technologically advance the microwave into new, unfounded product and process territory before the foreign competitors do it and we lose the market completely. Now that's the real time-to-market competitive technology strategy issue that needs to be on the world-class eManager's mind.

SUGGESTIONS FOR FURTHER READING

I have used extensive references throughout this chapter so that you can follow up on those issues you are particularly interested in. I would also recommend a number of articles I have written for various publications:

"Advanced Technology and Integrated Systems", *Logistik 92 Conference Proceedings* (June 1992, Singapore).

"'Free' PM Technology", *PMI (Project Management Institute) Seminar/Symposium Proceedings* (October 1987) pp. 433-435.

"Getting The Best Of Technology Transfer", *Production and Inventory Management Review* (March 1985) Vol. 5, No 3.

"Production Technology Transfer: A US-Japan Example", *1992 International Symposium on Pacific Asian Business Proceedings* (January 1992) pp. 114-116.

APPENDIX 10.1: EXAMPLES OF UNITED STATES GOVERNMENT
TECHNOLOGY DATA SOURCES

Federal Laboratory Consortium for Technology Transfer (FLC) and *News Link*
newsletter:
FLC
P O Box 545
Sequim, Washington 98382-0545
(206) 683-1828

National Aeronautics and Space Administration (NASA) and *NASA Tech Briefs*
magazine:
NASA Tech Briefs
41 E. 42nd Street, Suite 921
New York, NY 10017-5391

Technology Transfer Division:
P O Box 8757
Baltimore/Washington International Airport, MD 21240

COSMIC (software):
Suite 112, Barrow Hall
University of Georgia
Athens, GA 30602
(404) 542-3265

NASA Industrial Applications Center:
823 William Pitt Union
University of Pittsburgh
Pittsburgh, PA 15260
(412) 648-7000

NASA Industrial Applications Center:
University of Southern California
3716 S. Hope St., Sw. 200
Los Angeles, CA 90007-4344
(213) 743-6132

US Army Electronics Research and Development Command:
US Army Electronics R & D Command
Night Vision and Electro-optics Laboratory
Fort Belvoir, Virginia 22060

Lawrence Livermore National Laboratory:
    Lawrence Livermore National Laboratory
    Technology Information System
    P O Box 808, Mail Stop L-275
    Livermore, CA 94550

Naval Weapons Center:
    Naval Weapons Center
    China Lake, CA 93555
    (619) 939-9011

Journal of Technology Transfer
    The Technology Transfer Society
    611 North Capital Ave.
    Indianapolis, Indiana 46204
    (317) 262-5022

Chapter Eleven

A Value-Adding Strategy

Happy is he who is able to learn the causes of things.

Virgil

Let me tell you about a little trip I'm taking. I got up this morning in Maui, planning to return home to the mainland a couple days early. Last night, I learned that I needed to return home sooner than previously planned. Anyway, I tried to call the airlines to get my flight rescheduled. I call the 1-800 number of the airline (the name has been left out to protect the stupid) and after over twenty tries I finally got through. This was *waste generation point number one*. I had less trouble than this trying to place calls in most developing countries. Anyway, I talked to the airline reservations people that had booked my flight and they told me that I could change the flight schedule for a fee. There were plenty of seats available. However, since they only actually flew the flight from Honolulu to San Francisco, I would have to call the airline that handled the Maui to Honolulu leg of my journey myself and make the flight changes.

For *waste generation point number two*, I proceeded to call the second airline and made the changes without difficulty. I thought I was on my way. Little did I realize that the fun was only beginning. I entered the world of lines known as the airport. Consider below the process I encountered.

Waste generation point three — I waited in line to have the luggage passed through a quarantine inspection, necessary for all checked luggage.

Waste generation point four — the check-in line in Maui. The check-in went fine, but the attendants refused to check my luggage all the way through to San Francisco since I didn't specifically have the second ticket in hand. I flew to Honolulu.

Waste generation point five — I waited in a long line to go through the security checkpoint.

Waste generation point six — I waited in line to get on the plane. This line was exceptionally long because the plane was loaded on a first-come first-serve basis.

Waste generation point seven — arrival in Honolulu. After arrival in Honolulu I waited for the luggage which should have been checked through to San Francisco to begin with.

Waste generation point eight — I loaded the luggage onto a luggage cart and walked it from the in-state terminal over to the airline terminal for the flight to San Francisco. Upon arrival I went to the airline counter to check the luggage (another line). After off-loading the luggage I was told that I needed to reload the luggage and go to another counter to first get the tickets reissued.

Waste generation point nine — I waited in line and got the tickets reissued. They gave me my old tickets with some scribbling on them and told me to go check the luggage. Later I was to return for my credit card, after they had a chance to charge me for the cost of rescheduling the flight.

Waste generation point ten — I went back to the counter where my luggage was to be checked. After off-loading the luggage I was told that I needed to reload the luggage on the cart and get another agricultural clearance. The pink sticker I received in Maui didn't count in Honolulu. I needed a yellow sticker.

Waste generation point eleven — I waited in line to get my yellow sticker.

Waste generation point twelve — I finally got my luggage checked, but not without another line.

Waste generation point thirteen — I waited in line to get my credit card back and then was sent to get my seating assignment.

Waste generation point fourteen — I got in line to get my seating assignment.

Waste generation point fifteen — I was on my way, almost. Next I got in another long line to go through the security check.

Waste generation point sixteen — Honolulu airport isn't that big, but for some reason they decided to have the check-in counter at the opposite corner of the airport from where the gate was. The walk was good exercise.

Waste generation point seventeen — I got in line to get on the plane.

If it is as complicated to build a television as it was to get from Maui to San Francisco, the United States is in serious economic trouble. It would seem reasonable that at point number one I should have been able to eliminate points two to fourteen. Some additional improvements, like combining points three, four, five and six and combining points fifteen, sixteen and seventeen at each airport into one step each would also have been helpful. That would have reduced the process down to three value-added points rather than seventeen over-lapping waste-generating points.

This story is true. It really happened to me. I'm on the plane from Honolulu to San Francisco right now. And I'm traveling within the United States, not to some remote developing country that supposedly doesn't know how to do things correctly (I say this with sarcasm).

ARE YOU VALUE-ADDED?

I was invited to a factory in Malaysia and asked to comment on a comparison between this factory and a competitor. Both factories had the same number of employees and the same amount of equipment. However, one factory generated about one-third the output of the other factory. The manager of the plant said, "I don't understand it. Our employees work every bit as hard as the employees of the other factory. Why is our output so low?"

After walking through the plant and making a few observations I asked the plant manager to observe a couple of the employees. I wasn't focusing on any employee in particular. I simply wanted the manager to observe the manufacturing process. I asked him to watch these employees and observe how much of the employee's time was spent adding value to the product and how much of the employee's time was spent in waste. Waste can include:

- moving product
- positioning product
- walking from inventory to production
- preparing tooling
- filling out reports.

The plant manager was amazed at how inefficient his employees were, but he soon realized that it wasn't his employees that were inefficient — it was the process. It doesn't matter how hard the employees are working, if they are working on waste, the output of the plant won't go up.

Waste occurs in all the resource areas. Any time the process occurs it effects resources. If it does not add value to the company, it is waste. For example, waste exists in:

- materials inefficiencies like inventory
- energy inefficiencies
- machinery utilization inefficiencies
- marketing
- financing
- information systems
- accounting systems
- personnel
- manufacturing[1]
- invoicing

---

1. Plenert, Gerhard, "Successful Factory Management Systems", *Produktiviti,* (July-August 1992) Vol. 42, pp. 2-6.

- purchasing
- decision-making.[2]

A world-class value-added strategy is a waste elimination strategy. The literature is thick with individuals that have taught us the importance of adding value. One of the first writers on the subject is Frederick Taylor. More recently, the Japanese production philosophy of JIT has focused on waste elimination. And other authors like Dertouzos, Lester and Solow have stressed this issue as well.[3]

> The principle objective of management is to secure "maximum prosperity" for the employer and the employee. . . The close, intimate, personal cooperation between management and men [employees] is the essence of modern scientific or task management. . . When the elements of scientific management are used without the true philosophy of management, the results could be disastrous.
>
> Frederick Taylor

> An alternative definition of QC would be, "Everyone doing what should be done, in an organized, systematic way".
>
> Kaoru Ishikawa,
> Founder of the Japanese Company Wide Quality Control (CWQC)[4]

Value-added strategies also apply to the process of management. Managers who are not focusing their activities on achieving the goals of the organization (rather, they are focused on fighting fires) are non-value-added managers. Reconsider the discussion of world-class manager characteristics as found in Chapter 4.

It has been argued that the United States is becoming a service-oriented society.[5] Unfortunately, this also means that we are giving away some of our value-added potential. It means that we are losing some of our industrial capability and along with it we are losing our technological implementation capability, an area where the United States is already very weak (see Chapter 10). Generating waste, as a nation, means an ever decreasing balance of trade

---

2. Shays, E Michael, "Cleaning Up Waste in Decision Making — Breakthrough Thinking: A New Way of Attacking Problems Can Produce Startling Results", *Business Quarterly* (Winter 1992) Vol. 56, No. 3, pp. 43-45 (see also Nadler and Hibino books on Breakthrough Thinking, cited earlier).
3. Taylor, Frederick Winslow, *The Principles of Scientific Management* (New York: W W Norton & Company, Inc.) 1967.
4. Ishikawa, Kaoru, *Introduction to Quality Control* (Tokyo, Japan: 3A Corporation) 1990.
5. Plenert, Gerhard, "Megatrend or Megadisaster", *OR / MS Today* (December 1994) pp. 24-26.

and an ever increasing budget deficit. We need to focus on value-adding industries, such as strengthening our know how and our engineering capability, improving our innovativeness, and improving the productivity and quality of our output, in every area.

I find adding value, or waste elimination, an important strategy for life in general. If, for example, your personal goal is to have a successful, close, well-rounded family, then you need to establish a waste elimination strategy. This can be translated into eliminating items that deter from the important areas that you want to add value in. For example, this may mean watching less TV and spending more time on family activities. The same is true whether your focus is on, for example, your career or your spouse.

Talk is cheap, unless you're talkin' to a lawyer.[6]

FOCUSED WASTE ELIMINATION

A waste elimination strategy needs focus, just like all strategies do. The focus needs to be:
- on the goal
- on the critical resource
- on supportive resources.

The focus of a value-added strategy should be on the goals. For example, if the goal is customer satisfaction, then customer service becomes the driver. The customer defines customer value-added.

We also need to be careful on the second and third points, because waste elimination in the supportive resources may result in adding waste to the critical resource process. This was exemplified by the earlier example of how improving labor efficiency is often done at the expense of increased materials inefficiency and vice versa. The priority for waste elimination should always go to the critical resource first.[7]

In addition to all the other characteristics already discussed, waste elimination should include:
- flexibility, responsiveness, the ability to convert functions or processes as needed
- capital investment that supports value-added changes
- a focus on searching out positive changes

---

6. I saw this on a T-shirt in Maui!
7. For more details see Darryl V Lanvater article "Resource Planning: For Manufacturing, Business and the Enterprise" in Wallace, cited earlier.

- reducing the time-to-market
- concentration on customers' expectations
- thinking of the worker as a customer and involving the workers in the improvement process
- high productivity where technology is the servant of the process
- efficiency in the operational measures of performance, like quality, low inventories and high throughput
- overall integration.

AMETEK began its improvement process with a management seminar on total quality awareness. The top management commitment, starting with the president, focused on being "the best you can be". AMETEK felt it had to change its fundamental way of managing in order to stay competitive in the future. It established the following set of goals:

1. increase customer satisfaction

2. improve operating value drivers

3. increase employee satisfaction.

AMETEK licensed the Westinghouse Technology Improvement Process and adapted it for its own use. It developed a six-step methodology to improve process efficiency and thereby reduce cycle times and re-engineered a complex manufacturing process to do it. The steps are:

1. commit to performance improvement

2. select and scope process

3. analyze current process

4. design new process

5. implement new process

6. manage process performance

7. return to step one and repeat the cycle.

AMETEK, after three years of total quality improvements, has reduced cycle times by 89 per cent (from 22.5 days down to 2.5 days), reduced operating costs by 27 per cent, and has shown a 280 per cent increase in on-time deliveries (from 25 per cent to 95 per cent).[8]

---

8. This information came from a presentation by Hay Wun Wain of Total Quality Management for AMETEK in November 1994.

VALUE-ADDED PROFITS

If I am building a television, and in the TV I have a tuner and a power supply, it costs ten dollars to make each of these products. However, I can sell (or buy) the tuner on the open market for fifteen dollars and the power supply for twenty dollars. The power supply offers me ten dollars of value-added profit, whereas the tuner only offers me five dollars of value-added profit. As part of my value-added strategy, I should build all the power supplies myself, and have someone else produce the tuners (assuming I don't have enough capacity to build both). That way I would maximize my value-added profits. This is a strategy that the Japanese have understood for a long time. The overseas Japanese plants tend to get the low value-added components while the Japanese keep the high value-added profit items at home in their own factories.

In a world-class value-added profit strategy, we need a revised focus that centers on waste elimination and value-added profits creation. We need to realize that time and competition erodes value-added profits because the competition will drive the value-added profits down. Therefore, continuous value-added profits require continuous innovative changes. The function of the operations department, other than to create output, is to continually incorporate innovative, lead-edge, value-adding, profits oriented change.

VALUE-ADDED STRATEGY

A world-class value-added strategy is focused on the *three Cs*:

customer — focus on what the customer considers value-added, designs with the customer in mind and incorporating customer inputs, customer is always right, customer service orientation

competition — being competitive: this critically involves the employees and aspects of the internal organization

change — continuous, constant, positively directed changes in process and product.

Building on this focus, the value-added emphasis would next incorporate all the external influences. These influences need to be thought of as partners-in-profit. They include vendors, competitors, government, unions, stakeholders and the local community. These partners in profit would incorporate issues such as technology, regulations, the environment and globalization.

World-class eManagement must work on building and continuously improving a company's value-added capabilities so that it can outperform the competition by establishing a value-added strategy along five dimensions:

1. speed — the ability to respond quickly to customer or market demands and to incorporate new ideas and technologies quickly into products (and services)

2. consistency — the ability to produce a product (or service) that unfailingly satisfies customers' expectations

3. acuity — the ability to see the competitive environment clearly and thus anticipate and respond to customers' evolving needs and wants

4. agility — the ability to adapt simultaneously to many different business environments

5. innovativeness — the ability to generate new ideas and to combine existing elements to create new sources of value.[9]

> There is no true implementation of Total Quality or any other organization-wide improvement initiative without focus on both the customers and all the details involved in providing products and services to customers. This is true across all industries.
>
> Mark D Gavoor, Colgate-Palmolive Co.

Numerous publications exist that can be used to add detail to the development of a value-added strategy.[10] But the key principles to a value-added strategy are already found scattered throughout this book.

> Change the question from "How can productivity be increased?" to "What do we have to do to beat the competition?"
>
> William Wassweiler[11]

SUMMARY

We believe that if we improve customer satisfaction, we could improve customer retention and market share and gain higher revenues. So we surveyed our customers. They told us that we needed to be better at resolving their problems, to become more consistent with our transportation service, and to reduce the cycle time on our responses to them.

9. Stalk, G, Evans P and Shulman, L E, "Competing on Capabilities: The new rules of Corporate Strategy", *Harvard Business Review* (March-April 1992) pp. 57-69.
10. Olsen, Robert E, "Developing a Manufacturing Strategy for the 1990s", *APICS 34th International Conference Proceedings* (October 1991) pp. 403-405.
11. Wassweiler, William, "The Factory With a Future", *APICS — The Performance Advantage* (September 1991) pp. 26-28.

Our marketing and sales people needed to understand our customers' businesses.

Kent Sterett,
Union Pacific Railroad

A value-added (waste eliminating) strategy, which focuses on customer satisfaction, is an integral part of the drive toward world-class eManagement status. And the elimination of waste starts with a commitment from the top to make sure all processes in the organization are value-added, including the job of the CEO.

Part III

Value Chain Management

Chapter Twelve

Measurement Systems that Motivate

Many think they have an open mind, when it's merely vacant.

Dorothy arrived at a crossroads in the *Wizard of Oz* and she asked the Scare-crow which way she should go. His response was: "That all depends on where you are headed; if you don't know, then any road will do!"

As we develop the road map that will guide us on our journey to world-class management status we started with a vision and mission statement, both focusing on our core competencies. Then we developed a corporate and business strategy focused on what we are trying to accomplish. Next we need to develop a measurement and motivation strategy that conveys to the work force what it is that we are trying to achieve. This measurement system is the primary focus of this chapter. But before we discuss the measurement system, let's discuss two elements that tie closely into the measurement process — integration and information.

A STRATEGY TOWARD INTEGRATION

Everything was said that needs to be said — but since no one was listening it needs to be said again.

Integration is a topic which reminds me of the speaker who needs no introduction but demands one. One major fault with this book is that it segments world-class eManagement tools (in the American way). But, in reality, none of these tools have stand-alone value; they all need to be integrated together. We need to involve (integrate) people and systems utilizing the best of each and eliminating the waste in each, thereby maximizing the value-added.

We have several changes that need to be made within our organizations so that we can overcome the barriers to integration. These are:

- focused goals
- over-the-wall organizations
- organizational structure
- physical
- process/technology
- employees' abilities
- team/empowerment culture

- information systems
- measurement and motivational systems.

The last two items on this list will be discussed in the second and third sections of this chapter. Team/empowerment culture is the subject of Chapter 14. However, the first six items will be discussed briefly in this section.

Focused Goals

Chapters 5 and 6 thoroughly discussed goals, including the development of goals using:
- core competencies
- vision statement
- mission statement
- corporate strategy
- business unit strategy
- plan of operation.

Also, Chapter 5 discussed the measurement of goal performance using tools such as quality, productivity and efficiency.

In this chapter I want to re-emphasize the importance of focusing these goals and measures on the same target (remember Robin Hood). Being world-class is having a focused enterprise integration strategy where all aspects of the company are shooting for the same target, yet they are each empowered to develop their own road map to get there. Focused goals also emphasize the need to integrate people, as discussed in Chapter 4 and again in Chapter 14. World-class integration is needed which incorporates customers, vendors and employees (from CEO to line workers).

Additionally, part of an integration plan should include focusing the goals on a time-based strategy, as discussed in Chapter 10.[1] With correctly defined goals, we won't need the help of the scarecrow to direct us down the best path to world-class performance.

Over-the-Wall Organizations

We've heard the story before, but we still haven't learned the lesson.

> Departmentalized, hierarchical organizations don't communicate, and can't compete.

---

1. Monnin, Michelle, Roger Miller and Brian Schaenzer, "Are Your Goals and Measurements in Line with Your Time-Based Competition Philosophy?", *APICS 37th International Conference Proceedings* (APICS) October 1994.

Enterprises have numerous internal barriers. One of the biggest is over-the-wall organizations. In this type of organization, each department works independently. For example, marketing generates a forecast, without regard to customer wants. Engineering designs a product, without integrating with marketing or the customer. Engineering throws their designs and marketing throws their forecasts over-the-wall to production, who in turn modifies both sets of numbers to satisfy capacity and produceability, again not communicating with either. This type of independency game goes on throughout the enterprise.

World-class enterprises have realized that integration is the key to success. The organization needs to be borderless, both vertically and horizontally. *Vertically borderless* organizations have lost job titles and hierarchal definitions (see the next section under organization structure). *Horizontally borderless* organizations have lost department definitions along functional lines and have organized themselves along process lines. These organizations don't have a marketing department and a production department, rather, they have an automotive department and a television department. Within this process department structure, all employees are encouraged to work together, eliminating traditional functional barriers. The marketing and engineering employees have their desks on the shop floor right next to the production people. The process group is empowered, as a team, to change almost anything, as long as it focuses toward the goal targets given to them.

Borderless organizations are organic. This means that they are not rigid but grow and evolve as the needs of the organization changes. Employees may change functions and roles. They are encouraged to communicate with anyone within or without (customers, competitors, vendors) the organization, whatever it takes to get the job done and to get it done right.

Integration requires teaming across functional boundaries (see Chapter 14). Teaming encourages communication, and communication encourages integration. World-class borderless, organic organizations require integration processes to be a part of their strategic plan.[2]

Organizational Structure

Hierarchical organizations have a rigid and proceduralized structure for communication. In the rapid move towards world-class high-speed time-to-market strategies, which involve employee empowerment, we have discovered the need to break down these traditional barriers. Employees shouldn't have to talk to their boss, who in turn talks to their boss, who communicates with another functional area to the boss there, who communicates to their subordi-

---

2. See Bell, Robert R and Burnham, John M, *Managing Productivity and Change* (Cincinnati, Ohio: South-Western Publishing Company) 1991, which has excellent chapters on leadership and communications.

nate supervisor, who communicates with their employee, who gives the information to the supervisor, who communicates with their boss, who . . . anyway, you get the picture. The result has been to eliminate as many levels of the hierarchical structure as possible.

The elimination of power levels has generated a concern about span of control. A manager is only supposed to be able to manage four or five employees effectively. However, by reducing the number of levels, managers now have ten or fifteen or more direct subordinates. The solution is found by changing the role of the manager from that of drill sergeant to one of facilitator. The eManager no longer directs activity. Now the eManager leads or orchestrates activity and empowers the employees to run their own organization.

The issue of centralization versus distribution also comes into play. With fewer levels, the CEO comes a lot closer to the line employees. This offers increased centralization. However, empowerment allows the localized teams of employees to make localized decisions. This offers decentralization. If the CEO has his or her role defined correctly, they will realize that they are also facilitators and the new centralization needs to remember its role and not attempt to obstruct localized efforts at making the company successful.

Physical Integration

Physical integration means physically putting the CEO and plant manager's desks in the middle of the factory floor. It means removing physical walls, suits and ties and other physical distinctions that draw attention away from empowerment, teaming and integration. It may mean physical relocation of plants or of machines within the plants, so that the enterprise can become process, rather than function focused.

Process and Technology

Process integration is where the company organizes around a process that it accomplishes. For example, if one of our processes is building televisions, then all aspects of the organization that go into building televisions are organized together. Therefore, we would house:

- information systems
- accounting
- marketing
- engineering
- production
- purchasing
- customer support
- logistics

- technology development (see Chapter 10).

This doesn't suggest that we should eliminate some of the synergistic benefits of large purchasing, accounting or information systems groups. However, we need to have representation from each of these groups, which are involved in our functionally empowered team.

Employees' Abilities

> People are lonely because they build walls instead of bridges.
>
> Joseph Fort Newton

We tend to get so busy driving our employees that we forget to communicate with them. If we would do the unheard of, sit down with our employees during working hours to find out what they think, feel, like, dislike, etc. we just might learn something about ourselves and the enterprise. We need to interview our employees on a regular basis, not just the ones we want to reprimand but also the ones that are doing a good job for us. We can learn a lot from all our employees. This should be a personal, one-on-one interview searching for ideas, opinions and feelings. Don't be disappointed if the first couple of times don't seem fruitful. The employees are still trying to figure out what you are up to. They don't trust you any more than you trust them. Give it time and you'll be amazed at what you'll learn.

> To see our people talking about something that they know more about than anyone else — their jobs, and how to make them better — is exciting. It gets to you . . . We've got people here who are stars — who really want the opportunity to participate and to plot their own course.
>
> Shigeo Shingo,
> Toyota

Another key step in the employee integration process is teaming, which is expanded on in Chapter 14. The interaction and synergy of teaming to focus on solving problems has, for a long time, been an effective method of change improvement in Japan. Teaming also taps the abilities to solve problems and integrates them into the overall operation of the enterprise. But it takes time. For example, looking at the teaming process for Toyota we see in Figure 12.1 where it has taken thirteen years to get from ten to forty-seven suggestions per employee. However, the total history for the small-group (team) improvement process at Toyota goes back much further than that. The effectiveness that the process has achieved is now obvious. Employees are integrated into the process and their abilities are an integral part of the company. Employees are empowered to make a difference — they are empowered to change.

Figure 12.1: Toyota's Small Group Inprovements

Year	Number of Suggestions	Suggestions Per Person	Adoption Percentage
1976	463,000	10.6	83 %
1979	575,000	12.8	91 %
1980	860,000	18.7	94 %
1985	1,000,000+	24.0	95 %
1989	2,000,000	47.0	96 %

Source: Shigeo Shingo's book *Study of the Toyota Production System from an Industrial Engineering Standpoint*, p. 114. This book has been listed in earlier chapters.

People integration requires training. To take advantage of our employees' abilities requires education in how to find changes and implement them. Employee integration requires the strengthening of the abilities of employees at all levels. Horizontal integration of the staff is not enough, Vertical integration between management and staff is just as important. Anyone in the company should feel free to talk to anyone else, no matter what level or job function. Only then can the abilities of the employees be cashed-in and effectively shared.

The role of the employee has been discussed in nearly every chapter of this book. The focus on employee integration in order to effectively take advantage of their abilities has been discussed since the days of Henry Ford and is still a critical discussion today. People integration requires people. And people take time, not time for them to learn, but time for them to understand and to trust the change process. People integration takes patience. Without it, however, all other forms of integration are merely hi-tech exercises.

THE OVERALL INTEGRATED ENTERPRISE

Many of the tools for integrative change have already been discussed and more is explained in Chapter 7. But the common theme throughout all the literature that discusses enterprise integration is:

* management commitment
* time — employee commitment to integration is slow
* supportive structures and systems such as teaming
* internal measurements such as benchmarking
* integrative technologies such as information systems.

World-class enterprise integration starts at the top with management commitment and reaches the bottom with teaming and empowerment. It eliminates walls and barriers between departments and functions, but it also realizes that the integration process, especially the employee aspects to the integration process, takes time. Therefore, world-class enterprise integration is a long-term commitment to change.[3]

A DATA-INFORMATION STRATEGY

Always be sure you're right, then go ahead.

Davey Crockett

Are we an information society? The United States seems to think so. However, before we get too wrapped up in collecting data and disseminating information, we need to remember that the Japanese use little or no computer power to schedule the production floors of their world-class competitive factories, whereas the United States uses a lot of computer power. That doesn't mean that data and information are bad, it means that often our obsession with data collection is unfocused. Collecting data because we love data, or generating information because of the prestige attached to having a computer report, is a waste. It has no value-added.

An effective world-class integrated information strategy has focus, just like any other functional area of the organization. The focus needs to be targeted on the goals of the organization.

Building an Information Target

When developing a measurable target for all levels of our enterprise, we need to match the target to the function. For example, a target of customer service is interpreted differently for the different aspects of an organization. Customer service for the production department is measured in the number of production related problems with sold products. The engineering department is measured on design related problems causing ineffective product performance. For the customer service department the measure should be related to response time and follow-up satisfaction. The measures of performance need to be tied back and broken down to measure the teams that are responsible for the various aspects of the operation being evaluated. Of course, positive responses and compliments should also be recorded.

---

3. Sandras, William A, "Integration: Productivity Thrust of the 1990s", *APICS 34th International Conference Proceedings* (APICS) October 1991, pp. 400-402; Barber, Norman F, "Creating Organizational Integration", *APICS 33rd International Conference Proceedings* (APICS) October 1990, pp. 40-44.

Bringing the information system on target means that the information system should focus on the area of performance that we want to maximize. I was working with a company that had incorporated a very elaborate quality system. The slogan of the company focused on its high level of quality. They had the plaques on the wall, the Statistical Process Control Systems in place and quality personnel trained. However, the quality problems still remained enormous. When they asked me for an opinion on what was wrong I asked them to show me the paperwork that the employees filled out. The employees were asked to fill out and report on their job start and stop times and the quantity of units produced. They were measured on efficiency and they were rewarded (bonuses paid) based on this efficiency measure. The question I posed to the organization was "Are the employees rewarded for quality?" I was given some blue-sky answer about pats on the back and plaques. But the bottom line is that the employees were being rewarded to perform based on quantity, not quality, and that's what the company got. Haven't they ever heard the old saying:

You get what you pay for!

Building an information target does not have to be hard. Let me try to simplify it for you. For example, if we are trying to build cars, and our goal is profitability, then we can analyze the contribution that each of the plant's resources has on the profitability of the car. We will get numbers like labor 8 to 10 per cent, materials 50 to 60 per cent, machinery 5 to 10 per cent and burden 20 to 40 per cent.

From this example it should be obvious that the resource that is contributing the most to the profitability of the car is the materials resource. The materials resource is our critical resource. Therefore, if we have a goal focused on profitability, we would want to make sure that the information system measures individual performance on materials efficiency, whether it's in purchasing, storing or materials waste in the manufacturing process.

Cadillac, a recent winner of the Baldridge award, had numbers similar to the ones just listed. However, it revised its goals and shifted to a focus on customer satisfaction. It needed to re-evaluate the contribution of its resources on this new goal and to identify its new critical resource. It did this through an extensive customer survey process. For example, it asked customers what is more important in a car seat — is it the fabric (materials), the stitching (labor) or the contouring (engineering)? For Cadillac, the overwhelming new critical resource was engineering and it had to revise the information systems focus to reflect the importance of this new resource.

Information Tools

There are numerous information tools available to us. They include types and processing of information and information analysis and organization tools. Before we discuss each of these areas of information tools, let me list a couple of brief definitions:

data — the collection of numbers, figures, measurements, reports, etc. that occur — what goes into the data processing system

information — processed data rearranged into a summarized report, chart, graph, or screen display — the output of the data processing system.

Types and processing of information

There are numerous ways data is collected and the processed information is disseminated. For collecting the data we use qualitative methods, such as surveys, reports, interviews and so on which collect success stories or problem reports. We also use quantitative methods like statistical sampling, time reports or units of production. There are numerous devices for collecting the data such as like computer keyboards, sensors and time clocks.

Once the data is collected, there are various tools for processing the data, such as spreadsheets, word processors, data base management systems or manual reports. The data is summarized, sorted and grouped. Then the output information is generated using summary or exception (displaying only the errors) processing. The output is in the form of reports or computer screen displays.

The type of information that is generated is reports on success, failures, or, better yet, tendencies towards success or failure which anticipates situations before they happen. The information may be financial, like exchange rates, or it may be technological or operational, like inventory levels. Next, the information is made available to all areas of the organization through a variety of transfer processes. These include:

eMail — an electronic, international, information messaging system

fax — transmitting images over the telephone system

teleconferencing — a method of having meetings in multiple locations using television type images

electronic data interchange (EDI) — data directly transmitted between locations, like between vendors and customers for order processing

image processing — source document images available on any computer terminal

networking — multiple computer access to the same database without data transfer requirements

information superhighway — a network tool that allows data and information of all forms to be processed and transmitted from anywhere to anywhere

integrative technology — for example, computer integrated manufacturing (CIM) is an information systems tool that integrates accounting, personnel, finance, marketing, production, engineering, robotics, inventory storage and retrieval, and numerically controlled machines all into a common data base.

The focus of information processing systems should be the same as for all operational environments. Information systems should focus on facilitating change, increasing value-added and eliminating waste.

The information processing system should do a self-check to see if it is in fact collecting data that focuses on goal-directed changes. If not, then it is generating waste. Not all data and information is "good" by it's nature. Waste data and information is time consuming and resource consuming. One way to make sure that the data collection/information generation system is not generating waste is to involve the system users in the decision process. Ask the sources of the data if there are any problems in the data collection process: Do you understand the purpose of the data collected? Do things happen that circumvent the accuracy of the data? Is there a better way (more timely, more accurate, more meaningful) to collect the data?

Similar questions could be asked of the people who receive the information. We should ask questions such as "Is the information presented to you in the form that you use it (sequence, timeliness)?" "Is there too much information? Is something missing?" "Should some pieces be consolidated?"

As with all technologies, if the users (customers of the technology) aren't involved in the development of the technology, there's very little chance that they'll buy-off on it. In information systems technology, as with most changes, ownership is very important. If the users of the system fees ownership of the system, they will tend to insure its success.

Information analysis and organization tools

Information systems should be a step toward better integration. There are numerous tools available that help in this integration. Some include the systems approach, object oriented programming and software modularization. Let's consider them in more detail.

The systems approach — the systems approach is a tool used by many of the Deming and Baldridge award winners and by ISO 9000 to document and analyze a particular process. The systems approach is a tool whose usefulness is not limited to information systems only. For example, if we are analyzing the invoice processing within our enterprise, we would take all the pieces of paper, all the phone calls, all the paper transfer steps and we would draw these steps on a wall with little boxes and circles around them, and with lines connecting them to show the sequence of the flow. Then we would put times next to each box to indicate how long each step takes. We would continue this diagramming process until we had all the steps and all the pieces of paper diagrammed. Then we would look at this diagram and ask, "Why do we do this?" or, "How does this step help in achieving the goal of this process?" for each step in the process. We systematically, step-by-step challenge and redefine the process eliminating waste and focusing on value-added. The systems approach has also been characterized by looking to the future, rather than the past. We would focus on how it should be, rather than on how it is and try to correct it. Future looking systems analysis is highlighted in the following steps:

- focus on the key tasks
- define the ideal system
- concentrate on the process and the speed (time)
- assess ways of improvement towards the goal focus
- build in simplicity
- be sure every step is value-added (waste eliminating).

Another systems tool is flow-charting, which defines the logical sequence for a process to occur. Flow-charting defines the decision-making process that occurs in any series of steps. Again, with flow-charting we are trying to logically identify the steps in a process, and to identify and eliminate waste (processing steps) in the process.

Object oriented programming — object oriented programming is a new computer systems development tool which focuses on building information systems that are event and goal oriented. Programming is a series of events, not steps, that focus on the overall goal. For example, we may focus on systems development that will help us create a better quality car in less time.

Software modularization — software modularization is a strategy that attempts to avoid the duplication of efforts. We build a software product that has building blocks, each of which can be rearranged onto different systems to achieve different purposes. The Japanese have long been masters of this process utilizing a modular software data bank where all software is available through a computer network and can be used by anyone on any machine.

Modular software avoids point solutions. This means that software that focuses on one specific solution cannot find multiple uses. The software is generalized so that it can be cross-utilized. In the United States, we still have many forms of incompatible software. For example, small systems software, like the PC, is not useable on medium sized systems and their products are not useable on large systems. The reverse is also true. Additionally, within similar sized machines, the software is not transferable. Unfortunately, even within the same vendor, on the same sized machine, the software is often not transferable. Even though a nation-wide data bank of software across all sizes of machines many be nice, it really isn't feasible. However, software modularity within your organization is feasible and should be part of the information strategy for your enterprise.

Figure 12.2: The Information Flow

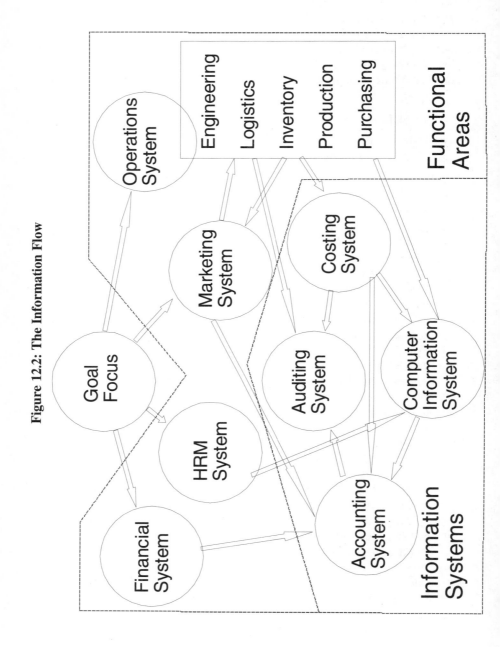

The Integrated Information Flow Diagram

Information integration can get very complex. However, as stated several times already, one of the keys to information integration is simplicity. In Figure 12.2 we see the information flow for an organization. Note that systems like the accounting system, auditing system, costing system and computer information system are supportive information systems whose role is not to run the company, rather their role is to supply information to the functional areas of the organization.

In Figure 12.3 we see the feedback mechanisms that help management stay goal focused. The feedback informs the various functions of the organization of what elements are successfully goal focussed and which are generating waste. The information systems areas need to be re-evaluated regularly to assure that they are integrated and value-adding aspects of the organization. A lot more detail is available on this integrated information flow process.[4]

The Short-Sightedness of Information Systems

Information systems are short-term systems. An investment in an information system should not be thought of as lasting more than five years, and often less. There are several reasons for this.

Technology obsolescence — the hardware and software are constantly being updated and changed and the newer is usually better and greatly overpowers the older.

Data portability — whatever you collect data on today will become an inaccessible media in five to ten years. For example, how many computers do you know that can read the punched cards or magnetic tapes that were used fifteen to twenty years ago? Even the diskettes (portable disks) that were used on computers ten years ago are now unreadable to the new disk drives. Additionally, even if these data storage medias were readable, the data itself is often software specific and is unreadable to the newer software products. We have gone from the diskettes, to the hard disks, to the CD Roms and beyond. Data can be transported from one to the next, but the conversion costs are high and the software is often not convertible at all.

Systems failure — old systems technology, like old technology of any sort, is noncompetitive. To be competitive, we need to keep updated in our software technology. This is a continual, never-ending series of changes.

---

4. See my book, *Plant Operations Handbook,* which has been cited in earlier chapters, for more detail on the information flow processes. See also my publication "Total Integration of Accounting and Manufacturing Information", *APICS 34th International Conference Proceedings,* op. cit., pp. 366-367; and Sheth, Jagdish and Golpira Eshghi, Global Operations Perspectives (Cincinnati Ohio: South-Western Publishing Company) 1989.

Figure 12.3: The Feedback Flow

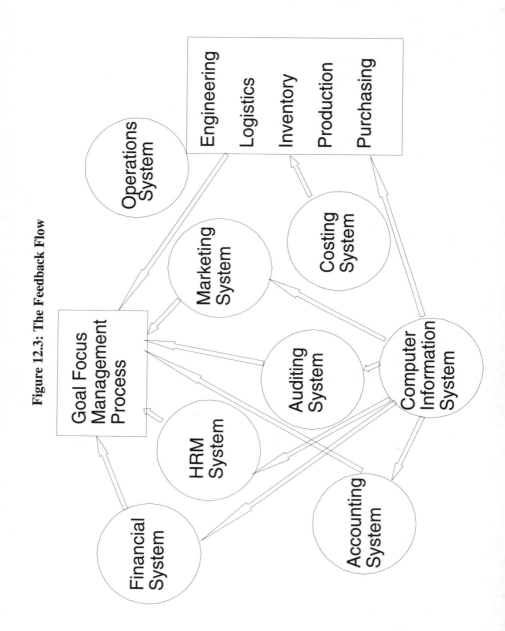

Additionally, as processes within the enterprise are updated, supportive systems need to updated.

Objective/goal defeating systems — "cost accounting systems are the enemy of efficient and productive production departments."[5] This statements focuses on the usage of systems such as cost accounting, a system that has come to have its own agenda without regard for the needs of the production department. Systems of this type are goal defeating. Another example is that US accounting systems list labor as a cost of operation (a negative, bad thing) and inventory as an asset (a positive, good thing). This is just the opposite of what logic would dictate. And this type of thinking causes labor to be the first cost cutting measure whenever cost cuts are required. To make matters worse, inventory carrying (financing) costs, which are often so high that they can easily destroy the profitability of a company, are buried in burden. This means that these costs are considered as uncontrollable and they are therefore ignored as a cost reduction option. I have been in numerous situations where the inventory carrying costs are higher than the labor costs. These accounting structures are objective/goal defeating systems. The US is now re-evaluating its accounting-information systems looking to redefine the measures that are being used. The I-CAM project at Wright-Paterson Airforce Base in Dayton, Ohio is working on a project of this nature. Systems are in a constant state of flux. No system will last you more than a few years without being updated. Even something as basic as a word processing package is constantly coming out with updated versions. Realizing this, we need to plan for this constant change environment in our information strategy. We need to focus on short-term, not long-term focused development.

Software that Fits

The question often arises — do we purchase software or do we develop it ourselves? Purchased software never fits exactly, but self-developed software takes forever to get. The answer to this question lies in your core competencies. Is software development included as one of your core competencies? If not, don't do it! Even if the purchased software doesn't fit perfectly, remember that it's only about a five year solution and then you'll need to get another software product that doesn't fit perfectly. That's still better than spending three of those years developing your own software, only to find it to be obsolete two years later.

There are several organizations that offer software comparative services, similar to the *Consumer Reports*. For example, APICS (see Appendix 12.3) offers a ratings service for production systems alternatives. The Council of

---

5. This is a statement regularly used by Goldratt. To get more information about his philosophy, see the books and articles referenced at the end of Chapter 1.

Logistics Management (see Appendix 12.1) offers a software ratings and comparisons report for logistics software products. What you need to do is get a hold of the software ratings service for the type of software you are interested in and look through their features and functions list to select about four or five products that seem to fit your needs. Order additional information from these organizations, possibly even demos. Test the software products with your own data to see if it works. You must use your own data because I have encountered situations where a software product was purchased, only to find out that there weren't enough decimal places of accuracy, or there wasn't a large enough description field for chemical formulas. Only after testing the software in your environment, using a team of future users of the software to do the testing, are you ready to purchase and install the software.

Is There an Information Revolution?

There is definitely an information revolution! The time and volume of data necessary to be competitive requires information accessibility. However, we need to remember integration, focus, simplicity, modularity and time. And we also need to remember that the purpose of the system is to facilitate change, increase value-added and eliminate waste.

Let me leave you with some additional reading, if you're looking for more details on information systems development. Savage discusses a process for information systems restructuring and Baker and Cleaves discuss improving information systems to achieve world class status.[6]

A MEASUREMENT STRATEGY FOCUSED ON MOTIVATION

Never get so busy making a living that you forget to make a life.

Anonymous

Now that we've learned about world-class integrated information systems, we are now ready to discuss how these systems should be used to measure and motivate performance. Measurement systems have a much greater purpose than to supply feedback to the accounting or costing systems (see Figure 12.2). Measurement systems are the motivation systems of an enterprise.

---

6. Savage, William G, "Implementing an Integrated System: Restructuring the Business Not Just Automating It", *APICS 34th International Conference Proceedings* (APICS) October 1991, pp. 382-386; Baker, Tom and Gerry Cleaves, "New Computer Solutions: World-Class Performance Through Improved Planning and Scheduling Integration", *APICS — The Performance Advantage* (October 1991), pp. 28-31.

As I have already mentioned several times:

Misdirected measurement systems generate misdirected results.

World-class measurement is motivationally directed measurement, which is focused on the enterprise goals.

AT&T has focused its sights on the Malcolm Baldridge Award process. It has used the Baldridge criteria to develop goals and to focus its measurement system. So far, it has won three Baldridge awards and one Deming award in the areas of both service and manufacturing, and feels it is just getting started. Within the Baldridge criteria there are defined areas of performance. Developing measurement systems within each of the AT&T organizations helps achieve the appropriate levels of performance. It started the process by initiating an internal Chairman's Quality Award (CQA), as a stepping stone toward the Baldridge Award. It didn't want to make the goal focused measurement process seem unrealistic, so took it one step at a time, using the CQA to initiate an internal movement toward the quality process using the same categories as the Baldridge Award program, which are:

- leadership
- information and analysis
- strategic quality planning
- human resource development and management
- management of process quality
- quality and operational results
- customer focus and satisfaction.

AT&T initiated specific measures at the business unit and division level for each of these categories, as well as three company wide measures of:

people value-added (PVA) — this is an index measuring employee's perceptions of leadership quality, overall job satisfaction and diversity practices

customer value-added (CVA) — this index measures the satisfaction of AT&T's customers relative to that of its competitors' customers

economic value-added (EVA) — this is a measure of financial value-added performance.[7]

Forbidden fruit is responsible for many bad jams.

Anonymous

---

7. This information was taken from a presentation by Lyle Tippetts in Guatemala. Lyle is the Quality Director of the Caribbean/Latin America region of AT&T.

Competitive measurement and motivation systems have become highly emphasized in the literature in recent years. I have included some examples for future reading in a footnote. The Cooper article offers a fast way to decide if your cost system gives you bad information. The Eccles article stresses that within the next five years every company will have to redesign how it measures its business performance. He notes that "one high-tech company has reorganized 24 times in the past four years to keep pace with the changes in its markets".[8] Additionally, my book *The Plant Operations Handbook* has a couple of chapters on measurement systems that are appropriate for motivation. Review the discussion on management styles in Chapter 4 of this book.

> Over the years, the design of performance measurement systems has focused primarily on financial and accounting information and led to the emphasis of efficiency criteria dealing primarily with direct labor. . . If . . . firms intend to compete, the role and scope of performance criteria must change . . . An increasing number of companies are responding to the competitive challenge and are acknowledging the need for more effective performance measurement systems.
>
> Wisner and Fawcett

In Japan, there are numerous measures of performance, all directed at the goal. For example, vendors are measured on quality, quantity, timeliness and sometimes cost. The best and worst vendors are listed on a board and unanticipated rewards (bonuses) may be paid to the winners.

Measurement and motivation theory has a long history of disagreements. Some believe non-financial rewards are the best motivators, others believe that only financial rewards motivate. Perhaps one of the first motivation theorists was Maslow and his hierarchy of needs, which says that individuals have different needs at different levels of success in their lives (see Figure 12.4). His paper suggests that the best motivator is dependent on the level of the employee and differs at different stages of their lives.[9] This is a very people oriented perspective on measurement and motivation.

---

8. Cooper, Robin, "You Need a New Cost System When...", *Harvard Business Review* (January-February 1989) pp. 77-82; Tarr, James D, "Developing Performance Measurement Systems That Support Continuous Improvement Goals", *APICS 37th International Conference Proceedings* (APICS) October 1994, pp. 416-420; Tincher, Michael G, "World-Class Performance Measurements — How to Get Started", *APICS 37th International Conference Proceedings* op. cit., pp. 424-428; Eccles, Robert G, "The Performance Measurement Manifesto", *Harvard Business Review* (January-February 1991) pp. 131-137; Winser, Joel D and Stanley E Fawcett, "Linking Firm Strategy to Operation Decisions Through Performance Measurement", *Production and Inventory Management Journal* (1991) pp. 5-11.
9. Maslow, Abraham H, "The Theory of Human Motivation", *Psychological Review* (1943) Vol. 50, pp. 370-396.

Figure 12.4: Maslow's Hierarchy of Needs

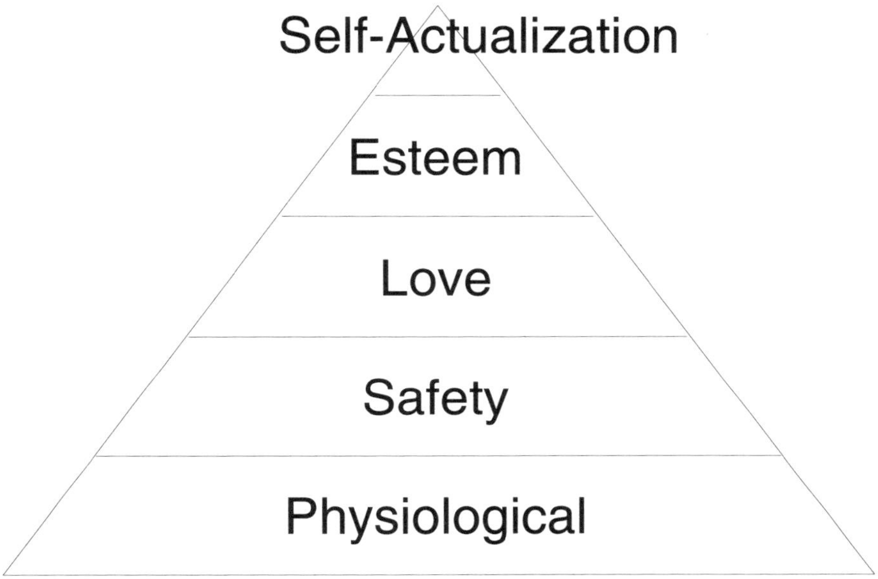

Self-Actualization

Esteem

Love

Safety

Physiological

> There is not one best motivator, it differs from person to person and for any one person, the best motivator changes over time.

Maslow's theories still have respect today. However, we now have new motivators in the form of self-managed work teams, full disclosure of all information to employees and empowerment.

The new employee power seems to be a motivator in itself. However, when the employees are rewarded for the successes of their decisions, the motivation cycle seems complete. I have listed some additional readings in case you want more information about measurement and motivation.[10]

> The eManager that motivates employees to work the hardest is the eManager who works the hardest!

---

10. Brown, Thomas J, "Measuring Performance for Strategic Improvement", *APICS 34th International Conference Proceedings,* op. cit., pp. 107-112; Abair, Robert A, "Super Measurements: The Key to World-Class Manufacturing", *APICS 34th International Conference Proceedings*, op. cit., pp. 113-115; Henson, Holly E, "Performance Measurement in the New Manufacturing Environment", *APICS 34th International Conference Proceedings* op. cit., pp. 126-128; US Department of Labor, *Road to High Performance Workplaces: A Guide to Better Jobs and Better Business Results 1994* (US Department of Labor — Office of the American Workplace) 1994.

We need to measure. The tax collector wants measures, the stock holders want measures and management want measures. However, by simply measuring for the sake of measuring and forgetting the motivational aspects of the measurement, we lose control of the direction in which the workforce is moving. We want to motivate our enterprise towards world-class excellence and a strategy towards motivational measurement is an important big step.

Types of Measures

The number of types of measures is enormous and I can't discuss them all. They include, for example:

- statistical quality sampling
- job performance
- financial totals and ratios
- materials usage and inventory levels
- throughput
- costing
- productivity
- efficiency
- quality.

We have already discussed how most of these measures are focused on short-term financial control rather than focusing on motivators to change and improvement (see Chapter 5 on goals). We need long-term, world-class measures that motivate long-term improvements, like process measures.[11]

The best measurement systems focus on results (quality output delivered to the customer), but several stages of measurement are required to check our progress towards this final measure. There are two categories of progress measurements, *discrete measures*, for assessment, and *continuous measures*, for control or improvement.

When developing a measure we need to realize that 85 per cent of operating problems have common causes (extrinsic) that are related to the process (how things are done) and not to the individual doing the step. Therefore, we need to focus more on measures that will improve the process and focus on measures that will motivate employees to look for improvement opportunities (continuous measures). The 15 per cent of the problems that are special causes (intrinsic) can not always be prevented, but we can reduce the effects of the variation caused by these special case situations by again focusing on the

---

11. The Maryland Centre for Quality and Productivity focuses on "strategic process measurement" as the best way to quality results. See earlier reference.

process. Therefore, in order to maximize the improvement effort, we need to focus on continuous measures that look for process improvements.

> The best process is not a stable process but a capable process, one that is capable of becoming better.

Additionally, I want to highlight a few new measurement systems. The fact that we have new measurement techniques does not outdate the old ones. In fact, I would prefer the old methods in many of the cases, because they focus on the desired motivation. I want to highlight these new methods, because, although they can be helpful, they are not the cure-all for all problems and need to be used appropriately. The new measurements that I want to briefly discuss include activity based costing, activity based management and benchmarking.

Activity based costing (ABC)

Activity based costing is a new costing approach that focuses on measuring the cost of all activities involved in, for example, a marketing, engineering, production or shipping process. ABC is a move away from measuring only labor and materials costs and burying everything else in burden. ABC is a move toward an approach where we measure all cost activities. Unfortunately, companies like IBM, the master of data collection, have backed off ABC because the data collections process is unnecessarily burdensome. The ABC strategy has shifted to one that uses ABC to evaluate the contribution of resources toward the goal, and then, once the critical resource has been established, focusing the data collection process on the critical resource(s) only.[12]

Activity based management (ABM)

Activity based management is similar to ABC in its focus on measuring all the activities that the enterprise is engaged in. However, ABM focuses on understanding and attacking the drivers of the activity costs, whereas ABC focuses on the costs themselves. Just like with ABC, ABM should be used to identify the cost drivers, but should not be used as an ongoing measurement tool.

Benchmarking

Benchmarking has two forms: internal and external. External benchmarking is where an organization compares its performance aspects with other

---

12. See Wallace, Thomas F, *World Class Manufacturing* (Essex Junction, Vermont: Omneo) 1994.

organizations. As discussed earlier in this book, external benchmarking is good as long as your enterprise has a long way to grow. It is also valuable in understanding the competition. However, if you are on the verge of becoming world-class, then there comes a point where copying other companies is not valuable. It becomes time to take the innovative step which leap-frogs you ahead of the competition.

Internal benchmarking is always helpful. Here we are comparing past performance with current performance and planning an appropriate future performance. It can also be used as a cross-departmental comparison of performance. Benchmarking assistance is available from several sources. For example, APQC (Appendix 12.3) has a Benchmarking Institute, which has an extensive database of comparative data. Canada and Mexico have similar organizations (see Appendix 9.2).

When considering criteria for change measurements, let's look at a couple of examples. Motorola uses a specific set of three criteria for evaluating measurements. All activities must focus on total customer satisfaction, total cycle-time reduction and total defects reduction per unit of work.

Lowenthal, in his book, focuses a chapter on "Evaluating the Improvement". He lists six foundation criteria in developing a measurement system that evaluates change.[13] They are:

1. validity — the desired results

2. completeness — thoroughness

3. comparability

4. inclusiveness — cover a wide range of activities

5. timeliness

6. cost-effectiveness.

In Appendix 12.4 there is an article based on a recent research study funded by the American Production and Inventory Control Society Education and Research Foundation. In this research an experiment was performed which demonstrates the direct relationship between measurement and motivation. This article demonstrates the before and after effects and the changes made in the process.

A world-class measurement strategy is one that is focused on the goals of the enterprise and motivates employees at all levels towards those goals. World-class measurement tends to not be an individual, labor efficiency oriented measure. Rather, it tends to be a team measurement of quality output. The development of an effective world class measurement and motivation strategy is a critical part of a shift towards world-class management status.

---

13. Lowenthal, Jeffrey N, *Reengineering the Organization: A Step by Step Approach to Corporate Revitalization* (Milwaukee, Wisconsin: ASQC Quality Press) 1994.

THE QUALITY VERSUS PRODUCTIVITY CHALLENGE

If you have a job without aggravations, you don't have a job.

Malcom Forbes

What performance strategy is the best? Some claim it is productivity, others quality, but most organizations still evaluate performance based on efficiency or cost. We'll need to look at and compare all of these. But first let's consider the man whose house was next to a river, which started to flood. A truck came by to pick him up and the man refused the ride and said, "Faith will save me". As the water worked its way up to the level of the windows, a boat came by to pick the man up and again, refusing the ride, he said, "Faith will save me". Eventually the water got up to the level of the roof. As the man sat on the roof, a helicopter came by and offered him a ride. And guess what? He refused the ride and said, "Faith will save me". The man eventually drowned and as he met Peter at the pearly gates he asked him, "Why didn't I get saved, I had faith?"

Peter responded, "I sent you a truck, a boat, and eventually a helicopter, but you wouldn't take any of them!"

Performance strategies take a lot of faith. Most managers feel that if you "believe" in quality or productivity hard enough, you'll eventually "be saved". You believe in them because they are right and eventually the right has to win out over the evil. Well, just as the true believer learns, religion and faith in God is a lot more than just believing. It's a lot of work too. If you don't perform on your faith, your faith is worthless.

Even so faith, if it hath not works, is dead, being alone.

James 2:17

So when we look at the performance evaluators of quality, productivity, cost and efficiency and as we try to implement them into our strategy, we need to do more than just hang plaques on the wall. We need to understand them, define them and then implement them using goals, strategies and measures. Let's start by defining each of them.

Quality

Quality is such a funny concept. For some organizations, quality means that we have a plaque on the wall that quotes some cute slogan. For other organizations, quality means that you've put a sticker on the bag that you give your drive-through customers which says that their order has been double checked. In reality, nothing has changed internally for either of these organizations. They both work to the same level of quality as they did before the plaque or the sticker. And I still have to do my own double check of the double-checked drive-through order because invariably one out of two of the orders will be wrong. The sticker didn't seem to motivate any change in the behavior of the employees. And why should it? No one ever asked me, the customer, how the employees were performing. It seems that the measure of quality performance is determined by the number of stickers that are getting used up and has nothing to do with the customer.

The best quality manager is no quality manager.

No! I'm not anti-quality! I'm opposed to some defined individual being responsible for quality. Everyone in the enterprise should be responsible for quality. The role of a quality manager should be to work themselves out of a job. The world-class quality manager should develop such a corporate fever and consciousness for quality that everyone becomes a quality manager. Unfortunately, most quality managers see their role as one of "trying to keep their job and get a raise" and therefore their intentions are somewhat suspect. But before we fire the quality manager, let's define what quality really is.

> You never get promoted when no one else knows your current job. The best basis for being advanced is to organize yourself out of every job you're put into. Most people are advanced because they're pushed up by the people underneath them rather than pulled up by the top.
>
> Donald David,
> former Dean, Harvard Business School

The traditional definition of quality in most parts of the world is that:

> A quality product is one that meets internal specifications.

If you're a manufacturer, quality means that the end product meets engineering specifications. If you're a service organization, quality means that you're doing the job the way the boss wants it done. That expectation of what the output should be becomes your quality "standard". And we proceed to set up elaborate measurement and non-trust systems to make sure that we achieve our internal measure of quality. We measure quality under these conditions by using measures similar to the number of rejects coming from the internal quality department.

World-class quality is quite different. World-class quality is customer excitement. A definition would be:

> Quality is when your customer is so thrilled with your product that they would go out of their way to get your product from you.

So how do you measure quality under this definition? You ask your customers and you ask your competitors' customers what they think of your product. Once you have defined what is important to your customer, that becomes your "customer expectation standard". We then measure our performance against this standard. For example, if quick response is important, you measure response time. It is the conformance to this standard that allows, for example, in many of the customers' eyes, the Saturn to be of equal quality as the Lexus or the Mercedes.

To measure quality performance to "standard", numerous gurus and systems have established their mark in quality literature. Figure 12.5 is a quality definition line showing how many of the gurus and systems stack up against each other. On the chart we compare the *systematic* against the *vague*, and the *theoretical* against the *"tool box"* approach to quality. On the chart you find:

- quality gurus — Deming, Juran, Crosby, Ishikawa, Taguchi and Shingo
- quality systems — total quality control (TQC) and just-in-time production (JIT)
- change systems — total quality management (TQM) and process re-engineering
- quality awards — Baldridge Award (US government), Deming Prize (Japan), Shingo Prize (US manufacturing) and NASA Award (US government).

Appendix 12.2 offers some insights into the focus of each of these gurus. The quality systems and change systems options will be discussed next. The quality awards were discussed in an earlier chapter.

> Does it seem reasonable for the United States government to be the issuer of a quality award, when they, with their characteristic rudeness and unresponsiveness, are the epitome of non-quality? Wouldn't we prefer that our congratulations come from someone who knows something about, or can at least spell, quality?
>
> Gerhard Plenert

Quality Levels

Quality, in the narrow sense ("C" level quality), is what you as an enterprise feel that your product should be. In a slightly broader sense ("B" level quality), quality is what your customers feel your product should be. And, in the broadest sense, quality is what society as a whole feels that your product should be ("A" level quality).

Quality is added value. In the narrow "C" sense, quality is adding value (eliminating waste) to the internal organization. A quality product is one that fits as closely to specifications as possible, generating as little waste as possible during the process (i.e. making as few mistakes as possible in the creation of the output). Similarly, in a "B" sense, quality is maximizing the value-added

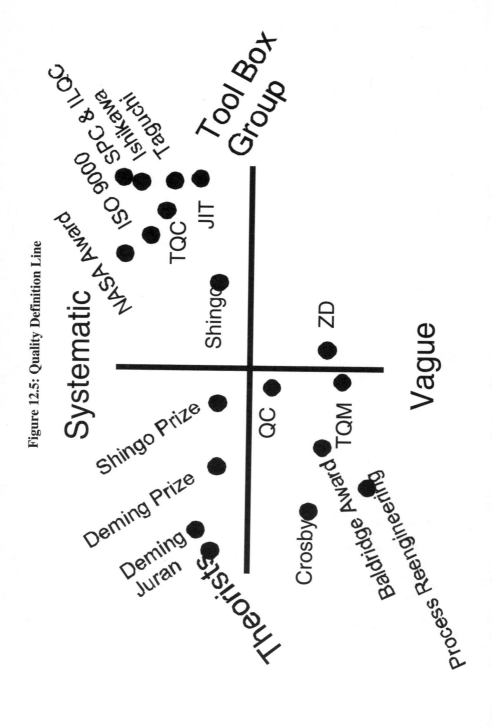

Figure 12.5: Quality Definition Line

to the customer. "B" quality is when your customer goes out of their way to buy your product because they feel confident that you will maximize the value-added for them.

In the broadest "A" sense, quality of your product includes "C" level quality (internal valued-added) and "B" level quality (customer added value). Additionally, "A" level quality incorporates issues such as environmental consciousness, developing the infrastructure (schools and roadways) and utilizing home country employees and vendors as much as possible. "A" level quality is especially important internationally where the acceptance of your business into the community can be critically important.

Unfortunately, there is also a "D" level of quality, which a large number (probably the majority) of companies utilize. This is where companies have no quality program, no quality goals and no quality measures at all.

The Cost of Quality

Is there a cost of quality? Definitely! Quality costs time, commitment, risk, dollars and control.

Time — quality systems take years, not weeks or months, to implement. Additionally, quality systems take the time of numerous personnel that are committed to being educated and to making a quality difference.

Commitment — quality systems require the commitment, not just the involvement (remember the bacon and eggs breakfast), of top management or else no one will take the quality change process seriously.

Risk — a quality change is risky. All change requires a risk. Like the Florida Power and Light story, implementing change may cost you your job.

Dollars — as demonstrated in Figure 4.2 on page 78, there is a very definite short-term cost to any change program. A quality program requires training and the time of the employees, both of which have a price tag. The benefit of the quality change process is long term and, just like in Figure 4.2 on page 78, in the long term, the benefits will by far outweigh the initial costs.

Control — a world-class quality management system results in the loss of control. A manager that enjoys power will rebel at the need to empower the employees which changes the management role into one of facilitator, rather than one of traffic cop. The employees are the creators of quality improvements.

Quality Systems

The amount and variety of quality systems that exist is absolutely astounding. What happens is that we copy some little piece of a much larger quality system (usually for the Japanese), give it some Americanized name, try it out for about six months to a year, decide that it doesn't bring about a sufficient amount of improvement in that short amount of time, throw the system out and start the cycle all over again searching for some little piece to copy. We have a black and white approach to these quality processes. Either they prove themselves in the short run or they're no good. We don't even seem to consider the possibility that perhaps these systems are building blocks that need to be used together, rather than isolated entities. We will discuss a collection of these systems, most of which originate in Japan and most of which have been dropped by the US but are still alive and well in Japan.

One of the prime copycat processes that we are trying to imitate from Japan is the JIT production process. More factories have thrown this process out rather than have it implemented in the US. Rarely will a company give the system more than two years to prove itself. However, Toyota will readily explain that it took it 30 years to fully implement the process. Why do we think we can do it in two years?

Another example of short-sighted quality implementation is the Florida Power and Light example that I discussed in a previous chapter. Again, it was plagued by the short-sighted hurry-up bug believing that "faith" would save it.

For definitional purposes, let me list some of the more popular quality systems that have come and gone (some are lingering on).

Quality control circles (QC) — these are management teams that focus on quality improvements. This team concept has come and gone in a variety of forms. Lately we've been calling it empowerment. Chapter 14 discusses teaming in detail.

In line quality control (ILQC) — this utilizes the Japanese concept of having everyone trained in quality so that they understand and can inspect the quality of the products that they are receiving and sending out. This usually encompasses some of Deming's statistical processes for quality monitoring.

Zero defects (ZD) — this is a system that focuses on error elimination by catching the problem as it occurs and then continuously improving the process so that the error will not occur again.

Statistical process control (SPC) — this uses statistical sampling and control charts to monitor the process so that corrective action can be taken immediately when, or even before, the error occurs.

Total quality control (TQC) — this is the control of quality in all aspects of the organization using a variety of systems tools and statistical control tools.

Just-in-time (JIT) — JIT is the Toyota production philosophy focusing on materials efficiency and waste elimination in the production process.

Total quality management (TQM) — this moves the quality process out of the realm of "control" (baby sitting) quality and into the realm of "managing" (motivating) quality. TQM was discussed in detail in Chapter 7.

Process re-engineering (PR) — PR is a change system that promotes "rapid, radical, change" throughout the organization. This change model is also discussed in detail in Chapter 7.

ISO 9000 — ISO is a certification process initiated by the European Union. It requires that anyone who wishes to bring a product into Europe must get certified. ISO 9000 is a procedurization of the quality process. It documents that what you say you are going to produce is what you produce. It is not customer oriented, it is procedure oriented. Some of the more progressive (in terms of quality) organizations have seen it as a bureaucratic step backwards. Other, not so leading edge companies see it as a positive step which formalizes their quality process.[14]

Quality functional deployment (QFD) (sometimes referred to as quality systems deployment or QSD) — this is the buzzword that has been given to the organized Japanese way of implementing a goal directed quality change process. More is said about this change tool in Chapter 7.

Quality buzzwords are floating around by the dozen. If you haven't seen your favorite in this list, check the glossary at the end of the book.

Quality systems are building blocks and should be treated as such. They are not isolated entities. An enterprise should custom design a quality system for their use utilizing the systems listed above along with other tools like systems analysis and process documentation.

The Role of the eManager in Quality

Quality is not the function of a department, it is the function of the company. As long as we think about quality as someone else's job (like a quality eManager) we never get involved in it ourselves. However, being world-class requires that in today's competitive market we have to be totally involved in quality. This means involvement by every department, every employee and every job function. You've got to want to be involved in quality before a quality program will work. Involvement requires time: time spent in training,

---

14. To find an ISO certifier, contact one of the quality organizations listed later in this chapter. You might also like to read Voehl, Frank, Peter Jackson and David Ashton, *ISO 9000 — An Implementation Guide for Small to Mid-Sized Businesses* (Florida: St Lucie Press) 1994; Kanholm, Jack, *ISO 9000 Explained — 65 Requirements Checklist and Compliance Guide* (Florida: St Lucie Press) 1994; Ewing, Suzanne E and Glenna K Russell, "Recipe for ISO 9000 Certififcation", *APICS 37th International Conference Proceedings,* op. cit., pp. 477-479; Parisher, James Wilson, "Documentation for ISO 9000: What is the Right Balance?", *APICS 37th International Conference Proceedings,* op. cit., pp. 501-505; Kuhn, Ralph R, "How to Meet Europe's ISO 9000 Standard by 1992", *APICS 34th International Conference Proceedings,* op. cit., pp. 232-234.

time spent in teams and in meetings discussing quality improvements, and time spent sharing and co-ordinating the quality effort.

But there are two types of customer to deal with — the internal customer and the external customer. Internal customer quality is employee conscious, empowered and participative quality. The employee is the internal customer of the company, and should be treated as such. This means that you as an eManager need to think of fellow employees as your customers in that you pass information and product on to them. The quality of what you pass on to them needs to be a quality product and you should expect to receive a quality product from those who pass information and product to you.

External customer quality is customer participative quality, as described earlier. The end user customer is consulted to find out how they perceive quality and then we satisfy their perceptions with our performance.

Is quality a good measure of strategy performance? Definitely! Especially when it's tied internally to the employee and externally to the customer. There are lots of quality organizations that would be delighted to help you prepare your quality initiative. There is a listing of them in Appendix 12.3.

The Measure of Quality

Defining what quality is for you and your customer is the first step in the development of a quality measure. Are we focusing on "A", "B" or "C" level quality? Next, we need to come up with ways in which to measure this definition. I will offer some examples of quality measures so you can see how some "A" and "B" level companies have approached this issue. For example, Canadian National measures the following quality items in the service sector: on time delivery and punctuality, competitive prices, no damaged goods, right container equipment available, correct billing and good communication.

FedEx measures the following items and attaches the corresponding weights to them. The weights are determined by customer service determining "what is important to the customer". These weights are part of the FedEx Service Quality Indicators (SQI). They are:

- lost packages (ten points)
- damaged packages (ten points)
- delivery on the wrong day (five points)
- tracing required (three points)
- late pick up (three points)
- complaints re-opened (three points)
- delivery late on the right day (one point)
- invoice adjustment requested (one point)
- missing proof of delivery information (one point).

In the FedEx system, the customer is often unaware of a failure. Some things may be troublesome to one customer but are not a concern to another. However, since FedEx has stated that its quality goal is 100 per cent customer satisfaction, it has established a standard that strives to satisfy all customers.[15]

United Parcel Service (UPS) is looking for financial returns in terms of increased sales. It is accomplishing this by giving its drivers free time to talk to the customer. UPS believes that the customer wants interaction and that this "hand holding" aspect of customer service will develop sales leads.

World-class Quality

In moving from the role of general manager to world-class quality eManager, several points need to be made.

1. We need to establish a *quality culture* where all of management, from top management to the clean-up crew, are trained in how to recognize and improve quality. They need to have quality goals established and these quality goals need to focus on the business strategy. The workforce needs to think, feel, eat, sleep and breathe quality. They need to be motivated to be on a constant lookout for quality improvements. They need to be excited to find opportunities to make a quality difference in the organization.

2. Quality needs *direction*. It needs to be part of a strategic plan that focuses on a specific objective.

3. Quality is not short term, it is a *long-term commitment*.

4. Funding and staffing need to be available to do the necessary *training*. Remember the learning curve of Figure 4.2 on page 78.

5. The workers, not the managers, produce quality. *Empowerment* of the employees allowing them to improve quality and rewarding them by giving them the benefits of the improvements (recognition, financial rewards) is the only way to motivate quality change. For example, Jan Carlzon, when he took over SAS (Scandinavian Airline System), gave the front line employees the freedom and authority to do whatever it takes to improve quality service. He kept them informed, opened up communication lines and give them direction.

World-class management requires a strong focus on quality, both internal and external to the organization. Quality is customer satisfaction, and customer satisfaction is world class.[16]

---

15. FedEx offers a document called the *Quality Profile* which outlines its quality programs including SQI.
16. Again see my book *The Plant Operations Handbook*. See also "Making Quality Pay —

PRODUCTIVITY

During an age when Christianity dominated Rome, a devastating plague was destroying the population of the city. St Augustine testified to the population that the only way to end the plague was to close all theaters, because these displeased the Lord. The theaters were closed, but the plague continued. Faith in the wrong messenger caused useless effort to be placed in the wrong areas. Similarly, faith in the wrong types of productivity can cause us to expend a tremendous amount of effort trying to correct a symptom while at the same time totally ignoring the real problem. Let's take a closer look.

What is productivity? We could say that:

$$\text{Productivity} = \frac{\text{Output}}{\text{Input}}$$

The output part of the equation is easy. It's net sales (gross sales adjusted by returns). It's the input part of the equation that gets confusing. For example, the US uses labor productivity as its measure of productivity performance when it compares itself with other countries, and is by far the best in the world with this measure. We generate more per productive labor hour than any other workforce in the world. Just look at our agriculture output. Less than 3 per cent of the US labor force, which is about 0.1 per cent of the world's population, generates about a quarter of the world's agricultural output. Similarly, the US is just as impressive in technology development numbers, but meaningful numbers are much harder to come by. So why, if our productivity is so impressive, do we have an ever increasing deficit? Simply because we are measuring the wrong type of productivity. We are putting our faith in closing theaters.

Some other alternative types of productivity calculations exist and they should be considered. Some examples are given below.

1. *Labor dollar productivity*, where labor dollars rather than labor hours are used as the input number, would adjust for our high cost of labor and bring the productivity numbers down slightly.

2. *Total factor productivity* would include the costs of all input factors, like materials, energy and equipment in the productivity calculation. This model is discounted in the US because of the claim that materials and energy cost the same for everyone so they wouldn't significantly effect the calculation. However, in a global economy, this is not a valid assumption.

3. *Value-added productivity* is where the input is the difference between the purchased materials costs and the sold materials costs. The best way to

How Companies are Rethinking the Management Buzzword of the 1980s", *Business Week* (August 8 1994).

describe this process is to again look at our radio building analogy. If we are building a radio, and in the radio we have a tuner and a power supply. Both components cost ten dollars in raw materials, but the tuner can be sold on the open market for fifteen dollars and the power supply can be sold for twenty dollars. We earn ten dollars for every power supply, and only five dollars for every tuner. Value-added productivity would suggest that we have someone else produce the tuner and we build the power supply ourselves, thereby maximizing the value-added productivity. The value-added productivity model is a favorite with several foreign firms (primarily Asian) that I am familiar with.

4. *Change productivity* measures the change (as opposed to absolute number values) in output over the change in input. This would show labor productivity improvement, or value-added improvements. This is an area where the US is very weak. The US has high total productivity, but we are losing ground to the rest of the world. By comparing our productivity growth with the productivity growth of the rest of the world we would get a better feel for where we are going (future), rather than where we are (present) or where we have been (past).

With so many productivity measures, does productivity really have any meaning? Unfortunately, not too much as an external measure. However, internally it can be an extremely useful measure. If we monitor our own total factor productivity, or value-added productivity, from one year to the next, we can learn a lot about our own ability to remain competitive.

Productivity Improvements

The key to productivity improvement is to improve the performance of your input, whatever that is. Hopefully, you are using a meaningful productivity measure such as total factor productivity or value-added productivity. That being the case, productivity improvements revolve around the value-added factors. We need to add value to the output in every step of the enterprise while at the same time reducing the inputs. Reducing the inputs primarily means reducing the waste in the inputs, such as unnecessary processing steps and unnecessary time. We need to minimize or eliminate functions that do not add value to the output product. We need to eliminate waste in as many resource areas as possible, a waste being any non-value-added activity.

World-class Productivity

Is productivity a world-class performance measurement tool? Definitely![17]

---

17. Examples of further reading would be Drucker, Peter F, "The New Productivity Challenge", *Harvard Business Review* (November-December 1991) pp. 69-79; Bell, Robert

As long as we focus on our own internal productivity improvements and don't become over confident by comparing ourselves with other countries. Value-added or total factor productivity, especially changes in productivity measures, are enormously valuable in letting us know if we are getting competitively better at utilizing our resources to maximize the benefit to our customers and our organization.

We need to become high productivity performance workplaces. For example, the National Productivity Board of Singapore claims that 62 per cent of Singapore's economic growth is directly the result of productivity gains since the 1970s.[18] We need high productivity performance that is focused on the right productivity measures. For more details on productivity improvements see Appendix 12.3 for a list of productivity improvement organizations that sell literature and offer seminars and conferences on the subject.

EFFICIENCY AND COST

The lash may force men to physical labor; it cannot force them to spiritual creativity.

Sholem Asch

Efficiency and cost are internal (to the organization) measures of performance to standard. Almost always, efficiency is the comparison of labor performance against some standard rate of production. For example, if you produce 100 units per hour but the standard rate of production, based on some historical average for your function, is to produce 80 units per hour, then your efficiency is 125 per cent and you would get a good bonus.

Cost is a measure of reducing the inputs into a process, primarily accomplished by reducing the labor force or the materials purchasing costs. Most companies develop costs around three categories: materials, labor and burden. Materials are considered to be an uncontrollable cost which is minimized by price bidding the vendors. It is uncontrolled because all the competitors can come up with the same materials cost minimizations. Burden is also considered to be uncontrollable and is simply allocated over all the enterprise's output. That leaves labor as theoretically the only controllable cost that can be minimized. So cost cutting, as a performance measurement tool, usually means labor cost minimization. An example may help to illustrate the fallacy of this cost evaluation process. In most forms of discrete manufacturing, we get the following cost breakdown:

R and John M Burnham, op. cit.; Grove, Andrew S, *High Output Management* (New York: Vintage Books) 1983.

18. National Productivity Board of Singapore, "Singapore: The Guiding Light of Productivity", *Productivity SA* (September-October 1994) pp. 11-13.

labor — 8 to 10 per cent

materials — 50 to 60 per cent

burden — 30 to 40 per cent.

Cost reduction would focus on improving the 10 per cent labor cost component. However, using these numbers, if we focus on a 10 per cent improvement in labor cost, we would get an overall cost improvement of less than 1 per cent. However, if we were to reduce burden cost by 10 per cent we would receive a 3 to 4 per cent cost reduction overall. Obviously, the benefit in cost reduction is in the larger percentage players of materials and burden. The traditional labor cost cutting focus is misdirected.

Additionally, by improving labor cost by 10 per cent, we may end up costing by more than the one per cent overall cost savings that we thought we gained. To understand let's consider a production line where we are focusing on being labor efficient (minimizing labor cost). In order to keep labor busy we need to have plenty for them to work on (more materials). The more materials we have, the more inventory carrying costs we incur. I have experienced numerous situations where this inventory carrying cost has increased materials cost by more than the labor savings gained. The result is that improved labor efficiency has, in total, resulted in increasing the cost of production.

Similarly, improving materials efficiency decreases labor efficiency. In order to be materials efficient, which means keeping the materials in the production process (being worked on) as much as possible and minimizing inventories, we can't always keep everyone busy (labor inefficiency). However, a 10 per cent increase in materials efficiency earns a 5 to 6 per cent overall improvement. Even if this results in costing a 10 per cent loss in labor efficiency, we will have a net gain in overall efficiency of 4 to 5 per cent.

Unfortunately, American management finds it very easy to tolerate inventory standing around and doing nothing but incurring cost (financing costs), but they go absolutely crazy if they see labor standing around doing nothing but incurring cost (wages). Some day we will wake up to realize that the inventory standing around is costing us more than the labor which is standing around.

Another example of a confused efficiency focus is to look at the factories that are being relocated overseas in an attempt to take advantage of a labor cost reduction. I am directly familiar with a plant that was transferred from Michigan to Mexico for this reason. The result was that labor cost was reduced. Unfortunately, material carrying cost was increased so dramatically because of the material transfer time of one to two months between the two locations that the labor cost reduction was by far outweighed by the cost increases that were buried in burden (interest costs). Even today, the plant relocation is considered a good move because the cost of labor is the only measure of performance that is used. The plant has been in the red every year since the move.[19]

Efficiency and cost are outdated forms of strategy performance measurement. Unfortunately, of the four measures under discussion (quality, productivity, cost and efficiency), efficiency and cost are the ones that are used the most often. For example, I know of several companies who have elaborate quality and productivity training improvement programs that they put their employees through. Yet, incentive pay and bonuses are based on employee efficiency and cost performance. Obviously, if the pay check is based on number of units output, regardless of whether the units are quality units or not, the employee is motivated to produce quantity, not quality, output.

Wickham Skinner also agrees with this assessment of the use of efficiency and cost. He states that the use of the efficiency and cost measures is keeping us from being productive. He stresses that the use of cost and efficiency as a measurement tool avoids competitiveness.[20]

World-class management would understand the inefficiency of using efficiency and cost as strategic performance measurement tools. The focus on labor performance to standard only ignores the larger, more value-added resource components of the organization's processes like technology or materials. The use of cost performance also tends to hide the real opportunities for adding value and eliminating waste. If you are still measuring efficiency and cost performance, you need to rethink what measures might be more rapid in moving your organization to world-class status.

You get what you pay for.

WHAT MEASURE IS BEST?

On my honor I will do my best . . .

Boy Scout oath

Why is the boy scout oath so important to us as children and so ignored by us as adults? Is being "best" no longer very important? Or maybe we are just giving it a new name. Now we are trying to be world-class.

At New United Motor Manufacturing, Inc. (NUMMI) in Fremont, CA, workers receive problem-solving skills before they go to work on the production line. The reason? New people breed new ideas and you can't find quality or productivity improvement opportunities if you're not trained to recognize

---

19. NAFTA has greatly reduced the transfer time to Mexico. However, the example given here is still a good one as there is still a significant transfer time to Mexico and the transfer time to Asia or South America, where many plants are being relocated, is still very large.
20. Skinner, Wickham, "The Productivity Paradox", *Harvard Business Review* (July, August 1986).

them. Part of this training includes team participation training. Employees learn to recognize safety, quality, productivity and cost saving opportunities. They are cross-trained to learn a variety of functions, so that they understand their fit in the big picture and so they understand their internal customers better. NUMMI has become a Stage 4 (see Chapter 6) company with effective empowered involvement of employees in the quality and productivity improvement process. As a result, in 1992, the average number of defects per 100 cars manufactured was:

- United States — 125 defects
- Asia — 105 defects
- NUMMI — 83 defects.

The answer to what strategic performance measure is best is actually very simple. In a move to world-class management status you should use customer based quality and total factor or value-added productivity change.

Quality and productivity are not achieved at the expense of the other. They go hand in hand, like two sides of a coin. Improving quality can be done in such a way so as to simultaneously improve productivity. It goes back to the slogan:

Work smarter, not harder.

Warner-Lambert's Technical Operations Division shifted to a focus on quality and productivity improvement. In 1983 it formally instituted what it referred to as its total production system (TPS). This incorporated extensive training programs, JIT production and SPC quality tools. The TPS program contained three essentials:

1. a focus on the improvement of production and administrative processes

2. the use of multi-discipline teams trained in problem-solving and statistical methods

3. the direction and management of local projects by the local management.

The TPS program focused on total productive output and, in their words, "was really a total success".

In 1988 it shifted this focus to the Total Customer Satisfaction (TCS) system. It saw the movement from TPS to TCS as a migration process, not as a replacement of good for bad. TPS was needed, and made a difference. But there came a point where TCS was needed to take that final, competitive, leading edge step. TCS was a step toward a continuous quality improvement process. It incorporated the 3 "M" quality process which identifies five essentials of quality improvement:

1. quality is defined as conformance to customer expectations

2. measurement of quality is done through indicators of customer satisfaction

3. the objective is conformance to expectations 100 per cent of the time

4. quality is attained through prevention and specific improvement projects

5. management commitment leads the quality process.

In developing the TCS program, Warner-Lambert started by developing a vision and mission statement focusing on the customer perspective. It then developed an implementation strategy for TCS using eight elements:

1. management leadership — open communication, empowerment, motivating innovation

2. organization — quality steering and improvement teams similar to the TQM process described in Chapter 7

3. education — quality education, training in skills, methods and techniques

4. develop a sensitivity for customer expectations — information analysis, customer surveys

5. quantifying conformance — identifying a measurement criteria, goals setting, improvement towards 100 per cent conformance

6. communication of achievements — awareness and recognition

7. action — projects and systems that bring visible improvements

8. annual plan — annually refocus the quality effort.

Some of the results of this migratory improvement process from TPS through TCS are outlined below:

	1984	1990
Cost of Goods as a Per cent of Sales	38.4	32.3
Inventory as a Per cent of Sales	14.1	8.4
Inventory Turnover	2.7	3.8
Dollar Sales per Employee	75.7	34.3
Dollar after Tax Profit per Employee	5.4	13.9

> The way we deal with each other, the way we respond to our phones and memos — everything in the process is designed to show our concern for our customers — internal and external.
>
> Dr Elias Hebeka,
> Warner-Lambert Technical Operations Division[21]

21. QPMA "Warner-Lambert Changes Focus and Comes Up a Big Winner", *Commitment Plus* (May 1991) Vol. 6. No.7.

WHERE TO BEGIN

Here's a test to see if you're on the road to being world-class.

Question 1. How good are you at satisfying your most crucial internal customer — your spouse and children (or parents if you don't have a spouse and children)?

Question 2. When was the last time you asked this internal customer how satisfied they are with your output? No! I don't mean sexual! What I am referring to is in every way except sexual.

If you can't add value to the lives of those people that you love, how can you bring meaning to the lives of those that you work with? Quality begins in the home. Do good there and you'll also feel good about yourself at work!

> Live joyfully with the wife whom thou lovest . . .
>
> Ecclesiastes 9:9

SUMMARY

> It is better to shoot for the stars and miss than aim for the gutter and hit it.

An operations manager was riding in a hot air balloon and because of intensive cloud cover, it had been days since he had seen the ground. Finally there was a break in the cloud cover and he looked down and spotted an information systems manager on the ground. He yelled down, "Where am I?"

The information manager responded, "Three hundred feet up in the air heading north." Just then the balloon drifted into another cloud.

The operations manager thought to himself, "That's just the type of information I always get. The information was completely accurate, but totally useless."

Good performance in both of the strategic areas of productivity and quality, on a continuing basis, won't guarantee a competitive position, but this would definitely be a good sign that you are moving in the right direction. Both productivity and quality, in a world-class setting, if they are goal directed towards customer satisfaction, will focus on waste elimination (value-added increases). The two strategies work together to simultaneously drive your enterprise toward world-class competitive status.

With a handle on what strategic performance measures we should use if we are to become world-class eManagers, let's now move forward to investigate the other areas of strategic competitive advantage.

Like most things in life, there is no one best solution for integration, information or measurement and motivation (don't forget to read Appendix 12.4). The best solution for you is usually not found by simply copying someone else's solution. And it should not be focused on operational efficiency. Rather, it should be focused on the goal, which, in a world-class setting should be the customer or the employee.

> To find out how to improve productivity, quality, and performance, ask the people who do the work.
>
> Peter F Drucker

APPENDIX 12.1: SOME SOFTWARE ANALYSIS OPTIONS

The American Production and Inventory Control Society
(APICS)
500 West Annandale Road
Falls Church, Virginia 22046-4274
(703) 237-8344

Council of Logistics Management
(CLM)
2803 Butterfield Road
Oak Brook, IL 60521
(708) 574-0985

APPENDIX 12.2: QUALITY GURUS

The gurus of quality all agree on the need for a focused and concentrated effort towards achieving quality improvements in order to be world-class competitive. However, they disagree dramatically on the best road to getting there. This appendix will not attempt to explain each of their philosophies in detail, it will just give you a little background in each and offer you tools to research each of these gurus further.

Ishikawa bases his quality program on seven tools. These are in-process tools that monitor the ongoing flow of the process. The tools are:

- Pareto charts
- cause and effect diagrams
- stratification
- check sheets
- histograms
- scatter diagrams
- control charts.

Taguchi uses "off-line" methods for quality improvement. He focuses on things that can be done to improve the product or the process through off-line studies. Shingo focuses on the Toyota production philosophy known as just-in-time (JIT).[22]

Deming has a series of "points" that he feels are the quality tools of success.[23] These are not so much tools, as a prescription for quality systems reform. They are:

1. create consistency of purpose toward improvement of product and service — develop a plan to become competitive, stay in business and provide jobs

2. adopt a new philosophy — we are in a new economic age and can no longer live with commonly accepted levels of delays and mistakes

3. cease dependence on mass inspection — require statistical evidence that quality is built-in which eliminates the need for inspections on a mass basis

4. end the practice of awarding business to vendors based on the price tag and instead, depend on meaningful measures of quality along with price; move towards single suppliers for any one item

5. improve constantly and forever the system of production and service, thereby improving quality and productivity, and resulting in decreased costs

6. institute modern training methods

7. supervise never-ending improvement through leadership

8. drive out fear so that everyone may work effectively for the company

9. break down organizational barriers so that everyone works on problem solving as a team

10. eliminate arbitrary numerical goals, posters and slogans for the workforce which seek new levels of productivity without providing the means

11. replace management by-the-numbers with never-ending improvement

---

22. Shingo, Shigeo, *Study of the Toyota Production System from the Industrial Engineering Viewpoint* (Tokyo: Japanese Management Association) 1981; Shingo, Shigeo, *Non-Stock Production and the Shingo System for Continuous Improvement* (Tokyo: Japanese Management Association) 1988.

23. See, for example, Gitlow, Howard S and Shelly J Gitlow, *The Deming Guide to Quality and Competitive Position* (Prentice-Hall) 1987; Walton, Mary, *Fourteen Points and Seven Deadly Diseases from the Deming Management Method* (New York: Perigee Books) 1986; Deming, W Edwards, "Improvement of Quality and Productivity Through Action by Management", *National Productivity Review* (Winter 1981-82) Vol. 1, No. 1, pp. 12-22.

12. remove barriers that rob employees of their pride of workmanship

13. educate and retrain everyone

14. create a structure which will push the prior thirteen points every day.

Deming has identified five deadly diseases of the quality process. They are:

1. lack of constancy of purpose and lack of goals

2. emphasis on short-term profits

3. evaluation by performance, merit rating, or annual review of performance

4. mobility of management — avoid job-hopping managers

5. running a company on visible figures only.

Deming focuses on people working smarter, not harder. eManagers need to remove 85 per cent of the defect-creating elements that are "systematic" and require management intervention. The workforce will eliminate the rest if they are allowed to, and motivated to do so.

Juran has developed a "breakthrough sequence" of quality improvement steps.[24] They are:

1. breakthrough in attitudes by proving to the employees that changes are needed

2. identify the vital few projects using Pareto analysis

3. organize for a breakthrough in knowledge using a steering group and a diagnostic group

4. conduct the analysis

5. determine how to overcome resistance to change

6. institute the change

7. institute controls to monitor and follow-up on the changes.

Crosby also has a series of fourteen points for quality improvement.[25] He focuses on showing that quality control is something that happens in the management office and not just on the factory floor. Quality begins with the people — all the people! They are:

1. management commitment

---

24. Juran, J M, *Juran's Quality Control Handbook* (ASQC) 1988.
25. Crosby, Philip B, *Quality is Free* (New York: McGraw-Hill) 1979; Crosby, Philip B, *Quality Without Tears* (New York: McGraw-Hill) 1984.

2. quality improvement team

3. quality measurement

4. cost of quality evaluation

5. quality awareness

6. corrective action

7. establish an *ad hoc* committee for a zero defects program

8. supervisor training

9. zero defects day to kick off the program

10. goal setting

11. error cause removal by error acknowledgement within 24 hours

12. recognition through non-financial prizes and rewards

13. quality councils

14. do it over again every twelve to eighteen months.

APPENDIX 12.3 : PRODUCTIVITY AND QUALITY CENTERS

For your reference I have included a listing of productivity and quality centers. They include:

The American Production and Inventory Control Society
(APICS)
500 West Annandale Road
Falls Church, Virginia 22046-4274
(703) 237-8344

Quality and Productivity Management Association
(QPMA)
300 N. Martingale Rd., Suite 230
Schaumburg, Illinois 60173
(708) 619-2909

GOAL / QPC
13 Branch Street
Methuen, MA 01844-1953
(800) 643-4316
Association for Quality and Participation
(AQP)
801-B West Eighth Street

Cincinnati, Ohio 45203
(513) 381-1959

American Society of Quality Control
(ASQC)
611 East Wisconsin Ave.
Milwaukee, WI 53201-3005
(800) 248-1946

Council of Logistics Management
2803 Butterfield Road #380
Oak Brook, IL 60521-1156
(708) 574-0985

American Productivity and Quality Center
(APQC)
123 N. Post Oak Lane
Houston, Texas 77024
(713) 681-4020

International Productivity Service
200 Constitution Avenue NW
Room N5409
Washington, DC 20210
(202) 523-7464

APPENDIX 12.4: HOW A MEASUREMENT SYSTEM CHANGE MOTIVATES PERFORMANCE IMPROVEMENTS

(summarized from 1999 APICS Education and Research Foundation Study: *Performance Measurement Systems and How They Are Used As Employee Motivators*)

Background

The author has long felt that the key to successful performance is not in systems and procedures, like ISO Certification. Rather, successful performance is found in a meaningfully structured measurement system which is focused on results rather than on data collection. With this idea in mind, the author received an APICS grant funding research focused on the relationship between motivation and measurement, with the belief that:

The measurement system directly effects employee performance.

The author went to work for Precision Printers, Inc., a company which was structured and focused on volume. Quality was secondary and was not used as a measure of employee performance. A shift was made to eliminate the volume measure and focus on quality performance in the belief that driving for quality will result in volume increases, but driving for volume will not improve quality. The transition from volume to quality occurred as a series of stages:

- production planning training
- total quality management (TQM) training
- goal/measurement system redesign
- the "quality week"
- team based empowerment
- ongoing continuous improvement programs.

Each of these areas will be discussed, but first we should have a little background about Precision Printers, Inc. (PPI).

Company Background

PPI opened its doors in 1982 as Marshall Marketing under the guidance of its founders Don and Frank Marshall. Later the same year it changed to the name Precision Printers. The garage it started in was replaced five short years later by a 5,700 square foot facility. By 1989 it had taken its initial $100,000 per year in sales with four employees to $1 million in sales and nineteen employees. It accomplished this by acquiring customers like Freightliner, Infocus, Fender Musical and Grass Valley Group/Tektronics producing primarily overlays and membrane switches.

In 1992, with the acquisition of an aggressive new customer, IGT, the face of PPI changed drastically. IGT doubled the sales and moved PPI into the world of high volume mass production with stringent quality and registration requirements. Additionally, many of the existing customers have also increased their business.

By 1994 PPI had grown to 50 people. In 1995 it was honored with receiving ISO 9000 certification and by 1996 had grown to $5 million in sales. In 1997 it had grown to the point where it needed to make a second move to the their current 16,000 square foot premises. Currently PPI has 108 employees.

PPI believes that thrilling the customer means delivering a product that is on time and defect free, or it should be free. PPI has incorporated systems that focus on a competitive, leading edge stance in technology. This technology includes the internal systems and procedure technologies such as:

- ISO 9000 certification – PPI was recognized by *Quality Digest* for its excellence in achieving certification

- implementing a facilities wide total quality management (TQM) system which involves everyone, from CEO to the newest employee
- a corporate wide enterprise resource planning (ERP) system that is manufacturing resources planning (MRP II) based to improve production scheduling and responsiveness
- a quality initiative that focuses the entire company on continuous improvements through teaming
- improved quality testing procedures with tools like integrated switch testing and bar coding
- involving and integrating the customer into its processes through site visits and improved communication.

The Transformation

The transformation that occurred at PPI was to take the volume/revenue based measurement system out. They had built up $1 million of unshipped customized finished goods inventory because the measurement system focused on revenue to be produced. The measurement transformation that took place changed the focus of the company to quality units produced while at the same time limiting inventory to no more than 30 days.

The measurement change was initiated by implementing an extensive training program which focused on production/inventory management. The training focused on how inventory build-up was destroying profitability. It showed that managing inventory was more important for profitability than managing labor. It showed that quality could only improve if it was measured and motivated by an incentive program. It showed that the current defect rate was costing the company money and chewing up valuable capacity. It taught the employees about how quality should be measured and that quality improvements came from the employees, not from management. TQM training was also included and focused on cross-functional team building with empowered ownership.

The next phase of the program required an implementation point which was set up as a "Quality Week". During this week the goal was "To Produce Only Perfect Parts". The employees were given the freedom to tear anything apart, move anything, or get with anyone. It didn't matter if only one part was produced, but that part had to be perfect.

PPI also had to reconstruct some new goals and objectives. Quality was the new goal and was defined as:

- defect rate reduction
- customer complaint reduction
- improved delivery performance
- cycle time reduction

- inventory level reduction.

All of these measures have a direct effect on profitability and customer satisfaction.

The week began with a great deal of fear and trepidation. Management was concerned that the employees would just stand around, not knowing what to do. However, what happened was that the employees were excited. They had always wanted to have the time and freedom to attack the machinery and figure out why things happened and how they could be fixed. Teams formed spontaneously. Management basically had to get out of the way before they got run over. The employees enjoyed the experience and several of them commented about how much fun they were having. The following is an example of some of the improvements that were made during a typical "Quality Week" day (this is the actual performance report that was distributed). Some of the abbreviations are as follows (since this is an actual company document I chose not to change it):

parts prep — parts preparation department which cleans, folds and stacks product for shipment

touch switch — the touch switch assembly department

reg lam — registered lamination department which laminates materials to metals

pos $ sheets — positive dollar sheets are a reporting mechanism that track costs

PCU — pre-cut department prepares materials by cutting them down to production sizes.

QUALITY WEEK - DAY 2

THOUSANDS AND THOUSANDS OF IDEAS AND SOLUTIONS

Think about it . . . 10 things a day multiplied by 200 working days equals 2000 things that got done. WOW!!! Because of the success of the last two days, a company meeting at 2:00 PM today has been called to see what the next levis is

Figure 12.6: Awards Issued

TQM TEAM	WHO	ISSUE	ACTION	PRIZE
Parts Prep/ Touch Switch	Josh, Wendy, Nancy B, Scott, Sherri, Stevere	Parts sticking together, moving protective cover from windows	Slip sheeting instead of recovering windows	$20
Die Cut, Touch Switch, Quality, Print	Justin P, Rob, Jeff, Steve, Joe, Judy, Matt, John V, John C, Skip, Brandon, *Josh Derek, Wendy*	Touchswitch conductive layer registration	Season polyester prior to print to reduce variation	$20 Music Certificate
Stencil	Bill, Ralph, Tyson, Karl	Masking tape falling apart, shredding into ink	Use box tape	$20
Print Coordinators	***Judy, Heath, Mike, Greg, Jesiah***	***Wrong ink getting into wrong screen***	***1-3 cans of ink at each press, provide only the necessary amount of ink***	***Movie Passes***
Reg Lam	Skip, Randy, Stacy	Difficult assemblies – requiring highly skilled hand/ eye co-ordination	Making tabs and jigs, improved quality and efficiency	$20
Touch Switch	Gerhard, Karen, Steve, Rich P	Order requirements, late list qty's, WIP qty's	Using correct tools to track quantities and due dates, filling out pos $ sheets, using 456	Movie Passes
Touch Switch	Nancy, Scott	Clean room environment	Made a cleaning schedule	$20

The awards in bold above were ideas implemented from yesterday's update. I'm sure there were more!

IDEAS:

➢ Someone interested in a job has the opportunity to spend a little time in the area of interest

➢ Job switching / trading

➢ Identify the areas

> ➢ Artwork drying racks – cleaning films in the loop

> ➢ Clamps for the vacuum table (exposure room) in stencil – safety and stability and better locking

> ➢ Preventing adhesive from tearing when pulling large amounts of parts out of the matrix (parts prep)

> ➢ Advanced work orders to PCU from purchasing may help PCU be able to schedule their work better

This is great stuff! I am sure more "out of the box" ideas will make themselves apparent. One of the things noted were the statistics and data and measurements used yesterday confirming the effectiveness of the solutions. Having valid and accurate measurement makes it easier to showcase our efforts. Keep it up everyone!

The Quality Week program taught the employees about teaming, goal setting and empowerment. At first they were skeptical, but once they saw the rewards for their performance, they became seriously involved in the process of improvement. The ongoing continuous improvement process that was kicked off by quality week is still today spontaneously forming teams and attacking quality and performance issues.

The total transformation from volume to quality took about eight months. The first three months were spent in preparation for the shift to quality (quality week) and the last three months were focused on the implementation of the transition. Some of the measurable results can be seen on the following figures. Figure 12.7 shows how the defect rate was steadily increasing from May to about October of 1997. Then, around November, there was a sudden shift, both in the direction of the trend and in the level of the defects. This figure demonstrates the most dramatic effect of the quality improvement process.

Figure 12.8 records customer complaints and shows how they were decreasing because of the new emphasis on quality. Figure 12.9 shows that on time shipment performance had also improved in that there were less late shipments. This is directly related to Figure 12.10 which shows how quality improvements directly reduced cycle times. All these improvements are directly linked together, including the performance on the finished goods inventory (FGI) which has been steadily going down. Cycle time reductions reduced lead times which made the organization more responsive to customer demands. Cycle time reductions also reduced on time performance. It is interesting how all these performance efficiencies were triggered by a measurement system modification.

Figure 12.7: Defect Rates

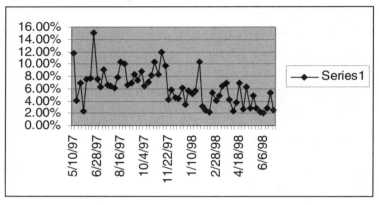

Figure 12.8: Customer Complaints

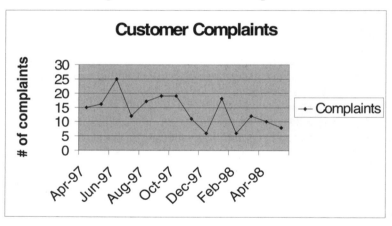

Figure 12.9: On Time Shipments

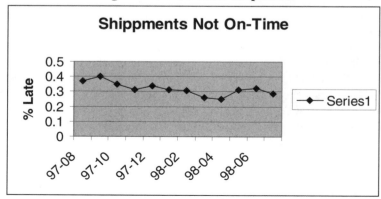

Figure 12.10: Cycle Time

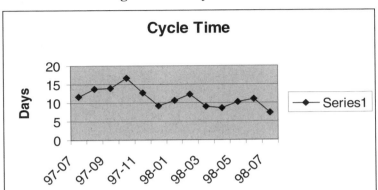

Figure 12.11: Finished Goods Inventory Balance

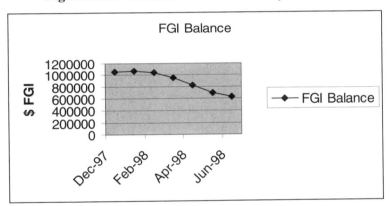

Some non-measurable results of the shift to a quality measurement process include:

- a strong shift from departmentalization to inter-departmental efforts
- engineers working on the production floor
- spontaneous teams are organized to solve specific problems
- the culture of the company has been shifted to being "one big family"
- greatly improved communication
- greatly improved customer relations.

Summary of the Research Findings

The findings of this research project include many additional lessons learned at Precision Printers, Inc.

1. Corporate vision and mission statements (goals) tend to have very little to do with the measurement systems. Tradition does more to dictate the measurement methodologies than do goals. For example, companies have slogans and banners all over the company promoting customer-oriented quality, but employees are still measured and paid based on the number of units produced. These employees care very little about quality, since spending more time checking quality will directly reduce their pay check.

2. Financial measures promote short-term thinking. Managers are numbers focused and will do anything to make the numbers look good on the short-term. Long-term investments are discouraged since they negatively effect the short-term numbers by increasing debt and costs. The result is that a "fix and patch" strategy wins out over a "replace with newer technology" strategy because the earlier costs less on the short term.

3. Blanket corporate-office dictated international measurement systems don't reflect the local management style or culture and are often demotivating rather than motivating as desired.

4. Measurement systems are still thought of as data collection systems and all data is considered to be a good thing. For example, in one company they have been running SPC for one year now and they wanted some recommendations on what they should do with all the data. When told to throw it out since SPC is a process tool for continuous improvement, not for data collection, they were very frustrated. Many companies have not yet realized that the measurement system is what directly motivates employee response and that measuring (like units produced per minute) the wrong things brings the wrong results.

5. There seems to be no understanding of the relationship between goal achievement and resource efficiency. For example, in most discrete manufacturing, labor is less than 10 per cent of the value-added product content, and materials is over 50 per cent. Yet, when cost cutting measures are enacted, we still hack more on the 10 per cent and tend to ignore the 50 plus per cent. In one situation I encountered a company that increased labor productivity by 10 per cent (employee throughput) at the cost of decreased materials efficiency (lower inventory turns) by 5 per cent (increased labor efficiency required more materials availability). Simple mathematics shows us that the increased labor efficiency increased profits by 1 per cent overall (10 per cent times 10 per cent) and that decreased materials efficiency hurt profits by 2.5 per cent overall (50 per cent times 50 per cent). Therefore, increased labor productivity cost the company a 1.5 per cent reduction in profitability.

SUMMARY

This research project has been very enlightening and the initial premise has been proven by the Precision Printers, Inc. example:

The measurement system directly effects employee performance.

Employees tend to focus on keeping their jobs and getting a raise and they consider the measurement system as the primary tool in determining their personal goal achievement. Employees have the ability to make any measurement system look good. The trick is for management to identify what that measurement system should be in order to maximize corporate goal achievement.

SUGGESTIONS FOR FURTHER READING

Abair, Robert A, "Super Measurements: The Key to World-Class Manufacturing", *APICS 34th International Conference Proceedings* (October 1991), pp. 113-115.

Baker, Tom, and Gerry Cleaves, "New Computer Solutions: World-Class Performance Through Improved Planning and Scheduling Integration", *APICS – The Performance Advantage* (October 1991), pp. 28-31.

Barber, Norman F, "Creating Organizational Integration", *APICS 33rd International Conference Proceedings* (October 1990), pp. 40-44.

Bell, Robert R, and John M Burnham, *Managing Productivity and Change* (Cincinnati, Ohio: South-Western Publishing Company) 1991.

Boyst Jr. III, William M, "HRM — Key to the Integrated Management Revolution", *APICS 34th International Conference Proceedings*, APICS, (October 1991), pp. 354-357.

Brown, J. Thomas, "Measuring Performance for Strategic Improvement", *APICS 34th International Conference Proceedings* (October 1991), pp. 107-112.

Cooper, Robin, "You Need a New Cost System When . . .", *Harvard Business Review* (January-February 1989), pp. 77-82.

Crosby, Philip B, *Quality is Free* (New York: McGraw-Hill) 1979.

Crosby, Philip B, *Quality without Tears* (New York: McGraw-Hill) 1984.

Deming, W Edwards, "Improvement of Quality and Productivity through Action by Management", *National Productivity Review*, Vol. 1, No. 1 (Winter 1981-82), pp. 12-22.

Drucker, Peter F, "The New Productivity Challenge", *Harvard Business Review*" (November-December 1991), pp. 69-79.

Gitlow, Howard S and Shelly J Gitlow, *The Deming Guide to Quality and Competitive Position*, Prentice-Hall, 1987.

Greising, David, "Making Quality Pay – How Companies are Rethinking the Management Buzzword of the 1980's", *Business Week* (August 8 1994), pp. 54-59.

Grove, Andrew S, *High Output Management* (New York, NY: Vintage Books) 1983.

Eccles, Robert G, "The Performance Measurement Manifesto", *Harvard Business Review* (January-February 1991), pp. 131-137.

Henson, Holly E, "Performance Measurement in the New Manufacturing Environment", *APICS 34th International Conference Proceedings* (October 1991), pp. 126-128.

Juran, J M, *Juran's Quality Control Handbook*, ASQC, 1988.

Kanholm, Jack, *ISO 9000 Explained – 65 Requirements Checklist and Compliance Guide* (Delray Beach, Florida: St. Lucie Press) 1994.

Lowenthal, Jeffrey N, *Reengineering the Organization: A Step by Step Approach to Corporate Revitalization* (Milwaukee, Wisconsin: ASQC Quality Press) 1994.

Monnin, Michelle, Roger Miller, and Brian Schaenzer, "Are Your Goals and Measurements in Line with Your Time-Based Competition Philosophy?", *APICS 37th International Conference Proceedings* (October 1994), pp. E1-E3.

Maslow, Abraham H, "The Theory of Human Motivation", *Psychological Review*, Vol. 50, 1943), pp. 370-396.

National Productivity Board of Singapore, "Singapore, The Guiding Light of Productivity", *Productivity SA* (September/October 1994), pp. 11-13.

Plenert, Gerhard, "Expanding the Value-Added Cost Component", *Advanced Manufacturing Technology* (October 1989), pp. 86-94.

Plenert, Gerhard, "Integration – Manufacturing's Hidden Buzzword of the 1990s", *International Productivity Journal*, 1991-III (Fall 1991), pp. 11-16.

Plenert, Gerhard, "Solving Indefinable Problems With Backward Utopian Iteration", with R W Kaiser, *Kybernetes*, Vol. 19, No. 4, 1990, pp. 59-62.

Plenert, Gerhard, *The Plant Operations Handbook* (Homewood, Illinois: Business One Irwin Publishing) 1993.

Plenert, Gerhard, "Total Integration of Accounting and Manufacturing Information", *APICS 34th International Conference Proceedings* (October 1991), pp. 366-367.

QPMA, "Warner-Lambert Changes Focus and Comes up a Big Winner", *Commitment Plus*, Quality and Productivity Management Association (May 1991), Vol. 6, No. 7.

Sandras, William A, "Integration: Productivity Thrust of the 1990s", *APICS 34th International Conference Proceedings* (October 1991), pp. 400-402.

Savage, William G, "Implementing an Integrated System: Restructuring the Business Not Just Automating It", *APICS 34th International Conference Proceedings* (October 1991), pp. 382-386.

Sheth, Jagdish, and Golpira Eshghi, *Global Operations Perspectives* (Cincinnati, Ohio: South-Western Publishing Company) 1989.

Shingo, Shigeo, *Non-Stock Production and the Shingo System for Continuous Improvement*, Japan Management Association, Tokyo, 1988.

Shingo, Shigeo, *Study of the Toyota Production System from the Industrial Engineering Viewpoint*, Japanese Management Association, Tokyo, 1981.

Skinner, Wickham, "The Productivity Paradox", *Harvard Business Review* (July-August 1986).

Tarr, James D, "Developing Performance Measurement Systems That Support Continuous Improvement Goals", *APICS 37th International Conference Proceedings* (October 1994), pp. 416-420.

Tincher, Michael G, "World-Class Performance Measurements — How to Get Started", *APICS 37th International Conference Proceedings* (October 1994), pp. 424-428.

U.S. Department of Labor, *Road to High-Performance Workplaces: A Guide to Better Jobs and Better Business Results – 1994*, U. S. Department of Labor – Office of the American Workplace, 1994.

Voehl, Frank, Peter Jackson, and David Ashton, *ISO 9000 – An Implementation Guide for Small to Mid-Sized Businesses* (Delray Beach, Florida: St Lucie Press) 1994.

Uhlemann, William R, "Management Integration for Your Focused Factories", *APICS 34th International Conference Proceedings* (October 1991), pp. 207-210.

Wallace, Thomas F, *World Class Manufacturing* (Essex Junction, Vermont: Omneo, An Imprint of Oliver Wight Publications, Inc.) 1994.

Walton, Mary, *Fourteen Points and Seven Deadly Diseases from the Deming Management Method* (New York: Perigee Books) 1986.

Wisner, Joel D, and Stanley E Fawcett, "Linking Firm Strategy to Operation Decisions Through Performance Measurement", *Production and Inventory Management Journal* (Third Quarter, 1991), pp. 5-11.

Chapter Thirteen

Training and Education – The Learning Organization

When you're through learning, you're through.

Vernon Law, Pitcher,
Pittsburgh Pirates

Let's expand your vision. Figure 13.1 has ten circles (coins) in it forming a triangle. The triangle points upward. Moving only three circles make the triangle point downward. Appendix 13.2 will train you how to change directions. Once you have been trained in how to do it, the shift in directions becomes easy.

Give a man a fish and you've given him a meal; teach a man to fish and you've fed him for the rest of his life.

There are dozens of motivational speakers in the world. One point they all agree on is the value of education. World-class management is positive, growth-oriented change. And change requires learning; learning what's wrong and

Figure 13.1: Ten Circles

learning how to do it better. If I were to list all the literature that focuses on learning, it would require volumes on the subject all by itself. So I'll just include a few of my favorite quotes and stress what you've already heard a million times:

- you can't change if you don't recognize the need for change
- you can't change if you have no focus on what to change
- you can't change if you don't identify what to change
- you can't change if you don't know how to change
- you can't change if you don't know what your alternatives for change are
- you can't change if you are not empowered to implement change.

Nearly all the steps outlined above require education and training. Education and training teaches you and your employees how to change, focuses their changes and helps them make value-added, goal-focused, innovative improvements.

> The ability to think straight, some knowledge of the past, some vision of the future, some skill to do useful service, some urge to fit that service into the well-being of the community — these are the most vital things education must try to produce. If we can achieve them in the citizens of the land, then . . . we shall have brought to America the wisdom and the courage to match her destiny.
>
> Virginia Gildersleeve

The most feared aspect of change is that it takes time. Managers think of training as lost production time, rather than as adding value to the labor resource. As long as we think of the short-term costs — time — and ignore the long-term benefits — a value increased employee that will make long-term improvements — we won't be world-class.

> The best way to help your employees is to give them a fishhook rather than the fish.

A world-class organization is a learning organization. Using this theme, Steiger offers four techniques of change:

1. change has to be a group atmosphere
2. change must be in the leadership methods
3. the vehicle of change is education and re-education
4. the cornerstone of performance is measurements.[1]

---

1. Steiger, Larry Dean, "The Learning Organization", *APICS 34th International Conference Proceedings* (APICS) October 1991, pp. 188-192.

In another article by Tobin, a learning organization is one that lays the foundation for innovation, efficiency and competitiveness. A learning organization has the following three characteristics:

1. an openness to new ideas

2. a culture that encourages and facilitates learning and innovation

3. widespread understanding of the organizations' overall goals and how each person's work contributes to them.

> Learn to unlearn.
>
> Benjamin Disraeli

To create the learning organization, a company must establish five foundations:

1. visible leadership committed to change

2. basic skills which include the mastering of a broad range of technical and non-technical skills such as communications, teamwork, business skills, and self-motivation and improvement skills

3. overcoming functional myopia (blinders) and focus on the goals

4. effective teamwork

5. managers as resources, teachers, coaches, facilitators.[2]

An inadequate investment in human resource development (HRM) is one of the major failures in United States businesses. We have thousands of years of experience available to us in our employee base, yet we barely and rarely tap into it. World-class eManagers have learned how to tap into this experience base by opening communications and by education and training in methods of how to utilize this experience in order to make innovative changes within the organization. Top-down, authoritarian organizations miss out on a great opportunity for innovative change. Empowered organizations tap into this opportunity.

Learning organizations need trained trainers and educated educators. There is value in having those employees closest to the job or function be the ones that teach about it. However, they need to be taught how to teach so that the teaching process is a value-added process, not one that takes twice as long as necessary and accomplishes half as much as needed.

> At Chrysler, we see the role of human resources [education and training] as twofold — to provide leadership and programs that contribute

---

2. See Tobin, Daniel R, " Building a Learning Organization" in Wallace, op. cit.

importantly to the direction and performance of the corporation, and to promote a participative work environment that results in enhanced employee job satisfaction and the production of quality goods and services.

Robert A Lutz,
President, Chrysler[3]

Learning, education and training occurs in groups and through individual effort. Both should be encouraged. It isn't always necessary for an employee to sit in a classroom to be learning. The classroom adds synergy to the learning process and offers the student the opportunity for interaction through questions. However, the inquisitive employee may not have the classes available for what he or she wants to learn. Or perhaps they want to delve into a subject deeper than that offered by the classroom. They should be encouraged to learn, no matter what the setting.

The more you know, the more you realize how much you don't know.

In a classic article on learning organizations, Senge focuses on several key characteristics that world-class eManagers of these types of organizations must have:

- a world-class eManager must teach "an accurate picture of current reality" which is just as important as "a compelling picture of a desired future"
- a world-class eManager must be a leader who takes on the roles of designer, teacher and steward of the big company ship that he or she is sailing
- a world-class eManager requires a new set of skills in order to build a shared vision, build and test models, and utilize systems thinking.[4]

He is educated who knows how to find out what he doesn't know.

George Simmel

One master example of a learning organization is Motorola, Inc., winner of the 1988 Malcolm Baldridge award as an entire corporation. After winning the prize, Motorola went on to push its suppliers to become world-class by telling them that they must be Baldridge Award worthy if they were to remain suppliers for Motorola. One of the results of this threat is that AT&T went on to win three Baldridge awards and the Deming Prize. I have had the benefit of working with Motorola numerous times, doing training as far away as Malaysia,

3. Ulrich, Robert A and A Young, "A Shared Mindset", *Personnel Administrator* (March 1989) p. 45.
4. Senge, Peter M, "The Leader's New Work: Building Learning Organizations", *Sloan Management Review* (Fall 1990) pp. 7-23.

and have found its focus on education inspiring. The following information comes from Robert W Galvin, chairperson of the board for Motorola (see book by Bell and Burnham listed in the bibliography).

Motorola sees its driving thrust as one of constant renewal. Its management travels throughout the organization offering seminars, speeches, etc. Additionally, to strengthen the focus on education and to ensure that 100,000 employees have the skills necessary to achieve the company objectives of 100 per cent customer satisfaction, Motorola has set up its own training center at a cost of over $170 million. Motorola training focuses on:

- training in awareness
- training in processes
- sharing experiences
- bringing in the best teachers of the new ideas
- how to better design for quality
- how better to design for manufacturability
- how better to analyze for quality results with such techniques as statistical process control
- how to improve problem solving skills
- studying the latest techniques in cycle time management — saving time can improve quality
- teaming the best people to employ these trained skills.

> I want to point out . . . that these investments really are costless, as we have gained through greatly reduced manufacturing costs — over $250 million savings in 1987 [one year] — and are continuing to improve. . . [training for the six-year period of 1983 through 1988 cost about $220 million — including the building of the training center]
>
> Robert W Galvin, Chairman, Motorola, Inc.

CHANGE ORIENTED ORGANIZATIONS

> You can get anything in life that you want, if you help enough other people get what they want.
>
> Robert Schuller, Minister

Industrial organizations are formed in order to open the door for learning through courses, seminars, conferences, certification, books, magazines and other literature. They also offer the opportunity for networking (meeting together and chit-chatting) and benchmarking (comparing yourself with others in your industry). I have already listed several of these organizations in this book, such as QPMA, APQC, ASQC, APICS and so on (see Appendixes in Chapter 12). However, you need to identify the organizations of this type that can help you "learn" about the advances in your industry. Some additional HRM organizations are included in Appendix 13.1.

Using conference proceedings from APICS, I will list just a few of the invaluable discussions on education and its role in competitiveness. There are dozens of these types of conferences (with published proceedings) every year.[5]

> Developing a "World Class Manufacturing" (WCM) work force requires the accumulation of new skills while simultaneously "unlearning" old (bad) habits.
>
> Michael R DiPrima

> In each stage of life we do the best we can. We may look back and say "why?" but each stage was really a learning stage for where we are now. And now, we are learning for tomorrow.

SUMMARY

We must regain our leadership role through education.

> Mike Ashapa

Education and training is so important to a world-class setting that will motivate change that it requires a chapter all to itself to emphasize it, even if it is a short one. A world-class organization is a continually learning organization, continually searching for opportunities for self-improvement for every employee in the organization.

> Not having a formal training program appears to be a guaranteed way to limit or even prevent success.
>
> Henry Alex Hutchins,
> Applied Industrial Cybernetics

---

5. Lamfers, Patricia, "Education: The Future of Our Competitiveness", *APICS 34th International Conference Proceedings* op. cit., pp 13-15; DiPrima, Michael R, "Education for the World Class Manufacturing / JIT Organization", *ibid.*, pp. 16-19; Ashapa, M R, "The State of Manufacturing Education in the Untied States", *ibid.*, pp. 27-29; Hutchins, Henry Alex, "Measuring the Results of Training: A Case Study", *ibid.*, pp. 37-40.

APPENDIX 13.1: LEARNING ORGANIZATIONS

Center for the Effective use of Human Resources
Human Resources Research Organization
66 Canal Center Plaza, Suite 400
Alexandria, Virginia 22314
(703) 549-3611

National Workforce Assistance Collaborative
National Alliance of Business
(202) 289-2984

Human Resources Research Organization
66 Canal Center Plaza, Suite 400
Alexandria, Virginia 22314
(703) 549-3611

APPENDIX 13.2: CHANGING DIRECTIONS

Figure 13.2 shows how to change directions. Now that wasn't so hard, was it?

Figure 13.2: Ten Circles Solved

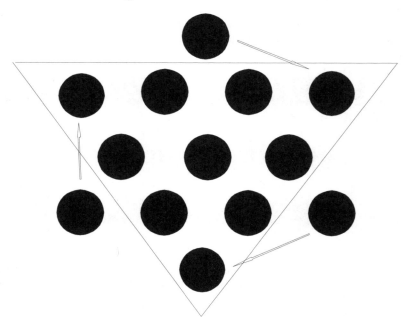

Chapter Fourteen

Teaming Skills and Personal Skills

> You see, really and truly, apart from the things anyone can pick up [the dressing, the proper way of speaking, and so on], the difference between a lady and a flower girl is not how she behaves, but how she's treated. I shall always be a flower girl to Professor Higgins, because he always treats me as a flower girl, and always will; but I know I can be a lady because you always treat me as a lady, and always will.
>
> Eliza Doolittle in *My Fair Lady*
> George Bernard Shaw

This is a chapter about you, the manager. To be a world-class eManager, you need to be a world-class person and you need to be able to find the world-class potential in everyone you deal with.

A world-class eManager is one who doesn't have to offend someone else, or make someone else look small, in order to make themselves look good. A world-class eManager looks good because he or she is good! A world-class eManager builds themselves up by building others up.

I often get the reaction that management has nothing to do with your personal life. These reactions come from individuals who approach management as a function where you keep a distance from your employees. World-class management is becoming one with your employees. A world-class eManager is involved with all the employees. He or she knows them by name, knows how many kids they have and even knows some of their personal struggles. A world-class eManager is a friend to the employees.

How do you become a friend to your employees? By being sincere and trustworthy. Terms like hypocritical, self-centered and unethical are not terms that fit a world-class eManager. In this chapter we will highlight some of the appropriate world-class characteristics without getting preachy.

The world's best reformers are those who begin on themselves.

The best definition of a world-class eManager that I have ever encountered is:

A world-class eManager is the type of manager we would like to be managed by!

THE WORLD-CLASS PERSON

> . . . if any man among you seemeth to be wise in this world, let him become a fool, that he may be wise.
>
> 1 Cor 3:18-19

To be a world-class eManager you need to be a world-class person. A world-class person is one with an unshakable value system; one that can be counted on and one that will stick up for you when you need a friend. Some characteristics of a world-class person are:

- integrity — ethical and honest
- standards and value system — goal focused, loving, humility, morality, obedience
- society value-added — job-enrichment
- leadership — example, enthusiasm, compromising, understanding, self-replacing, environmentally conscious, worker safety conscious, open, sharing, having fun.

Integrity

Integrity has many definitions, but one I like is:

> Integrity is saying what you do, and doing what you say!

Integrity avoids the secretive and sneaky, and is up front with everyone. Integrity is not trying to manipulate anyone by telling them what they want to hear. It is caring more for your word than for the fine print of the contract. Integrity is feeling good about doing good. It's leaving a negotiation process with a clear conscience. As someone once said:

> Integrity is hard to define but I sure recognize it when I see it!

Integrity is having a value system that would make the Pope proud. I'm not asking you to be the Pope. But I am suggesting that we need to have the people around us respect and trust us as if we were more than we are now. We need to have a set pattern of values that we stand for, and which are more important than our job, or money. Only then can we have integrity.

> If you don't believe in something you'll follow anything.

Earlier in this book I discussed non-trust systems, which are systems that were established in order to prevent fraud. I mentioned that the non-trust systems in most corporations, which incorporate computers, accounting, finance, etc. are costing us more than the fraud that they were set up to prevent. Additionally, the biggest fraud that occurs now days is the result of the manipulation ("getting around the system") of the non-trust data collection systems that we set up.[1] We would be better off in all ways, including financially, if we were to just eliminate the non-trust baloney.

We need to realize that non-trust systems are developed by individuals who don't trust others, because they know the kinds of things they would do given half a chance. If we have integrity, and demonstrate to others the value of integrity, we could save a fortune in time, complexity and money by simply trusting people.

> Reputation is made by what you fall for; character is made by what you stand for.

Being ethical is part of having integrity. Ethics primarily attacks manipulative business transactions where you focus on being the winner. Being ethical suggests that the results of business transactions should be a win-win situation for all sides involved in the negotiation process.

Recently there has been a great deal of concern about the lack of ethics in United States business. In an article in *New Accountant*, C William Thomas suggests that younger managers are becoming less ethical and more manipulative. The article suggests that environmental costs and competitive demands are focusing us away from ethical business practices.[2] For example, we may install a chemical plant in India to avoid US worker safety regulations, or we may move a steel products factory to Mexico to avoid pollution regulations. Similarly, an article by Bok suggests that our methods of training new managers, with a focus on analytical processes, brings a blindness to the decision-making process and forgets the ethical people concerns of the decision process. We do what the numbers tell us to do, rather than what our conscience tells us to do.[3]

> We should view personal standards as the "bedrock" of ethical conduct, because all corporations or other entities are made up of people.
>
> C William Thomas

Being honest is part of integrity and ethics. However, I want to draw attention

---

1. Plenert, Gerhard, "Don't Trust the Numbers", *Journal of Systems Management* (October 1989), Vol. 40, No. 10, pp. 34-37.
2. Thomas, C William, "Are Young Managers Less Ethical?", *New Accountant* (March 1991) pp. 3-10.
3. Bok, Derek C, "Social Responsibility in Future Worlds", *Computers and People* (September-October 1982).

to this critical element because it's probably the most important. Honesty is the first step to integrity. Everyone feels that the world should be honest with them, even though they often feel the need for a little dishonesty in their own lives.

Standards and Value System

Having standards and a value system incorporates the direction of your own life. Without it, no one, including you, knows where you stand, and no one stands with you. A standards and value system includes goals and the other characteristics we will be highlighting in this section.

A world-class person's life is goal focused, not just in business, but in all areas. Personal goals should be long range (ten years out), mid range (two to five years out) and short range (within the next year) and should include:

- educational
- business
- social
- ethical, moral or religious
- family
- entertainment/vacation /travel
- physical.

Personal success defines success in any other area. You can't be successful in business if your personal life is a mess. It inevitably effects your business abilities as well. If you can't manage your family, how can you possibly expect to be world-class at managing your business? Your personal life and the life of your family are the foundation of a successful business career.

A goal-focused life is a life that has meaning. With a life that has meaning, you can find purpose in your job. Managers without meaning in their life work in order to keep their jobs and get a raise. Managers with meaning in their life work for the joy of it.

> Life is like a jigsaw puzzle, but you don't have the picture in front of the box to know what it's supposed to look like. Sometimes you're not even sure if you have all the pieces.
>
> Roger von Oech[4]

Being loving encompasses a whole list of attributes, such as compassion, empathy, forgiveness, concern about other's feelings and opinions and having

---

4. von Oech, Roger, *A Whack on the Side of the Head* (Stamford, CT: US Games Systems, Inc.) 1990, p. 51.

a wise and understanding heart. Loving is caring about others. And, as the Bible says, love is having charity in your heart.

Humility is one of those difficult attributes to define, because if you think you're humble, then you not. Humility is realizing that we are all equally children of God and that He sees us all as equals, regardless of what luck life has dealt out for specific individuals. Humility is looking at an employee and realizing that individual could probably do your job better than you do, but you just happened to get there first.

Being moral is being the kind of person that you want the boys who date your daughter to be. Being moral is being a leader in your family, community and church. It's standing up for your beliefs on issues that affect our society, such as sex, family, alcohol, drugs and religion. It's making a difference in the education process, especially as it effects your children.

Being obedient is being respectfully submissive. It's not being a puppy dog, nor is it being blind. It's expressing your opinion, sharing your ideas and then supporting the decisions of your superiors, even if you think they made the wrong decision. Being obedient is not undercutting your superiors' decisions. Of course, I'm talking about judgemental differences, not ethical differences.

Society Value-added

The importance of being society value-added suggests that you are more than just self-interested. In most parts of the world, it is the betterment of society, not the individual, that we all work for (see the section titled "What in the World is Ethical?"). An individual that does not contribute (add value) to society is considered a waste to society. I have been challenged in many countries by the statement "The thing that's gone wrong in the United States is that you are graduating more and more non-value-added individuals in your schools than ever before, and these non-value-added individuals contribute nothing to the economic and social growth of the United States." I'm not sure how to answer this challenge, but it does give us something to think about.

> I have already observed that students in professional schools grow more and more preoccupied with the needs and problems of the clients they serve and less and less concerned with the impact of their profession on the larger society.
>
> Derek C Bok,
> President, Harvard University

Secondary to, but right in line with, being society value-added, is your role in becoming increasingly value-added. Often this is called job-enrichment. This suggests that you are getting more than a pay check out of your job (job retention). It suggests that you are becoming more valuable and, simultaneously, your job is becoming more fun. Job-enrichment suggests that you are broadening the role of your job, thereby making the job and you a more valuable contributor to the goals of the organization (adding more value) while at the same time enriching yourself.

Leadership

The last major category of a world-class person who hopes to be a world-class eManager involves becoming a world-class leader. As we discussed in Chapter 4, a leader focuses on being an example, rather than being a cattle herder. A leader is a servant to employees and serves them as if they were important to him or her.

I was in the local mall early one morning and I walked by a jewelry store. In the store were six employees, half asleep, totally bored and completely tuned out, pretending to listen to a manager who seemed to be preaching a never-ending sermon. It struck me that the only person who was enjoying this browbeating was the manager. Everyone else was planning to go back to work and do things as they had always done them. Most of management is very much a "do as I say, not as I do" philosophy. A leader has a "do as I do and as I say" philosophy because they are both the same. The leader is doing what he or she is saying. The leader manages by example.

A leader with example offers direction. They focus on doing rather then telling and, whenever telling is necessary, they make sure to do what they tell. A leader is also enthusiastic. A leader has goals and has a vision.

A leader is compromising, yet determined and decisive. There are some things worth fighting for, such as ethics, honesty, integrity and morality. And there are some things not worth fighting for, like the procedure an employee uses in solving a problem. Employees, such as our children, don't do things the way you would like them done. But, in many cases, it's the end result you want, not the road travelled. So don't take the fun, that is, figuring out how to do a job, away from the employee. Let the employee have some fun, as long as the results are correct. Besides, you may be surprised to find out that they did it in a better way than you. Therefore, as a leader we need to be compromising, yet determined and decisive (not wishy-washy). There's a favorite saying of mine that I often use when someone gets stressed out about minor procedural differences. It's simply:

> Don't sweat the little things!

A leader is understanding. If we expect an employee's job to take precedence over a family crisis, we are only fooling ourselves. The family crisis will effect the quality of the results, and we will lose the commitment of the employee to us. However, if we take an employee's problem seriously, and try to help them out, we will gain a friend for life. Often this takes patience. Which brings me to another of my favorite sayings:

> We get too caught up in the thick of thin things.

A leader is self-replacing. Leaders prepare others to take their place. They realize that they can only move up the ladder if there is someone who can take their place. Additionally, the best leader can disappear for a day or so and not be missed. His or her presence is not as important to the operation of the business as is the confidence that has been instilled in the employees to proceed without him or her.

> All indispensable managers end up in the same place — the cemetery.

Leaders are environmentally conscious in the broad sense. They care about the pollution in the area where they live, but they also care about the growth and development of the community. They care, for example, about the effect that labor force changes will have on the community.[5]

> Organizations must attempt to achieve harmony between managerial attitudes and behaviors in relation to environmental demands.
>
> Thomas J Zenisek

Leaders are worker safety conscious, not because some government agency tells them to be so, but because the employees are their friends and they don't want to see their friends at risk.

Leaders are open in all areas, like sharing ideas, offering compliments and meting out criticism. They don't have secret agendas, nor do they hide the truth. Oneness breeds confidence. I'm not suggesting that you do what my friend did, by telling a female employee that she had a poor taste in dress styles. He was just joking, but he got punched out just the same. Oneness is letting the employees know where they stand and letting them know what goals they are shooting for.

Sharing is caring. Share your life with your employees so that they will share their life with you. However, in the end, you should do a lot more listening then talking. And you should ask a lot more questions than make statements. People don't what to hear your opinions about how they should behave, nor do they want to have you pass judgement. What they want is a listening, caring

---

5. Zenisek, Thomas J, "Corporate Social Responsibility: A Conceptualization Based on Organizational Literature", *Academy of Management Review* (1979), Vol. 4, No. 3, pp. 359-367; Sikich, Geary W, "Environmental, Occupational, Health and Safety Regulations Threaten Many Corporations in the '90s: Reducing Environmental Vulnerability", *New Accountant* (March 1991) pp. 8-42.

ear. Avoid phrases like *you should have, you could have* or *why didn't you...*

One of my favorite phrases at work is *have fun!* I use it so much that employees have given me tee shirts with it written on. Basically, I believe that you shouldn't be working if you can't have fun doing it. And if what you're doing isn't fun, then make it fun! Don't be dull and boring. Bring in donuts for everyone once in a while, for no good reason at all. Sing a song out loud, for no good reason at all. Play the *Lion King* sound track extra loud, for no good reason at all, and better yet, dance to it. But be careful, having fun is contagious. Employees may actually enjoy working for you.

> . . . men are that they might have joy.

2 Nephi 2:25,
Book of Mormon

We have discussed the characteristics of a world-class person. When we look through recent literature, we are overwhelmed by self-improvement books. They seem to be never ending and I have listed a few of them already. One of the best series, that has become very popular, is the group of books by Stephen R Covey. One of his books is titled *The Seven Habits of Highly Effective People*. In it he suggests characteristics that we can use to become world-class people, even though he doesn't use that terminology. He suggests that highly effective people tend to:

1. be proactive — have initiative — lead out in your life — choose, don't just react

2. begin with the end in mind — understand your destination — creativity

3. put first things first — personal management — personal productivity

4. think win-win — realize the interdependence between you and others — develop interpersonal leadership

5. seek first to understand, then to be understood — emphatic communication

6. synergize — develop creative co-operation by valuing the differences

7. encourage renewal — sharpening the saw — develop a spiral of upward growth — consistently grow.[6]

Covey stresses that highly effective people lead their lives according to principles and values that are universally valid. The ability to lead is an outgrowth of applying these principles in solving problems. In a follow-up

---

6. Covey, Stephen R, *The Seven Habits of Highly Effective People* (New York: Simon and Schuster) 1989.

book, *Principle-Centered Leadership*, Covey discusses the characteristics of a world-class eManager who has principle-centered leadership. These leaders are:

- continually learning
- service oriented — life is a mission which includes helping others
- radiating positive energy
- believing in other people
- leading balanced lives — a wide variety of interests
- seeing life as an adventure
- synergistic — the interplay between parts produces more than the individual parts
- exercising the four dimensions of being for self-renewal — physical, mental, emotional and spiritual.[7]

I had a friend, who was trying to search for the perfect spouse, tell me that the secret to finding the perfect marriage partner was that we should spend at least as much time being Mr or Ms Right, as we spend searching for Mr or Ms Right. How can we find someone who is right for us if we're not right for anyone. Similarly, how can we find the perfect employee if we stink as an employer or as a boss? We need to be world-class people in order to become world-class eManagers.

> To make a difference, we need to be different!
>
> . . . Of those to whom much is given, much is required. And when at some future date the high court of history sits in judgement on each of us — recording whether in our brief span of service we fulfilled our responsibilities to the state — our success or failure, in whatever office we may hold, will be measured by the answers to four questions —
>
> were we truly men of courage . . .
>
> were we truly men of judgement. . .
>
> were we truly men of integrity . . .
>
> were we truly men of dedication?
>
> John F Kennedy

---

7. Covey, Stephen R, *Principle-Centered Leadership* (New York: Summit Books) 1991.

FINDING THE WORLD-CLASS POTENTIAL IN EVERYONE

One man practicing sportsmanship is far better than a hundred teaching it.

Knute Rockne

World-class management is learning that the company doesn't exist for you only, but for the benefit of everyone. An excellent comparison is to realize that internationally, any time a trade barrier is reduced, the cost of trade transactions goes down. Similarly, whenever we reduce barriers between employees, we reduce the cost of transactions between employees. The world-class eManager is the open, honest manager who is willing to share. This manager is not obsessed with being protective of his or her ideas.

World-class eManagers recognize that you cannot over-communicate when running a business. The more you share, the better will be the tools that employees have available. They are team oriented managers, taking advantage of the synergistic effects of team interaction.

World-class eManagers are world-class people that are confident enough in themselves to eagerly search out the potential in the people around them. They trust themselves and the people they deal with. They are not paranoid individuals who build non-trust systems all around in order to protect themselves from their employees, customers and vendors.

One approach to a relationship would be to constantly follow your spouse around (a non-trust system) so that they don't talk to the wrong people, say the wrong things or get any bad ideas. The other approach is to build a two-way trust relationship where both parties respect and trust each other to not engage in any behavior that would disrupt the trust relationship. As world-class eManagers, we need to build similar trust relationships with all our business associates.

World-class human relations, where we search out the potential in everyone, is built upon an effective, caring, human resources management (HRM) system.[8] An effective, people centered HRM program, that incorporates the people oriented characteristics we have discussed, looks toward what employees are becoming, rather than what they are right now. This type of system realizes that a better person makes a better employee. In a recent article, Boyst listed several needs of a world-class HRM system. These are:

- focus on continuous improvement
- build a new work-place environment
- rethink performance evaluations

---

8. Petrick, Joseph A, and Diana S Furr, *Total Quality in Managing Human Resources* (Florida: St. Lucie Press) 1995.

- focus on team-building
- job rotation and life-long learning
- rethinking compensation.[9]

I like the husband, who, after complementing his wife on a recent educational achievement, said to her, "I like you just they way you are becoming." Being world-class is finding the world-class potential in everyone we interact with.

> This above all: to thine own self be true,
> And it must follow, as the night the day,
>
> Thou canst not then be false to any man.
>
> William Shakespeare

WHAT IN THE WORLD IS ETHICAL?

> . . . the wisdom of this world is foolishness with God.
>
> 1 Corinthians 3:19

Does the United States define what is ethical for the entire world? We seem to have taken it as our role, since we place sanctions on other countries if they don't follow our ethical standards. For example, if a country has human rights offenses, we place an economic sanction on them, even though we had to fight our most destructive internal war in order to get rid of slavery in our own country. Or if a country cuts down too many trees, we place sanctions on them even though, in the last couple hundred years, we destroyed more of our own forests (by percentage) than any other country in the world. We tell other countries not to pollute, but we go into those countries and set up factories that are toxic and high-risk health hazards. So what is ethical? It differs from country to country. And the United States is not always right.

I am not trying to say that ethical standards are contradictory. I am saying that not all countries and peoples believe in the same ethical values. For example, is it ethical for the US to limit the economic growth of another country? If not, then why do we use economic sanctions to force their behavior? Let me give you some other examples.

- In the United States, we believe everything should be defined in black and white, as good and bad. As discussed earlier in this book, this is a very Christian perspective. A Hindu perspective would be that there is a lot of good and bad in everything, and it is the grey area in between where we live

---

9. Boyst, William M, "HRM — Key to the Integrated Management Revolution", *APICS 34th International Conference Proceedings* (APICS) October 1991, pp. 354-357.

most of our life. This black and white versus grey perspective has a significant effect on how decisions are made. For example, the United States would prefer to win, whereas other cultures would prefer to compromise.

- The United States focuses on a hurry-up, quick results philosophy. Other countries, like Japan, prefer the think-it-through-before-you-react approach to problem solving. Is intentionally moving too slow in a business transaction unethical?

- Many countries see their government officials as the tools for getting things done. Therefore, it is appropriate to hire them as consultants. However, in the United States, involving the government in this way is considered a conflict of interest or perhaps even a bribe. Is it unethical to use government officials as agents in the business transaction?

- I have already mentioned the difference between the Christian rights-of-the-individual ethical system as opposed to the Asian rights-of-the-society ethical system. For them it is unethical to work in a profession that is non-value-added. Yet we send many of our non-value-added self-fulfilling people to these countries to engage in business transactions.

The list of ethical differences could go on and on. Rather than continue, I again refer you to the book by Schumacher that you should consider reading. Although it is a little dated, and a bit controversial, it is still very eye-opening.[10]

> For what is a man profited, if he shall gain the whole world, and lose his own soul?
>
> Matthew 16:26

BECOMING A WORLD-CLASS EMANAGER

> Our scientific power has outrun our spiritual power. We have guided missiles and misguided men.
>
> Martin Luther King, Jr

As already discussed, a world-class eManager is an ethical manager. The topic of ethical management has received an enormous amount of recent attention. For example, *Time* magazine devoted their 25 May 1987 issue to ethics with the cover page headline of "What ever happened to ethics? — Assaulted by sleaze, scandals, and hypocrisy, America searches for its moral bearings." In March 1994, *New Accountant* wrote to future graduates and young managers

---

10. Schumacher, E F, *Small is Beautiful* (New York: Perennial Library) 1973.

with the cover page headlines of "Does Ethics Stand a Chance? — Are young managers less ethical?" However, in the search for world-class ethical managers, *Business Week*, on the cover of their 1 August 1994 issue, considered "Managing by Values — What is an ethical company?" Then, using Bob Haas, CEO of Levi-Strauss as the example, they attempted to demonstrate that ethics are back in style. Bob Haas focused on "responsible commercial success" with programs like paying for the tuition of a contractor's underage workers in Bangladesh.

In an article by Petrick and Manning, they offer steps to improving the organizational ethical climate. They are:

- improve the quality of the leader-follower exchange which involves the establishment of a collaborative relationship where support is provided for ethical conduct
- reduce delays in the enforcement of organizational ethical guidelines
- improve personal ethical conduct by having empowered individuals who can analyze and resolve ethical conflicts on site and by offering training that develops responsible ethical decision-making skills
- leaders need to model the behavior they want to see in others.[11]

> In today's global economy, the need to be internationally competitive in the work environment is an ongoing challenge for organizations. Part of that competitive edge is developing a reputation for superior productivity based on managing human resources with integrity.
>
> Petrick and Manning

From this chapter we have learned that the world-class eManager is a world-class person first. Additionally, a world-class eManager:

- adds value to society through his or her efforts
- is environmentally conscious
- is employee safety conscious
- looks to help employees develop their world-class abilities
- focuses on eliminating waste and increasing value-added
- focuses on being productive, rather than protective of ideas, opinions and territory — doesn't let innovation get tied up in ego
- gives employees time for self-evaluation (time to think), self-renewal and self-improvement
- cares about the personal aspects of the employees' life

---

11. Petrick, Joseph A, and George E Manning, "Ethics for Total Quality and Participation: Developing an Ethical Climate for Excellence", *Journal of Quality and Participation* (March 1990) pp. 84-90.

- focuses on breakthrough thinking — working smarter, not harder
- understands and utilizes the change process to influence positive, goal directed changes through leadership.

> All victory and glory is brought to pass unto you through your diligence.
>
> Doctrine and Covenants 103:36

A world-class eManager is a lot more than tools and talent. A world-class eManager knows how to manage his or her life, knows how to lead his or her family, knows how to make a difference in the community and, last of all, knows how to lead employees. A world-class eManager builds in themselves and, through example, in their family, friends, employees, customers, peers, vendors and anyone else they come into contact with:

- integrity
- standards and a value system
- society value-added
- enthusiasm
- understanding
- environmental consciousness.

And most important of all, a world-class eManager has fun doing it!

> The future will demand true leaders who can bring out the best in people.
>
> Adolphson, DeVries and Rinne[12]

PERSONAL SKILLS

We can't put our faults behind us until we face them.

The world cares very little about what a man or woman knows; it is what the man or woman is able to do that counts.

> Booker T Washington

Two women were walking through a forest when they happened to pass by a lake and a frog croaked up at them, "Help, I am a tall, handsome author, but

---

12. Adolphson, Don, Matthew DeVries and Heikki Rinne, "Rethinking Business: A Broader Sense of Responsibility", *Exchange* (Fall 1994) pp. 5-9.

an evil witch turned me into a frog! If one of you will give me a kiss I can turn back into an author."

One of the women bent over to pick up the frog and the other woman quickly spoke up, "You're not really going to kiss that frog are you?"

The first woman, as she picked up the frog, said, "Of course not. A talking frog is worth a lot more than an author.".

I've known a lot of managers who have turned out to be frogs, but the frog can be turned into a world-class eManager (a leader) if he or she has the right tools to work with. Without the right tools, they may stay a frog forever. This chapter will now discuss what some of the basic tools are. This is a "basic" set, and is by no means a complete set of tools. Just like everything else that this book discusses, this basic set of tools is continually changing.

This chapter discusses what the personal skills of a world-class manager should be, such as oral, written and verbal communication, personal characteristics and computer literacy. The tools will be discussed in two groups, in order to show their relevance, but there is considerable overlap between the groupings. The groups are:

1. categories of skills

2. areas of skills.

When the time for decision arrives, the time for preparation has passed.

Categories of Skills

The perpetual obstacle to human advancement is custom.

John Stuart Mill

There are four major categories of world class management skills. These are people skills, creative skills, change oriented skill and basic tools of the trade.

People skills

The importance of people skills in world-class management performance should be thoroughly ingrained into your belief system by now. I mention it again in this chapter because it cannot be forgotten.

The Quality and Productivity Management Association (QPMA) (listed in Appendix 12.3) has established a set of nine leadership standards that they feel leaders will need in the year 2000. These are:

1. priorities and values that focus on organizational effectiveness, anticipating and exceeding customer expectations, giving employees a sense of purpose and pride, guiding relationships by vision, core values and critical goals

2. open and honest communication, external and internal to the organization

3. agility in dealing with change

4. a pursuit of knowledge and learning for the leader and everyone else in the organization

5. innovation and creativity

6. commitment and courage

7. systematic approach to performance and solving problems by assessing what needs change, anticipating what should happen, organizing to get the change implemented, empowering those necessary, ensuring that the change gets done

8. teamwork

9. empowerment distributed throughout the organization.

Creative skills

World-class leaders need to foster creativity. In the books by von Oech listed in previous chapters, the author emphasizes the need for us to forget the routine and to open our minds to new and creative ways of thinking. He focuses on snapping your mental locks and opening yourself to new and creative ideas. Some of his suggestions from *A Whack on the Side of the Head* are:

- look for the "second right answer"
- don't be blinded by "what's logical"
- break the routine and "don't follow the rules"
- avoid the "practical" and look at situations through someone else's eyes
- get out of a world of specialists where "people know more and more about less and less"
- avoid "going along with the crowd" and "be foolish" once in a while.

In von Oech's book *A Kick in the Seat of the Pants* he suggests that we need to play roles in order to be more creative. He suggests four roles:

1. explorer — "get off the beaten path"

2. artist — ask "what if" questions and look for hidden analogies

3. judge — find "what's wrong" with the idea to work the bugs out of it

4. warrior — fight for your idea or it won't get implemented.

> Every child is an artist, the problem is how to remain an artist after he grows up.
>
> Picasso

The authors Nadler and Hibino, also listed earlier, wrote the books *Breakthrough Thinking* and *Creative Solution Finding*. They stress that conventional thinking is dead and that we need to search out methods of creativity.

Change oriented skills

Our most critical and also most abused resource in life is *time*. Time makes change impossible to avoid. Therefore, a world-class eManager takes change by the horns and controls it, rather than having it control the manager. We need to avoid being protective and possessive of the status quo. We need to influence and manage change by being a positive influencer and motivator of the change process. We need to position an organization for continuous success by motivating the change process. Some of the business aspects of technology and time management have already been discussed.[13]

Being world class allows us to understand the time pie. The time pie says that there is only a limited amount of time in our life and we need to define how we want to cut the pie (see Figure 14.1). The cuts of the pie define our priorities in life. Expecting the pie to become bigger is unrealistic. The only thing we can control is how we cut the pie and if we try to shove more into one piece of the pie, then other pieces of the pie need to become smaller.

I find it disappointing when some people make statements such as: "I know I spend a lot of time at work and away from my family (or kids). But when I'm with them I spend 'quality' time with them." This statement is used as if somehow quality made up for a lack of quantity. It's like having an employee come to you and say, "I'm only going to put in four hours today, but I'll make it quality time." We want the full eight hours out of our employees, just like our kids want the quantity time, as well as the quality time, out of us. Why don't we focus on making our work time more quality time and less quantity time, rather than hurting ourselves in those areas where the quantity time is needed?

> What counts is not the number of hours you put in, but how much you put in the hours.

To become world-class eManagers we need to develop change management skills, which focuses on managing our most critical resource — time. And it requires us to motivate the change process within our enterprise.

---

13. An additional book you might like to read is Thomas, Philip R, *Time Warrior* (New York: McGraw-Hill) 1992.

Figure 14.1: The Time Pie

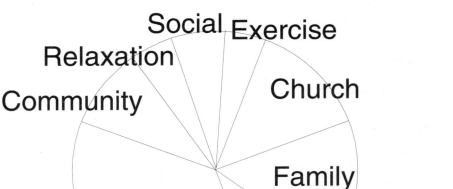

Basic tools of the trade

The list of basic skills of a world-class eManager is enormous. However, I would like to stress a few:

- computer skills — you can't live without them anymore
- measurement skills — an understanding of the measurement process and the reports that go along with it, like balance sheets, profit and loss statements, market share, financial ratios, operational ratios, efficiency, productivity and quality
- communication skills — reading, writing, listening, speaking
- creative problem solving and open-minded thinking.

Fifty-one percent of being smart is knowing what you are dumb about.

Ann Landers

AREAS OF SKILLS

The world is full of willing people, some willing to work, the rest willing to let them.

Robert Frost

World-class managers need to develop a set of skills that make them effective managers in each of four areas:

1. individual performance skills
2. job functional skills
3. enterprise management skills
4. beyond the enterprise skills.

I will list several of the skills that are necessary in each of these areas. APICS (listed in Appendix 12.3) offers the Certification in Resource Management (CIRM) which focuses on the manager's ability to manage an enterprise's resources in these same four categories. Some of the necessary skills are:

- *individual performance skills* — oral and written communication skills, listening and reading skills, ability to focus on the core problems, negotiation skills, computer literacy skills (like utilizing a word processor, spreadsheet, electronic mail and the Internet) and teaming skills like team leadership, membership and organization (the ability to accomplish change through teaming)
- *job functional skills* — understanding the business processes (how you and your job effect the total corporation), identifying and organizing the interactions that relate to business processes and activities, understanding the perspective of other functions and the ability to recognize and integrate organizational functions
- *enterprise management skills* — the skills necessary to search out the core competencies and develop a vision, mission, strategy, and critical success factors, a human resource perspective, an understanding of how the change process effects the enterprise, the ability to develop corporate and division strategies, an understanding of the tools necessary to make strategic and operational decisions (such as break-even analysis, make-buy decision analysis, return-on-investment analysis and cost-benefit analysis), the skills necessary to develop a focused measurement system and the ability to develop a focused information, productivity, quality, training and technology strategy
- *beyond the enterprise skills* — an understanding of globalization and localization, legal, governmental, union and environmental understanding, an understanding of stakeholder influences (such as employees, owners,

customers, vendors, financial institutions, agents and dealers and the local community), an understanding of the time phasing of an enterprise, through start-up, growth, maturity and decline, and an understanding of how the change process effects the world around the enterprise.

Being a world-class eManager is being well-rounded in your set of skills. It means stepping back and looking at the big picture once in a while rather than getting wrapped up in the details. It suggests a focus on building effective change while still stressing the goals of the enterprise.

> Straighten up your room first, then the world.
>
> Jeff Jordon

TEAMWORK SKILLS

> He has the right to criticize who has the heart to help.
>
> Abraham Lincoln

A father and his son took daily walks through Central Park in New York City. Every day they would walk past a statue of General Sherman who sat in full military gear upon his horse. As they walked past the statue, the father would tip his hat at it and say, "Hello Sherman".

The son would imitate this gesture making a mock salute and saying "Hello Sherman".

One day, while walking past the statue the father tipped his hat and the son did his salute. Then the son asked the father, "Who is that sitting on Sherman?"

Isn't that the way it is? Each of us has our own perspective on what we see and we don't discover other people's perspectives unless we communicate with them. That's what teaming is all about. It is communicating with others so that everyone can benefit from the synergy of ideas.

I was working on teaming problems at Applied Magnetics Malaysia (AMM) in Penang, Malaysia. The work force is composed of 60 per cent Muslim, 30 per cent Buddhist and 10 per cent Hindu. The management was American (Christian) plus a mixture of some of these other cultures. I was brought in to discuss multicultural team building. The resistance against open communication that existed in these cultures was enormous. It took a lot of time and patience to finally get the mixed culture teams to work together, avoiding culturally offensive occurrences. However, we ended up with teams of employees who have such a dramatically different way of looking at life that many of the ideas generated were extremely innovative and often even revolutionary.

Within the United States we don't have the cultural diversity, nor do we have the team relationship building problems that we have in Malaysia. However, I have found that the teams in the US are seldom as effective as the teams in Malaysia. Why? I feel that the biggest reason is that we in the US are not willing to give team building the time it requires. We simply don't have the patience. Instead, we throw a bunch of people together and tell them to get creative without establishing the proper team dynamics. We create "groups" of people, rather than "teams". This chapter will discuss some of the aspects of team building, but by no means all of them. However, I want to stress immediately that effective team building takes time. People need to get used to each other before they will open up to each other, even in the United States. And without the proper time commitment, all the other elements of team building won't do any good.

There are numerous teams in your life. The first, and most important, team is the quality circle of your life — your family. All the characteristics of effective teaming need to exist in your family if you expect it to perform well. If you can't get this primary quality circle to work out well for you, you have little hope of having the work circles in your life being effective.

> To keep your marriage brimming
> with love in a loving cup
> Whenever you're wrong admit it
> Whenever you're right shut up
>
> Ogden Nash

Teaming is a shift of management styles. It's a move away from the authoritarian (workplace communism) toward the participative (workplace democracy) — more details can be found in Chapter 4. There are lots of different forms of teams, like quality circles, management circles, decision teams, total quality management teams and small group improvement teams.

The key element of all teams, no matter what you call them, is participative interaction between people. Remember:

> Being able to talk things out makes us better able to act things out.

We will now go forward and discuss some of the other elements of teaming.

> Tell a man there are 300 billion stars in the universe and he'll believe you. Tell him a bench has wet paint on it and he'll have to touch to be sure.
>
> Jaeger

THE PURPOSE OF TEAMS

The purposes for establishing teams are many. A few of the most important are:

- to effect change/increase value-added/eliminate waste
- to build workforce cohesiveness
- to focus efforts
- to take advantage of synergistic perspectives
- to involve employees in the change process
- to build corporate-wide integration.

To Effect Change/Increase Value-added/Eliminate Waste

With teaming we are attempting to implement positive process improvements through people involvement. When people have an ownership of the change, they are more committed to the success of the change. For example, in Japan teaming means watching out for each other. Each employee sees themselves as an inspector searching for ways to improve the process. In Hitachi, teaming generates 40 to 75 value-added and waste eliminating improvement suggestions per employee per year.

To Build Workforce Cohesiveness

When employees know and understand each other they are much better at integrating. I've known people who have worked side-by-side for years and don't even know each other's names. Employees work better together if they know each other personally.

To Focus Efforts

Teams build a united focus. The team is given a charter with a goal and the members work together toward that goal, each doing their part. Employees are working together, rather than each going off in their own directions.

To Take Advantage of Synergistic Perspectives

As with the Applied Magnetics Malaysia example earlier, the synergy of a team effort results in more effective and creative solutions. The mixture of perspectives opens people's minds to new alternatives.

To Involve Employees in the Change Process

Teaming helps to reduce the size of the no-mans-land that exists between management, who are making decisions, and the workforce, who are implementing the decisions. Teaming is a shift from the authoritarian to the participative. It is a shift from workplace communism to workplace democracy. Under authoritarian management, the role of management is to plan, lead and control, and the employees do the work. Under the participative style, management plans (defines the goals) but the team (including the manager) does the leading, controlling and performing.

In a case study on the TRW-Thomasville Operations we find the authoritarian to participative shift with the following differences:

- authoritarian management — set goals for subordinates, define the standards and the results that are expected, give them the information they need to do the job, train them how to do the job, apply discipline to ensure conformity and to suppress conflict, persuasive leadership, develop and install new methods, reward achievements and punish failures

- participative, goal-oriented management — participate in problem solving and goal setting, give them access to the information that they want, create situations for optimum learning, mediate conflict, allow employees to set challenging goals, teach improvement techniques, enable employees to pursue and move into growth opportunities, recognize achievements and help them learn from failures.[14]

> World Class companies involve people, making them a part of the solution rather than a part of the problem. . . When involvement strategies are effectively implemented, they absorb people, committing them to the company and its future.
>
> Bell and Burnham[15]

To Build Corporate-wide Integration

Teaming builds sharing and focuses the entire organization on a common objective. Teams are composed of cross-functional team members which results in a corporate-wide integration. This integration is both horizontal and vertical, vertical in that many functional areas are mixed together into the same teams and horizontal in that the manager is now a team member right next to the employees and job titles are, hopefully, dropped.

One new way to perform this integration is through *teamnets*. Teamnets

---

14. Bell, Robert R and Randall B Duffy, "TRW — Thomasville Operations" (Tennessee Technological University) 1981 is a field case study.
15. Bell, Robert R and John M Burnham, *Managing Productivity and Change* (Cincinnati, Ohio: South-Western Publishing Co.) 1991, p. 13.

integrate the concept of teaming and networking and are networks of teams that cross all functional boundaries in order to focus on a common objective.[16]

> Never look down on anyone unless you're helping him up.
>
> The Rev. Jesse Jackson

THE BENEFITS OF TEAMING

I was talking to a manager about his planning process and he said to me, "You know what the problem with our planning process is? There are people who have left brains, and there are people who have right brains, and sometimes I feel like my planners fall into the middle category."

This confused me so I asked him, "What's the middle category?"

He responded, "No brain!"

I felt confident that with this type of attitude, he was not destined to get a lot of co-operation from his planners in the future. This type of authoritarian, dominating, "I know it all and everyone else is dumb" attitude is what teaming attempts to get rid of. Teaming focuses us on the abilities of the workforce.

Reviewing the published literature, some of the specific benefits that managers cite for creating teams include:

- improvement in the quality of the decision process
- improvement in the quality of the decisions
- an operations oriented focus to the decision process
- improved relationships overcoming personal differences
- improved training
- stronger employee commitment, more motivated employees
- employees get a management perspective to the decision-making process
- a greater awareness occurs because of the interaction process.

We have already referred to Toyota's successes in team building in previous chapters — it averages 50 improvement suggestions per employee per year (about one per week). Toyota uses quality control (QC) circles as its quality improvement teams. It is the synergy of QC circles that has created the environment where these suggestions can flow easily.

> The puzzle to me . . . is that almost every manager in almost every organization supports teamwork. In fact, many feel it is essential. But

---

16. See the article "Crossing Boundaries with Teamnets" by Jessica Lipnack and Jeffrey Stamps in the Wallace book, cited earlier.

very few organizations institute an organizationwide program to ensure team effectiveness . . . managers at all levels must learn to overcome the resistance to instituting a systematic team building concept.

William G Dyer

STEPS TOWARDS EFFECTIVE TEAMING

To understand the teaming process, we will start by considering the phases of team development:

- forming — initial orientation
- storming — conflict and confusion
- norming — consolidation around tasks
- performing — effective teamwork performance.[17]

Sadly, many teams are disbanded before achieving the performing stage. Teams prior to the performing stage are considered groups and have not evolved into a form that will take advantage of the synergistic benefits of teaming.

There are stages of teaming and employee involvement, as outlined below:

1. circle stage — organizing a team together to discuss quality problems (QC Circles) is one of the first stages and here the team is utilized for idea generation[18]

2. empowered stage — next, as we allocate authority and responsibility to the teams, we empower them to carry out their suggestions

3. fully-functional stage — the final phase is where the teams set their own goals and directions, keeping them in line with the goals of the enterprise and consensus management in self-managed teams is fully integrated; these are like the TQM teams.

In developing total workforce involvement, the team needs to be able to share and blend ideas from differing backgrounds and come out with something more and better than the individual team member could have accomplished alone. This type of *team interaction* builds integration and requires a couple of things.

---

17. Mears, Peter and Frank Voehl, *Team Building* (Florida: St. Lucie Press) 1994, p. 11.
18. Some additional information on QC circles can be found in the Bell and Burnham book, listed above. See also Hart, Marilyn K, "Quality Control Training for Manufacturing", *Production and Inventory Management Journal* (Third Quarter 1991) pp. 35-40.

1. First the team members need to come from cross-functional areas. This means that many differing perspectives are considered. It is important to include both insiders and outsiders. Insiders are team members that are directly involved in the area that the team is focusing on. Outsiders are individuals that do not have a direct interest in this area. The insiders know the technicalities behind the area of interest. The outsiders can look at the situation with a border perspective. Often the outsider is in a better position to question "Why are we doing this at all?"

2. The second key consideration of team effectiveness is team member interaction. The team members need to feel comfortable with each other. This may require social activities and time. Comfortable interaction won't occur the first time a team meets and probably not the second, third or fourth. But in order for team effectiveness to take place, this comfortable interaction will have to occur eventually. Perhaps extra meetings will be necessary at first in order to build this comfort.

> . . . world class manufacturers have found that the best way to tap into and channel their peopleware power is through the collaborative, cooperative, synergistic effort of people working in groups (teams).
>
> Charles G Andrew[19]

With an effectively organized team, we need to establish a *measurement system* that defines the team's performance. During the circle stage, the measurement still comes from management. However, in the fully functional stage, the team establishes their own goals and their own measures of performance.

Numerous tools have been suggested for establishing measurements. For example, activity based costing is felt to be the most thorough, but it is also the most cumbersome and lacks focus.[20] Other tools, like critical resource performance measurement, which is goal based, has demonstrated itself to be much more focused and therefore more effective.

Effective teaming requires the establishment of an *environment of success*. The enterprise needs to have a top-to-bottom commitment to teaming and empowerment or the effectiveness of teaming will be short lived. Additionally, the teaming process requires a time commitment and a lot of patience.[21]

---

19. Andrew, Charles G, "Team Building: The Competitive Edge for the 90's", *APICS 34th International Conference Proceedings,* op. cit., pp. 406-410.

20. Farmer, James R, "Activity Based Accounting and Performance Measurement", *APICS 34th International Conference Proceedings,* op. cit., pp. 156-160.

21. Nelson, Mel, "Team Building: Not the Way Daddy Taught Ya", *APICS 34th International Conference Proceedings,* op. cit., pp. 52-56; Shea, Gregory P and Richard A Guzzo, "Group Effectiveness: What Really Matters?", *Sloan Management Review* (Spring 1987) pp. 25-31.

THE THREE FACES OF TEAMING

A world-class eManager that utilizes teams needs to view their roles from three perspectives — team developer, team leader and team member.

Team Developer

The world-class eManager needs to understand how to define and establish a team. This includes designating a purpose for the team (defining a team charter), selecting the appropriate members of the team and recognizing that it takes time for the group to become an effective team.

Team definition also requires the outlining of the levels of responsibility and authority of the team (empowerment). Team empowerment is necessary because change is necessary.[22] Without it, the interactive politics between the changer (management) and the changed (employees) destroys effective change processes. But empowerment is more than authority; it is also responsibility (responsibility diffusion). The team is rewarded, or penalized, for their decisions. Therefore, they become very committed to the change process.

Some examples of the benefits of empowerment include:

- General Electric increased productivity by 250 per cent in empowered plants
- Corning decreased defect rates from 1,800 parts per million down to nine parts per million
- AT&T operator service has increased in quality by 12 per cent
- Senco S/A (Brazil) has shown inventory cycle improvements of 300 per cent.

An effective team should have internal and external members. The internal members are those in the know about whatever is being studied and should be the majority of the team members. For example, if we are considering a product development team, the team should include engineering, manufacturing, marketing, finance, purchasing and customers.

An external member would be someone who is not in the know about what the team is analyzing. This individual should challenge the obvious, because they are not familiar with the obvious. This generates a "rethink" attitude amongst the team. External members of the product development team could be inventory control clerks, maintenance supervisors, custodians or HRM personnel.

With a proper mix of team members, a synergy of ideas will be established.

---

22. Williams, Blair R, "The Realities of Empowering Teams — A Case Study", *APICS 34th International Conference Proceedings,* op. cit., pp. 319-322; Hall, Robert W, "Empowerment: The 1990s Manufacturing Enterprise", *APICS — The Performance Advantage* (July 1991) pp. 26-58. Again, also refer to the Wallace book which contains an piece by Steven R Rayner entitled "Making Employee Empowerment Work".

The quality of the decision process has demonstrated itself to be higher when team members can openly discuss problems that are normally hidden in the data of just one individual.

Team Leader

The team leader needs to focus on establishing trust amongst the team members. The different functions that have been integrated into the team have a natural distrust for each other. This lack of trust prevents openness (the storming phase of team development). The team leader needs to ensure that mutual understanding and respect can exist so that trust can develop. This requires a controlling of conflict so that disagreements don't get out of hand or become personal.

The team leader needs to make sure that all members of the team are heard. Each of the represented functional areas need to get a chance to share their ideas or the hoped-for synergistic benefits cannot occur.

When the team arrives at the performing stage of team development, the team leader needs to back off of the leadership role and regroup into a note taking, minute taking mode that lets the ideas roll freely.

Team leaders need to foster the synergy of the team by:

- listening to and clarifying the presented suggestions
- supporting all ideas — there are no dumb ideas
- differing and confronting problems openly and encouraging others to do so also
- looking for the quality, value-added ideas
- offering feedback on the teaming process, looking for and suggesting areas for improvement.

Team Member

During the performing stage of team development, the manager should become a team member, sharing in, but not dominating, the creative process. Additionally, a manager may be asked to take on the role of team member for a team of which he or she is neither the developer nor leader.

Whatever the role, whether developer, leader or member, the world-class eManager needs to understand and perform in each of these roles effectively, becoming a team player, not an authoritarian figure.

> No matter how well it is directed, the team will perform only as well as the individuals on it.
>
> Andrew Grove,
> President, Intel

THE REQUIREMENTS OF SUCCESSFUL TEAMS

As an attempt to consolidate many of the teaming ideas that have been presented throughout this book, here are some of the requirements of successful teams (note that I will only discuss those items that have not already been thoroughly discussed elsewhere):

- empowerment
- problem identification and problem analysis skills training for all team members
- team membership and participation training
- time to evolve from grouping to teaming and to develop interpersonal relationships
- no job descriptions or titles within the team
- team motivated performance measures rather than individual performance measures
- gainsharing where the employees share in the benefits of the improvements
- management by team established objectives
- treating workers as customers
- long-term change management focus
- team cohesiveness through common goals and change ownership
- a defined problem resolution process like the SPS process used in TQM
- a feedback and performance rating mechanism.

A successful team is an excited team that sees both challenge and opportunity in the teaming process. There is a massive amount of literature available on effective teaming. I have suggested just a few that will assist you with additional details.[23]

WORLD-CLASS TEAMING

The way we run our department is by thinking of ourselves as a small business . . . Before we went into teams, we were all functionalized . . . Today the associates do everything . . . We have far fewer people doing even more work.

Evelyn Carney,
AMEX Pioneer Team Member

---

23. See Wallace for an article by Grace L Pastiak "Energizing Your Workforce With High Performance Teams". Additionally, St Lucie Press (Florida) has a whole series of books on "Teams".

Successful, world-class teaming is something similar to the TQM teaming process. TQM teams are focused and organized around a charter. They have a quality council that is the kingpin team of all the teams. The quality council is a team that sets up teams, rather then a manager setting up teams, and these teams are established with a specific focus. There are several types of teams required in a TQM environment. These are referred to as the three "P" teams — project, product and process. With their charter, the teams are empowered to implement change focused on increasing the value-added and eliminating the waste.

Teaming does not make better managers — teaming makes better employees. A world-class eManager uses teaming to empower employees to be more effective. The manager becomes more effective by following all the principles of this book, of which teaming or employee involvement is a critical element. Teaming does not replace good management, but world-class management is difficult without an effective, team oriented organization.[24]

At the AMEX Investment and Insurance Services Group, Inc., a top-down view transformed the organization from a traditionally run insurance company into a company with a reputation for quality services and products. The process started in 1988 when the president, Sarah Nolan, teamed a group of experienced employees together with a charter to "set up a parallel business from scratch, throw out all the preconceived notions and discover new and better ways to run a financial services company".[25] This group was reintegrated into the main office in 1990. By mid-1991, 60 per cent of the employees were involved in teams.

> I was looking at the attendance records for 1990, and they had improved twenty-seven percent over 1989. I think it's because you feel such a strong responsibility to your team and your customers.
>
> Pat Haskell,
> AMEX

Xerox felt the need for change, pushed by the global marketplace, competition, the number of products and services, the complexity of products and services and customer demands. It established a strategic imperative that would unleash the power, creativity and motivation of the people and place decision-making closest to the customer. It started by setting a vision:

> Xerox, the document company, is the leader in the global document market, providing document services that enhance business productivity.

24. See Schonberger, Richard J, "Work Improvement Programmes: Quality Circles Compared with Traditional Western Approaches" in Sheth and Eshghi, cited earlier.
25. QPMA, *Commitment Plus* (April 1991)Vol. 6, No. 6, pp. 1-4.

The new standard of productivity and the effort to bring decisions closer to the customer, established a focus on world-class productivity through work process improvement. The primary tool for accomplishing these improvements was employee empowerment. Xerox developed a TQM type plan showing where it was (current state), where it wanted to be (vision) and how it was going to get there (transition plan). The transition started by initiating the development of the empowered work teams consisting "of four to seven people who share responsibility and accountability for providing their external and internal customers with innovative products and services that satisfy their requirements". The empowered teams were allowed to define their own work processes. They had the authority to make decisions on who they did work for and how they managed interpersonal relations. The manager, or team leader, took on the role of facilitator, communicator, integrator, mentor, teacher, coach, leader, monitor and feedback provider. Xerox soon learned that empowerment not only increased customer satisfaction and productivity, it also increased employee satisfaction.

Xerox found that the most difficult part of empowerment was not in orienting and training the employees, but rather, it was in getting the management to let go of the decision-making authority. Managers were to be the enablers in the transformation process. They needed to communicate the vision of empowerment to the employees. Then, through their actions, they needed to help the empowered teams to make their own decisions. This transformation is a gradual process, but well worth the time and effort, if you can just get management to let go.[26]

World-class teaming is not a fad, it is the trend for the future and world-class eManagers will understand and capitalize on the benefits of empowered teams.

> . . . they (the team) decided to use a "rotating coordinator." He or she is not in charge, but is responsible to co-ordinate the efforts of the team. The co-ordinator handles the distribution of the work and projects throughout the team, complaints and disagreements between team members, vacation schedules to some extent, and so on.
>
> The teams are not yet at the point where they are hiring and firing, but we're moving in that direction.
>
> Norma Bermudez,
> AMEX

---

26. The Xerox information was taken from a presentation that Ted Allenbach of Xerox Corporation gave in Guatemala in 1994 titled "Developing Quality Management and Self Managed Work Teams in a Service Organisation".

SUMMARY

The highest reward for a man's toil is not what he gets for it but what he becomes by it.

John Ruskin

In an episode of the *Twilight Zone* a stranger gave a woman a box. The woman was told that if she pushed a button on the box she would receive $2 million. At the same time, someone "she doesn't know and who doesn't know her" will die. After a period of soul searching, the woman decided to go ahead and push the button. The stranger returned, gave the woman the check, and asked for the box back. The woman wanted to know what he was going to do with the box and the stranger replied, "Take it to someone you don't know and who doesn't know you."[27]

Are we so blind that the $2 million would mean more to us than the life of another? Perhaps we need to do a little soul searching of our own. Remember, in order to be a world-class eManager we need to be a world-class person. And world-class teams are TQM empowered teams that act as agents for change. World-class eManagers, who are agents for change, recognize the positive value of utilizing the brains, and not just the brawn, of the workforce.

> Modern Man's seven diseases
> wealth without work
> pleasure without conscience
> knowledge without character
> commerce without morality
> science without humanity
> worship without sacrifice
> politics without principle, and
> rights without responsibility
>
> Mahatma Gandhi

---

27. Found in Adolphson, Don, Matthew DeVries and Heikki Rinne, op. cit., pp. 5-9.

Chapter Fifteen

Integrating the Value Chain

> Politicians are the same all over. They promise to build a bridge even where there is no river.
>
> Nikita Khrushchev

It's time for another puzzle. Take sixteen matchsticks and arrange them as shown in Figure 15.1. There are five equally sized squares. By moving only two of the matches, rearrange the diagram so that all sixteen matches are used, but we are left with only four equally sized squares. The four squares have to be the same size as in the ones already in the diagram. (Hint: four squares, with four sides, when there are no sides in common, will take 16 matches.) What I'm asking you to do is to simplify the diagram. Take some of the complexity out of it. Can you do it? The solution is found in Appendix 15.1.

> Want a peek at the topic that will dominate the discussion in Internet circles for the next year, just as portals and e-retailing set the pace a year ago and business-to-business commerce dominates the landscape today? Think supply chain.
>
> Richard Karpinski

Figure 15.1: 16 Matches Make 5 Squares

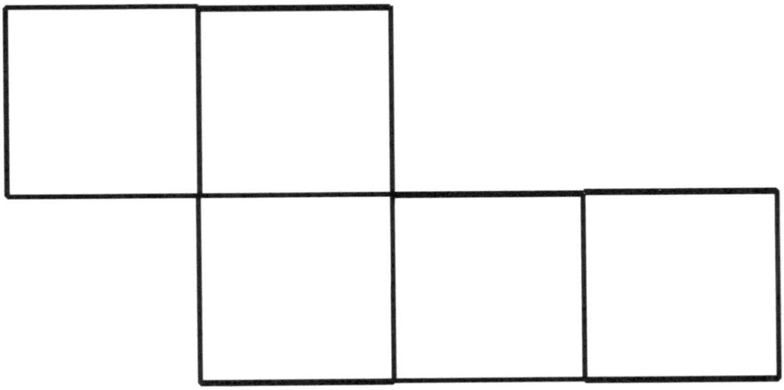

BUSINESS DRIVERS ARE CHANGING

Past experience should be a guidepost, not a hitching post.

When Thomas Edison was working on improving his first electric light bulb, the story goes, he handed the finished bulb to a young helper, who nervously carried it upstairs, step by step. At the last possible moment, the boy dropped it — requiring the whole team to work another twenty-four hours to make a second bulb. When it was finished, Edison looked around, then handed it to the same boy. The gesture probably changed the boy's life. Edison knew that more than a bulb was at stake.

James D Newton

The march toward the enterprise of the future (next generation enterprise — NGE) has been steady and sure. But what is the business impetus for this change? There are numerous factors pushing organizations in this direction.

Global Competition

Organizations are no longer constrained by geography. Customers are anywhere and everywhere. Worldwide markets present unparalleled opportunities to grow and succeed, but they also introduce new threats. A competitor a world away can compete for local business. Organizations must take a global view or risk being overtaken by those who do.

Convergence

In their efforts to remain competitive, enterprises are facing convergence along multiple dimensions. Concepts and entities that have been traditionally distinct are merging. Let us look at some examples.

- Customer, supplier, and partner integration — the lines are blurring between enterprises and their customers, suppliers and distribution channels. Competition is being defined with respect to extended enterprises and the value networks they command, not in terms of individual organizations. This convergence has major implications for maintaining or establishing competitive positions.

- Advertising, information, entertainment, retail integration — the lines between these functions are also blurring, as competitors approach customers with packages of information and services.

- Voice, video and data integration — competitors are increasingly able to provide speedy, personal service plus accelerated development and introduction of new products and services.

These trends are changing the landscape of competition and the fundamental relationship between an enterprise and its customers, suppliers and partners. Customers and their goals are constantly changing. Today's innovations will become tomorrow's expectations.

Deregulation

Deregulation is changing entire industries, for example, utilities and financial services. Telecommunications deregulation has been a major factor in the growth of the Internet economy and it will continue to present opportunities as well as uncertainties. The applicability and interpretation of existing regulations is clouded by the blurring of political borders and jurisdictions. The trend toward privatizing industries formerly controlled by national governments further enhances the climate of deregulation.

Demand for Personalized Services

Customer expectations are changing. Increasingly, customers are demanding to be treated as individuals as they have become sophisticated users of the cutting edge interfaces on the Internet (see below).

- Personalized products — they want mass customization, i.e. products built to order and customized to their needs. For example, personal computers are shipped pre-configured with the buyer's chosen software; consumers can create CDs that contain their choice of specific musical selections. Eventually, all products and services will be customized.

- Customer-centric services — customers want personalized service and a single point of contact for consolidated services. They demand a consistent, high-quality experience each and every time they interact with the enterprise. Furthermore, through behavioral predictions driven by customer information, enterprises can tailor customer interactions based on the *value* of the customer.

- Targeted, permission-based marketing — customers want targeted, one-on-one marketing, tailored to their interests and needs.

Moreover, in addition to individualized treatment, customers are demanding rapid response to their requests.

Disintermediation and Reintermediation

Increasingly, enterprises are able to interact directly with customers, eliminating the need for intermediaries. Examples include travel services and brokerage services. New types of intermediaries are also being created. For example, eMalls and eCatalogs are changing the nature of government and corporate procurement. In some cases, new enterprises replace traditional intermediaries (for example, web based auctions compete with traditional newspaper-based classified advertising).

Technology Makes it Real

Technology is no longer an option — it is a requirement for meeting today's business challenges. It is impossible to achieve the necessary scale, speed and consistent quality without it. Furthermore, using technology merely to support connectivity is no longer enough. The next generation enterprise will use technology extensively to leverage its base of knowledge.

At the same time, technology must be used intelligently, in support of a realistic business model. An enterprise must be careful not to add unnecessary complexity through ineffectual or wasteful use of technology.

High Power Computing and Universal Connectivity

In the next generation enterprise, high-speed computers drive sophisticated electronic analyses and provide lightning fast response to customer requests. Massive online storage enables enterprises to maintain extensive customer information and to organize and access enterprise knowledge. High-speed networks ensure that everyone is connected to everything. Browser technology lets every application work on every desktop or laptop.

Analytical and Decision-oriented Tools

Powerful analysis and decision software allows organizations to analyze customer data, understand trends and patterns, and define customer-centric sales, marketing and support strategies. Enterprise-level decision tools help ensure that chosen strategies are consistently applied and produce planned results. Technological optimization techniques help manage risk, resources (such as inventory) and processes (such as the supply chain).

Electronic Payment

Electronic payment technology speeds the exchange of money for products and services. It applies at the enterprise level (for example, through electronic data interchange or electronic funds transfer) as well as the consumer level (for example, through smart cards, electronic wallets, and electronic billing and payment collection).

Web Standards

Emerging standards, such as XML, support substantive communication and the exchange of data between enterprises. Web browser standards facilitate application interoperability across enterprises.

Security

Electronic commerce and enterprise integration depend on secure interactions. Security infrastructures protect sensitive enterprise data (such as inventory data, financial information and process knowledge) and personal consumer data (such as credit card numbers) while allowing the exchange of information necessary to conduct meaningful transactions.

SOLUTIONS FOR THE NEXT GENERATION ENTERPRISE

As we have already seen from Chapter 3, the enterprise has moved through a migration of being single-enterprise-centric (see Figure 15.2) to being network-enterprise centric (see Figure 15.3) next generation enterprises (NGE). Organizations that successfully become next generation enterprises are going to be the economic winners in the next few years.

NGEs need to define new, integrated, customer-centric business models by providing products and services that focus on:

- the interface between the enterprise and its customers (which can be either consumers or other businesses)
- the interface between the enterprise and its suppliers and partners
- the enterprise itself, the way it creates and leverages knowledge and the status of its evolution into a next generation enterprise.

Next generation enterprises need to achieve their business goals in a new competitive environment. The primary solution areas are shown in Figure 15.4. Note that Figure 15.4 offers an overly simplistic view of the enterprise and its links to customers, suppliers and partners. The picture implies that each entity is holistic and independent. In fact, as each element of this diagram evolves into a next generation enterprise, the overall level of integration will be magnified and enhanced. By integrating with its own customers, suppliers and partners, each entity will also integrate with its customers' customers, its suppliers' partners, its partners' customers and so on. The result will be an economically powerful and seamless value network — of next generation enterprises.

Enterprise — Customer Integration

Next generation enterprises become more customer-centric. Interactive customer value management products help organizations use customer information to provide each customer with:

- a consistent, high-quality experience each and every time they interact with the enterprise

Figure 15.2: Independent Enterprises

Figure 15.3: Business Redefinition through Networks of Extended Enterprises

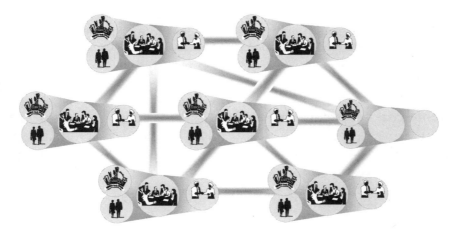

Figure 15.4: Independent Enterprises

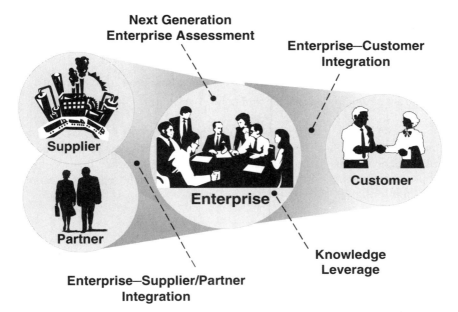

- personalized products and services
- targeted marketing, based on customer interests, preferences and history
- a rapid response to requests.

Examples of next generation enterprise successes in this area include:

- An interactive customer value management system helps US Bank use statistical models to analyze customer data — the bank can predict the needs, behaviors, risk and value (present and potential) of each customer and this information allows the bank to determine the best products and services for each customer.
- With an Internet lending system, the Bank of Montreal offers online, immediate transaction processing and credit decisions to all Canadians whether they speak English or French and whether or not they are current Bank of Montreal customers.
- The Kansas Department of Revenue enacted radical tax reform aimed at serving the state's taxpayers (that is, customers) with technology solutions that provide easy access to policy information, support electronic filing of returns and streamline the processing of returns.

Enterprise — Supplier/Partner Integration

Next generation enterprise solutions focus on the integration between companies, helping clients share customer information with suppliers and business partners to:

- improve product quality through continuous feedback
- build to customer order, creating a "mass customization" environment
- integrate planning, purchasing and control systems.

For example, working with AMS (American Management Systems), Orange County, California, has implemented one of the first web-based bidding and procurement systems in the state and local government market. It streamlines the procurement process by allowing more than 20,000 vendors to access contract information and submit bids via the Internet.

Knowledge Leverage

Next generation enterprises must bring their organizational knowledge to individual employees and to help them use it to advantage. The result is improved business performance through enterprise integration and reinvention. Next generation enterprises need to:

- integrate systems across the enterprise
- implement processes to continuously reinvent enterprise strategies
- optimize self-disintermediation and outsourcing.

For example, Shell Oil Company has developed an innovative hazard communication system, an intranet application that provides members of the Shell community with easy access to critical health and safety data about hazardous materials in the workplace. AMS developed a team collaboration system for Cummins Engine Company. The system provides a secure electronic environment that helps cross-functional engineering and manufacturing teams communicate and develop new products more efficiently.

> . . . there has been a growing impetus to find ways to manage the "extended enterprise" — to build collaborative relationships and improve both the flow of materials and information throughout the value-creating pipeline.
>
> John H Sheridan, "Managing the Chain", *Industry Week*,
> 6 September 1999, p. 52.

NEXT GENERATION ENTERPRISE ASSESSMENT

A next generation enterprise assessment is valuable in order to help organizations develop a strategy for the future. This service evaluates a client organization and its people, processes and technology internally and externally based on a next generation enterprise maturity model ranking. It helps identify and prioritize the steps needed to become or remain an industry leader in the face of staggering competitive business and technology changes.

> What you do for yourself may start you up in the world. But from there on up, it's what you do for others.
>
> Burton Hillis

VALUE CHAIN INTEGRATION

A few years ago at the Seattle Special Olympics nine physically or mentally disabled contestants assembled at the starting line for the 100-yard dash. As the race began they all started out in something less than a dash, but with the excitement and enthusiasm necessary to run the race to the finish and win. Unfortunately, one boy stumbled on the asphalt and tumbled a couple times. He began to cry. The other eight contestants heard the cry and they slowed down and looked back. They all turned around and went back — every one of them. One girl with Down's Syndrome bent down and kissed him saying, 'This will make you better.' Then all nine contestants linked arms and walked across the finish line together. Everyone in the stadium stood up applauding and the cheering went on for several minutes. People who were there to see the event are still telling the story. Why? Because deep down we know this one thing: what matters in this life is more than winning for ourselves. What truly matters in this life is helping others win, even if it means slowing down and changing our course.

As told in church by Sandra Titera

Although this story was told with a spiritual message, it also holds an unbelievable amount of relevance when considering the enterprise of the future. The race is no longer won by the individual enterprise that runs entirely on its own merits. The race for the next generation enterprise is won by the enterprise who links arms with their network of partners and realizes that value is gained through an integrated network of value-adding partners. Next generation enterprises are willing to slow down and look back to help a partner. The value of the network occurs when they all cross the finish line together, otherwise the value network has failed.

. . . an "extended-enterprise-management" approach is called for – in which supply-chain partners behave almost as though they are part of a single organization.

John H Sheridan

SUMMARY

In the years to come, the world's economy will be dominated by networks of extended enterprises, working together to provide real value to customers. Competition will be defined in terms of these enterprise networks. To meet the challenges of this global, convergent economy — and even to survive — today's organizations must transform themselves into next generation enterprises. They must fully embrace their customers as individuals, effectively integrate with suppliers and partners, and use enterprise knowledge to empower workers to implement new business models and exciting new strategies for success.

A word to the wise ain't necessary — it's the stupid ones who need the advice.

Bill Cosby

SUGGESTIONS FOR FURTHER READING

If you would like to know more about this subject, there is a wealth of information available, both in book and article form and on the web. I have given you a few pointers below.

Building the Next Generation Enterprise. Available at <http://www.amsinc.com/> (October 1999).

Encyclopedia of the New Economy. Available at <http://www.hotwired.com/> (20 October 1999).

Foster, Reg and Sandy Devine, *The Next Generation Enterprise.* (Presentation to AMS Senior Staff Conference, October 1999).

Gilpin, Linda and Mark Schroeder, *What's Next in eCommerce? The Next Generation Enterprise (NGE)!* (Presentation to European Knowledge Centers Associates Conference, September 1999).

Grochow, Jerry and Mark Raiffa, *The Next Generation Enterprise: Working with the Techno-Business Organization of the Future.* (Presentation at AMS Senior Management Meeting, June 1998).

Keres, Tamara and Bill Catherwood, *Next Generation Enterprise.* (Presentation to European Knowledge Centers Associates Conference, September 1999).

O'Connell, Teri. *Electronic Commerce Overview.* (AMSCAT Research and Discussion database, July 1999).

Plenert, Gerhard, *World Class Manager* (Rocklin, CA: Prima Publishing) 1995.

Plenert, Gerhard and Shozo Hibino, *Making Innovation Happen: Concept Management Through Integration* (Del Ray Beach, FL: St. Lucie Press) 1997.

Raiffa, Mark. *The Next Generation Enterprise: Helping Clients Build the "Techno-business" Organization of the Future.* (Presentation at New Principals' Day, July 1998).

Sheridan, John H, "Managing the Chain", *Industry Week*, 6 September 1999, pp. 51-66.

APPENDIX 15.1: FIVE SQUARES TO FOUR

Figure 15.4 has the answer showing which two matches to move. Did you find this problem challenging? If you can solve this one, you can probably solve more environmental problems than you are willing to admit. How are they related? They both take analytical think time.

Figure 15.5: 16 Matches Make 4 Squares

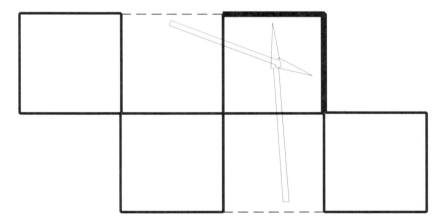

Part IV

eManager

Chapter Sixteen

The eManager Test

> The haves and the have-nots can often be traced back to the dids and the did nots.
>
> D O'Flynn

I had a friend die not too long ago and this made me think: how would I like my obituary to read? This may not be the cheeriest thought in the world, but try it anyway. Stop what you're doing, get a piece of paper, sit down and write your obituary. How would you like to be remembered? What are the first things that you would like people to think of when they're trying to come up with good things to say about you? Perhaps you would like them to say that you were always smiling, or that you were fun to be around? Would you like them to say that you cared more about others than you cared about yourself, that you were selfless and kind? Would you like them to say that you were a great with your family and that your spouse adored you? Would you like to have been considered a hero to your kids? Would you like to be considered a valuable contributor in your church or community? Would you like to have your employees and colleagues say that they enjoyed working with you so much that they hated to go home each day? Think about it! What would you like people to say about you at your funeral?

Stop right now and write your obituary!

Now that you've written your masterpiece, read it through and ask yourself if this is really the way you are. Do you need improvement? If you need improvement, and who doesn't, then why aren't you working towards that improvement?

The obituary you have just written is your long-term goal. It's the eternal target that you're trying to hit. However, if you're not there now, you'd better start planning out a course of action that will get you there. Once you get your target defined, that doesn't mean that you're going to die. That means that you have a good goal to work towards.

Being a world-class eManager is not easy. No one promised you that it would be. But it's worth it! And it's never too early to get started.

> Know the difference between success and fame. Success is Mother Teresa. Fame is Madonna.
>
> Erma Bombeck

HOW TO GET READY

Getting ready is the secret of success.

Henry Ford

My mother told me that I was getting a "pouch" on my belly. I guess she meant that I was getting overweight. Anyway, a friend told me that if I went to the spa for a half hour each day I could easily solve my problem. So I decided to go. I went to the spa faithfully for two months, every day, for about a half an hour. It was painful watching all those people jogging, doing aerobics, riding bicycles, lifting weights and swimming, but I was committed. I faithfully went every day and watched them. But, when the two months were up, I didn't notice any improvement in my "pouch" so I gave it up!

This spa story seems a little silly, but it's exactly what I see happening in management all the time. Managers will sit back and "watch" their employees strain through the motions of implementing a new system, then, after two months, they will give up on it because they decide that it isn't worth it, never asking the employees if they wanted it to begin with and never asking them if they wanted to stop after it had been running. Management wasn't committed to the change and, therefore, in management's eyes, it wasn't working.

Committing yourself to becoming world-class is much like committing yourself to any change. It goes back to the bacon and eggs breakfast story where the chicken is involved in the breakfast, but the pig is committed to it.

Getting ready to become world-class is getting serious about changing. It's becoming an active participant in the change process. It's working out at the spa and not just sitting there and watching. It's working with your employees as they try to implement change and not just observing them. It's getting committed to becoming world-class. It's doing something!

As we briefly discussed in the last chapter, you can't change everything at once. The purpose of this world-class test is to help you define the areas where you need work. Once you have them listed, sequence them by priority. Then attack the list, one step at a time. Attempting to tackle everything at once will only frustrate you. Attacking the changes in priority sequence will help you to feel success at each step in the improvement process.

Now you're ready. Move forward with the test, and remember, you won't see any improvement (just like at the spa) if you're not committed to the change process.

I think society has changed tremendously in the last twenty-five years. Today everybody talks about their rights and privileges. Twenty-five years ago, everyone talked about their obligations and responsibilities.

Lou Holtz

THE TEST

I have categorized the world-class eManager success factors into sixteen categories. These categories are by no means complete, but they are the most important of the areas of world-class eManager change performance. These sixteen categories should set your direction for improvement, assisting you in problem identification and helping you focus your change process. They are summarized in Figure 16.1 on page 351.

1. *Change is your friend* — do you expect your employees to "follow procedure?" Does it frustrate you if your customer changes something about the products or services they expect? Do you use statements like, "This is how we've always done it?" especially when talking to customers? Do you keep doing a job the way "it's always been done" even though you don't think it makes sense?

If you answered "yes" to these questions, you've failed part one of the test. A world-class eManager is bored of the mundane, the repetitive and the systematic. A world-class eManager enjoys identifying change and looks for opportunities for positive, goal-based change. A world-class eManager enjoys the challenge of change. A world-class eManager is a change eManager, understanding resistance and fear and how to overcome them. A world-class eManager understands the models for change, like total quality management (TQM) and process re-engineering (PR) and can systematize the change process with tools like systematic problem solving (SPS).

Be aware that a halo has to fall only a few inches to be a noose.

Dan McKinnon

2. *Taking advantage of time* — do you feel overwhelmed by all the things you have to do? Are you satisfied with the amount of time it takes for your company to respond to a customer request? Are you comfortable with the products and services your company provides? Do you feel that you are spending enough time with your spouse and family?

Once again, "yes" answers constitute failure. A world-class eManager doesn't get stressed out about all the things that need doing. Most of them will go away by themselves. A world-class eManager focuses on doing the *right things*, which are prioritized based on the goals, rather than worrying about doing *everything right*. And one of the right things to do is to focus on customer and family responsiveness. The world-class eManager has the patience to do the right things blended with the competitive urgency to keep things moving.

Patience accomplishes its objective, while hurry speeds its ruin.

Sa'di

3. *Innovation and creativity* — do you believe that there is one best way to do a job? Do you prefer to follow a process that someone else is using because it works for them, rather than developing your own ways of solving the problem? Do you prefer telling your employees (or children) what to do rather than telling them to come up with their own way of doing it?

Once again, the "yes" answers are bad! Enjoy the creativity suggested by authors like Nadler and Hibino or von Oech! A world-class eManager prefers to innovate (innoveer) rather than duplicate (copycat), because he or she realizes that there is not one best way. Even the best can be improved upon.

> We can easily forgive a child who is afraid of the dark; the real tragedy in life is when men are afraid of the light.
>
> Plato

4. *Defined goals* — do you know what you or your companies core competencies are? Have you reviewed the business plan of your company and do you understand how it relates to you? Do you have a written personal and corporate vision, mission and strategy? Do you know what your target is?

This time "no" is the bad answer. A world-class eManager has goals in his or her personal life, family life and professional life. This manager knows what their employer expects of them, which should have an emphasis on positive, goal-directed change focused on customers and employees.

5. *Measurement oriented toward motivation* — do you motivate your personal performance and the performance of your employees using appropriate measures that are goal directed? Are you personally motivated by goal directed measures? Do you motivate your children so that they want to please you, rather than making them afraid of you?

Once again "no" is the loser. World-class eManagers utilize measurement systems as a motivator and keep a focus on the goals. They understand the types of measures and establish a measurement environment that motivates change in the critical resource relative to the overall goals.[1]

6. *Continuous education* — are you too busy to "read the instructions?" Do you just want to know enough to get the job done, and no more? Is the work your employees are doing too valuable to allow them time to share ideas or to get cross training? Do you feel that it's not necessary for your

---

1. Smith, L O, "Motivation! What Can I Do?", *APICS 34th International Conference Proceedings* (APICS) October 1991, pp. 379-381.

employees to have a big picture understanding of what's going on, that it's more important that they get their job done?

> Education makes people easy to lead, but difficult to drive; easy to govern, but impossible to enslave.

Lord Brougham

This time the "yes" answers are bad. A world-class eManager promotes cross training and a big picture understanding. Even training that on the surface seems irrelevant broadens one's perspective. For example, a world-class eManager should have a handle on the analytical tools that are available and should understand the terminology listed in Appendix 16.1.

> Stay in college, get the knowledge.
> And stay there until you're through.
> If they can make penicillin out of moldy bread,
> They can sure make something out of you!

Mohammed Ali

7. *Empowered teaming* — do you believe that you understand your employees' job function better than they do? Do you believe that you have the best understanding on what improvements need to be made? Do you believe that paid employee discussion time is a waste of time and money? Do you feel that a team should produce some positive results within the first month of its existence or else is should be disbanded? Do you feel that teaming is good for other people, but that you operate better as a loner?

This time "no" is the right answer. A world-class eManager takes advantage of people power. A world-class eManager is a Theory-Z, participative manager who is excited about developing the circles in their life. A world-class eManager understands the three faces of teaming — developer, leader and member, and is an active participant in each of these faces.

> Many hands and hearts and minds generally contribute to anyone's notable achievements.

Walt Disney

8. *A people person* — do you enjoy being around other people? Do you enjoy listening as much as you do talking? Do you feel good when you pay someone a compliment? Do you feel bad when you neglect someone (this includes spouse, family, employees, peers or bosses)? Are you conscious of the stakeholders that are around you? Do you prefer leadership

by example as the management style that you and your employees are managed under? Does it make you feel good (not envious) when someone does better than you at something?

"Yes" is the right answer. A world-class eManager is stakeholder conscious, whether it is the stakeholders in his or her personal or professional life. A world-class eManager looks for opportunities to pay compliments, but is also open and frank about expressing concerns. A world-class eManager realizes that employee ownership of changes is important to the success of the change, and therefore is willing to set their own pride and ownership aside.

> Failure is an event, never a person.
>
> William D Brown

9. *Self improvement* — do you feel that profitability is more important than a long-term relationship, whether it is with employees, customers, or family? Do you feel that once you give your word on something, you'll stick to it unless you feel the situation changes? Do you feel that you have no responsibility for or interest in the success of your employees? Do you feel that the success (financial or nonfinancial) of your peers (or spouse) gains you nothing directly? Do feel that if you don't "toot your own horn", no one else will? Do you feel that learning about what other people do, even though you may never be doing it yourself, is a waste of time? Are you leery of what the future holds?

> I hope that I shall always possess firmness and virtue enough to maintain what I consider the most enviable of all titles, the character of an honest man.
>
> George Washington

"No" is right this time. A world-class eManager is a sunrise manager looking for opportunities for change. A world-class eManager understands the importance of change in their personal life and wants to develop personal and professional skills that will make them a more valuable person both at home and at work. A world-class eManager believes in the long-term benefits of virtues like integrity, trust, honesty, loyalty, morality, humility and charity. A world-class eManager is ethical!

> Don't talk about yourself, it will be done when you leave.
>
> Addison Mizner

10. *Focus on the family* — is your family (spouse and children) more important to you than your professional success? Is the success of your children

in their schooling more important to you than your next raise or promotion? Do you come home from work and become an active participant of the home (cooking, cleaning, helping the children with their homework, doing the dishes, etc.)? Do you enjoy picking up a present or a card for your spouse on your way home from work? Do you listen to, rather than command or instruct your spouse and children?

"Yes" is the right answer. A world-class eManager puts first things first. Success in the home can make failure at work seem trivial. Failure in the home will drag failure into your work life as well. A world-class eManager is a home participant and is not controlling. A world-class eManager likes to come home and not spend all their time worrying about what they should be doing at work. A world-class eManager will walk into the home after a long day and become a participant in the home, not plop themselves in front of the TV or go into their home office, disappearing from conscious existence as far as the family is concerned. A world-class eManager is a world-class person and will come home from work, seek out their spouse, grab them and make them feel like they have been terribly missed all day (it doesn't matter if just one works or if they both work). A world-class eManager should even bring a present home for the spouse and kids every once in a while.

> Man is the only animal that fears children.
>
> Sparrow

11. *Productivity and quality* — do you know what your customer wants out of your products or services and did you gain this knowledge by directly asking the customer what they want? Do you understand and focus on value-added or total-factor productivity, rather than on labor productivity? Does your company have a written and clear definition of what quality means to them? Is quality and productivity a part of the measurement/motivation system of your enterprise and does it measure performance at all levels of the organization, right down to the janitor?

The correct answer this time is "yes". A world-class eManager has a clear definition of what productivity and quality means to them. Productivity should focus on waste elimination or value-added creation and quality should focus on customer satisfaction. There are many different types and categories of value-adding and customer satisfying and a world-class eManager understands and takes advantage of all of these in order to be world-class competitive.[2]

12. *Globalized but localized* — does your enterprise have separate domestic

---

2. Fargher Jr, John S W, "Assessing Your Organization's Potential for Quality and Productivity Improvement", *APICS 34th International Conference Proceedings,* ibid., pp. 375-378.

and international divisions? Does your corporate vision, mission and strategy focus on centralized, top-down, official declarations on how things should be done? Are repatriated expatriate managers (managers that return to the US after an overseas assignment) treated like outsiders and shoved off to some secondary, non-critical management role until a place can be found for them? Does the corporate office go through extensive effort to make sure that the local offices know what is expected of them down to the minutest detail?

The answer should be "no"! A world-class global eManager focuses on a centralized global strategy development with localized strategy implementation. A world-class eManager would see the enterprise as a global entity, not as a domestic entity that occasionally has international transactions. A world-class eManager would encourage localized leadership and ethical systems without sacrificing the corporate morality.

13. *Information and technological utilization* — are you excited to learn about new technological developments? Are you convinced that the old ways still beat the new fangled ideas all the time? Do you know how to search out new technology ideas? Are you discouraged because new technology changes faster than you can keep up with it, and therefore you avoid it? Do you encourage your employees to read and learn about what's new?

The answers are "yes-no-yes-no-yes". Do you find this fun or frustrating? New technology is often both — fun and frustrating. A world-class eManager realizes that there is a risk in technological change, but that the long-term competitive benefits of technological improvements greatly outweigh many of the disadvantages.

14. *Integration* — do you enjoy working with other departments because it broadens your perspective? Do you understand how information flows throughout your organization, not just for your department? Do you encourage your employees to talk to people at all levels in any department without coming to you first? Do you feel free to talk to the CEO without a special appointment?

This time the answer should be "yes" in all cases. A world-class eManager understands the benefits of and encourages integration, both horizontal and vertical. They understand the flow of information and how it effects and motivates employees throughout the organization. A world-class eManager avoids over-the-wall settings and encourages enterprise-wide integration.

15. *eCommerce prepared* — do you have a website that allows more than order placement (for example order tracking or capacity management)? Does your order processing system respond immediately to the customer with a realistic schedule? Is order processing information and capacity

information shared immediately with all vendors, and is there information in turn made available to you? Do you have both B2B (Business to Business) and B2C (Business to Customer) interfaces?

The answer should again be "yes" in all cases. A world-class eManager understands the need for an Internet presence that interacts and supplies finite capacity schedules. A world-class eManager assists vendors and customers in the development of the web abilities so as to optimize the performance of the entire supply chain/value chain.

16. *Supply chain focused* — do you enjoy working with vendors and customers because it broadens your perspective? Do you understand how information flows between organizations, not just for your department? Do you encourage your employees to talk to and visit customers and vendors? Do you help your suppliers and customers become web-enabled and help them to develop an integrated sharing of order processing and capacity information?

Again, all answers should be "yes". A world-class eManager understands the benefits of and encourages business to business integration, both with the suppliers and with the customers. They understand the value and flow of capacity and order demand information. A world-class eManager avoids over-the-wall vendor and customer relationships and encourages inter-company integration.

WHAT TO DO FIRST

In the Old Testament (Second Kings, Chapter 5, Verses 1 to 14) is the story of Naaman, the "captain of the host of the king of Syria" who was a powerful and influential man. However, he was also a leper. He went to the prophet Elisha to be cured of his leprosy and was told to wash in the River Jordan seven times and his "flesh shall come again." But "Naaman was wroth and went away." He expected some great demonstration by the prophet, or some fantastic deed that he needed to accomplish, not something so direct and simple. However, eventually his servants convinced him to go down and be washed seven times, which he did and was cured.

The Naaman story is an excellent story of how we look for the dramatic, the exciting and the exceptional. We are often not satisfied with the beauty of the simplistic. This is also true when it comes to becoming world-class. Here we need to focus on the simplistic and the easy. When we look for what to change we should change the easy things first. Do the things that will give us the most sought after results. We should not try to do everything, nor should we try to do the dramatic. We should focus on doing the simplistic that will give us the biggest bang for the buck.

I have listed what I feel are the sixteen success factors for world-class eManagers in Figure 16.1. Other books, like Covey's book *The Seven Habits of Highly Successful People* or Miller and Schneck's book *All I Need to Know About Manufacturing I Learned in Joe's Garage* also have their lists of characteristics that are needed in the world-class manager. Whichever list you use (of course I think mine's the best!), the most important thing is that you begin the change process immediately!

So what should you do first? You should commit yourself to changing first, and then begin the change process!

MEASURING YOUR PERFORMANCE

Even when you lack self-confidence, keep in mind that if you want a woman to think you're a prince, you should treat her like a queen.

Marilyn vos Savant

I have a cousin who, when she was about three, came to her aunt to ask her for help in going to the bathroom. The aunt said, "Look at Joe, he's only two years old and he can go to the bathroom by himself."

The cousin responded, "Yes, but he's got a handle."

This is the story that came to mind when I thought of getting a personal handle on your individual performance. However, the point I need to make about measuring your progress towards becoming world class is this:

To know if you are getting better, measure yourself against yourself.

Don't measure yourself against someone else. They are on a different road, using a different road map. Don't think they have a better handle on the situation than you do. Maybe the end objective is the same but they are coming from one direction and you are coming from another. This can be discouraging, frustrating and highly misleading. What you need to do is to make sure that you are getting closer to the final destination (world-class status) by checking your map (goals and strategy) and monitoring your progress. But I'll guarantee you that unless you get going, you'll never get there!

SUMMARY

Now that you have a list of things that need to be changed, prioritize them and start changing. First, as mentioned in the last chapter, identify the areas where you need improvement. Sequence the necessary changes in order so that you would either:

- have the most fun to least fun
- need the most help
- have the biggest benefit on your future performance.

This list can then be used to sequence your changes. Pick the top ones first. Doing those things that will make you feel the most successful first will help you develop positive feelings about your efforts. Then go on down the list. You can't do it all at once. But you can get started, one small step at a time and have fun doing it too!

This process of changing towards world-class eManagement status shouldn't be the funeral that you wrote your obituary for. Rather, this should be a rebirth for the:

New, world class you!

Figure 16.1

The Success Factors of World-class Management

1. *Change is your friend* — a world-class eManager enjoys identifying change and looks for opportunities for positive, goal-based change. And a world-class eManager enjoys the challenge of change.

2. *Taking advantage of time* — a world-class eManager focuses on doing the *right things,* priorities based on the goals, rather than worries about doing *everything right.*

3. *Innovation and creativity* — a world-class eManager prefers to innovate (innoveer) rather than duplicate (copycat), because he or she realizes that there is not one best way.

4. *Defined goals* — a world class eManager has goals in his or her personal life, family life and professional life.

5. *Measurement oriented towards motivation* — world-class eManagers utilize measurement systems as a motivator and keep a focus on the goals.

6. *Continuous education* — a world-class eManager promotes cross training and a big picture understanding.

7. *Empowered teaming* — a world-class eManager takes advantage of people power.

8. *A people person* — a world-class eManager is stakeholder conscious, whether it is the stakeholders in his or her personal life (spouse, family, friends) or in their professional life (employees, peers, bosses, customers, suppliers).

9. *Self-improvement* — a world-class eManager is a sunrise manager looking for opportunities for change. A world-class eManager understands the importance of change in their personal life and wants to develop personal and professional skills that will make them a more valuable person both at home and at work.

10. *Focus on the family* — a world-class eManager puts first things first.

11. *Productivity and quality* — a world-class eManager has a clear definition of what productivity and quality means to them.

12. *Globalized but localized* — a world-class global eManager focuses on a centralized global strategy development with localized strategy implementation. A world-class eManager would see the enterprise as a global entity, not as a domestic entity that occasionally has international transactions.

13. *Information and technological utilization* — a world-class eManager realizes that there is a risk in technological change, but that the long run competitive benefits of technological improvements greatly outweigh many of the disadvantages.

14. *Integration* — a world-class eManager understands the benefits of and encourages integration, both horizontal and vertical.

15. *eCommerce* — a world-class eManager understands the need for an internet presence that interacts and supplies finite capacity schedules to customers and vendors.

16. *Supply chain* — a world-class eManager understands the benefits of and encourages B2B (business to business) integration, both with the suppliers and with the customers.

APPENDIX 16.1: BUSINESS TERMINOLOGY WORTH UNDERSTANDING

This is a partial listing of business terminology that a world-class eManager needs to be familiar with. The terms in this list are all used in this book and focus only on the examples discussed in this book. However, there is additional terminology in each of the specialized functional areas that exist in any business. As part of the educational process, a world-class eManager should be familiar with the terms in this list. The index at the back of the book will assist you in finding where these terms are used.

Goals

Customer based goals
Employee based goals
Financial goals

Operational goals
Primary goals
Secondary goals

Strategic Planning

Aspirations statement
Business plan
Business areas (BA)
Business unit strategy
Core competencies
Corporate strategy
Enterprise resource planning
Government
Growth maintenance

Joint ventures
Life cycle
Mission statement
Plan of operation
Strategic alliances
Strategy models
Stratification
Subsidiaries
Vision statement

Measurement

Benchmarking
Cycle time
Efficiency
External quality
Motivation
Non-value-added

Pareto
Performance
Productivity
Standard industrial
    classifications (SIC)
Value-added waste

Change/Innovation

Breakthrough thinking
Change models
Change manager
Change productivity

Continuous change
Motivating change
Recognizing change

Change Analysis Processes

Flow-charting
Process re-engineering (PR)
Quality council
Resistance
Showcasing

Systematic problem solving (SPS)
Systems approach
T-Model
Total quality management
(TQM)

Time

Cycle time
Time pie
Time-based competition

Time-life cycle
Time-to-market
Time-to-market technology

Competition

Customer

Vendors

Globalization

Culture
Deregulation
Developing country
Exchange rates
Internationalization
ISO 9000
Localization
Nationalism

Newly industrialized economies (NIE)
Political
Religion
Tariff
Taxes
Trade theory
Trade barriers
Transnational

Productivity/Quality

Cause and effect diagrams
Company wide quality control (CWQC)
Conformance
Control charts
Decision teams
Deming award (Japan)
In line quality control (ILQC)
Internal quality
Labor dollar productivity
Malcolm Baldridge National Quality Award
NASA Award (US Government)

Parieto charts
Parieto principle
Quality improvement program (QIP)
Quality systems deployment (QSD)
Quality functional deployment (QFD)
Quality levels
Scatter diagrams
Shingo Prize (US Manufacturing)
Statistical process control (SPC)
Toolbox
Total quality control (TQC)
Total factor productivity
Value added productivity
Waste
Zero defects (ZD)

Technology

Business to business (B2B)
Business to customer (B2C)
Computer
Computer aided design and manufacturing CAD/CAM
Computer integrated manufacturing (CIM)
Digital cash
ebusiness
eCatalog
eCommerce
EDI
EFT
Electronic signatures
eMail
eMall
Encryption systems
Enterprise resource planning (ERP)
Facilities and equipment technology
Group technology
Internet
Knowledge leverage
Process technology
Product technology
Pure research technology
Systems and procedures technology
Technology transfer
URL
WEB
WWW

Management

Activity based management (ABM)
Authoritarian manager
Cash manager
Centralized
Circle
Commitment to excellence (CTE)
Conflict manager
Cool manager
Crash manager
Crisis manager
CRM
Customer value management
Decentralized
Departmentalization
Disintermediation
Diversification
eManager
Enterprise of the future
Enterprise value management
Feedback
Focus
Focused management
Hierarchical organization
Integration
Leader
Leadership
Leverage
Management by objectives (MBO)
Maturing
Networking
Next generation enterprise (NGE)
Over-the-wall
Participative manager
Reintermediation
Sunrise manager
Sunset manager
Supplier value management
Supply chain management
Theory-X manager
Theory-Y manager
Theory-Z manager
Value chain management
Value management

HRM

Ethics
Gainsharing
Honest
Humanistic
Humility
Innovation
Innoveering
Integrity

Job-enrichment
Morals
Non-trust system
Society value-added
Value system
Values
Virtue

Stakeholders

External customer
Final customer

Internal customer

Teaming

Employee involvement (EI)
Empowerment
Management circles
Quality control circles (QC)

Small group improvement
activities
Three "P" teams
Total quality management teams

Accounting

Activity based costing (ABC)

Cost

Manufacturing

Bottleneck allocation
methodology (BAM)
Certification in resource
management (CIRM)
Design for automated
assembly (DFAA)
Economic order quantity
(EOQ)
Four stages of
manufacturing
Green manufacturing
Integer programming (IP)

Just-in-time (JIT)
Kanban
Linear programming (LP)
Manufacturing resources planning
(MRP II)
Material requirements planning
(MRP)
Optimized production technology
(OPT)
Schedule based manufacturing
(SBM)
Theory of constraints (TOC)

Logistics

Speed sourcing

Information Systems

Artificial intelligence (AI)
Data
Decision support systems (DSS)
Electronic data interchange
    (EDI)
Expert systems (ES)

Information
Information flow
Information management
Information technology
Image processing
Object oriented programming

General

ABC analysis
Borderless company
Borderless organization
Communication
Environment

Management science
Operations research
Physical integration
Subcontractors

SUGGESTIONS FOR FURTHER READING

Some of these books and articles I have mentioned before, but they have relevance for the issues I have just discussed.

Beddingfield, Thomas, and Thomas Waechter, "Attaining World-Class Manufacturing Status", *APICS 34th International Conference Proceedings* (October 1991) pp. 472-476.

Covey, Stephen R, *Principle-Centered Leadership* (New York: Summit Books) 1991.

Covey, Stephen R, *The Seven Habits of Highly Effective People* (New York: Simon and Schuster) 1989.

Fargher Jr, John S W, "Assessing Your Organization's Potential for Quality and Productivity Improvement", *APICS 34th International Conference Proceedings* (October 1991) pp. 375-378.

Miller, William B, and Vicki L Schenk, *All I Need To Know About Manufacturing I Learned In Joe's Garage* (Walnut Creek, CA: Bayrock Press) 1993.

Nadler, Gerald and Hibino, Shozo, *Breakthrough Thinking* (Rocklin, CA: Prima Publishing) 1990.

Nadler, Gerald, Shozo Hibino and John Farrell, *Creative Solution Finding*

(Rocklin, CA: Prima Publishing) 1995.

Smith, L O "Motivation! What Can I Do?", *APICS 34th International Conference Proceedings*, op. cit., pp. 379-381.

von Oech, Roger, *A Kick in the Seat of the Pants* (New York: Harper & Row) 1986.

von Oech, Roger, *A Whack on the Side of the Head* (New York: Warner Books) 1990.

Chapter Seventeen

eManaging

> We may not know what the future holds, but we can hold on to the future!

It is time we quit playing copycat by trying to copy some wonderful idea from Japan or from some competitor! It is time for us to innovate ourselves ahead of our competition! It is time to change ourselves from the inside out and to manage that change so that we can become world-class in our lives, our families, our enterprises and our future! Let's bring the world-class that is within us out into the open! Lets become world-class people!

No matter how you look at world-class eManagement, the first and most important characteristic of a world-class eManager is to be willing to sit down right now and identify how they are going to change! Use the test in Chapter 16 to identify areas of change, prioritize the changes, to boldly go where you've never gone before, one small step at a time. Use the building block approach to make a difference.

Get the big perspective of where you are, where you want to be (goals) and how you're going to get there. Be patient — never, never, never give up! Manage your changes, don't let changes manage you. Listen to what people (stakeholders) are saying, learn from them and then innovate out ahead of your competition.

> It was pride that changed angels into devils; it is humility that makes men as angels.
>
> St Augustine

Jack Smith, CEO of General Motors, gives five turnaround tips:

1. establish a vision for the whole company

2. set clear expectations for performance at each level of the organization

3. construct realistic strategies that don't require rocket science

4. develop the capability to execute by reorganizing people and reallocating assets

5. focus everything — all assets, all decisions — on the customers, as they are the ultimate arbiters of success or failure.[1]

The major trends that are shaping the future of business include:
- time management — cycle time performance
- all companies will have an eCommerce and eBusiness presence
- customer centric product markets
- value optimization will define competitiveness
- supply chain performance will be the measure of competitive success
- quality will be defined on a customer-by-customer basis
- the family is back — more work will be done at home
- new employee benefits
- the personal face of business
- growth of environmentalism
- the nation's mood — back to reality.

> Riches are not from an abundance of worldly goods, but from the contented mind.
>
> Mohammed

Learn from examples like:

> The "e" in e-commerce is misplaced; it's "d-commerce" or "f-commerce" — distribution or fulfillment. You can't email a sweater to somebody.
>
> Kevin Silverman,
> ABN Amro

Fingerhut has grown up as a database marketer and as the second largest catalog retailer in the US (behind J C Penney). It has transformed itself to become a successful online retailer with one-stop e-fulfillment. But this giant learned its lesson the hard way. It found its catalog growth wasn't what it expected. Its warehouses were half empty and it had to rethink its retailing model. Utilizing its new Fingerhut Business Services Inc. (FBSI) division, it was able to leverage its core competencies in direct marketing and supply chain management making it a premiere e-fulfillment services provider. When Federated Department Stores purchased Fingerhut in February 1999, Fingerhut found itself

---

1. Taylor, Alex, "GM's $11,000,000,000 Turnaround", *Fortune* (October 17 1994) pp. 54-74.

with the capital it needed to expand the eCommerce efforts. Fingerhut now runs ten eBusinesses and boasts the largest end-to-end direct-to-consumer infrastructure in the US. It offers turnkey end-to-end customer fulfillment networking (CFN) thereby facilitating web based businesses to become eTailers. Large retailers like Wal-Mart, who do not have the competency to do its own one-on-one order management, use Fingerhut to manage this process.[2]

British Gas Services (BGS) controls the dominant market share as the provider of installation and maintenance services for domestic gas appliances. However, a concern about losing this market share found it overhauling its customer fulfillment structure with a focus on eliminating bureaucracy, developing superior customer service and leveraging its core competencies by cross-selling. The lessons that it believed it learned during this transformation process include:

- the importance of virtual integration to transforming a service into a customer-focused solution
- the value of delivering knowledge at the point of customer contact
- the positive impact of eliminating non-value-added stages from the supply chain
- the value of aligning physical capital to support digital capital.

The new measure of performance at BGS was "quality of service" as defined by the customer. As a result, it has experienced increased margins in all main product areas, a 36 per cent decrease in complaints (1997 to 1998), its first ever year of profitability (1998) and a 3 per cent increase in market share.[3]

> Price is not the transforming event. The transforming event is the ability to deliver personalized information to the customer in real time, at virtually no cost.
>
> David Pottruck,
> co-CEO, Charles Schwab & Co.

Charles Schwab & Co., Inc. is one of the few so-called dinosaurs of industry that has been successfully able to transform itself into a web business. The company has repeatedly positioned itself in the forefront of business revolutions as a technology pioneer. In this case, the revolution was on-line trading, offering customized service delivery. Its value proposition focuses on a "better customer experience and improved profitability through the flawless delivery of customized service in real time". As a result it can boast:

2. De', Arindam, "Fingerhut" (Alliance for Converging Technologies) 1999. This can be found at http://cfn.actnet.com/pdf/fingerhut.pdf
3. Hancock, Denis and Michael Conlin, "British Gas Services" (Alliance for Converging Technologies) 1999. This can be found at http://cfn.actnet.com/pdf/britishgas.pdf

- 6 million page views per day
- a greater market cap then previously possible
- industry leader with 25 per cent of the online trade market
- 2.8 million active online accounts
- Cost savings of $100 million per year.[4]

The examples of supply chain performance, world-class management and eCommerce integration are endless.

> You could be a great retailer, (but) if you don't have technology . . . if you don't have good delivery infrastructure and capability . . . you're nowhere on the Internet.
>
> Elizabeth A Vanstory,
> vice president, Office Depot.com

Office Depot has positioned itself as the premiere office supplies supplier through an integrated supply chain, customized eCatalogs, web based order placement and customer on-site deliveries. As a result, it claims:

- it is the largest office supply retailer on the internet
- customized web pages for more than 37,000 clients
- 13,000 products are available
- 50 per cent internet business growth per quarter
- inventories increased by 1 per cent while overall sales increased by 13 per cent.[5]

> UPS handles more e-business shipments than anyone, shipping more than fifty-five per cent of all goods ordered over the Internet
>
> UPS website

UPS re-engineered its delivery system model to focus on customer fulfillment. Since then UPS has dominated the market for the eBusiness package delivery service with a focus on satisfying end-customer needs. This transformation required extensive investment in partnering with software development companies. Its themes have been to grow the web based businesses, focus on the core competencies and "plug and play" customer service.

---

4. Lee, Michael, "Charles Schwab" (Alliance for Converging Technologies) 1999. This can be found at http://cfn.actnet.com/pdf/schwab.pdf
5. Lee, Michael, "Office Depot" (Alliance for Converging Technologies) 1999. This can be found at http://cfn.actnet.com/pdf/officedepot.pdf

As a result, the lessons learned have included:

* empowerment of employees and customers with real-time information
* creating a virtual integration network using web based interfaces
* using information partnering to speed up the process
* expanding into higher value-added services.[6]

Other examples of world-class performance exist that do not necessarily have all the components of eManagement but which demonstrate that even if everything does not apply, you can still find opportunity for improvements. For example, Ford, Sharonville was scheduled for shutdown but was saved by utilizing Employee Involvement (EI), which required a letter of understanding with the United Auto Workers (UAW). Since the 1986 threatened shutdown, quality has improved by 53 per cent.

L-S Electro-Galvanizing used laid-off steel workers and teaming to create the organizational design of the company, including the administrative systems. It effectively utilized goal based measurement and motivation systems including profit sharing and gainsharing.

Albertson has focused on quality and productivity improvement through training. It feels that its most important product is customer service.

> He who merely knows right principles is not equal to him who lives them.
>
> Confucius

Marriott International feels that associates are the key to success. It feels that if the hourly employees are taken care of, then they will in turn take care of the customer. Marriott focuses on the core expectations of the employees and attempts to gage employee satisfaction, which is the prerequisite for quality service.

Boise Cascade feels that understanding and implementing the best strategies for the deployment and diffusion of quality initiatives is the key element in successfully managing an enterprise transformation toward quality.

Wallace Co., a 1990 winner of the Malcolm Baldridge Award, developed sixteen strategic quality objectives and matrixed them against the seven Baldridge Award criteria. It used the Baldridge template to help the company become world-class. The results include an increase in market share from 10.4 to 18 per cent, on-time deliveries went from 75 to 92 per cent and a 69 per cent increase in sales volume.

---

6. Conlin, Michael, "UPS" (Alliance for Converging Technologies) 1999. This can be found at http://cfn.actnet.com/pdf/ups.pdf

The name of God is Truth.

Hindu Proverb

Hewlett-Packard's statement of corporate objectives is — "The reason HP exists is to satisfy real customer needs."

Hollis L Harris, president and chief operating officer of Delta Airlines, Inc. states that "We operate on the age old adage that if you take care of the customer, the profits will take care of themselves." And then there's Motorola, the company that other companies are afraid of being compared with. Motorola was the first winner of the Malcolm Baldridge Award and it immediately required all its vendors to be Baldridge contenders. CEO George Fisher says, "I personally think the renewed focus on quality, cycle time and customer satisfaction is far more important in the long run (to our global competitiveness)." Motorola emphasizes high goals and follows through as the means of satisfying the customer. However, it is doing more than just stating these goals — it is making sure that all the desired standards get implemented and that they are all focused on the objective of "total customer satisfaction."[7]

A man should first direct himself in the way he should go. Only then should he instruct others.

Buddha

So what type of manager are you? By now you should know where you are, where you're trying to get to and how you can get there. The question is — are *you green and growing or ripe and rotting?*

The key word in that phrase is *growing*. To be world-class is to be growing (positive change)! And if you're growing, both in your personal life and in your professional life, you're on your way to becoming world-class!

In a world in which we are overwhelmed with a blizzard of messages, we can easily lose sight of which messages are really important. But, realistically there is only one message that can never be ignored. It is the message of God, the one message which gives meaning to all others. Read the Bible and encourage others to do so. It's got a message for each of us.

William M Ellinghous,
President, AT&T

---

7. Denton, D Keith, "Lessons on Competitiveness: Motorola's Approach", *Production and Inventory Management Journal* (Third Quarter, 1991) pp. 22-25; Thomas, Sam, "Motorola's Six Steps to Six Sigma Quality", APICS 34th International Conference Proceedings, (October 1991) pp. 166-169.

SUGGESTIONS FOR FURTHER READING

If you would like to know more on this subject, then the references given in the footnotes will be useful. You might also like to look at the following articles:

Denton, D Keith, "Lessons on Competitiveness: Motorola's Approach", *Production and Inventory Management Journal*, Third Quarter, 1991, pp. 22-25.

"31 Major Trends Shaping the Future of American Business", *The Public Pulse*, Vol. 2, 1991, pp. 1-8.

Taylor, Alex, "GM's $11,000,000,000 Turnaround", *Fortune*, October 17, 1994, pp. 54-74.

Thomas, Sam, "Motorola's Six Steps to Six Sigma Quality", *APICS 34th International Conference Proceedings*, October 1991, pp. 166-169.

Index